Target: JFK

TARGET: JFK
THE SPY WHO KILLED KENNEDY?

ROBERT K. WILCOX

REGNERY
HISTORY

Regnery History™ is a trademark of Regnery publishing; Regnery®
is a registered trademark of Salem Communications Holding Corporation

Cataloging-in-Publication data on file with the Library of Congress

ISBN 978-1-62157-487-3

Published in the United States by
Regnery History, an imprint of
Regnery Publishing
A Division of Salem Media Group
300 New Jersey Ave NW
Washington, DC 20001
www.RegneryHistory.com

Manufactured in the United States of America

10 9 8 7 6 5 4 3 2 1

Books are available in quantity for promotional or premium use.
For information on discounts and terms, please visit our website:
www.Regnery.com.

Distributed to the trade by
Perseus Distribution
250 West 57th Street
New York, NY 10107

ALSO BY ROBERT K. WILCOX

To Robert

Contents

INTRODUCTION

I could hardly believe what I'd just read. An Argentine-born American clandestine named René A. Dussaq was allegedly intimately involved in one of the most momentous and disturbing events in America's history—the assassination of President John F. Kennedy. Dussaq had been a celebrated and much-honored war hero, a public speaker of note, a member of an Olympic rowing team, and in his post-WWII life a military instructor and a mentor to fellow Prudential insurance agents. How could it be possible that he had also participated in one of the twentieth century's greatest crimes?

His father had been an important Cuban diplomat around the turn of that century, a pacifist Sufi holy man involved in the creation of the League of Nations and a man who urged international unity and worked for peace. In contrast, his son, René, had been a soldier of fortune; "a man of violence in my younger years," as Dussaq himself admitted. But he was more widely known as a respected businessman and charismatic military leader, a master of many languages renowned for his icy calm in the face of mortal danger. While these are traits common to able assassins, the charge that René Dussaq had been involved in the killing was virtually unbelievable.

Yet there it was in my hands; passage after passage inscribed in secret diary entries written by René Dussaq's close friend and clandestine colleague, Douglas Bazata. Like Dussaq, Bazata had been a decorated OSS commando and spy. As vaunted Jedburghs—the forerunners of today's tough, daring, courageous, and deadly U.S. Special Forces—both Bazata and Dussaq had been OSS assassins. It was a profession that Bazata had practiced for several governments after World War II. He was an undeniable part of René Dussaq's murky, mysterious past. If anyone shared Dussaq's secret, it would have been Bazata. He and Dussaq had trained together in the OSS, conducted missions during World War II in concert with one another in occupied France, and created a freelance mercenary group in postwar Europe.

Bazata wrote that the two men had known each other since the late 1920s, meeting first as young men in Cuba, where Dussaq had been involved in revolution. In his diaries, Bazata, to preserve his friend's anonymity by disguising Dussaq, referred to him variously as "Peter" or "Paul," after the Biblical apostle who had undergone a conversion on the road to Damascus. There were so many references in the diaries about Peter/Paul that inevitably Bazata stumbled and accidentally wrote "René" or "Dussaq" several times instead. The more I read, the more obvious it became. There were too many instances, life parallels, and similarities for it to be mere coincidence. It *had* to be Dussaq to whom Bazata was referring. Suddenly, stories I'd heard about the Argentine-born adventurer, who had recently died in Los Angeles, loomed large.

What role had Dussaq really played, besides "machine gunner" and spy, in the various early Cuban and other Latin American revolts?

What forced him to flee the Latin civil wars and, in 1933, surface in Hollywood, where he became a movie stuntman and, after World War II, an actor, undercover agent, and later a successful insurance executive?

What really occurred the night of February 23, 1933, when the car the young, newly-arrived Dussaq was driving careened over a Los Angeles cliff, killing socialite Daisy Canfield Moreno, oil fortune heiress and wife of Spanish-born Antonio Moreno, the reigning Hollywood Latin-lover of the era? There were persistent rumors that Moreno was gay and that Daisy was threatening him with divorce, thus cutting him off from her huge inheritance. Had Dussaq, the burgeoning stunt driver and wing-walker, himself desperately in need of money, accepted a devil's bargain to save the troubled Moreno's career and access to his wife's fortune?

As World War II in Europe and Asia widened, was Dussaq acting as a U.S. spy—or perhaps one for a foreign government—during his Atlantic and Pacific sailing ventures as a treasure hunter and deep-sea diver? Were his well-attended public lectures, which centered not only on his own exploits but also on the need to respect each nation's right to self-determination, particularly Latin American nations, a clue to deeply-held political beliefs? Was his outrage at the traditional U.S. interventionist policy towards the Latin nations, especially Cuba, the motive, as Douglas Bazata believed, for Dussaq's involvement in President John F. Kennedy's assassination?

Why had the U.S. Army wanted to court martial Dussaq after he returned from extraordinary and successful missions as a WWII Allied resistance leader, by then known as "Captain Bazooka," behind German lines? Was it because he'd gone AWOL (as certain documents indicate) following the tragedy that befell his wife following his return to America after mistakenly being reported dead?

Or had the threatened court martial had a more sinister genesis?

After the war—and after personally being honored by President Truman himself—was he, as he claimed, only an undercover agent for the FBI hunting down Hollywood communists? Or was he, as his postwar commanding officer in Germany charged, a double-agent?

And if he was a double-agent, for whom was he spying?

Did Dussaq simply work undercover for the CIA after the war? Or, as Bazata claims—presuming Dussaq *was* CIA—was his real job to "penetrate" the U.S. spy agency? The CIA, in its standard reflexive response intended to conceal anything potentially damaging to it, will neither confirm nor deny any association with Dussaq.

Did he also work for Cuba, which Bazata notes that Dussaq oddly and occasionally claimed as his birthplace, but also his political passion and love? Had he secretly helped Fidel Castro mount the 1950s Cuban Revolution? And had he directed a reluctant but complying Bazata to alert high-level U.S. intelligence authorities that Kennedy was to be murdered in retaliation for the CIA's bungled attempts—undertaken with JFK's approval—to assassinate Castro?

Bazata had credible evidence to support his claims.

Bazata had an extraordinary letter he allowed me as his biographer[1] to copy before he had died. At the time, writing about Bazata, I knew little about Dussaq and hadn't thought much about the letter. It was signed by Lou Conein, the infamous OSS-CIA agent and acknowledged overseer of the 1963 assassination of Ngo Dinh Diem, the U.S. puppet-ruler of South Vietnam. In the letter, Conein swore that Bazata had communicated four separate times to him prior to Kennedy's death that the murder plot was in motion. Conein wrote, "You referred to this assassination as 'The Execution', noting always that your source of information was an anonymous 'Paul', whom you obviously knew extremely well. You also referred to this tragedy as 'Operation Hydra-K.'"

Was it the memory—and guilt—of the JFK assassination that caused Dussaq to often wake screaming, as his widow told me he did, or rather was it only terrible World War II flashbacks, as she believed but never knew for sure?

Relentlessly private, Dussaq would never say.

Who were the government men who came to him in 1979, as Dussaq was approaching seventy, and tried to pressure him into helping free the hostages being held by radical Iranian Islamists in the American embassy in Teheran? According to a friend at Prudential, they had reduced Dussaq—the man who had done a handstand atop the Empire State building and willingly jumped into the cauldron of Nazi-occupied France—to tears as he related their visit. The friend was shocked to see

René Dussaq standing before him, his composure gone, stammering, weeping. "They wanted me again—after all I'd done for them," he quoted Dussaq as saying.

Operation Hydra-K. The very phrase was chilling. What did it mean? Hydra, for the serpent-like water monster possessed of many heads from Greek mythology, and K for Kennedy? Or was it just a sinister though meaningless phrase? Of course, Dussaq *was* a weapons expert and, like his friend Bazata, a trained assassin. All this information was contained in Dussaq's army records. I had them—at least those that could be pried loose from the government or others obtained from friends or family. A paratrooper in the famed 101st Airborne before joining the OSS, Dussaq had taught all manner of weapons use and clandestine skills, including snipering, the most necessary of skills required for the Kennedy killing. I knew he had personally killed several Nazis, including a Gestapo chief during one of his arrests while operating in concert with the French Resistance in occupied France. Apparently, after being tortured, Dussaq had agreed to write and sign a confession, revealing names. Instead of putting the pen brought to him to paper, he'd used it as a weapon and fatally stabbed his interrogator and escaped. As a crack marksman with steel nerves, he had all the qualifications required of an effective assassin. Most of those who knew Dussaq echoed what Bazata wrote: "He was the most extraordinary person I was ever to know."

But I still couldn't believe it. I *didn't* believe it. I needed convincing.

PART 1

"BAZOOKA"

1

The Commando

MAY 23, 1944

René Dussaq was worried. He watched concernedly in parachute harness, jump boots, and shock helmet as the plane's crew decided what to do next. It was approximately 1:30 a.m. over Occupied France. Thirty-three years old, tall, and athletically lean on a muscled frame, he was the lone "Joe"—purposely so named and segregated for security—waiting to be dropped from a roaring, four-engined B-24 bomber, modified for such human "insertions" and war cargo deliveries. The big "Liberator," painted black for night camouflage, was winging low in a moonless sky at five thousand feet in anticipation of getting code from below and then parachuting the Joe and containers and packages, mostly arms and explosives, to waiting resistance fighters.[1]

But the signals being beamed weren't right.

"We had great difficulty in identifying the [code letter] they were sending from the ground," he wrote in an after-action report.[2] Consequently, the bomber crew was "stooging," flying a repeated circling pattern, uncertain of what to do next. They were over a large forest-surrounded clearing in a mountainous area of rural Central France. There was a river nearby and a village north in the distance. It was dangerous. They had been spotted by searchlights earlier as they'd snuck in low from the English Channel. Flak had been fired at them. Was the enemy still tracking? Nazi nightfighters were always a threat. The longer they stayed, the more likely they'd be discovered again by the wrong people. And what if the reception was a trap? The blinking red and white signal lights they were seeing below were suspect, and they couldn't make contact with their S-phone, a wireless communication device specifically designed for the secret drops. Its signal passed narrowly between the plane and the ground and back, making detection hard for monitoring Germans who might be in the area.

But they'd been over the site too long.

Time was running out.

Since the Japanese attack on Pearl Harbor, Dussaq had been trying to enter the fighting. A celebrated adventurer and lecturer in a television-less time when speaking events were prime entertainment, he'd tried to enlist in the Army Air Corps, the Navy, and Marine paratroops. He was a licensed pilot, "dare-devil" wing-walker, deep-sea diver, and treasure hunter. He'd knife-fought sharks for the movies, and jumped from insanely high perches like ship masts. But the services had balked. South American by birth, he wasn't a U.S. citizen, which posed a potential security risk. Finally, the Army, desperate for bodies in the war emergency, took him as a grunt infantryman. "It was important for me as a foreigner to try to prove myself to be as good as any American-born guy," he later said of his determination.[3]

Quickly, talent obvious, he had been picked to give motivational speeches to new recruits at South Carolina's Camp Cross training facility and was noticed for his leadership abilities. Even if it was cleanup duty, he bagged more garbage than anyone else, said his second wife. With a resemblance to film star Gilbert Roland—the dashing Mexican-born actor he'd once doubled for in a high-dive pirate movie—he had a commanding voice, a sensational smile that gleamed brightest when he was challenged, and he used wit and humor in his lectures. "It's very disconcerting to a speaker when the audience is asleep," he'd chide exhausted recruits newly arrived at the camp.[4] Naturalized on July 24, 1942, in nearby Spartanburg, South Carolina, he'd been recommended for Officers' Training School, and, by early 1943, had become a lieutenant instructor with the soon-to-be famous 101st "Screaming Eagles" airborne division. Within months he was a standout paratrooper being eyed for recruitment by the Office of Strategic Services (OSS)—the U.S.'s newly formed spy agency, forerunner of the CIA.

"Lieutenant Dussaq [was] born in Buenos Aires, Argentina, of a Cuban father and an Argentinean mother," wrote George K. Bowden, a top-ranking OSS official in Washington, to his counterparts in London who were looking for tough, quick-thinking agents to become clandestine airdropped operatives—the cream of "Special Forces" in today's parlance. "He was educated in France and Switzerland...speaks six foreign languages [and] could pass as any national except Anglo-Saxon. ... He is a remarkable athlete [having mastered] boxing, wrestling, knife fighting, dueling, rowing...and a variety of unusual and hazardous work of a physical nature. ... He is keen, adaptable...intelligent...and a dirty fighter conversant with jujitsu and the commando type of close combat fighting. ... Waldo Logan [of Chicago's Adventurer's Club and backer of some of Dussaq's earlier sea-borne expeditions] says that he is the only man he has ever known who is entirely without fear."[5]

It wasn't true. Dussaq carefully hid his fears in order to defeat them. But few knew that. He'd publicly demonstrated steel nerves for the newsreels before arriving for special training in England. "On the day before we shipped out of New York," wrote fellow fighter Bazata, "Pathe News [one of the era's large newsreel organizations] paid him $100 for standing on his hands on a ledge at the top of the Empire State Building [the city's tallest at the time, windswept and acrophobic]. It created a bit of a scandal and was quickly hushed-up."[6] The OSS was supposed to be secret and its members invisible—especially its special-ops parachutists. But

Dussaq was his own man. In fact, he had almost exited OSS when its vetting officers indicated he had to be watched because of possible Nazi ties. On a pre-war trip to Chile, he'd listed for customs "Nazi HQ" as his primary residence. He had also disclosed in OSS interviews that it was possible "his family in Santiago [Chile] had pro-Nazi tendencies."[7] The address listing was surely a joke. As Bazata noted, his friend enjoyed tweaking questioners, especially self-important authorities. "He was always smiling and would say incredibly negative things, with his big grin, about people who were standing right alongside him."[8] But despite the fact that he had eventually been approved by OSS security, the inference and personal probing had privately irked him. "Privacy," he'd complained, "isn't easy to come by."[9] He prized it. And when he learned that his "Screaming Eagles" had been ordered overseas, he'd tried to stop his OSS transfer and rejoin. Getting in the fight quickly was still his primary aim.

What happened to bring him back to OSS is unclear. Records available give little clue. But the clandestine agency had strong influence in the White House and usually got what it wanted. By early fall 1943, he was in the British Isles training with "Operation Jedburgh," OSS's first commando-type special mission, and showing why he'd earned the nickname "Human Fly."[10] A fellow "Jed" trainee recalls that instead of properly exiting a practice parachute gondola five hundred feet up by the required method of dropping through its center "Joe-hole"—as he would have to do in the B-24 in which he was now flying—he'd decided to "liven things up by taking a swan dive over the side." The sudden absence of his weight tilted the basket, unintentionally dumping his unprepared trainee partner who luckily, in the short time allotted, opened his chute but still landed badly. Stunned, "remaining motionless on the ground [as] we all ran toward him," wrote the witness, the hapless partner regained his senses and, surprisingly, limped off without hard feelings. It was Bazata, tough to the core, who would become one of the most decorated Jeds.[11]

"As a jumper, he was by far the most experienced we had," writes Bazata, who regarded Dussaq almost as a mentor except that they were roughly the same age. "For some reason [which] I never discovered...Dussaq had a very special status in O.S.S. He was allowed to be even further isolated within an already isolated group. ... When the rest of us were supposed to be doing physical drills, he was never around. I learned that he could usually be found off in the woods, standing on his hands on a branch of a tree or simply communing with nature."[12] Dussaq's father, Emilien Talewar Dussaq, in addition to being Cuban Consul in Geneva, Switzerland, was Sufi General Secretary, a world spiritual leadership position he'd been appointed to in 1922. Sufism, or Islamic mysticism, basically seeks union with God through, among other ways, ascetic harmony, such as meditation or food deprivation. Interestingly, ancient Samurai warriors also practiced asceticism as a way to toughness. Although René listed Catholicism, his mother's religion, as his own on military forms, he revered his father and even bizarrely kept close a photo solely of Emilien's bulging bicep—the upper arm a weight-lifter might curlingly flex for the camera. He probably had the snapshot with him as he waited now to jump into Occupied France. Like his father, physical fitness was near religion to the son. "Not that he needed conditioning," writes Bazata. "The hand-standing acts, which he demonstrated frequently, proved this." For instance, when a dispute occurred at a rowdy Jed dinner celebration—attended by, among other dignitaries, General Omar Bradley, U.S. field commander on the upcoming D-Day— "Dussaq stopped it by climbing on the table and walking its length on his hands, eight wineglasses held by their stems between his fingers. No one can argue when he's dumbfounded."[13]

Not everybody, however, was impressed. Fellow Jedburghs, named for a Scottish town of medieval warriors known for their ferocity with axes, were a competitive bunch, mostly hell-for-leather talents like Bazata. Some resented Dussaq's suave, aloof derring-do, especially because, infuriatingly, Dussaq, with his trademark pencil-thin mustache and confident Latin good looks, could back up his boasts. "Brash...pushy and a showoff," was how some of the Jeds regarded him, according to Thomas L. Ensminger, author of *Spies, Supplies and Moonlit Skies*, in an email to me. The book details missions such as the one Dussaq was currently waiting to jump into. And when the British spy agency, the Special Operations Executive (SOE) which conceived of and basically ran the multi-national Jedburgh operation (Jeds included French operatives and other nationals), evaluated Dussaq, its report said he was "a very flamboyant, verbose, domineering personality, with little sympathy or tolerance for others. He is extremely self-centered, with a tendency to exhibitionism, and is unlikely to be capable of disinterested service.... His enthusiasm might well flag unless he could keep in the limelight."[14]

Whatever the truth of that evaluation—fact, prejudice, or British-American rivalry which often flared during World War II—Dussaq kept pressing for insertion into the war. And when a need arose, the Brits, who snatched him from the Jeds, didn't hesitate to grant his wish. They needed his talents and skills badly. Upcoming Allied plans demanded it: in addition to the joint OSS-SOE Jedburgh missions, SOE had numerous other clandestine "circuits" already operating in Nazi-held France. The circuit Dussaq was assigned to was code-named "Freelance," a small group of Brits. It, as the Jeds were, was to aid D-Day, the much-anticipated invasion of Europe upon which victory, Allied planners knew, crucially hinged. All these fighter insertions, like Dussaq, were to aid and train local "Maquis," the French term for the Resistance. Fighters like Dussaq were to train the "Maquisards," help terrorize the occupiers, and help destroy German-aiding industries commandeered in France. Especially, they were to slow down and hopefully stop Nazi reinforcements to the invasion front once the D-Day invasion began.

Freelance, which Dussaq was soon to join, was headed by the French- and German-speaking British Major John Farmer, codenamed "Hubert." It included former Paris newspaper correspondent Nancy Wake, a gutsy, French-speaking New Zealand–born operative who the Gestapo labeled "the White Mouse" because of her illusiveness.[15] Women, less threatening—and thus disarming to soldiers and others in authority—made good operatives in the right situations. Farmer, Wake, and others in the circuit were working with a charismatic Maquis leader code-named "Gaspard."

Strong-willed and physically imposing, Gaspard, whose real name was Emile Coulaudon, had been taken prisoner when the Nazis had invaded and quickly subdued France in 1940. But he had escaped back to his home city of Clermont-Ferrand in Auvergne, the mountainous region south of which Dussaq was now circling, and started a resistance against the occupiers who had surged to include thousands of fighters banded in small, scattered units throughout the province (or "Department," as the French call their state-sized divisions).[16]

A quickly mustered draftee in the French Army, "Col. Gaspard" lacked serious military training, as well as weapons and supplies for his men. Nevertheless, under his inspirational leadership, his fighters had killed many Germans and, among other successes, had destroyed important liquid oxygen plants at historic Massiac, a place of ancient streets and churches, and burned to uselessness forty thousand tires stacked for the Germans at the large Michelin plant in Clermont-Ferrand. Thus, when Gaspard had requested help from London, the Freelance mission had been dispatched. And when Farmer had requested another operative—and quickly—Dussaq had been tapped.[17] Now, waiting concernedly in the plane as the crew debated his fate, Dussaq decided he was not going to be denied.

"The dispatcher may have told me that I should not jump," he later wrote for officials, conjuring a weak cover for what he had done. They were going to dump the supplies and move on, he explained. "During the conversation that ensued...because of the noise in the plane...I just could not make myself understood...I am not quite sure that the dispatcher gave me the signal...but when they decided to make their run to drop the packages and opened the hatch, I was resolved to jump."[18]

There was no way they were going to stop him—orders or not.

He stepped to the noisy "Joe Hole" and disappeared.

2

"I've Come for a Room"

esides the disorienting darkness of the night, Dussaq had leaped into
a strong downwind, which had taken him many miles from the
clearing where those who he was told were supposed to meet him
should have been waiting.[1] From briefings in London he knew generally
where he was—somewhere amidst the forested lowland and river-carved
gulleys of Central France near Mennetou-sur-Cher, so named because
it was on the Cher River. It was well north of Vichy, seat of the collaboration government formed after France's defeat. He may have landed
near where, in 1924, as a precociously athletic fourteen-year-old, he had
ventured while traveling in peacetime from Geneva to Paris, some 250
miles north, as assistant coxswain for the Swiss Olympic rowing team.[2]
But those were happier days. Occupied France was now thick with local
Nazi-cooperating paramilitaries, known as "Milici," who knew the
countryside well, and often were more savage with prisoners than the

Gestapo, who counted on them to help track the Maquis and its enablers like himself.

To make matters worse, not only had Dussaq parachuted in alone—a rarity—but he was one of the few Allied agents who did so in civilian clothes, thereby relinquishing crucial protections guaranteed combatants under the Geneva Convention.[3] It's not clear why he did not wear a uniform. Available documents indicate only that his request was granted.[4] Maybe he or his handlers preferred stealth over protection? But if apprehended, he could be executed—and most probably would be—after being tortured for information. Neither the Germans nor Milici had shown any proclivity for mercy to "terrorists" and "saboteurs," as they surely would view him.

He had with him one hundred thousand Francs as well as fake papers and a memorized scenario saying he was "René' Alexandre Dufayet," a Paris businessman. The money was mostly for Gaspard to help finance Maquis operations. His SOE codename was "Anselme," to be used in radio communications back to London. His specific mission—to hook up with Freelance—was "Druggist." If he missed the reception committee, his instructions advised him to get in touch with "Samuel," codename for an operative already functioning in the area. Samuel would be found through a safehouse at 16 Rue de la Republique, Chateauroux, a town on the Indre River, a source of the lower Cher.[5] He had a secret code for contact—"I've come for a room"—"Whose room?"—"François.'" But instead of Chateauroux, he decided to try and return to the drop clearing, a decision that turned out well as Chateauroux was much farther away. "After a three-hour walk," he wrote, "I was able to establish contact with the reception committee which was still looking for packages that had been dropped all over the place."[6]

He must have stayed the remainder of that night in or near Mennetou, a town of eight hundred, the first he mentions in his report. He wrote that by daybreak, alerted by the circling, indecisive plane the night before, an estimated five hundred German soldiers from a local garrison were detected surrounding a camp of thirty-three Maquis in woods nearby. The prognosis was grave. Their leader, Dussaq wrote, came to him and asked him to take charge. To his surprise, some in Mennetou, although sympathetic to the cause, did not want him aiding in this particular instance. "My first realization that the Resistance in France was not as united as I had been led to believe" came when "the ex-mayor of Mennetou told me" not to do it. These Maquis, the man hissed, were communists. "I informed him...that I did not care a damn what they were, that the only thing that interested me was that Germans were there to be killed."[7] As British SOE expert Marcus Binney writes, what happened next was the action of a "quick-witted...impressive...soldier"—Dussaq. Taking charge, Dussaq had the surrounded thirty-three quietly withdraw through a small, presumably hard-to-see river bed in the center of the woods. When the Germans finally realized what was happening, they opened fire with, as Dussaq later reported, "no other result than the killing of some of their own men" in the crossfire—six, according to an estimate attached to his report.[8]

With the Germans now stirred like hornets, he decided it was best to try to find the safehouse at Chateauroux, a lengthy journey south towards the mountainous Auvergne Region where Freelance, his immediate objective, was operating. He probably had help from the Maquis he'd rescued. The address on the Rue de la Republique was a local rooming house, and although he quickly, upon arrival, connected with two supposedly helpful local Maquis, it wasn't long before things went haywire. The following day, he reports, he was rousted in his room by a Gestapo agent accompanied by a French police inspector and "three gendarmes," possibly Milici. Had he been betrayed? They wanted to see his papers. Complying, he was told to accompany them to headquarters. His account of what happened next strangely lacks important details. "Having received instructions in London never to go to any headquarters should [his papers when shown] incite suspicion," he writes, "I was able to get the inspector alone in my room"—how?—"and to inform him that I would be compelled to kill him were he to insist on his plan to take me to the police station. I did not want to shoot him immediately for fear of alerting [the Gestapo agent] who was outside with the three gendarmes." Why were they outside? Gestapo agents weren't usually so cooperative.

And why hadn't they found and confiscated his pistol? But the threat worked. The inspector, he writes, walked out of the room "calling off the gendarmes" and "gave me the opportunity to escape through the window."[9]

Whatever the missing details, Dussaq was now unquestionably a known and hunted terrorist. The Gestapo and Milici—despite being coerced or duped and unsuspecting earlier—would certainly have given alarm, if not chase, once he had bolted. Did he run wildly down streets, ducking into alleys, his pursuers shouting and shooting behind? Had he made it to nearby woods, avoiding road blocks and angry German soldiers? The woods probably would have been his best avenue of escape. One can only speculate because after the bolting, the next sentence in his report is that by nightfall he made "contact...with a Maquis group" who aided him in a journey further south to a safehouse in Montlucon, a fairly large industrial and communications hub, crisscrossed by rail and auto roads in roughly the geographic center of France.

The commune (as the French call such municipalities), which started as a medieval fortress for the Duchy of Bourbon, featured, among other historical sites, a fourteenth century castle on a cliff overlooking the headwaters of the Cher, which was in higher country than Chateauroux. In 1988, Dussaq told a magazine writer about another of his escapes from the Gestapo by "jumping from a train into a river."[10] He gives no other details. Was this on his trip south to Montlucon? It's possible. Questions aside, when he arrived, the picaresque city was, in its more industrialized areas, now important to the Nazis for help in tire production. A large Dunlop factory there produced synthetic rubber. The Germans had little natural rubber, and depended on such facilities to supply its war machine, especially tires for aircraft. In January 1943, workers rioted in Montlucon in protest of a nationwide Nazi order deporting able-bodied Frenchmen to Germany for forced labor. Many young Montlucon males escaped the roundup and joined the local Maquis. Once part of the Resistance, they returned to sabotage the forced Nazi industry and, in reprisal, were being avidly pursued. Dussaq was therefore entering a hotbed of resistance and retaliation.

"Each time I escaped," Dussaq told a newspaper reporter in 1949, "I assumed a new identity with falsified papers which would slow down the tracing efforts of the Nazis."[11] Thus, it was probably not very long, once he'd taken residence in the safehouse of a "Madame Renard," that he got himself a new name—the second of seven identity changes he claimed he would make while in occupied France. He probably had help from the local underground. As a fifteen-year-old, he was a Swiss tennis star, and, at seventeen, the Cuban national champion.[12] One of his opponents in international matches was the famous French net ace René Lacoste, nicknamed "the Crocodile" for his tenacity on the court. Lacoste would later become internationally known for his "Alligator" shirts. (I still wear them.) "The name [therefore, when he had to pick one] came immediately to mind," he told a reporter in 1995.[13] So by at least June 3, 1944—the date stamped on a French identity card I found at his house—he had become Alexandre René Lacoste, supposedly a teacher from Saint Santin, a town further south, the direction he soon hoped to be headed. With an undergraduate degree in letters and sciences, a master in Latin languages—both from the College of Geneva, in Switzerland—and attendance at, if not graduation from, Havana University Law School, he was well prepared to pose as an instructor or scholar.[14]

By June 6, 1944—the momentous D-Day invasion at Normandy—he had been undercover in the country for more than two weeks, and in Montlucon, probably one of those two weeks. What he did in Montlucon is mostly unknown. There is scant information available, but it appears it was while there that he experienced one of his most brutal personal World War II episodes—the grisly killing of a Gestapo officer who was torturing him. Years later he would recall the incident variously, and sometimes with conflicting details, to specific listeners: a colleague, two different newspaper reporters, and scriptwriters for CBS radio—the prevailing public media at the time.[15] In essence, the following is what he related: he was arrested because he was suspected of being Jewish. He protested that he was a Catholic, which is true—at least by birth. He was taken to Gestapo offices, and—according to the CBS radio script—while under torture, he agreed to sign a confession for being a spy with the Maquis and participating in a recent ambush of German soldiers. In the radio script, written in early 1947—not long after what happened—the Nazi interrogator, a vicious major, is whipping him across the face and back with a belt when Dussaq apparently caves and asks for a pen. But when it is handed to him, instead of signing, he plunges it into his torturer's throat and escapes in the bloody chaos.

The script was never aired because Dussaq himself nixed it. According to Western Union cables I found at his house, he had been promised script approval by producers but it didn't happen. "Regret to inform you," he wrote CBS, "unable to release radio script for broadcast." Curiously, the desperate killing does not appear in any official document I've seen. Was it fabricated for fame or fortune? Obviously, he was nixing both benefits with his Western Union cable, so that doesn't seem right. Throughout his life, evidence indicates, René appeared uninterested in fame or money—or at least, for whatever reason, wanted to keep his exploits private. "I prefer experience to riches," he would tell his second wife, Charlotte, a blonde actress and drama coach for Paramount Pictures. He rejected movie offers to dramatize his life, she said.

But such a killing perhaps explains Dussaq's extreme defensive behavior when he was finally contacted in Montlucon by Freelance operatives sent to fetch him. As the historic D-Day landings on Normandy commenced, intrepid Nancy Wake, following a harrowing two-day car journey evading Germans, Milici, and trigger-happy Maquis (who, she wrote, shot first and asked questions later), finally arrived to fetch him at Madame Renard's safehouse. After a tense few moments convincing the madame that she was with the resistance, Wake writes, "[Madame Renard] laughed and led me into the kitchen. She called to 'Anselme,' who came out of a cupboard pointing a Colt .45 clutched in his hand. We looked at each other in astonishment. It was René Dussaq, whom I had met during my training in England. He was also one of the men who had kissed me goodbye when I left on my mission. He was to become known as Bazooka."[16]

3

The Redoubt

The two-day trip south to Freelance's headquarters in Chaudes-Aigues, an ancient mountain town known for its therapeutic hot springs, was tense. "Dussaq nearly passed out when I said we would be going by car," writes Wake. "He sat in the back with his Colt at the ready, while I was in the front with the driver, a couple of Sten guns [British submachine guns] and half a dozen grenades."[1]

They drove on roads rising into the giant Central Massif rift of mountain plateaus towering above the Mediterranean lowlands of southern central France. Chaudes-Aigues, in the Cantal department, sat near the winding Truyere River, which meandered forcefully one hundred miles from the high ground down through a picturesque landscape of rocky ravines, shimmering lakes, deer-filled forests—and dangerous, trigger-happy fighters, friend and foe alike.

Even a swan can be deadly.

But they arrived unscathed.

■ ■ ■

General Eisenhower, the Allied Supreme Commander, estimated the value of the French Resistance during the war as "the equivalent of 15 divisions," writes British historian-journalist Alexander Werth. The general added, "they hastened victory by two months"[2]—a tall accolade. They did so primarily by attacking the Germans in coordination with the massive D-Day invasion. The attacks either delayed or stopped German reinforcements from going north and helping repulse the Allies. Part of that action was a plan championed primarily by the French to form "redoubts," or fortresses of fighters—preferably elevated in high ground—from which the Resistance could launch major attacks against the enemy. It was into this network of budding redoubts that Dussaq arrived with Wake and her driver.

Apparently Dussaq thought of himself as the vanguard of an Allied paratroop force that would soon be coming. (Planners rarely gave the big picture to operatives, unless the information, which might be extracted through torture, was essential for success. Sometimes they even gave false information to the operative in case it might be extracted.) "On arrival," says a Freelance history, he briefed Freelance boss Maj. Farmer ("Hubert") that "his mission was to act as liaison officer between the Maquis and any American parachute troops that might be sent to the area. As a second duty he was to find, when requested [presumably by London], landing grounds for airborne troops. And thirdly, [he was] to act as weapons instructor."[3] His hosts were quickly impressed with his ability to speak French like a native. He presented the local Chaudes-Aigues commander, Henri Fournier, with a Colt .45 pistol, which, according to Fournier's wife, was much coveted by her husband.[4]

Dussaq's arrival had to be welcome news to "Gaspard" (Emile Coulaudon), the overall Resistance leader in the region who had his headquarters on a mountain plateau near Chaudes-Aigues. That plateau was Mont Mouchet, one of the larger former, and now leveled, volcanic peaks that jutted throughout the southern Auvergne province. With news of the D-Day landings, Resistance leaders, including Gaspard, had sent out an urgent call for recruits to bolster the Maquis. Liberation was at hand! They needed every available man. The response had been overwhelming. By the time Dussaq appeared, potential new fighters from throughout the region were streaming into the redoubt. The Germans couldn't help but be aware of the buildup and had begun small, ominous probing attacks. An enemy assault was brewing.

Gaspard was undeterred. He appears to have regarded Dussaq as proof that substantial Allied help was on its way—something he'd been requesting for months, and which he thought, rightly or wrongly, had been promised to him.[5] His largely novice troops, armed with mostly Allied-supplied light weapons, like Sten guns, grenades, and pistols, were very much in need of heavier firepower, hopefully tanks and air support, and professional training such as Dussaq, a specialist in weapons and ambush, could provide.

Dussaq wrote, "I was introduced to a Colonel Thomas who was the commanding officer of the [redoubt at nearby Fridefont]," a village which was part of the overall Mont Mouchet network, and "immediately" told "to train his men in all the weapons they had, and in their tactical use…The lack of trained cadre [experienced key personnel] was pitiful. Even those who had been appointed company commander had not the training necessary for such a job. Furthermore, the majority of 'Maquisards' had joined the Maquis to hide from the Germans [the implication being they were not there to fight], and it was rather difficult to change them from the hunted into the hunter."[6]

He estimated the total number of Maquis in and around the redoubt to be seven thousand men and growing—but with a much smaller number, perhaps two thousand to three thousand, equipped and few trained to fight any kind of major engagement. "Having received information that the Germans were preparing to attack [in force], I did all in my power [along with the others in Freelance] to convince [the leaders, including Thomas and Gaspard] that it was suicide to try and maintain such a large group of men in one single spot with the types of weapons they had." They were sitting ducks. He urged breaking the troops up into small and mobile hit-and-run guerilla bands where they would be less vulnerable, and their light arms could be better utilized. But Gaspard, who continued to insist that all "they needed were tanks and cannons [and aviation support]...to defend their position," would not budge.[7]

It appears Gaspard still believed substantial reinforcements were on the way.

Alas—with the exception of periodic small arms drops by Allied air—they were not. Only a few days after Dussaq had arrived the Germans attacked on June 10, in the first of several devastating offensives that forever in that region of France would be remembered as the heroic Battle of Mont Mouchet. It was heroic because this rag-tag bunch of inexperienced anti-occupiers, led by a tiny core of professional fighters, held their ground basically until ammunition for their meager weapons ran out. Then they fell back to smaller redoubts in the area, eventually being routed and scattered. However, because they held on as long as they did, and kept an entire German Division, if not more, from going north to Normandy at a crucial time, they incurred a special wrath from the enemy who, in savage retaliation during the roughly two-week, on and off, conflict, massacred and mutilated dead and injured Maquis, and innocent French civilians, including women and children

It was one of the major unheralded battles of World War II—and in Europe, one of the nastiest.

And Dussaq was in the middle of it.

Even to this day, information on the battle is hard to acquire. It is mostly in French and much is disputed because of the remoteness of the battle and politics involved. When it began, with a coordinated attack by approximately ten thousand Germans[8] with artillery, tanks, and armored cars against perhaps three thousand Maquis on Mont Mouchet, Dussaq was in nearby Fridefont, a few mountainsides away, training new recruits. "From our headquarters we could hear the sound of the battle raging," writes Nancy Wake. "We could offer no assistance...The nature of the terrain between our position and the Maquis under attack made it impossible."[9] As Freelance's radio operator, Denis Rake, a heroic but controversial soldier,[10] sent coded messages to London begging for airborne help.

Wake, for her part, was handing out British army boots to new recruits who were then passed to head trainer Dussaq, "who all day long and far into the night would be instructing them on how to use our weapons."[11]

The ill-equipped defenders in the battle "were magnificent," writes Wake. They consistently inflicted "4 to 10 percent" more casualties on the Germans than the Germans did on the Maquis.[12] But it wasn't enough. By nightfall, Gaspar ordered a withdrawal to Chaudes-Aigues, perhaps only ten miles away as the crow flies, but much longer in actuality as anyone traversing between the two had to go up and down mountains and across rivers and lakes in the ravines, dangerously exposed. Dussaq, he writes in his after-action report, took "a company" of men to Clavieres, a small mountainside village used as an outpost by the Maquis, "to cover the withdrawal of the main body." He must have been involved in considerable fighting because, he recalls, "we sustained the loss of some 40 men, 25 missing and 15 certainly dead."[13] It was probably during this time that he acquired the name "Capt. Bazooka."

Among the supplies periodically airdropped to the area by the Allies were the new American anti-tank rocket launchers nicknamed "Bazooka." They were shoulder-fired and resembled a long pipe. A popular Arkansas comedian of the day, Bob Burns, had, as part of his country music routine, an instrument that resembled the tubular weapon. He called it a "Bazooka." The army adopted the comical name. Apparently, the Maquis had been having trouble using theirs. Dussaq writes that during the first Mont Mouchet attack "I heard severe criticism of our anti-tank weapons, the bazooka. I had the opportunity of showing [that the weapon] could easily stop any enemy armored car, with the result that from then on [they called him] 'Capt. Bazooka.'"[14]

If not during the retreat, it's possible he had received the nickname several days later. "Three days after the [evacuation]," he wrote, "we ambushed at the Pont du Garabit [a towering railway bridge over the Truyere River] two German trucks with 12 enlisted men, mostly Armenians, one German noncommissioned officer, one lieutenant, and a captain who just before dying told us they had lost 1,400 men at [Mont Mouchet]...On our side we could not tell exactly how many we had lost because few company commanders kept a list of those under their command. When the Maquisards fell in German hands they were killed and often mutilated with all personal identity papers removed. Often some boys would run away and hide during the course of an action and reappear 50 miles away two or three weeks later."[15]

The retreating Maquis regrouped around Chaudes-Aigues and St.Marital, another town nearby in the mountainous complex, served, among others, by the mighty Truyere River. Once again—against the urgings of their foreign advisors, including Dussaq—Maquis commanders massed on the plateaus and in the ravines, presenting inviting targets. Again rejecting advice to disperse, Gaspard vowed to stand and fight to the death. Furthermore, if the massing wasn't enough to invite assault, Chaudes-Aigues sat on a main road the Germans needed for transit to Normandy. That alone marked it for attack. Then, on June 12—two days after the bloody Mont Mouchet fight—local Maquis ambushed and killed SS Capt. Hugo Geissler, head of the Gestapo in Vichy. Geissler had been one of the leaders of the June 10 attack. His death inflamed the Germans, who were already bent on revenge. They rounded up and shot local civilians. On the day they attacked Mont Mouchet, they had massacred an entire village, Oradour, murdering 642 civilians, mostly women and children, many of whom were locked in a church and burned alive.[16] The Germans were savagely angry. Everyone knew it was only a matter of time before they returned—and with much greater force.

■ ■ ■

The second major attack against the redoubt—a makeup for the enemy's failings in the first—began in the early morning darkness of June 20. Roaring in was a huge force of approximately twenty-one thousand enemy soldiers—crack infantry, hundreds of armored cars and tanks supported by heavy artillery, dive bombers, and strafing fighters.[17] Dussaq, who was at Fridefont, wrote, "The Germans attacked from three sides simultaneously, placing their artillery batteries three miles north of Chaudes-Aignes" and "on a line running south of St. Martial."[18] Dussaq tried to get Col. Thomas to take his men and outflank some of the big guns, he writes, but Thomas bungled the job. Another Maquis commander, equally inexperienced, placed his men on the wrong side of a river, effectively taking them out of the fight. "Seeing that it was useless to make [such commanders] understand modern [guerilla] tactics...I then decided to move from one company to another and give them all the assistance within my power."[19]

It did little good. Despite "many individual examples of astounding courage," he wrote, "the complete lack of liaison between our different groups [spread out over several mountains in the complex] and the demoralizing effect of aerial bombardment and strafing" forced a rout.[20] The Maquis were nearly encircled; those not killed eventually scattered—scurrying into the woods, down rocky ravines, and into the lower river beds and pastures. For a while, Gaspard was deaf to pleas by his Freelance advisors to evacuate but eventually agreed after Wake, desperate for a way to make him comply, faked a communiqué supposedly from Free French authorities in London, but really just made up, ordering him to do so.[21]

Before the attack, Freelance headquarters, now at St. Marital, had taken in several downed Canadian flyers trying to escape back to England. As the defenses deteriorated, they, Farmer, Nancy Wake, the wife of one of the Maquis commanders, and radio operator Rake, fled to nearby woods and got separated. Dussaq, leaving from Fridefont, went looking for them. On the way, he observed a distant firefight and "decided to...find out what was going on." Encountering an abandoned position on the outskirts of the fight, he found a jammed machine gun. He was now close enough to see the enemy advancing. The gun had quit due to "a bad headspace adjustment." It was an easy fix for him. He was well-versed in machine gunnery. He started firing "short bursts" at attackers, killing some, until his ammunition was spent. Hastily retreating back into the woods, he was almost wounded by mortar fire aimed at a nearby road on which others were exiting. "They hit my hat with a fragment." "...one of the poorest demonstrations of mortar fire I have ever witnessed," he wrote with obvious bravado.[22]

In truth, he was fortunate to have escaped decapitation.

Unable to find those he was looking for, Dussaq snuck back to Fridefont to find it evacuated and the Germans entering. "Knowing then that the only road to escape left me was through the Vallee de la Truyere, I went in that direction." The valley was where most of the other retreaters were emerging. Later he made contact with Wake. Escaping the attackers, she, and apparently Major Farmer, perhaps others, were in a car on the road to Fridefont where they thought they could find refuge when attacked by a German fighter plane. "I could see [the pilot's] helmet and goggles as he banked to continue the pursuit, and I could hear the bullets whizzing as his aim got closer and closer. Suddenly a Maquisard who was hiding in the bush signaled me, shouting...jump. We flung ourselves into a culvert by the roadside as the plane flew overhead. The young man explained that Fridefont was...evacuated and Bazooka was waiting for me further down the mountain...I was delighted to find Bazooka. He always looked after me when he was around."[23]

With others in retreat, the reunited began the difficult trek north to Saint Santin, a distant village through the mountains towards Vichy where they hoped to regroup. "The Germans were patrolling all the bridges over the...Truyere which was deep, rapid and dangerous in most parts," writes Wake.[24] But the Maquis had an "ingenious scheme" for crossing the threatening water. Downstream from the bridges, they had areas secluded by heavy foliage. Several feet beneath the surface of the rushing water, they had "installed layer after layer of heavy slabs of local stone" and "covered them by secured dead tree trunks. [The stones] were not visible from above...All we had to do was remove our footwear, release the [concealing] logs...and cross in absolute safety."[25]

It took them four days to reach Saint Santin. German planes crisscrossed the skies above the trees and rocks concealing them, randomly dropping bombs presumably to hit or flush out Maquis. Luckily, none scored. But after two days of running and hiding, "we were all thirsty and starving."[26] They slept in barns, and were fed by locals, although sometimes they were turned away because of fear of reprisal, orneriness, and, according to Wake, prejudice against raggedy peasants, which, in their current state, many of them resembled. On their last leg, they met a subdued Gaspard leading another retreating group. Showing he had no hard feelings for those who had warned him, he "took my arm and walked the rest of the way with me and Bazooka."[27]

Safe in Saint Santin—at least for the time being—they learned details. Doctors and nurses attending wounded Maquis had been murdered in reprisal.[28] German Tartar troops from Eastern Europe, descendants of Mongols, had been mutilating the dead for plunder. Severed fingers, gold wedding rings still attached, had been found in dead Tartar pockets.[29] While they had battled, German convoys had slipped through at Chaudes-Aignes to head north to Normandy. "These convoys should have been ambushed," wrote Dussaq.[30] He confronted the leaders. "There was...a tendency on [their] part to justify their defeats...by blaming London for not equipping them with the proper weapons. I was very blunt in setting these gentlemen straight. Our efforts had been to discourage the massing [and encourage] guerrilla [tactics] to ambush...convoys, blow...up bridges and generally harass...the enemy. As for the weapons [sent by the Allies], they were excellent, and it was...not our fault if the men did not apply themselves...[to] learning all about them. To the credit of Gaspard, I must say that my bluntness did not alienate him but rather brought about a very fine understanding between us."[31]

At one point—it's not clear when—Dussaq writes that he asked for volunteers to return to Fridefont and "attack the Germans from the rear. I met with 100 percent negative answer, although I believe that Nancy offered to come with me."[32] At the time, Denis Rake was still missing. "I decided I would go back again to the woods in an effort to find [him]."

Dussaq had developed a relationship with the crucial radio operator—and not, it appears, the kind those in the know might suspect. Rake, who would later be awarded a British Military Cross (MC) for bravery, was an outspoken homosexual at a time when such admission could have landed him in jail or worse. Early on, Freelance had designated Dussaq, married and demonstrably heterosexual, to keep Rake out of trouble, a duty he'd apparently taken very seriously. Rake had already angered at least one French father who charged that the Brit had made audacious advances towards his son. Code-named "Roland" and a captain by rank, Rake "never concealed the fact that he was [gay]," writes Wake. "We could not close our eyes to the problems which would arise if we let him run wild amongst the good-looking young men in the Maquis."[33]

As far as the record shows, Dussaq, at least up to that time, was no friend of homosexuals. As a youth, he had defied his father and refused when the elder had wanted him to take dancing lessons in order to learn "the noble art of Terpsichore," a supposedly mind-and-body bettering exercise of sultry physical moves named for the ancient Greek Muse who first practiced it. One look at this "effeminate" male instructor, he wrote, "convinced me...I would have no part in an art" that was not "virile."[34] Ironically, becoming a professional dancer in 1936 on a bet—a friend had taunted that he didn't have the skill to do it—he'd started a fight with a rowdy audience member who had challenged his manhood with a homosexual slur.[35] But now in France he had acknowledged respect for Rake's "courage...He is a man who, although not a soldier"—a reference apparently to Rake's chosen profession as an actor and comedian—"has all the qualities that one would like to find in a soldier," and eventually joined in recommending Rake's later decoration, one of Britain's highest.[36] Rake, in turn, according to his biographer, Geoffrey Elliot, described Dussaq as "handsome, debonair and tough."[37] In his own biography, he gives the following descriptions of his designated protector:

> I remember very well a trip I made with him...there were Germans about, we moved mostly in the very early morning or late at night. One day...extremely tired, we stopped at a farmhouse and asked for help. We were very well received by the farmer and his wife, who invited us in for a meal...we sat around the kitchen table...The farmer's two small boys could not keep their eyes off us, especially "Bazooka."
>
> Bazooka was a great leg-puller, and he told the boys some really gigantic fairy-tales about what had happened to us in the Maquis. They looked at him wide-eyed. Then pointing to

me, he said in a sinister voice, "This one here is the real ogre.
You must be very careful with him; he eats little boys!" At
that moment, for some reason or other, I stood up, and the
boys who were sitting on the other end of my bench were
suddenly sent sprawling on the floor as the bench
tipped... They scrambled with shrieks and ran to their father
believing I was going to attack and eat them.[38]

Rake notes that Dussaq was "a heavy smoker, and the next day, after
we had left the farm, he found that his lighter would not work. He was
very put out and after we had walked several miles he decided to call at
a farmhouse and ask for matches and a drink of water. It was always...a
risk calling at a strange house. The occupants might be pro-Vichy or
pro-German [or] against the Maquis because they feared...repri-
sal...'It'll be best if we say we're escaped prisoners of war,' 'Bazooka'
suggested. 'We won't speak at all, just make signs.' So we went to the
door and knocked. A young woman opened it. 'Bazooka' said something
like, 'Light! Light!' all the time gesticulating with his lighter, which suddenly burst into flames. The young woman was so scared she slammed
the door in our faces. 'Bazooka', with a look of bewilderment...regarded
the lighter, which now worked properly, for a minute or two, and then
[cursed it] for having deprived him of a smoke for so long. Then he saw
the joke and we went on, both of us chuckling to ourselves for the next
mile or more."[39]

In another situation they were in a village where a lot of Maquis
resided and were invited to a party in a "local bistro." The party got loud
with people singing patriotic songs like in the movie *Casablanca*. But in
a corner, Rake noticed disapproval. "I overheard two elderly men saying
it would be a good thing if they could get these English out of the village
because they were dangerous and undoubtedly attracting the attention
of the Germans."[40] It made him angry, wrote Rake, and he started a
scuffle, which was quickly broken up.

The next morning an angry young villager came to where they were
staying, demanding that Nancy Wake, the first he encountered, explain

the previous night's "vicious attack" on his father. Seeing Rake, he challenged menacingly, "It was you, wasn't it?" Wake stepped quickly between them, warning the youth that it was obvious his father was either pro-German or a collaborator, and if he didn't behave himself, "I will personally see that [your father] is liquidated...The poor young fellow was quite taken aback and at once became very apologetic... 'Phew!' said 'Bazooka' when the young man had gone. 'I thought I was going to have to roll up my sleeves for you, Den-Den [Rake's nickname].' If it had come to that, he certainly would. I missed him terribly for quite a time after he had left us."[41]

Given Rake's proclivities, the statement of deep affection begs a question: Was there more to their relationship than just Dussaq's devotion to duty? Only one other aspect of Dussaq's life even hints so—his early 1930s involvement with Hollywood heart-throb Antonio Moreno, who allegedly was gay.[42] But that, as we shall see, is more about an apparent tragic accident, or worse, than a homosexual relationship. And nothing else I've encountered suggests Dussaq was anything but a devoted husband during the war.

■ ■ ■

It's unclear from available sources whether Maj. Farmer accompanied Dussaq to find Rake. Some indicate he did but there are contradictions. After two days and "some 170 kilometers" (approximately one hundred miles), writes Dussaq, "I found him [Rake], and on foot I led him [back] to Saint Santin."[43]—a journey described by biographer Elliot as "days of sheer hard slog up and down stony slopes and across the many streams and rivers which fissure the terrain, especially the Truyere. Its deep waters ran so fast through its rocky gorge that the Germans believed it impassable."[44] Making things worse was the fact that while crossing one of the Maquis's submerged and camouflaged "causeways," Rake, who had strung his boots around his neck, lost them in the rushing water. Earlier, on a previous mission in France, he had been captured and tortured by the Germans, which had left his feet injured. Now they were bare. Makeshift coverings had to be fashioned from available uniform cloth as "the baying of German tracker dogs" could be heard. Given Wake's condition—"lame, unfit, middle-aged," wrote Elliot—and Dussaq having to cope with it as well as his own hindrances—made their successful trek back "an extraordinary accomplishment."[45]

4

The Lion

EARLY 1920s

Young "Rajah"—the nickname René's father affectionately bestowed—
couldn't sleep. He was approximately ten years old, probably younger,
but certainly in the formative years when slumber comes quickly to
a tired youth. Yet he couldn't settle. He was tormented: "You're afraid to
do a handstand on our balcony," a voice within him challenged. "No I'm
not!" he countered—but he was. He just wouldn't admit it to himself as
he lay there alone in the silent darkness.

"Ever since I can remember," he wrote years later, "I have always
tried to give an impression of feeling in a way that I really did not feel.
The feeling of fear [troubled] me tremendously. The thought of being
afraid...would prevent me from having any peace of mind or peace of
heart. Whenever I thought I might be afraid of something I had immediately to proceed and prove to myself [and others, if need be] that such
was not the case."

His father, whom René, at that young age, regarded literally as God, had taught him and his older brother, Maurice, to stand on their hands almost from infancy—part of the elder's belief that physical prowess helped spiritual enlightenment. "After years of practice, doing a handstand had become to me as easy, practically, as standing on my feet." Now, laying there in the dark, he was compelled. "If I was ever to go to sleep, I had to sneak out of my room, go to the balcony, and do the handstand."

His apartment, either in Buenos Aires or Paris, possibly in Geneva—all places the family lived in those days because of his father's diplomatic job—was many floors up. From it, the plunge was straight to a stone pavement. A fall would kill or certainly maim him—more reason, he now decided, to go do it.

He exited his bed and hopped on to the balcony railing, hands first.

That account comes from an autobiography Dussaq began, probably before World War II, possibly right after, but never finished—at least as far as I know. Entitled *Adventure to Order*, I obtained it from his family.[1] Almost two hundred pages long, it deals mostly with his childhood and early adult years, ending with his adventures as a young deep-sea diver and treasure hunter in the late 1930s. True to his mysterious ways, it says next to nothing about his involvement in Latin American revolutions and purposely avoids[2] the 1933 auto crash and death of Los Angeles socialite Daisy Moreno in which he was the ill-fated driver. In those two ways alone it is disappointing. They are both mysterious events in his life I'd like to know more about. The manuscript does, however, shed light on how he became who he was.

He had been afraid of fear as long as he could remember. He fought it with an affected bravado and athletic ability. When he was five years old and his father had decided it was time he learn to swim, he saw a young man diving from a board. It scared him. So the fear became a challenge. He decided to dive even before learning to swim. His father, who encouraged the children to do as they wished—as long as they accepted the consequences—agreed.

In his childish mind, the son of God was protected, and even helped in his quests. "In all the years to come…I have always…consciously or unconsciously tried to prove that [the] faith I had in my father was justified…"[3] But belly-flop after belly-flop that day at Lake Geneva soon had him in tears. He wouldn't quit. Stubbornness and pride, he wrote—traits he'd carry throughout his life—prevented it. Even at that early age, he was a neophyte grandstander, a show-off, a budding conman in the sense that he would not admit that he wasn't capable—even if he wasn't. He kept diving until, at last—at least in his own mind— he was performing as the diver he'd witnessed.

He'd beaten the fear.

At least that was how he felt.

In time, Dussaq began to count on such successes. "Many were the times…when, out of a bluff, I claimed to be able to perform things, and…lacked the courage to admit that I had been merely bluffing."[4] But such "pride" and "arrogance," he wrote, forced "the hand of destiny" and helped him reap advantages like admiration from others and opportunity he felt he otherwise never would have gotten. This, in turn helped develop in him a resolve that could also be called courage. "For years I have bluffed," he wrote. "I confess it, for I do not feel particularly proud of it…But I do not recall to have boasted…to be ready to do a thing…and when the time came, to have backed down."[5]

Such resolve figured in one of his first transformations.

Sheltered in his formative years first by home tutoring and then by strict Catholic school, he received a rude awakening when the family moved to Geneva, Switzerland, and he was enrolled in public school there. For the first time he heard "dirty" stories that "shocked" him, and was bullied embarrassingly by older, bigger boys. In the past, his brother, Maurice, five years older, had kept such harassment away. But Maurice was now in college.

The sexual awakenings were the worst. They induced "terrible," "shameful" thoughts in his head for which, at that age and naivety, he was unprepared. The older boys instantly saw it and delighted in tormenting him more. Convinced he was heading for hell, he went to a priest, who made it worse. "Somehow I failed to express myself clearly...or he failed to understand...I left the confessional frightfully upset, feeling I was damned forever."[6]

René couldn't tell his family. He couldn't rest. His new problem grew to obsession. "The intensity [was] such that I became ill...For a month I stayed home, running high fever, wishing I would die, and yet fearing [death) because [surely] I would burn in...hell..."[7]

The ordeal was a crucible and eventually hardened him. "When I returned to school [sensitivity] seemed to have abandoned me...I became very bitter toward those who most loved me [his family] and of course toward those whom I held responsible for the agony I had just known. From that moment on, I seemed to have just one thought...To become so strong that I would make all those who had [tormented] me physically or mentally pay for whatever they had done."[8]

For several years Dussaq worked diligently in the gymnasium, took lessons in acrobatics, wrestling, and boxing, and, because he was still much younger than the bigger, stronger boys who manned the oars on the rowing team—he was only fourteen—he competed for and won the position of coxswain, the team member who shouted the strokes and navigated the boat. In Switzerland, contrary to most other countries, the coxswain was given important and crucial responsibility.

"Gradually [as he grew and became stronger] I started to impress some of [the] older boys, who up to that moment had made fun of me with the thought that if they stepped out of line I could take care of myself, either fairly or foully."[9] Still bent on revenge, but revering his father's advice, he asked him if he should challenge those who had hurt him. Never look for a fight, said his father, but be strong enough that people will see it and won't take advantage. However, "if by letting somebody do something to you and not taking a firm stand you [are] encouraging that person to repeat the same experience, it might be wise to put a stop to it."[10]

That was all he needed. But Dussaq does not give details of what happened next, other than the following: "Although my father's advice had been of a conciliatory nature, I felt that I would have no peace…until I would humiliate that same fellow as publicly as he had humiliated me…Although physically he probably was much stronger than I was, I went ahead with my plans and I startled him so much that I got away with it."

What had he done? Hit his tormentor so fast and hard that the older boy had gone down afraid to rise? Surprised him with a sucker punch? Scared or beaten him with a special tactic? Not that the details are so important—although I'd like to know them—but their absence is an example of the manuscript's defects.

Obviously, René's father was a major influence on him—especially in his younger years.

Born in Havana in 1882, Emilien T. Dussaq, whose own father (René's grandfather) was French, was a large man of great kindness, patience, and purpose. His family had land and businesses in Cuba. They had come from France in the 1800s. They ran travel services for steamships, the major mode of international travel in those days, import and export activities, and, because of their success, had significant land and agricultural holdings. "Dussaq & Company," later renamed to "Dussaq & Toral," offered a variety of services to and from the island nation and did so until at least the 1960s, according to references I found. But instead of joining his family's lucrative enterprises, Emilien chose the diplomatic corps, and was involved in the establishment of the League of Nations, the international organization formed after World War I to try to keep world peace.

But a personal spiritual quest eventually seems to have taken precedence in Emilien's life, and in 1922—at the age of forty—he was appointed general secretary of the Sufi Movement in Geneva. The appointment was made by Inayat Khan, the Indian Sufi leader regarded as the spiritual teacher who brought the Sufi Order to the West.[11] That, not his job as Cuban general consul in Geneva, appears to have been Emilien's main focus from then on.

"Father had that great quality of helping people not by his advices but rather by his example," writes René. "Never once did he ask us to do anything that he was not ready to do himself." For example, physical culture: the children would wake for school at 6 a.m. to see him exercising. "We would remain in our bed and look at him...admiring him in a very objective fashion...One of our favorite pastimes was to touch [his] tremendous muscular arm...because a child is at first struck by the physical expression of life." It was "astonishing" and, to a young mind, engendered "reverence...linked very closely to worship."

Underlying how important his father was in his life, René begins his autobiography by recalling the utter devastation of experiencing, at five years old, his father leaving the family for Argentina during World War I in order to sell property he owned to ease hard times brought on by the conflict.

"I was hanging desperately to one of my father's powerful legs as a man who is drowning [hangs] desperately on a buoy...It is the first emotion that I can remember...so intense at the thought of him going away without taking me...that [the] unreasoned love that I had for him was on the verge of turning to hatred...The very thought of parting with father without understanding [what] was driving [him] away...was so strong that everything else seemed to have no importance—[not] the encouragement of a loving mother, or the companionship of an older brother or older sister [which he had] was capable of relieving my head from that bursting feeling it had...[Those months] remained in my memory as the...most lonely...I probably have ever spent."[12]

Eventually Emilien returned and inspired his son on a new quest, what René called "mastery of the mind."

"Of all the things I admired in father [the most] was [his] tremendous power of concentration...At times of great strain and great financial difficulties father would remain cool and collected, ever trying his utmost to overcome whatever obstacles he met on the road of life and never once letting whatever disturbance that he might have interfere with his kindness and understanding of our own childish predicaments..."

"Father...would practice the training...given to all the great mystics of the Orient...When I asked him why he was spending so many hours at night in meditation, he would tell me that the purpose was to develop that mastery of the mind that [allows] man to concentrate or focus…on whatever subject he chooses, rather than to have whatever subject choose him." This ignited René. "I had on that occasion my first true glimpse of the mystery that is presented by man's mind. How can a man think according to his wishes and not have [different thoughts jumping] right and left…I wished very sincerely that I had that power of concentration."[13]

Eventually, given the dangerous tasks he'd be performing that demanded focus, I believe he found it. But even before that, he was to get another confirmation of his believed father-supplied invincibility.

A year after he had traveled to Paris for the 1924 Olympics, only to sit disappointingly on the sideline as an alternate, René was designated official coxswain on the Nautical Club of the Geneva team that won the World Rowing Championship. And that was after winning the Swiss high school singles tennis championship—a heady combination of accomplishments for anyone so young. The trip to and from the Paris competition ate heavily into his study time. In order to graduate, René took his school math examinations the day after he returned. His father had reminded him that he would want to plan his time carefully for studying or suffer the humiliation of repeating his senior year.

Unfortunately, he'd spent most of his free time exploring Paris and tossing floating corks into the Seine River in order to discover helpful currents and map the best course for the competition. The extra work, dubbed "brilliant" by his teammates, had enabled them in the win to set a speed record. But neglect of his studies meant he faced calamity when he returned.

To remedy the dearth, he took a gamble. He opted, in the short time of travel home, to study only the hardest question of approximately fifty he might be asked—a tough fifty to one shot that he would be right, he notes. "How comforting then it was to feel that one is the son of God…Although that faith I had was great, still there was an element of worry that I could not very well overcome [those odds]." Nevertheless, "I presented myself before my professor and he asked me to draw a question out of the bag."[14]

Extending his hand, "I held my breath." He needn't have worried. The paper he picked unfurled in heavenly glory. It was the one he'd studied—the hardest question of the exam! "Good old father!" he thought, hiding his emotion. "He never failed me—the only question I knew. Because of its difficulty, the professor offered me to draw again (saying) it was so difficult...I looked at him and an actor was born...I told him that as a faithful student of Geneva High School I had considered it my duty to study all possible questions and that I felt it imperative that I should answer this question whether difficult or not. I could hear the silent clapping of my fellow students."[15]

Years earlier he had asked his father, "If God created the world, why is there fear and doubt?" His father had answered with a story from the mystics.

There was an orphan lion cub who, right after birth, had been adopted by sheep. He ran with the herd, ate grass, and bleated, unaware of whom he really was. One day a ferocious lion attacked sending the herd fleeing. The little lion ran with the others, bleating cowardly. Puzzled, the big lion grabbed him. "What are you doing? You're a lion!" "Oh no," said his cowering captive. "I'm a sheep. I'm afraid of you." Disgusted, the big lion took him to a river and made him look at his reflection. For the first time, he realized the truth and after the shock subsided, he roared. "I'm a lion!" he said proudly. "Yes," said his teacher. "Now go act like one."[16]

In the same way, said Emilien, until one learns who he really is, he is afraid and confused. He also told Rajah, "You have an inclination toward accomplishment of physical feats."[17]

In René's mind, he was a lion.

5

Maquis

SUMMER 1944

Back in Saint Santin after Denis Rake's retrieval, Dussaq solidified his relationship with Gaspard. He "told me this," writes René. "'I am the head of the resistance in the Auvergne but I am not a trained officer. I have under me some career staff officers that I have accepted for the sake of harmony although they do not fit as guerrilla fighters. When in the course of your operations you come across officers who do not come up to par in action, let me know and I'll see to it that they be removed. On the other hand any man that you wish to recommend for promotion will be promoted.' I must say he kept his promise."[1]

But the situation in the small village was tense.

Even though Rake had returned, he was without his radio and codes, which had been lost in the hasty retreat. With communication to London thus impossible, the Maquis were more vulnerable and Freelance was unable to respond to Allied orders or make requests. Farmer sent Nancy

Wake over one hundred miles north by bicycle to Chateauroux to try to find, in effect, another radio.[2] Complicating matters, the Germans, in continued retaliation for opposition, had savaged local villages, including Clavieres, where Dussaq had helped cover the Mont Mouchet fighters in their retreat. The Nazis had executed the bulk of the small village's young men—nine by some estimates, more by others—and murdered the town's mayor, who had sought naively to negotiate under a white flag.[3] Saint Santin residents, including its mayor, feared the same retaliation and were accusing the Maquis of being responsible for the massacres.

Dussaq went to the mayor and demanded he gather the townspeople. "I spoke very bluntly as to the fact that if it were not for the French resistance and for those who were falling before the German bullies, France would not [because of the collaborating Vichy government] still be considered among the foreign nations as a fighting ally; [and further] that the Allies would win this fight with or without the resistance, and that it was advisable for all Frenchmen to put themselves at this early date on the side of the Allies in anticipation of victory day. The result of the talk seemed to be very satisfactory, for from then on we received the full collaboration of the mayor and all those under his rule."[4]

There is some mystery here. One document I received from the U.S. National Archives, entitled "Appendix to Dussaq ITG"—apparently a first interrogation shortly after he'd left France—indicates that he "had been accused of shooting boys that had fled away."[5] He mentions in his after-action report the problem of young Maquis fleeing battles and returning after the fighting, but does not indicate any retribution. On the contrary, he seems understanding of the problem. The interviewer indicating he shot offenders was probably mistaken. However, if Dussaq had personally dealt punishment, his speech to the townspeople would have had more power—they were dealing with someone who would not tolerate desertion or cowardice. Such retribution might have been the source of the disturbing memories his second wife had reported.

Whatever the truth, Nancy Wake returned from her grueling four-day bicycle trip exhausted, bloody-thighed from the incessant pedaling, and without a radio. But she had made contact with a resistance group that possessed one, and they had agreed to send a message to London explaining Freelance's situation. Unfortunately, she had been forced to exit before the message was dispatched, leaving them with only the hope that reinforcements might be parachuted in.

For Dussaq, there was an additional glitch—a troublesome communist "chief" of one of the disparate groups amongst their Maquis. He liked one of the group's young apolitical leaders and wanted to use him and some of the unit on ambushes. But the problematic chief, disparagingly called "the eye of Moscow," was always meddling for political reasons and hindering Dussaq's plans.[6] "Through his sheer stupidity," Dussaq wrote of the chief, "he caused me to miss a very good operation in Aurillac [a large town in their area from which the Germans operated]. In front of all the company and all those under his orders, I called him a jackass, and what amazed me most was the fact that all his subordinates seemed to agree with me, and yet they were unable to dislodge him from his position."[7]

■ ■ ■

Nancy Wake's contact with the group to whom she had biked appears to have been successful. In the next few weeks, a new radio was parachuted in—along with a second trained and highly valued radio operator. For whatever reason—probably increased pressure from London as the Allies tried to break out of Normandy—Farmer gave an order to split Freelance operations. He, Wake and, eventually, Denis Rake, moved to another location. Farmer—or those directing him to make the change—gave Dussaq a vote of confidence by leaving him in charge of the old territory. Thus empowered, Dussaq moved quickly to do what he liked best—attack. ("My only interest was to go after the Germans and kill them...")[8]

He had a local Maquis commander he respected, a "Commandant Carlian, a very fine French captain of the regular army." They set up units similar to "American paratroopers," the U.S. soldiers Dussaq was most proud of being a part. Within the units, they formed three-man ambush "parties" which would "constantly go out hunting Germans along national roads wherever the terrain would lend itself to such operations."[9]

With new false papers, he snuck into Aurillac in the foothills, and somehow—he doesn't say—"secured direct information from the German Kommandantur, which enabled us to ambush successfully a German column that was trying to leave the town to rejoin their forces in Saint Flour," an enemy-controlled hub near Fridefont and Mont Mouchet.[10]

While in Aurillac, he set up an assassination. "I made arrangements with a milicien [native Milice member] to kill La Haye, the head of the milice in Aurillac, and provided him with a silent gun." (Marcel Lahaye "was definitely the leader of the Militia" in that area, a French source later wrote me. But he fled around this time with the Germans and survived until executed by the French in June 1945.[11] So he apparently escaped any attempt on his life.) In addition, Dussaq wrote, he dealt with another problem. "My adjutant arrested a woman from the milice who had sold to the Gestapo 18 young men from the Maquis."[12]

No further details are provided.

In late July, as the Allies broke out of a stalemate at Normandy and began fighting into the French interior, Dussaq received orders to go to Ambert, near Vichy, heart of the French collaboration government—a particularly dangerous area to be resisting the authorities. His propensity for action only heightened—getting him into trouble. "We traveled in three cars in the company of Colonel Gaspard [other Maquis leaders, and Freelancers, including Farmer]. As we were approaching Ambert and crossing a national route south of Clermont-Ferrand [one of the region's largest cities], we observed a German truck loaded with troops and mounted with a machine gun. I immediately got myself into position and opened fire with my carbine, for which I was reprimanded, since our mission was to go to Ambert and not to attack the Germans."[13]

The reprimand didn't seem to change things much. Left in Ambert "to await the arrival of 60 parachutists [which the Maquis and apparently Freelance thought were coming]," he was idle for five days. The paratroopers didn't show. "So I took it upon myself to continue doing what I had done since my arrival in France: to look for Germans and attack them whenever feasible."[14]

6

"Crashing the Door"

LATE 1920s–EARLY 1930s

When René asked his father how to become enlightened, Emilien answered thusly:

"All people in the world have a different way of reaching the same goal...The very purpose of religion [is] to help people reach higher for an ideal...By bowing in reverence and humility toward that ideal and endeavoring to become one with such an ideal, man gradually would progress and evolve toward a higher state of perfection...The difference between people is not in the goal they are all [trying] to reach, but that some people are dragged toward it unconsciously and unwillingly."

"He told me that between the world in which I lived, with all its anxieties...and desires, and the spiritual world into which I seemed at times to be attracted, was a door—a closed door...I had the opportunity, if I chose, to use the door knob...and peacefully enter the room; or else try to crash into the room by bumping my head against the door," which, he said, was perfectly acceptable, "as long as I did not mind…the [results of the] crash through it."[1]

So what was the way for René?

"Well, he said, my [path] might not be favorable to your temperament…Some people, to realize and understand the spiritual life, must exhaust all their desires to experience life through the physical plane…Probably with [your] character it would be necessary…to go out in the world, follow your fancy…for perceiving life through many different experiences."[2]

It was the answer René wanted to hear.

Graduating from college in 1930, plans were for him to attend law school in Geneva, then, through his father's connections, go to work for the League of Nations' Disarmament Department. But he wanted to see the world, and with a two hundred dollar gift from a family member that year, he was off to Paris. He was unable to find work, which bothered him. He didn't like being a "loafer." An uncle, on business in Paris, advised him to join the family still in Cuba, where undoubtedly he had spent at least summers, and where he could work with his brother Maurice at a steamship company. On the way, he almost decided to stay in Spain. During a port stop he saw a play where the main actor portrayed an adventurer. "I began to see myself in him…. he was spending his life [traveling], working just enough to support himself and enjoying life from many different angles."

The lifestyle appealed to him.

He was also "struck" by the play's leading lady, a beauty, whom he tried to engage backstage after the show. "For the first time I became aware that…a young lady…might be worth [challenging] the world."[3] He gives no other details except that he came to his senses just in time to make it back to the boat before it sailed.

In Havana, Maurice, a manager in Dussaq family business by this time, got him a job as a book-keeper for the Holland-America Line. He worked "faithfully," he writes, "putting numbers on paper and *still* more numbers." On free days, he rowed and played tennis, rising quickly by 1931 to become the country's celebrated national tennis champion.[4]

Photos show him dandily-dressed, shiny hair slicked back, looking narcissistically, almost flirtingly, into the camera. "I had popularity, friends...success" but, "I was becoming more conceited, arrogant, selfish—the opposite of what I wanted." He was straying, he writes, from his "desire to be truly spiritual." He did things—unspecified in the autobiography—which he says he should not have done but "could get away with." It was unfulfilling, "monotonous...I needed excitement. I needed thrills. I needed to experience life in such a way that would make me...familiar with strong emotions."[5]

At least one incident surely gave him that—his first parachute jump— an exercise, as it was, that came unexpectedly. "I was riding with a friend in an open-cockpit biplane," he told *Washington Post* reporter Ken Ringle years later when he and a group of aging veterans re-enacted their jumps into France in commemoration of the fiftieth anniversary of D-Day. The friend "inverted the plane suddenly and I fell out."[6] Luckily, he had the parachute on. René sold insurance and enrolled in law school at the University of Havana. But it made little difference. He was unhappy. Something was missing. "Fortunately" he writes, "they started at that time a revolution to overthrow the existing government."[7]

Cuba's history is full of insurrection—not just Fidel Castro's successful 1959 communist coup, so prominent in modern times. Since the days of Spanish rule, Cubans, many of them descendants of slaves and slaveholders, resisted outside control. The early 1930s were no exception. The 1898 Spanish-American War won the island its independence—but with caveats. Cuba was not a rich nation to begin with, and the 1898 war left it devastated. Businesses, predominately American, bought at deflated prices the nation's prized asset— sugar plantations and production. That caused dissension. The Platt Amendment, named for the American senator who proposed it—a concession to America for help in winning its independence—gave the U.S., among other privileges, the right to intervene militarily in Cuban affairs.

Platt was a burr beneath Cuba's saddle.

The early twentieth century saw a succession of corrupt, puppet Cuban leaders cow-towing to foreign investment, mostly American, leading to more outside control. In 1924, a former butcher and soldier-turned-politician, Gerardo Machado, was elected president. He combined nationalism and moderate cooperation with U.S. interests—a political tightrope to walk—and built the island's central highway, which was an economic boon, especially for the foreign-owned plantations. However, by the time Dussaq arrived—presumably in November 1930, as an immigration record I found indicates[8]—the Depression had engulfed Cuba's one-crop economy and Machado, in an effort to strengthen his power, suspended constitutional rights. He became a hated despot and truly earned his derisive nickname "The Butcher." *Time* magazine, for instance, reported that he actually fed political enemies to sharks.[9]

Strikes, rising taxes, hunger, and turmoil characterized the Cuba to which Dussaq returned. Students and nationalists, many of them communists, constantly demonstrated in the streets against the administration, clashing with government troops who sometimes killed them, deepening the outrage. A young, mercurial, soon-to-be Cuban leader, Sgt. Fulgencio Batista, the dictator Castro would one day depose, sided variously with Machado—but also with the opposition—another tightrope walk reserved for only the most cunning (which Batista would prove to be). Machado, escalating his repression against what he called "agitators from Moscow," was finally overthrown and sent fleeing in August 1933.

The record of Dussaq's participation in all this is murky.

There is little doubt his revolution was the one against Machado. His OSS entry profile, for instance, says he "was a machine gunner...in the Machado Revolution."[10] Also the timing—early 1930s—means it could be no other. But in his autobiography, he relates little of what made him flee:

"Although I had no direct interest in this particular revolution...I thought that maybe to take part...would permit me to...live some of those emotions I was eager to experience. I got myself involved in...such a way that my brother felt it would be wise to absent myself...without further delay. [He agreed that] my idea of seeing the world might be...

best…at this moment. We discussed the subject on a Wednesday evening. The next morning, Thursday, I was on board a boat bound for California."[11]

Obviously, his exit was quick and forced. What happened? Had he shot or killed someone? Thrown a bomb? Was it worse—maybe something basely criminal, only marginally related to politics, if at all? One would think that he would detail such a dramatic experience in an autobiography. But at the time he was writing—the 1950s or earlier—his father was most probably still alive and a Cuban diplomat. Perhaps his silence was to shield Emilien and/or family members still in Cuba who might be hurt by such a disclosure?

Whatever, the family, it so happened, had a contact in Los Angeles— a very influential contact. Antonio Moreno was the first Hollywood "Latin Lover"—before the more famous Rudolf Valentino or Ramon Novarro, two Latin heartthrobs who followed. In early silent movies from 1912 until the late–1920s, Moreno was the swooned-over, handsome actor who starred romantically with the biggest female names— sultry Greta Garbo, Lillian Gish, Mary Pickford, and the "it" girl, "Flapper" (as in Roaring '20s) Clara Bow. Moreno's dark looks and smoldering on-screen persona was part of the matinee model adopted by screen Casanovas who came later.

Moreno was barely a teenager in Spain near Gibraltar with big dreams but no future when, around 1902, he met two rich travelers from America taking the "grand tour" of Europe, the traditional enlightenment trek made by young men of means in those days. One of the two was Enrique de Cruzat Zanetti, a Cuban-born Harvard graduate whom Dussaq, years later, would refer to as "uncle." It's hard to officially connect Dussaq and Zanetti as blood relatives or in-laws, although they may have been. But strong ties certainly existed. Zanetti was a patriotic Cuban and lawyer from a well-to-do family like Dussaq who was educated primarily in the U.S. As a New York attorney and champion of Cuban independence,[12] he was a contemporary of René's father and a Sufi principal in Geneva prior to Emilien taking over as head of the movement in Switzerland. The two Sufis surely knew each other, and such a connection, as spiritual and cosmic as both kindreds would have felt, could easily have sufficed to allow Zanetti being thought of as "family."

Zanetti and his companion on the tour, Benjamin Curtis, nephew of then New York City Mayor Seth Lowe, took a liking to Moreno, who earned money helping and guiding tourists such as themselves. The young Moreno lived with his widowed and religious mother, who wanted him to be a priest. But he dreamed of adventure and far off places, especially America. In a 1924 Hollywood autobiography probably ghosted for the star, Moreno tells how the two men paid for his schooling and eventually brought him to the U.S., where Zanetti shepherded him into various jobs, such as Manhattan gas meter-reader, until, after appearing on his own in New York stage plays, he went to Hollywood and became a star. Specifics are vague as to the exact relationship between Zanetti, Curtis, and Moreno, but there is no question that Moreno was indebted to Zanetti.[13]

At the height of his movie career, in 1923, Moreno married Daisy Canfield Danziger, a Los Angeles socialite and fabulously wealthy oil heiress, who, claiming adultery by her first husband, LA attorney J. L. Danziger, divorced him and united with Moreno barely a year later. The union made Moreno, already famous and well paid, extravagantly rich and prominent. The two were at the top of Los Angeles high society in what was a budding and exciting world movie capital. They built a palatial Mediterranean-style mansion with an Olympic-sized pool on top of one of the highest mountains in the exclusive Silver Lake section of Los Angeles. On weekends the couple threw lavish parties. On weekdays, as Antonio presumably toiled at the studios, Mrs. Moreno aided charities and causes, including the Red Cross, and helped stuntmen, not yet well organized, get insurance.[14]

"I had a letter of introduction given to me by my uncle addressed to Mrs. Moreno in Los Angeles," writes René. "At the time I did not speak a word of English but with my usual confidence I felt it would be a matter of hours for me to master the Shakespearian language."[15]

It took him considerably longer, he later acknowledges.

Slowly passing through the Panama Canal, he had an urge to explore the mysterious flanking jungle—"maybe it was the fascination the unknown held"[16]—but he curbed it. In Santiago, Chile, another stop on the way, he had a run-in with a conman.

The stranger was "dignified" and appeared "honorable," he writes. The fact that he spoke Spanish and said he loved Cuba, cinched it for René. "To find somebody who spoke my language...was sufficient to make me feel very friendly toward him." He invited Dussaq for a drink in a café. Eyeing a "slightly intoxicated" patron, the new friend whispered that they could have some innocent fun: challenge the unsuspecting drunk to a rigged dice game, relieve him of his money, after which, of course, they would return it. Why not? thought Dussaq. "The idea of fooling that man appealed to me."[17]

But after multiple losses, the drunk asked suspiciously—and, in hindsight, surprisingly sober—why the other two always won? His acquaintance signaled to René to "lose once in a while," which he did. Soon, he was cleaned out. When it was time to go, he thanked his companion for the amusement, and asked for the money back. But "this gentleman seemed to express surprise, as if we had been gambling in earnest. Obviously I had been taken for a ride." It's noteworthy that what happened next tends to belie the innocence with which Dussaq portrays himself in the story.

"I had in my left pocket a brass knuckle. I seized it, grabbed my elderly friend by the throat...and threatened to smash him with the knuckle should he not return the money immediately"—which he did, with interest. A brass knuckle is not the usual possession of most luxury liner travelers—unless, of course, one is an enforcer or thug (or had been involved in violent, perhaps nefarious, activities previously as Dussaq, it appears, had been.) But these were different times, and Dussaq was supposedly on the run and alone. Further mitigating the situation is this: "Although on the surface I might have given him the impression that I did not know fear, I had to use all my will power as soon as I had the money not to run away like a scared rabbit. Being an actor, I had to uphold my dignity, and I walked away from the scene with what I thought great poise and trembling knees."[18]

Fifteen days after departing Havana, René's ship apparently docked in San Diego,[19] and he soon made his way north to Los Angeles and residence at the very swanky Lido Apartments in the heart of downtown Hollywood. At the time, it was a five-story, newly-constructed building complex, posh, and fashionable. It would later earn fame—or more rightly, infamy—as the decadent cover art for the Eagles rock band album, "Hotel California," a place of broken dreams and prostitutes, drug addicts, even devil worshippers.

Yet when René arrived, newspaper ads proclaimed it "Hollywood's Smartest Apartment Hotel," which it was—a shining, new art-deco creation in the heart of Dreamland, mere blocks from the famous "Hollywood and Vine" intersection and Grauman's elaborately exotic Chinese Theater, a main tourist attraction with its newly-instituted "Walk of Fame," where top movie stars had their palm prints immortalized in sidewalk cement. Rudolph Valentino would dance the tango in the Lido's spacious and glittering ballroom while visible from the hotel's windows was the spectacular fifty-foot-high mountainside "H-O-L-L-Y-W-O-O-D" sign.[20]

"Hollywood," wrote Dussaq, "that was the place for me. Ever since I was a little child, I held the stars of silent days in great admiration. Hollywood [had] a certain mystery, and whenever I [was] confronted with mystery my desire was to solve it." The Depression, however, also engulfed Southern California—which may explain the relief he expresses in arriving there: "I managed somehow to get to Hollywood and check into a hotel right on the main boulevard. I called on Mrs. Moreno with [my] letter of introduction. She had known my family for years, and always remembered that her husband, Antonio Moreno, had been helped by a member of my family at a time he was…in Spain without any resources. She had ever been thankful…and when she saw me, it was indeed with the greatest of kindness that she extended to me her hospitality." [21]

Then the page in his autobiography goes blank. There's nothing more about the monumental event in his life shortly to occur. He just ends his thoughts there, as if deciding he won't discuss it, and jumps to a new chapter about his later adventures as a treasure hunter and deep-sea diver. For the rest of his life, he keeps what was about to happen basically secret. He apparently informs some in his immediate family, but even then the details are muddled.

I'm talking about the death of Daisy Moreno, for which Dussaq, accident or not, bore responsibility, and which basically changed his life.

He hadn't really started working as a stuntman yet—at least not in the way he would. In the chapters he'd later write, he recalls getting an early chance studio job to fight a shark. Upon arriving at the studio, the shark was waiting "malevolently" in a tank, and he changed into his bathing suit. But the creature wouldn't fight. He tried goading it like a bullfighter, but it just hung there in the tank staring at him. He finally refused to kill the "pacifist." It didn't seem fair. The producers solved the dilemma by replacing the animal with a rubber fake "cleverly manipulated [by] string. It was a lot better than the live fish; it put up a much better fight, and I did not feel like a murderer."[22]

But following Daisy Moreno's coming death, he might have.

According to the meager accounts and a few documents available (everyone involved is now dead), here is what happened.

Early in February, the Morenos, after ten years of marriage, separated. They had already moved out of the lavish Silver Lake mountain mansion, by then known as "Crestmount" (and today, "Paramour"). Antonio had taken up residence in the Hollywood Athletic Club on Sunset Boulevard, the tallest building in the movie city and home to many of the era's biggest unattached and often partying stars.[23] Daisy rented an apartment at the more subdued and newly-built Fontenoy, a tall, art-deco tower-like building also overlooking Hollywood. It was only a block from the Lido, where René was staying.[24]

Dussaq, twenty-one, and Daisy, forty-seven,[25] were practically neighbors. But there is no available information about what happened between them after René introduced himself—until February 22. On that night, only a few weeks after he'd arrived, Dussaq was a guest at a small dinner party Daisy gave at the Beverly Wilshire Hotel in the heart of Beverly

Hills. The party was for her daughter Elizabeth and young husband Frances Tappaan, newlyweds of about six months. Husband Tappaan, a well-known Los Angeles athlete and rising attorney, was a former all-American tackle on the University of Southern California's championship football teams of the late 1920s. He and Dussaq, given René's athletic prowess, probably had much to talk about—if Dussaq's English had improved.

Antonio, estranged, was not at the party. It ended, according to newspaper accounts, shortly before 1 a.m., in the first hour of February 23. Daisy, Dussaq, and the Tappaans returned together to Daisy's apartment at the Fontenoy in a limousine she had hired. On the way, Frances Tappaan told the subsequent official inquest, they decided to have a "ham and eggs supper" at the Tappaan's home in Moreno Highlands, formerly owned by and named for the actor, near where Daisy and Antonio's former mansion was. When they had sold Crestmount, some of the choice property was subdivided into the Moreno development and a parcel went to the Tappaans.[26]

But rather than go straight to the residence, Daisy, according to Tappaan's inquest testimony, "wanted to show Dussaq the city from a hill top." So they transferred to her car, described in the coroner's report as a "Cadillac Sedan," and in the *Los Angeles Examiner* as "a big touring car."[27] Neither paper gives the year or model. Because "Mrs. Moreno's arm was still weak from an operation," Tappaan told a reporter, Dussaq drove.[28]

Thus, Daisy in a passenger seat, presumably in the front, and Dussaq at the wheel left in the opposite direction from the Tappaans to drive west through the Cahuenga Pass and up onto a newly-opened largely dirt road winding around an Eastern slope of the Santa Monica Mountains named after a local pioneer—Mulholland Drive or Highway, depending on what parts one is on, and when. Today, it's mostly Mulholland Drive, famous as a movie location and a mountaintop two-lane road off of which stars like Jack Nicholson make their storied residences. At its top at night, running level and ribbon-like amongst the mountain peaks, it offers fantastic, twinkling vistas of Los Angeles, Hollywood, and surrounding valleys—except Daisy and René never reached the top.

About halfway there, probably at the second or third[29] of what today appears to be a handful of relatively well-defined curves on the rising road, Dussaq told investigators, "I noticed the lights were dim. The fog was thick"—not unusual in the mountains at that time of year. He decided to brighten the lights by leaning down and adjusting them—which apparently took his eyes from the road. But "instead of turning the lights on full, I turned them off."[30]

The next thing he knew they were hurtling from the road and crashing down a steep incline. They had burst through rotting wooden guard rails and gone over a steeply sloping cliff. They plunged approximately three hundred feet,[31] the car going head over heels at least once, according to a drawing of the accident in the newspapers, until the ordeal came to a halt at the bottom of a box canyon. Dussaq, still at the wheel, had his lower back broken in several places, according to the doctor who later treated him.[32] Daisy, during the horrific descent, was hurled from the car and died instantly or shortly after, her chest crushed and lungs ruptured, among other serious injuries.[33]

Dussaq apparently thought she was still alive because, despite his injuries, he "miraculously" and "heroically," in the words of reporters and his doctor, climbed the three hundred feet out of the canyon up to Mulholland and hailed passersby Harold Viault and his wife, who were returning to their house in the San Fernando Valley after a late night card game. "There was blood on his face and he spoke with a slightly foreign accent," Viault told reporters. He was staggering and "gasped, 'Woman dying, woman dying, get ambulance.'"[34] Despite his injuries, Dussaq reportedly climbed back down the canyon to try to aid Daisy.

Viault found two policemen at the bottom of the mountain as it met the Cahuenga Pass (not far from where Universal Studios now rise). They rushed up. By means of a rope and using the Cadillac's broken hood as a sled, the policemen were able to get Daisy, found in "a pool of blood," up to the road and, after it arrived, into an ambulance. It was too late. The coroner's report indicates she was already dead. Dussaq was taken to St. Vincent Hospital in Hollywood, where he was described by investigators as "semi-hysterical...sobbing...'Oh God, I cannot say more now. It is too terrible.'"[35]

Moreno, unaware, was contacted at the athletic club by investigators and, they told the newspapers, "could not believe it." Taken to the hospital to view Daisy's body, he "reeled" and had to be "supported." Later, "he visited the spot where the tragedy occurred," then went into "seclusion."[36] Another account says Moreno "took charge of everything, sending Dussaq to a hospital and arranging for the funeral."[37] At the inquest the following day, Frances Tappaan insisted that René had not been drinking and was absolved "from any blame."[38] Moreno, apparently still in seclusion, did not attend the inquest. Daisy, according to her written wishes, was cremated following a private Religious Science service a few days later attended by more than one hundred people.[39]

That wasn't the end of it.

According to at least one book, as well as a European magazine, among other publications, "rumors swelled" that Daisy had been murdered."[40] It's doubtful that the rumors—at least publicly—swelled back then. Most, feeding on bits and pieces surrounding the incident, probably cropped up in later years as writers and others looked back at it with lingering questions—which legitimately existed. For instance, a *Los Angeles Examiner* story quotes Good Samaritan Viault as saying that when he inspected the crashed car, its "left front light was still glowing"—an apparent inconsistency if Dussaq had extinguished the lights."[41]

The rumors theorize that Moreno, whose career as a major actor was waning since (and because of) the advent of talkies (his accent was a problem), was fearful that his wife was going to divorce him and thus cut him off from her money. There are reports of raging fights between them.[42] Daisy, it was said, was tired of her husband's dalliances with both women and men, and was preparing to legally be rid of him. He therefore enlisted newcomer Dussaq, a fellow Latin and friend of a friend (Zanetti), to assist him. The theory was bolstered by the fact that Dussaq was a relatively anonymous adventurer who might be receptive to kill Daisy by running the car off the cliff. Dussaq was in need of money and skilled enough in crashes to execute the plot and survive.

Fueling the rumors is the following.

Moreno may have been gay or bisexual. He never married after Daisy's death and was best friends with William Desmond Taylor, one of early Hollywood's giant directors who was mysteriously murdered in 1922. The crime is still unsolved. King Vidor, a contemporary of Taylor's and also a celebrated director, investigated the murder, according to Vidor's biographer, Sidney Kirkpatrick, who concluded that Taylor led a secret gay life. In 1986, following Vidor's death, Kirkpatrick published the director's investigation in the critically-acclaimed book *A Cast of Killers*.[43] The book portrayed Moreno as having something to hide —and to those interested in Daisy's death, by inference, as a type who conceivably could have killed his wife. He was known to be the last person to talk by phone to Taylor before he was fatally shot.[44] Shortly after the murder, observed *Gibraltar Magazine* writer Reg Reynolds, Moreno married Daisy. "There were suggestions that Antonio was bi-sexual and had only married [her] at the urging of the studio to protect his Latin lover image."[45]

The Los Angeles police were notoriously corrupt in the 1930s, "an era," in the phrase of a *Los Angeles Times* story, "when mayors were crooks and L.A. cops were bagmen and bombers."[46] An influential and wealthy person like Moreno, with the right connections, could have paid or had other means (blackmail?) to have evidence suppressed. I tried to get the police report on the accident, but was told by LAPD that such a report (or reports) had long ago been destroyed, standard procedure for cases officially closed and so far back. Curiously, supporting documents to the coroner's report I found on microfilm—which may have been police reports and subsequent investigations—were listed as "missing." When I asked the coroner official why, she said she didn't know but volunteered, "High profile case. You know how those can go." The implication was tampering.

Coincidentally, Daisy's mother, Chloe, a beautiful socialite of turn-of-the-centery Los Angeles, was murdered in 1906. As wife of Daisy's father, Charles A. Canfield, oil magnate and cofounder of Beverly Hills with Edward Doheny, Chloe, a former school teacher, was a social and charity leader in what then was mostly a rural, dirt-road ranch community. One day a coachman, Morris Buck, who had been fired from the Canfield mansion, showed up to ask for a loan that he felt he was owed. Daisy's father was in Mexico attending to oil interests. Chloe, alone except for some of the children, answered the door. She invited him in, but ultimately refused the request. Buck shot her several times. She died in her living room. A child ran for help. Buck fled, but angry neighbors found him hiding. The trial was sensational. Buck pleaded insanity, but was convicted and hanged. Daisy's father, grieving, died a few years later. Before he died, he deeded Daisy sparsely populated land including parts of the Santa Monica Mountains that became, after Daisy sold them, exclusive Bel-Air and Brentwood, where celebrities, including O. J. Simpson, involved in a sensational murder in 1995, lived.[47]

In recent years, Crestmount, now called "Paramour," has been rented out as a recording studio. Charges that it is haunted have added to the rumors that Daisy was murdered. For instance, when *Papa Roach*, a hard rock band, recorded *The Paramour Sessions* there, a band member claimed, "I was visited by inter-dimensional beings, had out-of-body sex with spirits from old Hollywood...and...know what it feels like to have a ghost walk through me...There were times that I was lyrically stuck, and I would go down to Daisy's grave—she was buried on the property—and just write whatever came to me."[48]

Another band that recorded there, *My Chemical Romance*, has members who claim similar experiences—sensations of being strangled, visions of fiery death, and deep depression.[49] Repeating the murder rumor, Wikipedia, in its article about the "Canfield-Moreno Estate," declares, "Some believe that the ghost of 'Paramour' is Daisy trying to make peace."

In the absence of hard evidence, however, I'm not persuaded. The conditions for an accident were very real that night—darkness, an obscuring fog, winding dirt road. It is hard to understand how Dussaq, as injured as he was, could have crawled up and down a three-hundred-foot sloping embankment. But that is the official record. All available accounts portray René as genuinely shaken and remorseful. Existing accounts indicate he performed like the hero he was destined to be labeled.

If there is more to be revealed it will be hard to discover. Moreno, after a diminished but continuing career as a character actor in movies like *Captain from Castille* (1947) and John Ford's *The Searchers* (1955), died in 1967. His witness is thus forever silenced. And Dussaq, curiously—but perhaps understandably—would effectively erase Daisy's death from all public accounts of his life.[50]

7

"I Will Kill You Myself"

LATE SUMMER 1944

The nearest town Dussaq knew to be garrisoning Germans was Thiers, a hillside community about thirty miles north of Ambert in the direction of Vichy. It had been famous for centuries—known for its fine knives and cutlery. The Germans used main roads to and from the town for important transport. Dussaq wanted to block the passage, but couldn't get help from the local Maquis leader. "Commandant Dangou," he writes, told him "it was not in his sector." So he settled on something less ambitious: to attack a small outpost just outside the town. "My adjutant and two other youngsters removed the outpost, killing five Germans and wounding one. The reaction of the German garrison was to declare a state of siege in Thiers. All night long they fired flares [apparently to illuminate attackers]. The next morning they [started an] evacuation of the…garrison. Not having the necessary personnel, we could not stop them…"[1]

With the Germans exiting, the communist Maquis, among other fighters around him, again became a problem. "I was in contact with [Commandant] Pigeon and a Capt. Alain commanding [Red] battalions of the sector and asked them not to move into Thiers hurriedly for fear of encouraging street-fighting, should there still be some hostile elements [remaining]." But afraid they'd miss spoils, "they ran headlong into the town, with the result that civilians were killed needlessly. They helped themselves to the booty left by the Germans at the College of Thiers and refused to share it with the [non-communist] companies which came to their assistance."[2] He charged that communist leaders were the only Maquis "which instructs the new recruits in a definite political line...that they should get all the weapons and...training possible [and not use them] now against the Germans, but later...to establish themselves in power."[3]

If this was true—and it has been reported elsewhere—then the communists had a future takeover of France in mind. But "in the ranks," he wrote, "the immense majority" of Maquis under the communists were not ideological. They just wanted to fight the Germans. So, presumably relying on men he could count on, "I recruited some French agents to obtain...information about Vichy," seat of the Nazi collaborators, "which was to be my next move. A large body of Germans was reportedly at the Hippodrome [large race track facility], which would have been a nice prize."[4]

He was aiming big—to kill a substantial number of the enemy.

Then, in late August, with the Allied liberation of Paris and the occupation collapsing, a sizeable German force with tanks moved into Vichy in order to force French puppet president, Marshal Philippe Petain, to move his government to Germany. Petain was resisting and keeping the German units in Vichy as they tried to cajole and threaten him. Apparently Dussaq decided the force was too strong for any resistance operation—at least for him anyway. But from his intelligence gathering, he writes, "I received information that at Issoire [a plains town] a strong German garrison was keeping [routes] open to German traffic between Saint Flour and Clermont-Ferrand," an industrial hub and capitol of the

Puy-de-Dome department where he was largely operating. "I decided then to attempt a bluff."[5] This, it appears, is what really started the legend of "Capt. Bazooka," for it was a very bold and daring plan that he writes he devised and executed.

Issoire, an ancient settlement dating from the Roman era, was closer to them than Thiers was. By this time, Allied troops were threatening from several directions. As an adjunct to the Normandy invasion, American forces had landed to the south near Cannes and were pressing upward into the interior.[6] Gen. George Patton, as well as Free French Forces, was dashing across France in the north, spearheading the push of Germans east. In previous actions, the Maquis with Dussaq had taken nearly four hundred German prisoners, including, according to Dussaq, "a Colonel Schultze, two German nurses, four medical officers and 12 wounded whom we had in custody at the hospital of Ambert."[7] He went to the colonel, and demanded he write several letters. He didn't give the Nazi any details, but what he had in mind was to go almost alone to the Issoire garrison, and pretend he was the advance guard of a huge allied army that would destroy the garrison and all in it if its occupants didn't surrender. Part of what he wanted written was to demand that the Germans not use hostages, as they were fond of doing.

"At first Colonel Schultze did not wish to comply…I informed him that my main purpose…was to stop the German practice of warding off any attack…by taking hostages and threatening [to shoot] them."[8] Earlier, he writes, they'd been tricked at St. Flour, another nearby town, when the Germans took forty hostages, and threatened to kill them and burn the town down if attacked. St. Flour's bishop, he writes, begged them not to attack. The Germans decided not to attack, but when they left, they still killed twenty-seven of the hostages.[9]

"I told Colonel Schultze to say in his letter…that should hostages be taken, I would see to it that the colonel, the two German nurses, the four medical officers, and the 12 wounded were killed, and…I would do it myself with my jackknife. When he informed me that…was not in accordance with the Geneva Convention, I answered that I was interested only in getting the [letter]. He tried a last great gesture by telling me that

I would pay dearly for that, for he believed in the star that guides Hitler. I answered that I was much stronger, for I believed in the 48 stars of my flag. He wrote the letter."[10]

A B-movie exchange? Over the top? Maybe he wanted to impress his British handlers? But the 1940s were a different era. The struggle wasn't ambiguous—as today's wars often seem to be. It was stark good vs. evil—do or die. People were more patriotic, and René had become a citizen only two years before.

Whatever the case, now came the hard part.

The local Maquis commander in the Issoire area was a "Commandant René." He commanded 350 men. Dussaq talked with him, and he agreed to put fighters "on the roads that the Germans would be likely to take should they get scared and [try to] evacuate." Next, he forced a captured German tailor to make an American flag, and put it prominently on a car that Dussaq described in later interviews as having been stolen from Pierre Laval, prime minister in Petain's Vichy regime.[11]

With his interpreter—brought primarily because the Germans had worked with him— and his "adjutant," as he called him—a "Lt. Grillon," whom he thought highly of—he drove to a position "some 500 yards" in front of the garrison and stopped "in full view of the Germans...I got out of my car, instructing the interpreter and my lieutenant to stay where they were, and started walking towards the garrison." Reaching the entrance, he halted. He didn't want to "walk straight in," he wrote, because "had the German commander demand[ed] [I] prove I was an American officer, I could not have done so." He didn't have an American identity card, "my uniform was not correct [and] I speak English with a foreign accent...[It] would have been very easy for the German commander to think that I was just [a Maquis] trying to make him think that American troops were there."[12]

Waiting, he heard a "short burst" of machine-gun fire "probably in my direction, " but he didn't move. He doesn't say how long he stood there, but eventually he stopped "a young man on a bicycle" entering the town and gave him two letters to take inside. One explained "that I was an American captain sent by my division which was surrounding the...garrison [and demanding] surrender or...fight it out." The other challenged "whether they were afraid to come out to talk with me."[13]

It was a brazen ploy that could have angered his prey.

The Germans answered that they needed more time.

He had given them a deadline and when it passed, "I decided that maybe the bluff had not worked; I returned to my car and as I was turning...around," saw Germans exiting from the rear of the garrison, "running on bicycles, trucks and what not."

Captain René was in the woods behind him "to help in case the Germans opened fire on me." Seeing the exit, he quickly ordered his fighters in. "It was not my intention to have Commandant René's men enter and occupy Issoire. I had asked him to keep his men on the roads, but it was useless. Mad celebrations [ensued] as if the war had come to an end."[14]

Dussaq's ruse had worked.

Almost single-handedly he'd sent hundreds of Germans scurrying and captured what is variously reported as 120 to 500 prisoners.[15]

However, the celebrations were short lived—at least for the Maquis. "No sooner were we in Issoire than we had news that a column of 129 trucks of Germans was ten miles south" on a road heading for the town. It was obvious that the Germans were coming back to reverse what had just happened.

"I immediately ordered that all the trees on the road" be chopped down and thrown across it as a road block. With "the few men we had," they rushed to intercept the column. "When the head of the [Nazi rescue] column arrived to where the first tree was blocking the road," the Maquis "engaged it with a bazooka" and "were able to put three trucks out of action, killing a few Germans and taking the rest prisoner."[16]

The action forced the remainder of the column, which had stopped, to turn around and retreat—but not for long. They returned with reinforcements at 3 a.m. that night. Again the Maquis, hitting them from other points, stopped most of them from getting through. "Only a few trucks reached Clermont-Ferrand," reported Dussaq. They were so intimidated by their attackers that they reported Issoire had been taken by a "division of American parachutists," the ultimate compliment to Dussaq.

And that wasn't the only accolade.

The bluff had worked so well that "The day after the action...I was given a radiogram from Colonel Gaston, military chief of the Puy-de-Dome, informing me that American parachutists were operating in Issoire and instructing me to get in touch with them."[17]

I can see the smile lighting Dussaq's face.

8

A Dangerous Business

LOS ANGELES, EARLY 1933

Emilien, despite his Sufi calm, was distraught almost to tears in Geneva when he learned of his youngest son's auto accident and injury. "I cannot have one moment of real rest [until I know] that my boy may fully recover...and be as fit as before," he wrote St. Vincent Hospital's Dr. William Molony. "Have not the kidneys been injured...and how long do you think it will take [him] to be on his feet again?"[1]

Dr. Molony, in his return letter, was reassuring. "I am very happy to tell you that his physical condition is all that could be desired and that his spirits are most excellent." In spite of fractures to "the first lumbar vertebra" and the "transverse process of several others" he "shows a wonderful spirit of pluck and endurance...and smiles under great adversity." There were no other injuries to René, wrote the doctor, and "we now have him in a body plaster cast in extreme hyper-extension in order that the space between the two adjacent vertebras may be widened to permit a return of the injured vertebra to normal."[2]

In layman's terms, Dussaq, apparently sufficiently recovered from any psychological trauma due to Daisy's death, was nonetheless trussed like a stick in cement, and according to his second wife Charlotte, stretched taut from head to toe and suspended in a hammock-like bed to minimize accidental jarring. He was hanging this way when the Long Beach earthquake, a legend of catastrophe in Southern California, struck. "I can only imagine what that was like," Charlotte told me.[3] The Long Beach earthquake occurred on March 10, 1933, just a few weeks into his multi-month hospitalization. With a magnitude of 6.4, it destroyed buildings throughout Southern California and killed 120 people, which must have provided quite a swaying ride—or conquest, as the case may have been—for a fear-challenger like René.

Beyond the earthquake, it wasn't all pain and discomfort for him— although there was probably a lot of that. Under the influence of the morphine injected into him, he writes, he was able to pursue the extreme focus and concentration of which he believed his father was such a master. "At such times I held a picture in my mind [undescribed] and enjoyed it steadily for hours without difficulty."[4] It would be later, as a deep-sea diver, that he would more fully understand such mind mastery, and why it aided in the midst of turmoil. "There is no storm under the water," Murshid Inayat Kahn, his father's Sufi master and teacher, once counseled him. "The sea is a marvelous parallel to the mind." When the waters are calm, one's reflection is placid, undisturbed and quiescent. In a storm, noted the mystic, it's distorted and upset. "If one allows the mind to become roughed by difficulties," the same happens.[5]

What else occurred at the hospital is anybody's guess. René doesn't say. Certainly, he would have preferred not to be there. Who paid his bills? Or came to see him? Moreno? There simply is no available information. He stayed perhaps six months, maybe less, which means sometime in the summer of 1933 he was recovered enough to be discharged—a handsome young man with a repaired broken back. He walked out, or rather, hobbled, into a Los Angeles increasingly affected by the Great Depression, and seemed to have been out of money. "I wound up sleeping on a bench in Pershing Square," a downtown Los Angeles park, he told reporters years later. "I washed dishes—when I was lucky...My parents gave me everything I wanted. But...I wanted to make good on my own. So I starved on my own. Once I went four days without eating."[6]

In 1933, it was common to have milk delivered to the doorstep of American homes, especially in the cool darkness before dawn. Charlotte said René was so hungry once that he stole a freshly-delivered bottle from the porch of unsuspecting residents. It appears this is the time that he became a stuntman in earnest, although some of the feats he's credited with later may have occurred earlier. For instance, in newspaper stories he is often said to have been an airborne "wing-walker."[7] But there is no record of him doing that in California. If it did happen—and I don't doubt that he did it—it was probably earlier in Cuba as he sought exciting experiences.

There's no question that after he left the hospital he was eventually able to get a job in Hollywood as a stuntman. One of the most celebrated adventurers of that era, John D. Craig, verifies it. Craig, like Lowell Thomas then, was a world-explorer and, in addition, an underwater photographer long before Jacques Cousteau became a household name with his sea-diving shows on television. Craig was a former successful teenage oilman who took the money and pioneered photography under the waves. In 1933, he was just establishing his reputation as the go-to man for Hollywood producers needing underwater action to splice into their sea adventures—things like shark fights, sunken ships, and monster squid and octopus encounters. Although he used hard-hat diving equipment—the big, bulbous suits much like today's astronauts wear—he was developing lighter, more flexible gear that would later become known as "SCUBA" equipment, and was looking for bold divers like himself to join his team.

In his bestselling 1936 book, *Danger Is My Business*, Craig describes meeting Dussaq on a movie lot. "They were shooting the

Spanish versions of *Mujer*.[8] The location was a garden-party set with an exotic swimming pool sequence. A fancy diver of exceptional physique doubling for the male star was plunging from the twenty-five-foot platform. He did four graceful swan dives before the director was satisfied. When he crawled out after the last one I noticed he lay for a long time on the pool edge. His face was a mask of pain as he staggered past me going to the dressing room. I caught a glimpse of him later fitting a steel back brace, and learned he had been released from the hospital…He was broke and had to get money somehow. The stunt dive offered quick cash, and the pain was preferable to the embarrassment of borrowing from friends."[9]

Craig made his pitch. In *Adventure to Order*, Dussaq writes that the adventurer was a man "one must like." He had an "open mind…open heart" and was "devoid of prejudice." Tall and thin, "a lover of discovery" prone to sea sickness, he accomplished what he did mostly by "sheer moral strength," was "stubborn to a degree of danger to himself" and "never backed down."[10] He was Dussaq's kind of man; basically fearless. The two hit it off. Despite having no deep-sea diving experience, said Charlotte, René told Craig he did, and signed on. Craig probably sensed the truth but didn't care. He was seeking spirit not resume. He and his crew were blazing new trails. What needed to be learned would be part of that. On his OSS application, René wrote that he left stunt work because he was "tired of it."[11] That doesn't sound right. He hadn't even spent a year in Hollywood, and this new job, while different in venue, was basically more of the same. Was he simply restless? Did he possibly just want to skip town?

Working with Craig were a handful of other adventurers: Max Gene Nohl, an MIT-educated engineer and salvage diver from Milwaukee who, in 1937, would set a world diving record of 420 feet in cold, winter-time Lake Michigan; Ernie Crockett, former Oklahoma cowboy and Hollywood cameraman who got tired of filming bathing beauties and Mack Sennett comedies; Douglas Campbell, a USC swimmer and boxer who graduated to tiger hunting and race car driving before joining Craig in

Egypt; and Jim Ernest, a "tall, good-looking" Englishman who claimed he had met Craig in Tahiti, which Craig wrote was probably bogus. "I suspected he was lying but it made no difference." Craig didn't care what the man's past was—only his heart. "Somehow I liked him instinctively." Ernest was a hard worker and could be counted on in a pinch.[12]

9

"Adventure to Order"

THIRTEEN FATHOMS, ATLANTIC OCEAN, 1938

Fear gripped Dussaq—fear like he'd never known—so startling and bone-chilling, he wrote, it was like the Raven suddenly knocking on Poe's midnight door—an ominous, frightening, death-knelling fear. He could feel the panic welling—panic he had always been able to keep at bay with pride, bluff, and charge.

But there was no bluffing here.

He was in trouble and alone—a diver's worst nightmare.

He was staring wide-eyed through his thick faceplate at a gigantic, waiting abyss—an abrupt five-hundred-foot drop almost straight down from the submerged seafloor ledge on which he was teetering. A hidden trench! He knew what a fall into it meant: suffocation as his air hose was ripped away and subsequent exit of the air cushion in his suit protecting him from the immense pressures at such depth.

He'd be crushed.

Craig had witnessed such a "horror" earlier.[1] He and Crockett were deep with a Japanese diver off the Philippines. A strong current had bashed the diver against a rock, wrapping him around it like a ragdoll on a fishing line, simultaneously wrenching the air hose from his suit. "He seemed to telescope into a dwarflike figure" as "tons of water pressure [forced] his torso [up] into his helmet," compacting it. They saw what seemed like "grey smoke" issuing from his smashed face plate. It was blood. When they got the body back to the boat, the dead diver "was a mass of smashed human pulp...like strawberry jam."[2]

Dussaq had not seen the ledge. He had trundled out on it in order to avoid sharp coral—another air hose menace. But as he'd emerged, seemingly safe, there it was gaping, like a colossal attacking sea monster, dwarfing everything in his tunneled vision, waiting huge-mouthed to swallow him whole.

He stumbled, teetering on the ledge's lip, half on and half off it, fighting the plunge as if in slow-motion because of the watery resistance. Momentum and the weight of his diving suit, he knew, would propel him, inextricably, helplessly, into the seemingly bottomless dark.[3]

■ ■ ■

The seabed to Dussaq was a mostly wondrous place. He had grown to love it after years of diving with Craig and the team in many of the world's oceans. It was a "dreamy fairyland," he wrote—evidence of God's stunning creation; orderly, structured, and "so beautiful—yet so dangerous." It had "a peculiar loneliness" where death for the diver was always just a professional mistake away, not to mention the everyday perils they all dealt with—sharks, barracudas, giant octopus, poisonous corals with slicing edges, treacherous currents, and the dreaded "bends," the agonizingly painful tiny nitrogen bubbles formed in one's tissues due to chemical changes in the body when a diver rose too fast. It, too, could kill. Add rotting wrecks that could trap a diver, and giant manta rays to the list. They'd seen a big ray kill a friend with its tail. A deep-sea diver had to know what he was doing, and be aware of his surroundings every minute.

Dussaq actually had a soft spot for sharks, which he said were misunderstood and "much maligned." They had been put in the ocean for a purpose. They were the "garbage cans of the sea." Only a few of them, especially the bluefin, which always seemed hostile and wily, worried him to any degree. Razor-teethed barracudas and the sharp-beaked octopus, especially if its tentacles detected soft, edible flesh, were, in his opinion, worse. Still, he tried never to turn his back on a shark. They were unpredictable. They attacked mostly as a diver was coming up, not on the bottom. Craig, however, like the natives, hated them. A barracuda though, "mean and sinister," was basically neutralized if you stayed upright. Its triangular, pointed jaws required an angled strike to do damage. They all were leery of killer whales—today's beloved "Orca"—which Craig wrote was "the most voracious, cruel, bloodthirsty thing that swims." It ate everything, hunted in packs, and "worked on whales like a man works on a steak." It would bite off a whale's tongue if it just wanted a tidbit. One cornered Crockett when he was filming. Luckily, the Oklahoman was able to get into a rock crevice where the killer whale's large "ugly head, with teeth like ice-cream cones" didn't fit. It eventually left.[4]

Off the Dominican Republic, where Dussaq was teetering now—in and around a huge, approximately forty-by-twenty mile underwater "island" of giant coral formations known as Silver Shoals—there was the added danger of what the West Indies natives called "Chubaco" or "deadly wind." It would spring up out of nowhere, engulfing a boat such as he was tethered to in a windy violence of darkness, cold, driving rain and huge waves. In such tropical tempests, he would often take great pleasure remembering Inayat Khan's soothing words, "there is no storm beneath the waves." Still he knew a Chubaco could end his life, either by sinking his ship, or through a sudden air-hose wrenching gust or rogue wave. They had procedures to prevent such disaster—at least the air-hose fouling—but accidents happen. Silver Shoals was the graveyard of some of the most treasure-laden shipwrecks in history—mainly due to hurricanes, and the fact that many of the giant corals, like monster toadstools or lily pads, jutted just beneath the surface and were unseen in storms when ships were forced off course. The jutting corals could rip open the strongest hull, especially ancient wooden hulls.

In 1642, as Craig tells it, a large fleet of Spanish galleons escorted by battle frigates set sail from Haiti for Spain loaded with what in today's conversions was probably hundreds of millions of dollars' worth of gold, silver, raw emeralds, copper, and platinum, used for ornamentation. It had been gathered from South and Central American countries and mule-trained across the Isthmus of Panama to the Atlantic where it was loaded on to the flotilla. It was this treasure that Craig and his adventurers were hunting when Dussaq blundered out on the edge of the underwater precipice. The Spanish knew the danger of the West Indies waters they would be sailing through to reach home—the hidden, uncharted reefs; the storms now called hurricanes; and lots of opportunistic pirates. Outlaws infested the island backwaters. If the reefs didn't get the treasure, pirates often would. The battle frigates were there to discourage the pirates. But when a hurricane arose it was every ship for itself. Resignedly, the Spanish expected losses, and just hoped some of the galleons would get through—even one getting through was worth it. Actually built into their shipping calculations was the expectation that only a third of the treasure would reach Spain. Most of it, they knew, would go to the bottom—or to the pirates.[5]

The area was that dangerous.

Forecasting weather satellites, of course, were nonexistent in the seventeenth century, and sure enough, shortly after the flotilla sailed, a hurricane hit, scattering the ships, most of which were splintered and sunk in and around treacherous Silver Shoals. Only a handful of survivors from the wrecks, floating on mangled remains, clutching fresh water containers they had managed to grab, made it to Santo Domingo to tell the tale. Several decades later, New Englander Captain William Phips, after trying twice and failing, recovered, with the backing of the English crown, a substantial amount of treasure from one of the galleons and became rich and knighted as a result.[6] In spite of that, through three more centuries up to the 1930s, attempts to find more of the treasure yielded only meager results—a few coins and artifacts and a lot more death and ruin. The sea quickly encrusted its booty in enveloping, disguising coral, and the area remained treacherous—and not only because of the weather and reefs. "The place swarmed with sharks," wrote Dussaq, who notes that Phips used slaves to dive on the wrecks, seventeen of whom were said to have been killed by sharks—a report Dussaq viewed skeptically. It was more probable, he wrote, that the novice divers' lack of skin-diving knowledge, coupled with the "bewildering" maze of coral-filled "caverns, tunnels and ravines" in Silver Shoals, did them in.[7] He had experienced the danger himself when they'd begun their search.

After extensive maritime research and small plane reconnaissance over the shoals, Craig had pinpointed spots he thought might be fruitful. They'd shipped out from Puerto Plata, Dominican Republic, anchored, and were in the second week of searching in a small row boat with a glass-bottomed viewing box attached when one of them spotted something and called René's and Craig's attention to it. Encrusted in coral, it nevertheless looked like a chain of some sort. "A tense silence fell upon us," writes Dussaq. "If this was chain, we had found the galleons...the place...where Spanish gold lay hidden...where conquistadores had sailed and drowned three hundred years before."[8]

He and Craig looked at each other, trying to hide their gleeful expectation. "I suppose I can do it," Dussaq said, anticipating Craig's unspoken question. But there was only one way—skin dive. "No man could go down [where they were looking] in diving [suit]." The corals, with "jutting ledges which could smash a [diver's] face plate," were too close, too encrusted. Besides, the schooner with their equipment was a mile away."[9]

He dove in. "I judged myself no more than fifty-five feet below the surface when I got to the point where I could touch the chain." Corals menaced him everywhere. "I hovered over the chain-like projection and pulled...hard. A piece broke away within my grip [biting] into my flesh savagely. I held on and made for the surface."[10]

In the row boat they huddled. Larkin probed the broken piece with a whittling knife. Metal soon showed. "It was petrified chain," alright. They brimmed with excitement. "I went down again. I was eager to follow the chain." It led to a "jutting promontory of coral rock" at the base of which "I found an opening through which the chain disappeared." It was a tunnel. It "intrigued me."[11]

But René was out of air.

Up top, he wanted to go back and explore the tunnel. "'You might get stuck,'" cautioned Craig, who in the next breath seemed to egg him on—"'but it's up to you. There can be no doubt we have found the place where one, at least, of the sixteen galleons lies.'"[12]

Dussaq needed little prompting, but he was tired. They decided to go back to the schooner where he could breathe pure oxygen from cylinders they had. The oxygen would enable him to stay down for maybe two minutes, he figured, which would be enough. They marked the spot with a floating empty gasoline can, and after fifteen minutes of Dussaq sucking oxygen, returned.

"I shot below the surface. The tunnel was pitch dark…it narrowed somewhat from the entrance width which was ample for a…man." He "[stroked] with speed, careful not to knock against any unseen projection." As he swam, he felt he was rising, and detected possible light ahead. A current "sought to drive me from side to side" but he swam harder, "fighting upward inch by inch."

A ray of light suddenly flickered above his head, then more. "I saw a mass of coral hanging downward. It looked like a giant chandelier…but there was no mistaking the shape. This was an anchor"—a galleon!—"at least ten feet in length and a magnificent sight. It gleamed through the pellucid water in shafts of green and violet, yellow and streaks of purple." He was in one of the sunken wrecks! René grabbed the outflung jagged point as a kind of celebratory pat, pausing momentarily in triumph, and then continued upward.

Suddenly he was out of the tunnel, reaching for the surface. But the moment's delay grabbing the anchor "had almost been my undoing" for he had somehow "gasped and swallowed [sea water]" in the celebration. "I emerged coughing, sputtering, choking. I regained my breath…in great gulps of air…Evidently I had come up at the [opposite] entrance of the mysterious flume, twenty-five yards from the point at which I had gone down. I was clinging to the broad edge of the [shoal's] outer barrier reef," beyond which was the open Atlantic, its deepest trench no more than one hundred miles away. He could see the row boat and the others frantically watching where he had gone down. "Evidently they thought me gone for all time since they expected my return by the same way as I had gone...I shouted. The three men responded with relieved surprise."[13]

But they couldn't get to him. Coral tops peppered the surface, blocking any passage. Usually, when he dove, he wore tennis shoes, but he was barefoot now. He'd have to walk on the corals to the boat. "I balanced carefully and endeavored to take a few steps...The corals, covered with their slippery slime, were razor sharp on the under side. I had no mind to slip and lacerate my shins, and I blessed my balancing instinct...for if I had never done a handstand on a roof's parapet or dropped to a trapeze hanging from a plane, I should have been in bad case."[14]

■ ■ ■

Nice reflection in hindsight, but now, as I pictured it, he was teetering on the edge of a murderous shoals trench—with no way to stop from plunging.

He went over.

"I felt myself falling into that dark, deep blue."[15] Prior to coming to the Dominican, "I had wondered what awaited us in the treacherous sea where many men had died—was treasure worth this? Was scientific knowledge worth it?"[16] Was the challenge worth it? Now he knew the answer. No!—a humiliating admission that he had been wrong, and worse—scared.

Too late now.

"The sudden change of pressure gave me a squeeze"—the first sign of being crushed into oblivion. "Then abruptly I was jerked to uprightness." It happened so fast he didn't think about it, just reacted. "I kicked backward and found a footing." His air hose, he soon realized, had miraculously caught on coral—miraculous not only because it was yanking him back, but because normally such a brush with the dangerous organism meant severance. At this moment it was the only thing preventing him from going over—"the first time I welcomed such an entangling…"[17]

Cautiously, his one foot holding, he moved himself, top heavy because of his oversized metal helmet, backward. Then the other foot, weighted with lead, grasped the ledge. He balanced again, stabilizing. Fleetingly, he wondered where the line was caught. He had to be careful not to cut it by any unnecessary tug or jerk. He tested his phone line but it was dead. Both the air hose and "signal phone" were connected—still no chance for help from above. When one thing goes wrong, everything does, he wrote.

For a moment he became panicky again. "Perhaps to have gone over that ocean canyon's rim would have been easier"—presumably, one guesses, than feeling such dread and fear. He doesn't explain the thought. He continued, "then I brought my imagination under smart control"— apparently a kind of automatic take-charge state switched on when in dire straits and there is still a chance of survival. "While my body broke out in sweat and my heart pounded…I stopped and took time…I must retrace my steps one by one, slowly; I must breathe rhythmically and little by little control the disturbing force. 'All is still and quiet under the sea,' reminded Inayat Khan, and thus I solved the unsnaggling of my line and pulled the signal clear."[18]

He writes no more about the incident—which is typical of actioners such as himself. Once out of danger—

Next.

■ ■ ■

There were other close calls.

According to the *New York Times*, which reported on the treasure hunt, "René Dussaq, French diver on the expedition, was rescued from almost certain death by Capt. Craig when Dussaq's foot was caught in a coral formation and his lines to the ship above became fouled." Without details, the story continues, "He was inflating his suit to rise out of danger and would have been shot to the surface, his suit exploding and dropping him back unprotected to the terrific pressure below when Capt. Craig held the diver and gave an emergency signal. 'We were scared to death all the time we were out there and I wouldn't dive there again for $50,000,000 unless I had better equipment,' Captain Craig said."[19]

Perhaps discussing the same incident, a reporter for the *San Francisco Chronicle*, in 1951, wrote, "Dussaq survived one weird mishap while testing a new-type diving gear...His oxygen gear jammed and pumped his suit up like a balloon. Helplessly Dussaq shot upward. At the surface his inflated suit exploded into little pieces. He dropped again like a stone to the ocean floor—with heavy lead shoes and no air hose or lifeline. He was accidentally saved by John Craig [who] in a normal diving suit with lifelines, had caught his arms in Dussaq's gear while trying to fix it. He went up and down with Dussaq. Then workmen above hauled up Craig, whose trapped arm involuntarily hauled up Dussaq. Dussaq walked away jaunty and unhurt."[20]

But the article says they were in the Pacific—half a world away from Silver Shoals.

Once, a Chubaco almost killed him.

As he waited for Craig and Waldo Logan, whose father had started Chicago's Adventurer's Club, to arrive (Waldo, an avid adventurer himself, was helping to finance the Silver Shoals hunt) René decided to take another underwater "siesta," as he called the contemplative bottom "rests" he'd grown to enjoy.

Increasing waves should have given him warning.

The weather was ominous and the schooner was "bouncing up and down" when he went over the side. He found a place he liked between two monster corals "and sat down, then lay, being careful not to allow the air in my helmet to creep down my suit and thus inflate the lower part of my dress, for such would put me in a most undesirable predicament, that of going back to the surface feet first"—a quick ticket to the bends.

It was here that he concluded that even if not conscious about it, he benefited from a mysterious protection.

After about ten minutes of relaxation, he writes, "I shall never know why I should have got to my feet at that moment, and from sheer curiosity make up my mind to look for the anchor of the schooner. I had not thought of such a thing before, not even to see if she had been put down in a good spot."[21]

He exited the coral cavern, and found the anchor without difficulty. But as he gripped the chain attached to it, he felt "a terrific jerk," and was suddenly yanked up off the sea floor and was dangling, "my feet and legs walking on nothing." Simultaneously, as if in slow motion, he saw the anchor "snap"—a bad sign, to say the least. He "hung [on] desperately to the chain and felt myself dragged rapidly [away]. Perhaps I was stunned ... [but] in a split second I realized what was happening." A wave had slammed the schooner so violently that it had broken the metal anchor like a twig. Luckily, he felt a pull. "The boys were getting me up. At last my head was above the water, but not above the crashing waves...It is strange to see how one's intuition will protect one at times from sure death. Indeed, if I had not had the urge to go and look at the anchor, and had remained where I usually was between those two huge coral growths, the same jerk that snapped the anchor would have snapped my life line as if it had been a thread..."[22]

10

Sunken Treasure

I t's hard to precisely track Dussaq in the mid to late 1930s—his most mysterious period prior to World War II. He appears and reappears in limited source material, including his own writing, in a hazy succession of incidents, mentionings, and actions sometimes difficult to put in exact chronological order. However, an early dive he participates in involved a vessel that had sunk off the Eastern U.S. during Prohibition. Max Nohl of the Craig team had learned of the treasure from an old diver, hobbling from the bends, who had approached him on a dock where he was engineering new diving gear.

The following is related by Craig:[1]

In the summer of 1923, said the diver, a 112-foot coal lighter, the *John S. Dwight*, used to transport fuel to ships, was hijacked off Newport, Rhode Island, by gangsters in speedboats. Two nights later, the gangsters, at gunpoint, used the eight-man crew and ship to hijack a half million dollars' worth of scotch from bootleggers on "Rum Row" off

Long Island, New York. They sold the loot that night for $125,000, but the buyers couldn't take delivery for days. Uneasy about the Coast Guard, which they thought might be on to them, they sold the same scotch to another criminal group who could receive it immediately, but they kept the earlier money. Double-crossed, the first group came after them. There was a night sea battle with explosions. Due to fog and bad weather, the Coast Guard couldn't tell what happened until morning's first light. They found eight dead gangsters floating in the water, along with the smoldering wreck of a speedboat, presumably used by the assailants. The *John S. Dwight*, with its valuable cargo, and its imprisoned crew unable to get out, was sunk on the bottom of the Atlantic Ocean. Nobody was found alive.

Worried that the cargo was still a temptation for more violence, Prohibition agents hired two civilian divers to blow up the ship's sunken remains. But the divers pulled a fast one, and didn't destroy the *Dwight*. Instead, they blew up a wreck nearby, leaving the treasure for themselves—to be retrieved at a later date. Officials had no clue. The old man informing Nohl was one of the two divers. His partner was killed in the later accident in which he was hobbled. He wanted to go after what they'd left, offering Nohl—and, ultimately, Craig and the team—the partner's cut. The scotch bottles had been capped to prevent sea water from entering, and there was also a lot of cash on board, the old diver assured. "It was a curious situation," writes Craig, "for the Navy had officially written the ship's obituary. The newspapers dug up the old story and wanted pictures"—and thus pressured authorities. "We finally convinced the Coast Guard that it was worth a try, and they assigned us the Coast Guard cutter *Algonquin* to supply power for our lights. With the help of the old diver, who had marked the spot well in his memory—sighting landmarks to get his position—we found the wreck." It was a mile and half off shore in 110 feet of water—not an easy depth. "Nohl and I went down."

Dussaq remained on top, presumably to supervise diver support. They quickly found the wreck. It was crumbling and dangerous to explore. "We could...fall through it, so we worked carefully"—but diligently—cognizant that "there was enough down there to make us all rich." They found the scotch—hundreds of bottles—and began loading the bottles into baskets, excitedly shouting "the good news to the crew above" who, after receiving the first loads, kept shouting back. "But something was wrong with the receivers in our helmets, and we heard only garbled words."

Enthused by their luck, Craig stayed down longer loading baskets than his mandatory safety time permitted. "And when I did go up, exhausted and groggy, René pulled off my helmet and screamed at me. 'You damned fool!' We've been trying to tell you guys for an hour that stuff is no good!'" It was one of only two times, according to Dussaq, the friends clashed. Sea water, ever dominant, had "eaten tiny holes in the caps." Woodworms [thus given entry] had destroyed the corks. The bottles were filled with Atlantic Ocean."

Discouraged but hoping to salvage something, they went after the paper currency, but it, too—not unexpectedly—was destroyed. It was all very disheartening. When anchorage lines were mysteriously cut by what was later determined to be a file, almost killing Nohl, who was below at the time being dragged dangerously as the boat drifted, they decided gangsters were still interested and abandoned plans to retrieve the remains of the imprisoned crew.[2]

■ ■ ■

In January 1936, while visiting London, writes Craig, he was asked to dive on the storied *Lusitania*, the Titanic-like British passenger ship torpedoed off Ireland by a German submarine during World War I. More than one thousand passengers died as a result of the May 7, 1915 attack, and besides millions in gold bullion and jewels that might be retrieved from the sunken wreck, important questions about the ship's demise remained. The Germans claimed the civilian liner, en route from New York to Liverpool, was secretly transporting munitions, which was why they had sunk it. The British denied the accusation (And they were later proven truthful—as the Germans were shown to be lying. They had simply taken an easy shot at an unarmed vessel.) In addition, stories of heroism, incompetence, and cowardice during the tragic sinking needed to be vetted. A dive would aid that.

Craig, hearing details when approached, became interested.

A year earlier, in 1935, a British salvage company, the Tritonia Corporation, had located with a diver the wreck at the bottom of the Celtic Sea. Its officials were preparing a salvage of the controversial ocean liner when Craig had come to London. They heard the adventurer interviewed on a popular BBC radio program, and decided he would be good to film their historic effort. They contacted him and offered a contract—but only if he could solve the major cinematic problems that existed in such a complicated and dangerous deep-sea shoot.

The huge ship lay on its side almost upside down in 312 feet of water—a waiting trap for divers. Until Tritonia's diver, protected from the immense water pressure by a bulky, metal suit, had discovered the wreck, the world depth record had stood for twenty years at 307 feet, and he had only reached the top of the ship. The salvage would put divers lower, thus setting new world records. No one had ever filmed at such depths. They would need underwater lights more powerful and water-pressure resistant than ever before. Suits for the cameramen would have to be as strong as Tritonia's, but less bulky and restrictive in order to get tough shots, such as inside the ship. The tethered lifeline, vulnerable to snagging and slicing, was always a problem. They decided they would need a new air mixture, because the usual nitrogen-oxygen combination was increasingly prohibitive at such depth.

All of Craig's team, including Dussaq, went to work on the problems. Dussaq's exact contribution is unclear. Over a year later, possibly more, they had developed, with General Electric's help, new, five-thousand-watt lamps that could withstand pressures at depths in excess of four hundred feet. Craig and Nohl, with data supplied by Dussaq in ongoing ocean field tests,[3] engineered a new, lighter, more maneuverable diving suit. For breathing it used portable canisters on the diver's back, rather than the restrictive, boat-tethered lifeline. It was the first "self-contained underwater breathing apparatus," or "SCUBA" gear, although it had an encompassing metal helmet and other deep-sea adaptations. Working in secret with the U.S. Navy and a civilian medical doctor, they created a revolutionary new oxygen mixture that substituted helium gas for nitrogen. Helium was lighter and less dense than nitrogen. It eliminated debilitating "nitrogen narcosis," or the "narcotic effect," and greatly reduced "agglutination," the clumping of blood particles responsible for the bends.[4]

The team, at the end of all this, was raring to go—but ran into a snag. Dussaq, he writes, "after making all the preliminary tests to prove the worth of the new Craig-Nohl diving gear," was in Chicago readying to ship the new equipment to England when he got a midnight call from Craig. The *Lusitania* salvage was shelved. The reason, said Craig, was "International complications."[5] In *Danger*, he explains: "Hitler had marched into the Rhine. [Italian dictator] Mussolini was invading Ethiopia. The British government [trying to appease Hitler] considered it best to let sleeping dogs lie"—at least for the time being. They'd ordered Tritonia to back off. "To salvage the *Lusitania*, with its attendant publicity, would be rubbing salt into German wounds."[6]

Instead, said Craig, itching to test what they had developed, the team would go to the Dominican Republic and hunt Spanish treasure—Silver Shoals, to be exact, where Dussaq would lie on the ocean bottom in blissful contemplation and nearly die in a coral-hidden, Caribbean trench.

■ ■ ■

By 1938, Nohl, wearing the newly-created "Craig-Nohl" diving suit, had set a world depth record of 420 feet in Lake Michigan. The *Washington Post* heralded the accomplishment with pictures of the two creators and a lengthy feature story mentioning Dussaq's help, and describing him as "Craig's personal aide whose diving career has taken him from Tahitian waters to the Mediterranean."[7] It's the only mention I'd found of Dussaq being in such far destinations, prompting me to wonder where else he'd traveled in his diving life that hadn't been disclosed. As 1939 neared, his whereabouts came back into public focus. He and Craig were some fifty-five miles out in the Atlantic off Chesapeake Cape, Virginia, hoping to lay claim to perhaps their most lucrative sought after treasure— what was said to be hidden in the wreck of the ill-fated steamship *Merida*.

On a foggy night, May 12, 1911, the *Merida*, a six-thousand-ton passenger freighter carrying mostly Mexican aristocrats fleeing revolution in their country, was struck amidships by the steamship SS *Admiral Farragut*. It sank hours later after drifting aimlessly in 220 feet of water. All 350 passengers on board were rescued by the *Farragut* crew. The treasures the ship was said to be carrying out of Mexico, estimated at the time of the accident to be worth at least several million dollars, maybe more,[8] went to the bottom. The wreck, according to insurance claims, included hundreds of bars of silver and copper stacked and stored in the purser's strong room, and jewels that once belonged to Mexican emperor Maximilian. The jewels were rumored to be cursed by angry nineteenth century temple priests in Burma from where they were allegedly stolen.

At least that's what Dussaq wrote in a series of syndicated articles about the dive distributed by the North American Newspaper Alliance (NANA), one of which I found in the *Daily Boston Globe*. "Those who believe in the curse," he wrote with an at-sea byline, "are inclined to blame it for the delay in [our] salvage operations."[9] Bad weather, postponements, disagreements between the captain of the salvage boat, an Italian vessel, and Craig and his team had combined by summer 1939 to keep the treasure hunt so far unsuccessful.

There had been problems from the start.

Writing in the then-popular *Coronet* magazine in 1946,[10] Craig said that upon arrival at Norfolk, Virginia (the closest main docking facility to where the *Merida* lies and headquarters of the U.S. Navy on the East Coast), Italian salvage ship *Falco*, commanded by Luigi Faggian, was already there—and with the same intentions: getting the Mexican treasure. The Italian salvage ship "was modern and suitable for deep diving," he noted, and Faggian who, in the early 1930s, "had retrieved six million dollars from the sunken [liner] *Egypt* in the Bay of Biscay, was known to us...The Italians had the jump on us."

But Craig had Dussaq.

"My companion adventurer" he wrote, "better understood Italians" and "managed to get a contract with Faggian for exclusive film rights"— and probably a percentage of the treasure. (I doubt they would have gone out just to make pictures.) However, "It was too late in the year for diving...so after the *Falco* located the wreck and marked it, we spent the winter collecting data to help in picture and salvage work."

By spring 1939, they were diving the wreck, and by summer—after blasting room after room with small bombs—the treasure room had nearly been reached. "The next blast would open the room. Everyone was excited; tension ran high."

Then Faggian—for a treasure hunter on the brink of finding the mother lode—began acting strangely, at least according to Craig in *Coronet*.

Instead of firing off the last dynamite blast, the Italian "decided to return to Norfolk for supplies. My picture instinct of 'shoot it now' was outraged," wrote Craig. "Yet try as I would I couldn't convince Faggian to go hungry for a couple of days and get the treasure while weather was good and we were on top of it."

They went back to Norfolk.

"Once in port, an engine broke down"—or so Faggian said. He "ordered a trial spin to check equipment," and put out to sea in the night. He "did not return for 10 days, during which," notes Craig, "perfect diving weather prevailed."

At wits end, Craig and his team, including Dussaq, "tried in vain to get out to the wreck." They finally decided "we had been tricked...Faggian didn't want foreigners aboard when he opened that treasure room. And then the tension broke." Washington newspapers bannered that they had been right. "Salvage Ship Recovers Crown Jewels," screamed the headlines.[11]

Now they knew they'd been duped.

But Faggian, when he finally returned, denied any subterfuge. "He was furious over the reports," writes Craig. "He swore he had no treasure—only a small silver bar and trunks of Mexican bullfighter costumes."

The loot was acknowledgement that he'd done as they'd suspected—gone back and blasted the room on his own. Strangely, however, he "insisted" Craig and the team go back with him to the wreck and film "the barren strong room." Wanting to check things out themselves, they did, sailing on September 1, 1939—a momentous day for the troubled world at that time.

"Before reaching the wreck-site the radio brought news of Germany's invasion of Poland." As happened regarding the *Lusitania* dive, politics intervened. "Immediately Faggian [whose country was allied with Germany] turned about. Within two hours of reaching Norfolk the *Falco* sailed for Italy, never to return...Did Faggian move the treasure from the hull to the sea floor, mark the spot, then pick up the loot on his way home?"

The answer to Craig's question remains a mystery because the *Merida* treasure, despite later attempts to recover it by others, has never been found. Dussaq, curiously, does not mention any of the Faggian controversy in his NANA dispatches—at least not in the ones I found. Perhaps he was just being gentlemanly, or maybe there were other reasons. A lingering question for me in his entire diving saga—especially if he did, in fact, dive secretly in Tahitian and Mediterranean waters—is: Given the war clouds rising in Europe and Asia, and the team's unique access to remote naval and coastal areas throughout the world, were Craig and Dussaq spying? If so, for whom specifically was Dussaq spying? He wasn't a U.S. citizen.[12]

These were the types of men—adventurers, explorers, engineers—who could easily spy while seemingly doing their jobs. Their work was good cover. Their cameras were good recorders. Despite the lack of hard evidence for spying, there are indications they might have been doing just that.

Referring to Craig's 1937 *Lusitania* dive, the *Encyclopedia Titanica*, a website which gathers information about the 1912 sinking of the legendary passenger liner *Titanic*, asks, "Is it possible that the [salvage Craig was arranging] was some form of reconnaissance?"[13] Its interest is in one of the assistants Craig signed to help him on the project. Thomas Arthur

Whiteley, an actor and adventurer, was to be a "co-director and film technician." Whiteley was a survivor of the earlier Titanic disaster—an obvious reason Craig would have wanted him.[14] But *Titanica's* question isn't in a vacuum.

Craig and the team, including Dussaq, had constant dealings with the Navy, Coast Guard, even the Army. Dussaq writes in *Adventure to Order* that while waiting for the others to arrive in the Dominican, he tested a Navy diving suit, the details of which, probably secret, are not given.[15] When Craig, who was in Ohio at the time, learned his wife in Los Angeles was injured, he simply called "friends in Washington" and arranged an Army plane to pick him up in Dayton and fly him quickly to the West Coast.[16] I couldn't do that. He obviously had clout and connections.

Throughout *Danger Is My Business*, Craig mentions military ties without giving details: he's using Navy manuals and charts,[17] has a collection of military pistols and weapons,[18] and he and Nohl basically did their helium-oxygen exploration at secret Navy facilities in and around Chicago—from where Dussaq was eventually waiting to ship equipment. In fact, writes Craig, "I had to go to Washington to ask the Navy if they would let me [make tests] in their diving tanks."[19] Would the Navy just open their doors? More likely, they would ask for something in return.

Craig had actually been accused of spying before—by "Islamic Riff Arab warriors" in Morocco when, as a young man traveling in search of adventure, he'd been captured in the desert. The warriors had thought him a spy for the French Foreign Legion, and told him he'd be killed if the Legion attacked. It didn't and, obviously, he wasn't killed—nor, he writes, was he a spy.[20]

But what spy reveals his activity?

Craig and the team often worked in proximity to Japanese divers and fishermen, primarily, it appears, off California and Mexico. But who knows where else they encountered them or others of the eventual Axis powers? Their proximity to the potential enemy certainly would have been of interest to the U.S. military which, at that time, was watching Japanese expansion with an eye toward halting it.

As mentioned earlier regarding the Italians, Dussaq's language skills and familiarity with European culture gave him, should he need them, important tools for intelligence work, as did his persona, dashing and personable as it was. His Sufi background, originating as it did in the Middle East and Asia, provided a philosophical connection with foreign enemies. Photos show him looking like Errol Flynn, the most dashing star of that era, laughing and joking with all manner of foreigners during this pre-World War II period. He had charisma and magnetism—ideal for swaying people and gaining their confidence.

In a 1938 article, Craig, who actually later became an intelligence officer in World War II, made passing mention of participating in "submarine salvage operations," but, again, gave no details.[21] It may have been a slip. That kind of work is usually done secretly, and with the military. Nohl, by 1939, after leaving Craig, created a diving equipment company, DESCO, which during World War II would make diving helmets for the Navy and special SCUBA gear for the OSS—Dussaq's next important destination.[22] Waldo Logan, the Chicago Adventurer's Club member who financed some of Craig's hunts—and who recommended Dussaq to OSS—tells of seeking treasure with the team on a remote island of interest to a Nazi submarine. The island was Mona, off Puerto Rico, near where they were diving on Silver Shoals.[23] At the beginning of the war, those Caribbean waters were hunting grounds for Nazi U-boats.

Does this mean Dussaq was doing something wrong? No. He might very well have been helping America. Or, as the record so far dictates, he might not have been a spy at all. On the other hand, if he was—especially if it was for Cuba, his adopted homeland—it might have a bearing on important mysteries about Dussaq following World War II.

11

Legend

FRANCE, LATE AUGUST, 1944

Following the successful bluff at Issoire, the German prisoners captured at the garrison were made to construct a landing strip, presumably for Allied-Maquis operations.[1] Since the D-Day invasion, Nazi strength in the area had, after initial moves against the Maquis, steadily dwindled as more German troops were needed for the heavy fighting north. "Bazooka" was sent to Clermont-Ferrand, where the Germans, seeing the writing on the wall, were already evacuating. Once the city—focus of a 1969 documentary about the occupation and aftermath, *The Sorrow and the Pity*[2]—was finally free and reclaimed, Dussaq, idle as he contemplated actions, was asked by Gaspard to speak at the opening of victory celebrations there. He declined. Gaspard "was much distressed," Dussaq wrote in his after-action report. "I had to explain that since the meeting had a political flavor, I could not participate in it."[3] Apparently Allied rules forbade such involvement.

Previously, in similar celebrations in Thiers, he writes, "I was put in a rather embarrassing situation because...they were performing what they called the 'Tribunal du Peuple' [People's Court] led by the FTP [communist Maquis]. When I arrived in the big public place where the tribunal was held, the [commander of the FTP] took the microphone and introduced me to the crowd as their saviour [sic], and seated me in the place of honor at the table of the tribunal. They carried on judgments for two hours by asking the crowd what sentences they would recommend for the guilty. Many women had their heads shaven, and a swastika painted on their skulls. Some men were shot. There again I excused myself as quickly as I could without offending anyone."[4]

But his elevated stature in the area continued. Chief of police of the region, "Le Colonel Prince," issued him a special identification card I found at this house with his picture—looking steely-eyed—asking all who were presented the credential to please help "Capitaine Bazouka" in carrying out his mission. The card was evidence that even after the Germans had exited, Dussaq was not done. An OSS "appendix" to his after action reports says, "Having no more Germans in his sector," he chased them all the way to "the Swiss border where he arrived too late."

That finally ended his mission. He had no more enemies to fight.

In the middle of September he was ordered to Paris, which had been liberated in late August, and flew to London on September 22, 1944. What else he did in France during that time is not publicly known. I've seen, I believe, all the official documents available on it (although I've not seen any French documents about him, which may or may not exist). His second wife, Charlotte, said he seldom talked about the war, even to her—a statement I've been able to verify in interviews with those still alive who knew him. "He blocked those things out and would go on to another subject."

Dussaq was not a braggart.

When he returned, he received a strange reception. OSS officials, to whom he ultimately belonged—although he was working while in France for the British—were surprised to see him, very surprised. They thought he was dead! I'd found evidence of this at his home. In a 1987 letter to him from Daphne M. Friele, secretary to the wartime Jedburgh commander, she recalled how she had listed René as "Known to be deceased."[5] How the mixup occurred she doesn't explain. Was it an honest mistake? Was it a purposeful deception by the British for some unknown reason? It wouldn't have been the first time. There's a third possibility, although it's a long shot. In a strange coincidence—including because Dussaq is such a rare name in America—there was actually another OSS operative with the last name of Dussaq who died in France while René was there. PFC Reginald Camille Dussaq was a driver-interpreter. Records say he died on August 25, 1944, in an army field hospital somewhere in France (not otherwise defined) after a "vehicle accident."[6] Since this is at the tail end of René's mission, and it appears he was reported dead from the start of his mission, this explanation doesn't add up. But stranger things have happened.

In any case, OSS officials, upon receiving him, were flummoxed. They had written him off, and because they had based his death on official records, were skeptical about his story. Was he now a spy who had been turned? It appears even his friends and family were uncertain about, if not mourning, his fate. They included his wife at the time—his first wife—Katherine "Kay" Applegate Dussaq, a Woman Airforce Service Pilot (WASP) and adventurer like himself whose story I will soon relate. Because he was working strictly with the British in France, he told a reporter in the 1990s, "I was out of touch with American forces for four months. They had no idea where I was or what I was doing. Some thought I'd deserted. They wanted to court-martial me."[7]

It's a curious situation. To investigate the matter, OSS sent Army First Lt. George A. Schriever to France. He interviewed key Maquis in Dussaq's sector, including "Colonel Prince," the police chief who had given him the special ID, and whose real name was Robert Huguet; "Commandant Bengali," a Maquis official who knew Dussaq quite well, having served with him throughout; and Lt. Grillon, Dussaq's constant "adjutant." All three validated Dussaq's report, including the bluffs at Thiers and Issoire. "Prince" said five hundred Germans had surrendered as a result of Dussaq's "ultimatum" at Issoire. Bengali was quoted in

Schriever's report as saying, "Bazooka never ceased to participate in the struggle against the common enemy using the...Maquis...under his orders...Confident and a trainer of men...he was an example of fighting spirit [and] knew how to give the irresistible impulse of American troops to our boys [under] Commandant René [at] Issoire."[8]

Grillon described the raid on the Thiers outpost along with the bluff and subsequent fights after Issoire, mentioning the auto "bearing an American flag," Dussaq making the German colonel write the demand letters, and the "Germans believing they were going to be attacked" and fleeing. Schriever added that he'd met with others who had served with Dussaq "and had many attestations of esteem for him—some quite extravagant. One man said: 'He may be Lieutenant Dussacq [sic][9] to you, but to us he is our Commandant Bazooka.'"[10]

No question that the on-scene investigation cleared Dussaq of any wrongdoing, and did not indicate any hyperbole or exaggeration in his report. Of course, it was one man's rendition—Dussaq's. Others might have seen what he described in different ways, but Schriever's report was good enough for American intelligence, which was always on the lookout for lies and deception.

He was awarded the Distinguished Service Cross (DSC) "for extreme gallantry and risk of life," second only in prestige to the Medal of Honor. The French gave him the Croix de Guerre with palm, a similar award for bravery and performance. He was also awarded a medal for participation in D-Day. Furthermore, in OSS archives at Carlisle Barracks, Pennsylvania, I found the following in a report about French operations: "Lieutenant Dussacq [sic] from California was known all through eastern France...and became a legendary character in that section. In many villages they tell you now that when he happened to spend the night in their town, they felt safe. He is the one who bluffed a general into believing that he was surrounded by American troops and the...general with about 1,500 men, surrendered. Dussacq happened to be the only American near there and he had a hard time finding American troops to take over the prisoners."[11]

And so the legend grew.

According to historian Richard Dunlop, a former OSS operative himself and author of *Donovan: America's Master Spy*, a biography of General "Wild Bill" Donovan, creator and head of the OSS, Dussaq was sufficiently revered by the intelligence agency, forerunner to the CIA, that he was personally escorted by General Donovan to meet in person, as a reflection of official esteem, President Harry Truman in the Oval Office of the White House[12]—the only OSS officer, to my knowledge, ever to have had that honor.

Today, however, French historians are challenging the legend—not Dussaq's courage or bravery, or that he helped the Maquis. They are reluctant to give him the credit for the surrenders at Thiers and Issoire. Gerard Crevon, whose father fought with the Maquis, and who has written about them, says Dussaq's name is absent from accounts by French historian Levy Martres, a former Maquis who Crevon feels is the prime authority on such matters. Moreover, while Crevon believes Dussaq did participate in negotiations at Issoire, he says that participation did not result in the immediate capitulation that Dussaq relates.[13]

While nationalism and revisionism may be influencing such views, Crevon and Martres are native and have local access to archives in France, albeit years removed, that I do not. So I cannot dismiss their views.[14] Yet, they are only disagreeing over details, not the total story. In any case, what René had been through in war, regardless of the details, was, in my opinion, less trying than the personal tragedy he was shortly to experience upon returning to America in late 1944.

12

A Man of Many Talents

PRE-WAR CARIBBEAN SEA

One day diving off the Dominican Republic, Dussaq got the dreaded bends.

He shouldn't have. He knew better. But in a peak of remorse at losing his favorite goggles, he disregarded some prime rules. Be prepared. Think things out. Don't jump in willy-nilly.

But he did.

It was daytime. His goggles, he writes in *Adventure to Order*, had somehow fallen overboard. He doesn't say how, but they were special—"used by the Japanese skin divers and only made by the workmen of their country." The two eye pieces protruded an inch and a half out. They were secured on the head with "hollow rubber bands" that had a "small bulb" filled with air where they joined the front. As the diver went deeper, the pressure outside squeezed the bands, putting more or less "atmosphere" into the eye spaces equal to the "pressure of water against the glass." Perfect sight. "It was ingenious and most effective."

He loved those goggles. They'd fallen in fifty-eight feet of water amongst corals so closely grouped, as one of the local crew members said, "it would take an eel to get between them."

No problem, thought René, rationalizing what he was about to do. He had to find them—and fast, otherwise they'd be gone, buried in shifting sand and moved by currents.

He dove in.

He believed they were near the anchor line, so he pulled himself down along it. "I know I was excited, and perhaps I had been overdoing it in the work of the last strenuous days." Without warning, at twenty-five feet, he felt a violent pain, not otherwise described. "I knew there were thirty-three feet of water weighing fourteen point seven pounds to the square inch [on] me, and something was going wrong." But he didn't stop.

"I hung to the chain grimly and dropped another ten feet, another twenty feet." When he got to the corals hiding the goggles, "I stretched out my hand and fished within the narrow space."

Nothing.

His lungs were bursting. He couldn't stay down any longer. He shot to the top. "The boat was bouncing as I threw myself upon the deck and breathed deep gasping breaths. I wanted those goggles."

He dove back in.

"Once more I experienced that peculiar pain of great violence." It wasn't paramount in his mind—only the goggles were. But torturously knifing bubbles spawned by a pressure-induced chemical change were forcing their way out of his blood stream into denser flesh and joints.

The pain increased but he didn't stop.

He reached the bottom.

Again, "I fished around until my groping fingers touched something smooth." The goggles! He grabbed them and shot upward. The pain got worse—terribly so. Breaking the surface, he barely made it to the boat.

Helpers pulled him up over the side. "Blood poured from my nose, my mouth, and my ears." He couldn't hear.

He now admitted to himself what was happening. "A trifle panicky, I shook my head." His hearing returned—not completely, but sufficient to realize he hadn't lost it. "I knew now I had a minor case of the bends. I never repeated [such] foolishness...but learned always to relax and come to the surface slowly."[1]

■ ■ ■

He didn't dive for a while, probably not for a month or two, maybe longer. Getting the bends was a bad experience, more so, I think, than he lets on in his unfinished book. He took time off. Also, treasure hunting, diving in general, and the adventurer's lifestyle in particular were not full time. They came in spurts, intermittently interrupted by Craig deciding what project to commit to, by lengthy planning and raising money for the project, and by unrelated pursuits elsewhere by members of the team.

Diving was an off-and-on job.

One night, during one of their extended breaks—Charlotte said it was while René was recuperating from the bends—a group of them were at a posh supper club featuring ballroom dancers as part of the entertainment. The dancers were talented. However, a wager arose, and the group left with Dussaq having made a twenty dollar bet—about one hundred dollars today—with Craig that he could pose as a dancer and do as well as the professionals.

He did better than that. The multi-talented Dussaq actually became a professional dancer and toured, according to one newspaper, for a full "season."[2] His partner was a lithe and attractive blond who resembled Ginger Rogers, the popular movie star often coupled in films dancing with Fred Astaire. The two were billed as "Patricia and Renée." Both the *Washington Post* and *Washington Times* ran picture features of the couple on November 4, 1936, in anticipation of their appearances at the

La Paree and Casa Grande clubs in D.C. "Patricia and Renée...are the highlights" of the show, said the *Post*—"ballroom dancing with a capital G [for] their grace." The pictures show them smiling in costume—formal ballroom mostly, and in one that appears to be matching dark and silky for Fandango, the Spanish courtship dance.

They were billed as having performed in "New York—Argentina—Cuba—Paris." But that seems unlikely, except that in *Adventure to Order*, Dussaq writes they danced on at least one cruise ship that docked, among other ports, in Havana—a "Holland Amerika [sic]" liner. The captain knew Dussaq's uncle. He said they had only three days of practice before beginning their act. He was constantly fighting with Patricia, who apparently wanted someone more effete, not a gruff "deep sea diver." During an early performance, he validated her fears. Somebody in the audience made a crack. He apparently stopped dancing and challenged the heckler to a fight—if he didn't actually come to blows with the guy. "Ok. I forgot I was a dancer," he scribbles in longhand. "If a fellow gets in your way, get him out of the way—the customer is *not* always right."[3]

In any case, he'd come to the point where he didn't see his future in ballroom dancing—or with Craig either. As he told a reporter, he liked the adventure and experiences diving and treasure-hunting provided, but he didn't "plan to continue [either] as a career. Instead, he wished to turn to the lecture platform and bring to the people of the United States the story of *his* [emphasis mine] people, the people of [Latin] America."[4]

Up to World War II, with television in its infancy, lectures were a popular form of entertainment. Experts, celebrities, humorists and radio personalities, among others, made a good living or added to what they already had speaking to audiences on all types of subjects. Comedians Burns and Allen did it. Royalty did it. Adventure, especially in the largely unexplored and increasingly militarily important undersea, was a big draw. Moving pictures in color added to the attraction. Craig, who had all of it, was in demand, and Dussaq had sometimes accompanied him at lectures and participated. He had a talent for public speaking, and decided to launch out on his own.

In the years with Craig, he'd matured and changed. In *Danger*, Craig tells a story about newly-hired Dussaq turning red-faced and embarrassed at hearing a woman—Craig's wife—cuss like a sailor when tricked by her husband and the crew. Dussaq had reacted, "She ought to be ashamed." But after years of life-threatening experiences, there was little that now ruffled or surprised him. Fear, the bugaboo of his youth, was no longer a concern. He knew exactly how to handle it. A diver, he writes, "flirts with sharks, dodges barracuda, is tempted to tickle the pulsing tentacle of an octopus with a diving knife, just to vary the monotony of a job which brings in the weekly paycheck."[5]

In contrast to the apathy of his revolutionary days, he had developed a political direction. It had to do with origins. He was Latin, born in South America with an identity honed in revolutionary Cuba, his beloved father's birthplace. Periodically in the 1930s, he traveled to Havana, sometimes on the ship's manifests listing "Cuba" as his birth place—even though he'd actually been born in La Plata, Argentina, near Buenos Aires. Was there more to it than just visiting family or being a dancer— or "artist," as he sometimes listed—on the ship? Could he have been working with the Cuban government? I don't know. But living in America and being, for all practical purposes, an American—although not yet naturalized—he decided that with his international experience and insight he could inform U.S. citizens about their Latin neighbors and how, because of misunderstanding, prejudice, and exploitation, Americans needed to change.

He got himself an agent, Harold R. Peat, a Canadian and bestselling author whose speaking stable included heavyweights Winston Churchill, Lillian Hellman, and H.G. Wells among other notables. Peat was impressed with Dussaq. "He is a made-to-order speaker for the World Adventure Series," wrote Peat in a brochure about a star-studded speaking event showing a picture of Dussaq, amongst headliners, hair slicked back and shiny, and a pipe studiously in his mouth. "He never sought adventure—it sought him."

Peat had him start out lecturing about his undersea adventures. The title of his presentation was, "Adventure to Order," the same he'd

eventually give his unfinished book. The reviews for Dussaq were terrific. They included praise like "Excellent;" "Far outweighed our
expectations;" "An outstanding young man of exceptional breadth…"
Dussaq's handsome looks, humor, even his slight accent, were major
assets. Bookings rolled in. By early 1942, training for war and still
lecturing on occasion, he'd appeared on "Town Hall of the Air," a
nationwide radio program, and told the *Spartanburg Herald* (South
Carolina) after lecturing there that he'd "once fulfilled 122 speaking
engagements" in as many cities.[6]

Early on, buoyed by the success, he switched to politics. "A South
American's view of South America," was how Peat titled the new thrust.
He traveled to Chile, Argentina, and Havana for research. No less than
New York gossip columnist Walter Winchell, a national star, used
Dussaq's humor in his syndicated column:

"René Dussaq, the deep-sea diver and former Hollywood stunt-man,
has just returned from South America with this story…Dussaq was sitting in a café in Caracas, Venezuela…and noticed pretty senoritas
engaged in animated chatter…Suddenly there was a big commotion…An ambulance was summoned and a tall, distinguished-looking
man was taken to the hospital…Dussaq later learned that the senoritas
had tiffed and one had said to the other, 'You're as pig-headed as Hitler!'
An attaché of the German consul's office…happened to overhear it.
Without a word, he slapped the girl across the mouth" and handed her
a card saying, "any brothers or male relatives" can meet him "on the
field of honor. The senorita, her mouth bleeding, stood up…'I have no
male relatives,' she said, 'but here's *my* card!' She picked up a cola bottle
on the table and struck him on the head with it…The nazi [sic] fell to
the floor and somebody called the ambulance…Dussaq adds that the
incident swept through the nation and inspired this saying: 'You can
stand up for Hitler but not for long!'"[7]

His basic message was that Americans didn't understand Latin America and exploited it to their peril. While diplomatic in his criticism, and
consistently praising democracy, the U.S. Constitution, especially equality for all, and the Declaration of Independence, he attacked "gun-boat"

and "big-stick" diplomacy, singling out U.S. Marines, whom professionally he greatly admired. "We don't believe in invasion," he told an audience in Wisconsin. "Don't insult us. Help us."[8]

He was particularly hard on American businesses investing in Latin America. He labeled them "money-mad," "exploitive," and "imperialistic." Naiveté was their only excuse, he told a South Carolina audience. Seeking the best deal at the expense of a long-term relationship, they "could not see that their contracts were too often made under the benevolent eye of a dishonest, unpopular government," which always had the locals wondering what kind of a country would deal with such scoundrels?[9] Alluding, it appears, to his earlier revolutionary activities, he said, "It has been established in Cuba that no government can succeed which does not have the recognition of the United States."[10] Americans "should be conscious of the duties and obligations that go with...democracy."[11] Differences between the two cultures are great, he emphasized. They are allies only because of a common enemy—the Axis.[12]

Usually, he would temper his remarks by telling a joke, acknowledging his desire to be naturalized "in this great country," or stating his belief that the problems were solvable and could be worked out. But in Moline, Illinois, according to his second wife, the audience got mad and called him "un-American." "It was a very conservative community," she said. "They didn't like him saying it was wrong for the U.S. government to prevent cattle from Argentina to come over the border."[13]

He never backed down. "He always spoke his mind," said Charlotte. And on Miami Beach, representatives of various South and Central American consulates protested his speech, accusing him of "trying to undo all the Pan-American good relations they have been working for." Their list of objections to his talk included his contention that "no government existed in Central America without Washington's approval, no true war of freedom and independence had ever been fought in Latin America," and "there has never been any social progress in Latin American nations."[14] In the running battle, which got into the newspapers, they called him a "fake," claiming that he couldn't have graduated from "The University of Havana...since the institution was closed [in 1932] by Gerardo Machado, the late Cuban dictator." Yet as far as I've seen, he never said he graduated from the University of Havana—only that he attended its law school. However, the way he left Havana— probably as a fugitive of the Machado Revolution—left room for all kinds of misunderstandings.

As a speaker, he was controversial, no doubt about it. It was possibly during one of these well-attended, sometimes tumultuous speeches that he met his first wife, Katherine Applegate Dussaq, beautiful and famous—a near fearless adventurer much like himself.

13

Katherine

In early 1933, as Dussaq lay trussed and suspended in a Los Angeles hospital recuperating from car crash wounds, Sears Roebuck's mail order, halfway across the nation in Chicago, began experiencing large losses from forged checks sent from backwoods in the Kentucky hill country. It was a wild and remote area with few roads and no electricity. "'Folks lived mostly up creeks," with suggestive names like "Bloody," "Fighting," and "Widow's Creek"—the last so dubbed because of feuding that left wives without their husbands. When the company sent two tough Chicago detectives to investigate the fraud, they were run out by "poorly clad, unshaven...characters with rifles who escorted them to the nearest railroad station." Back in the city—mobster Al Capone's— the failed investigators reported to their bosses, "there wasn't a chance of getting anything out of those hillbillies."[1]

However, Chicago at that time had an adventuresome crime fighter who did not agree with the shamed sleuths whose defeat had been publicized in the Chicago papers. Her name was Katherine Applegate Keeler, called "Kay" by her biographers (a nickname surviving family members object to). She was to become Dussaq's first wife—but not yet. A statuesque, strawberry blond "with an aloof dignity," she was, at age twenty-seven, a budding document examiner and handwriting expert—the first American female to practice that kind of CSI (Crime Scene Investigation) specialty so popular on television today.[2] Consulting with Sears Roebuck, she had a bold plan to solve the crime that had sent the defeated detectives packing. She knew the hillbillies prided themselves on purebred origins. In their minds, they were the original Americans. She and an assistant, Jane Wilson, would pose as doctoral students gathering anthropological research. That way they could gain entrance to the hostile homes, obtain signatures ostensibly as validation for professors under whom they supposedly were conducting the research, and later compare the signatures with those on the forged checks.

At first Sears balked. They considered the plan too risky and dangerous. But Katherine—headstrong, independent, and not one to heel when told no—persisted. She could do this, she assured them. They slowly came to regard her as a particularly strong woman who instilled confidence. After signing liability releases, the company's officials agreed.

Bold, gutsy moves were not new to Katherine Keeler. The Walla Walla, Washington native was descended from an important Oregon pioneer family—the Applegate brothers, who, with their wives and children in 1843, led "the first major wagon train from Missouri to Oregon."[3] She "came from a long line of strong, rare, and accomplished women," a relative emailed me.[4] One summer, while a psychology student at Stanford University, Katherine and a friend stowed away on a cruise liner by mingling with departing passengers. Discovered at sea, they were put off in Hawaii where they found jobs flipping pancakes in a restaurant window, and then working in a pineapple processing plant. In her spare time, Katherine "took flying lessons in a World War I Jenny," soaring thrillingly, it can be imagined, over Hawaii's tropical splendor, "and both girls sold articles about their adventures to newspapers."[5]

According to historian Ken Alder, she'd first attracted her noted husband, Leonarde "Nard" Keeler, pioneer in perfecting the "lie-detector" machine, not only by her "striking" good looks, but because she'd outsmarted him in a polygraph demonstration when both were students at Stanford.

Leonarde (named for Leonardo DeVinci), even in college, was already recognized for his polygraph skills. He'd helped authorities find lawbreakers with the new machine. An amateur magician as well, he would ask subjects to pick without telling him a card from a deck he displayed, and then say "no" to all the cards as he slowly dealt them. In this way, the subject, wired to his polygraph, would have to lie when the card inevitably appeared. The indicating spike would enable him to correctly identify the chosen card. But Katherine, Alder writes her family informed him, bucked the rules and didn't pick any card. Her mind, therefore, was blank—no tell-tale impulses of guilt to register on the machine. He was stumped—and everyone saw his befuddlement—a probable moment of amusement for Kay who, according to Alder, was known in college for her practical joking. After dating her awhile, Nard, writes Alder, wrote home to his father, that she was "startlingly brilliant...I only wish I had the keen mentality she possesses."[6]

Now, for Sears-Roebuck, she was betting on that—and her guts.

Entering "Bloody Creek" on rented horses,[7] writes Eloise Keeler, (Leonarde's sister) in a 1984 biography of her brother, "Kay" (as Eloise calls her) and Jane Wilson were met by a "tobacco-chewing mountaineer blocking their path with a rifle."[8] He demanded their purpose. Katherine responded, "We've been told [you are] direct descendants of the early Americans...This brought a glow to the face of the bearded man," and soon they were eating supper in his shack, measuring and recording notes about the "young'uns," and getting signatures. Their dangerous charade went on for several days. In the various shanties and cabins visited they spotted mail order phones, "a modern kitchen range [that] couldn't be used because there was no gas," electric trains with no electricity to run them, and a woman cooking—"in a fancy evening gown." Soon they'd seen a good number of the mail items acquired with the bad checks, and had gathered with their ruse many of the possessors' signatures.

Eventually—inevitably—some of the hill people, who may have been ignorant, but not stupid, got suspicious. One morning, a ten-year-old boy approached them with a rifle. "You ain't foolin' us," he said ominously. The two pretenders got the message but disregarded it because Katherine didn't think they were done. They kept on gathering signatures. However,the following day, on their way to another shack, they were surrounded by "a dozen scowling hillbillies carrying rifles" who said they weren't sure if the two were legitimate or not, but if they stayed any longer they might get shot by some "hothead." Folks were getting angry. Katherine decided it was time to leave. After returning to Chicago, she proved, through microscopic examination, that the phony signatures on the forged checks were written by many of the same people whose signatures they had gathered. A savvy ringleader in the area, indicates Eloise, had persuaded largely ignorant locals that receiving mail order items was as easy as signing fictitious names on small pieces of paper—the checks. Most of the 137 convicted of postal fraud, Katherine believed, probably were unaware of the laws they were breaking.[9]

Katherine's initiative and courage saved Sears major money—at least one million dollars, according to Alder.[10] That figure would be much higher in today's inflated values. It was her first big case as her husband's assistant in their crime fighting work at Northwestern University's Scientific Criminal Detection Laboratory, which, according to Alder, was the nation's first forensic lab.[11]

In the next few years she increased her reputation with participation in a string of highly publicized cases. Her work in matching minute bits of tape found at the crime scene of a bombing helped put a Southern Illinois coal mine terrorist behind bars. Taking on the notorious Chicago political machine, she proved numerous instances of voter fraud by phony ballot in Cook County elections. The signatures viewed under her microscope were shown to be mass produced, and in cases of "X"s used by supposedly illiterate voters, she identified—and showed to the judge and jury with enlarged photographs—tiny, repeated anomalies which proved the marks identical repeats.[12] The voter fraud work was so important that her articles about the cases in professional journals are still "landmark contributions to the literature on questioned documents," writes Jan Beck, a modern document fraud expert.[13]

In the midst of such professional exploits, Katherine took fencing lessons, becoming an expert sword dueler. She competed in at least one rodeo, was an excellent cook, according to friends whom she and her husband frequently entertained after work, and made much of her own fashionable clothing—the last two skills probably stemming from her rural Washington upbringing. Sister-in-law Eloise writes, "She had a remarkable talent for making a success of whatever she undertook...I've never known a more outrageously daring, complicated, or intriguing woman." She was "years ahead of the women's liberation movement"— strong, independent, competitive. She was also "unpredictable" with "quick changes of mood," and did not like being professionally second to anyone—even her husband, a large, cautious man who, according to his biographers, tended to quietly dominate.

When the Depression forced cutbacks at Northwestern, including at their crime lab, rather than stay on under deteriorating work conditions, she took the opportunity, reluctantly agreed to by Leonarde, to exit his lab and become her own boss—a move, according to biographers, that she'd been contemplating. She started her own crime lab with four female assistants. They were hailed as Chicago's solely "women detectives," a rarity if not a first for a forensic office. The venture took off immediately and prospered. In effect, although both husband and wife tried to downplay it, she and Leonarde became professional rivals, competing for much of the same business—a problem that certainly aggravated him. Their personal relationship, according to all accounts, began to deteriorate— irreparably, as it would turn out, mostly it appears because of Leonarde's penchant for control and drinking (a problem, according to biographers, that got worse as he got older), and Katherine's desire for personal achievement and adventure. They were both strong and independent personalities.

As Leonarde's polygraph work, nationally recognized, ran into mounting obstacles, Kay's new enterprise, helped by increasing publicity, thrived. The press loved her. She was smart, wily, a soft-spoken and pretty young woman fighting crime. It was a great story with shades of Wonder Woman. She was constantly in the news as an expert testifying in court, as a relentless crime fighter, or as a sexy commentator on the forensics of grisly crime—the perfect contrast for her glamorous looks and modern style. In 1939, the *Chicago Herald Examiner* produced a twelve-part series about her. It was promoted as, "The Girl on the Case."[14] It called her the "Terror of Killers," crediting her in her career thus far with solving "hundreds of crimes" and crowning her all-girl office as "the most modern private [crime] laboratory in the country."[15]

By this time, however, given her considerable accomplishment in crime fighting and document expertise, Katherine seems to have lost interest, or, in any case, to have moved on to other interests. As part of her new independence—and increasing personal wealth—she bought, according to Alder, a "honey of a car," a flashy Buick convertible. "Heads turned," he writes, as she drove by. She literally dove back into what must have been a dormant love—flying. He writes that she became "obsessed" with it. She bought a Piper Cub airplane and apparently spent most of her time at the airport. "Nard joked that he would have to take up flying again if he wanted to spend any time with her."[16] But it was no laughing matter. They were breaking up. "It was the core of Nard's nature to dominate," Alder quotes a close friend of Leonarde's, "and Kay refused to be dominated."[17]

Arguments over money, politics, how to spend time together, increased—with little to no reconciliation, although both Alder and Eloise indicate they tried. She was a fervent New Deal Democrat. He was a conservative "respectable" Republican. She was prone to send money home. He was tighter with what he had.[18] Trips together that had been relationship refreshers in earlier years no longer worked—or weren't even scheduled. Visiting the two, Eloise noted a difference. "Nard didn't seem happy…Kay was glum."[19] Shortly thereafter she moved out and eventually filed for divorce.

"Around that time," writes Eloise, "Kay met a dapper young Argentinian with a dark mustache, René Dussaq. More daring than Nard had ever been, René was a flyer, a deep-sea diver…a Hollywood stuntman.

Besides smashing up cars and careening them off cliffs [an allusion to the Daisy Moreno death, apparently unknown to Eloise], he'd once leapt from one plane in flight to another. In real life, he'd fought in two Latin American revolutions, participated in two duels—one with swords, one with guns—and spoke six languages. Kay, with her affinity for adventure, was almost inevitably attracted to this daredevil."[20]

I'd run across the duels but hadn't documented them. The leaping between planes was new, although certainly possible, probably in Cuba as he searched for meaning in life.

As for the attraction, did Cleopatra dig Antony?

14

My Beloved

t's uncertain how René and Katherine met. Most of their life together is a mystery—by all accounts and evidence, fervent and passionate in the beginning, tragic and haunting at the end. My guess is that they met because of either his desire to become a licensed pilot or his speaking in the Chicago area. He was there, or around the Great Lakes, numerous times in those years, not only as a deep-sea diver, but later lecturing, including at the world-renowned Field Museum downtown.[1] It was during this time that he worked for Waldo Logan, the Chicago millionaire and Adventurer's Club member who was financing some of his and Craig's treasure hunts, and who would eventually recommend René for the OSS.

Ironically, according to Eloise Keeler, Katherine and her husband, Leonarde, were in the Dominican Republic around the same time Dussaq and Craig were there diving on Silver Shoals.[2] Dussaq was often on the island dealing with top Domincan authorities, as were Katherine and

Leonarde, who had gone there to vacation on the yacht of millionaire Gene McDonald, founder of Zenith Radio Corporation. But it's hard to think the two met in the Caribbean. More likely, I can see her going to one of his lectures in Chicago, being attracted to the handsome and dynamic speaker—an adventurer like herself, which would have been part of the draw—and perhaps being introduced to him as a Chicago personality by one of the Field executives, or maybe even Logan, who might have known about her crime exploits —speculation, of course. Or it could have been simply him going to the airport where she kept her Piper Cub, and spent a lot of time, and meeting her that way. A resume for her from that time says she "instructed flying at Piper Aircraft."[3] His OSS application notes that he received a "C.A.A. Airman Certificate…issued in Chicago," on August 11, 1941.[4] And in a 1994 article, he's quoted as saying, "My first wife, also a pilot…taught me to fly."[5]

However they met, Leonarde Keeler, apparently separated from her by this time, found out they were having an affair. According to Ken Alder, Keeler, suspecting something, hired a private detective who "discovered that she had betrayed him"—perhaps a harsh characterization given their irretrievably estranged relationship. While "the detective's report has not survived," writes Alder, he (Alder) learned of it in papers of a close friend and confidant of Leonarde's, and therefore gives it credence.[6] Alder indicates that this revelation might have been the cause of a "crack up" Leonarde experienced right around that time. As different as the two were, Keeler still loved Katherine according to accounts—still had a torch for her—and was depressed over the breakup, although he tried to hide his feelings. But it was clear to observers that the marriage was over, and given Leonarde's controlling nature, it brought to mind a pertinent movie (or TV show?) proposal I'd found among Dussaq's papers.

Titled *The Katherine Keeler Story*, it had "by John C. Champion" on its cover page. Champion was a noted Hollywood producer and screenwriter who died in 1994. Describing the love triangle of Leonarde, Katherine, and René, it began, "No writer of fiction could have invented three more exciting characters than were brought together by life in

Chicago of the 1930's. Possessing all the attributes of a heroine—youth, beauty, brains and ambition," it said about Katherine, she "made love to two of the damndest men on earth. The one she met and married first was Nard Keeler. Physically large, with an ego to match...[he] promised to be almost everything...Instead he almost destroyed her...Insanely jealous...he threatened to kill her if she ever tried to divorce him. Fear, however, couldn't hold her. And shortly after obtaining her initial divorce decree [she] met a dashingly handsome young European who made her forget the vow she'd made of never falling in love again."

The dashing European, of course, was René, described by Champion, not only as a "world tennis champion" and deep-sea diver, but, like Katherine, having "a thirst for adventure. Angered by their happiness together and still deluded by the idea of reconciling, Nard confronted René. He warned him not to see Katherine again. Finding his warning unheeded, Nard sprung a pair of hoods from jail in exchange for their agreeing to beat René to a pulp. Instead, wrote Champion with the kicker, "when the fight was over, they were the ones who were hospitalized."

Proposals aren't necessarily strong on fact. Their objective is to entice potential backers, and Hollywood likes to use facts as a starting point only. But because I'd found the proposal at René's, I had to believe he had been the source. I could not find it produced anywhere, so true to what his second wife, Charlotte, had told me, he'd probably killed the project—part of his penchant for secrecy. But, as a writer, I've learned there are always at least two sides to every story. So this was perhaps René's side—as told to Champion, with whatever license the screenwriter took, or mistakes he may have made in retelling it.

Whatever the truth, René and Katherine left Chicago and took up residence together in Washington, D.C. From there, even less is known. The war, with America's entry after the Japanese attack on Pearl Harbor on December 7, 1941, seems to have taken over. They were married in Washington, D.C., on November 20, 1942. On René's OSS application, dated February 1943, while he was a second lieutenant in paratrooper training at Ft. Benning, Georgia, he gave their address as 2232 Hall

Place, Washington, D.C., which was also the address of Katherine's sister, Mrs. Wallace (Dorothy) Eckert. He included on the application that Katherine was working for the Navy. Her resume confirms that. It says she instructed flying in an Atlanta civilian pilot program, relatively near Ft. Benning, and between "January 21 and March 11, 1943," she was a "Junior Cryptanalyst" with "Navy Communications," part of naval intelligence. The last resume entry is, "Left to join husband in Columbus, Ga. He is with the 513th Paratrooper Regiment."

In Dussaq's papers, I found pictures of the two from this period. The most interesting—at least to me—is an 8x10 studio portrait of Katherine looking softly but convincingly into the camera, blonde hair shining from a side light, a hint of a smile on her lips. Its inscription: "To My Beloved René." Others are mostly snapshots from what appears to be a winter respite they took in the mountains. Georgia? North Carolina? In some they are skiing or walking on windless, sun-drenched snow. In others Katherine, obviously having a good time, laughs while sitting on a cabin bed, then studies a book or magazine in front of a lighted fireplace. Two others show them standing in front of what probably is the new convertible she bought. It has conspicuous white wall tires. Dussaq, a lieutenant's bar on his slightly-tilted Garrison cap, is in dress khakis with paratrooper boots and pant legs tucked in. Clutching his side, Katherine wears a light skirt suit, trim and fashionable. The other shows the two in embrace, laughing at the camera—maybe their last happy time together.

In a November 30, 1942 letter to OSS, Chicago's Owen A. West recommends both Katherine and René to the newly-formed U.S. spy organization.[7] For whatever reason, she did not become an OSS agent. Instead, she followed her long-time passion and became one of the select few women—something like 1,000 out of 25,000 applicants—picked for the Woman Airforce Service Pilots, or "WASPs. They were formed under the Army Air Forces as a civilian component—but with military organization and dress—to free men for combat while the women ferried planes, towed practice targets, and conducted preliminary airplane testing, training, and other noncombat, but nonetheless dangerous flying. She entered training at Avenger Field in Sweetwater, Texas on August 9,

1943, and received her wings on February 11, 1944—as her husband, far away, trained in Britain prior to jumping into France. According to WASP information on the internet and the Texas Women's University (TWU), Denton, which keeps files on them, her first duty station was at the Army air base in remote Sioux Falls, South Dakota.[8] Photos at TWU show her the tallest of six women posing before rows of one-story barracks they shared six to a room. Another shows her horsing around in a stupid costume with another woman pilot.

But when it came to flying, she was all business, and rose fast in the organization, becoming an executive officer, one the WASP's leaders. A roommate "remembers her as more mature than most of the young women who often were just out of college...She was a perfectionist...always neatly dressed...always knew what to do," writes Jan Beck, the documents expert.[9]A quote next to Katherine's picture in a WASP yearbook says, "I like efficiency." Eventually, she was sent back to Texas. In what appears to be one of the only informal communications from her in public circulation, Eloise Keeler says Katherine wrote the following on a postcard to an uncle of hers (Eloise) and Leonarde's. The postcard said, "Well—it worked. Was on my good behavior 6 weeks and got transferred to the West Point of the Air Corps—Randolph—as a staff pilot. But it may be temporary. Hope not as I like it a lot. Am getting checked out on twin engine stuff soon." Eloise hastens to add, "Whether Nard heard from her, I can't say."[10]

Which brings up the question, was she still in contact with her ex-husband?

One of the coincidental aspects of Leonarde and Katherine's break up was that right after their divorce became final in the summer of 1941, Leonarde, who threw himself into his work apparently to blunt the heartache, worked on a criminal case remarkably similar to the death of Daisy Moreno, who died in Dussaq's tragic 1933 car crash. As Eloise Keeler explains in *Lie Detector Man*, "A prominent businessman from another city had been driving with his wife when the car apparently swerved off the road and hurtled down a steep embankment. The man jumped to safety, but his wife was killed."[11]

Just as in Dussaq's LA accident, there were questions, and putting the businessman on the polygraph, Leonarde was able to eventually get the suspect to confess that just prior to the "accident," he'd bludgeoned his wife to death with a pipe. Thus revealed, the man, a small town newspaper editor who had bought an insurance policy on his wife also just prior to the crash, went back to his hotel room and jumped to his death from a window—a suicide that, according to Alder in *The Lie Detectors*, kept Keeler, who felt responsible, "liquored up" for days.[12]

It's only speculation, but could Leonarde, in preparation for this case, have learned about Daisy, and, trying to get back in his wife's good graces, informed Katherine about it, instilling in her doubts about her new and somewhat mysterious husband? René had, so far as I can tell, always kept the Moreno crash hidden—at least publicly.Could such a Leonarde-provided revelation explain, at least partly, why she was keeping in touch with the uncle? Doubtful, and a stretch, I admit. Breakups don't always cut all ties, especially if affection or good memories linger. Keeping in touch is not so unusual. However, Dussaq, as his story so far shows and will continue to show, *was* a secretive man.

Speculation aside, soon Katherine was literally sitting near the top of the WASP hierarchy, assigned as she was, in her last duty, to Army Air Forces Training Command headquartered in Fort Worth, Texas. For instance, taking part in a rare press interview with Jackie Cochran, the first female air racer who, as much as anybody, had founded the WASPs and was hopeful they would continue after the war, Katherine suggested that the U.S. might benefit by learning from Russian women pilots who had, by necessity, flown combat and shot down Nazi war planes. "After the war, Miss Cochran," Katherine asked during the wartime interview, "why don't you see what can be arranged in the way of an exchange program between our women fliers and Russia's women fliers?"[13]

But by late 1944, the organization was designated by Congress for dissolution, a sign that war-runners and the politicians, who held the purse strings, no longer saw the WASP's work or mission as necessary— which had to be a disappointment for Katherine, as well as her boss Cochran.

As the end of the organization approached, Katherine, aware of the imminent WASP demise, was working on post-WASP projects. One was to get formal recognition and benefits for her fellow women flyers, thirty-eight of whom by the end of its existence would give their lives in the performance of their duties—mostly in crashes, according to literature about them. The other project was helping to create a post-WASP organization, called "Fifinella," named after a playful fictionalized pilot demon, to continue the group's war-formed camaraderie and keep its departing members informed about each other and subsequent developments that might aid or be of interest to them. It was while flying across the country in pursuit of these final goals that Katherine died—and not without more mystery.

15

Into the Night

SUNDAY, NOVEMBER 26, 1944, WASHINGTON, D.C.

The weather was bad.

It was Thanksgiving, and a typical late fall afternoon—cold, wet, windy.

Katherine had been in the nation's capital seeing mainly Civil Aviation Authority (CAA) officials about her fellow pilots' futures after WASP deactivation. She wanted them helped in the future, and also recognized for their service in the past. Now she was leaving Washington National Airport alone in a two-seat, single-engine AT-6 advanced trainer. It looked like a World War II fighter plane—big, powerful, with a cockpit like a rectangular cage sitting atop the barrel-like fuselage. She had been flying cross-country in it from her Ft. Worth headquarters. Her destination now was Cincinnati, Ohio, where she planned to visit her oldest brother, Lindsay, and his family. He was an Army Air Corps major at Wright Field, Dayton, Ohio, near Cincinnati. Lindsay's daughter, a fourth grader named Katherine in honor of her noted aunt, was excited in anticipation of the visit. She idolized "Big Katherine."

Official business done, Katherine had in the cockpit somewhere her own personal WASP records and scrapbooks of pictures and write-ups about her life accumulated through the years. She planned to give everything to Lindsay, according to surviving family members —even her valuable WASP records. The reason is unknown. She and René had lived in Washington, and presumably had, if nothing else, her sister Dorothy's residence at which to leave the items. That was the "permanent address" René gave for both of them on military forms after he was married. But instead she was taking them to her brother. Why? Did she even know René was alive? It's a valid question since OSS had officially listed him as dead from most of the time since he'd left England. Most probably she did, one would have to speculate. Even if for some of the time during his absence she'd thought him dead, he'd now been back from France over a month and surely would have contacted her—although there's no hard evidence he did.

However, in a curious move, according to the surviving daughter of Katherine's nine-year old niece—Kristin Applegate-King, now an Oregon nurse—Katherine, before she left Washington on this day, had strangely brought the key to a safe deposit box to her sister Dorothy Eckert with instructions to take everything out of it "should anything happen to me." In the aftermath of what was about to occur, they—the surviving members of the family—never knew why Katherine did that, said Kristin. Either Katherine didn't tell Dorothy, who is dead now, or Dorothy, for whatever reason, wouldn't tell them (the surviving members). It was very strange. They just didn't know what was in the box or why Katherine wanted it removed. Was she anticipating some kind of problem, even danger? Or was the request simply the routine caution of a woman who knew she had a dangerous job flying airplanes and wanted to make sure whatever was in it wasn't lost?

One thing is certain—by this date René was on his way home, either physically or making imminent preparations to do so. It's reasonable—lacking any solid evidence to the contrary—to think that he was

looking forward to a long-awaited reunion with his wife after approximately a year and half of war-enforced separation.

■ ■ ■

Despite the weather—which was forecast to be worse at her destination—Katherine was given "IFR" (instrument flight rules) clearance. This meant officials with responsibility along the route of her
flight had okayed her to fly solely on instruments if visibility was
hampered—a probability on the flight plan she filed. They were anticipating continued bad weather—but not bad enough to disallow the
flight. Such a clearance is given to properly qualified pilots, which
apparently she was. From there it was up to the pilot to decide whether
or not to proceed.

For whatever reason—anticipation of seeing her brother and family,
more pressing WASP work to be done, or an eventual planned rendez-
vous with René—she took off shortly after 5 p.m. It was dusk. The plane
lifted into growing darkness and headed west into a fading, if not
obscured, sunset. Her route probably took her successively over the
mountains and forests of southern Pennsylvania and northern West
Virginia, and on over Ohio. By then, according to the accident report,
"The weather was more severe than forecast" and, probably flying IFR,
she began experiencing difficulties.

At 8:05 p.m., according to the report, she was talking via radio with
Cincinnati controllers at the area's Lunken Airport. This was at the
southwest tip of Ohio, just above Kentucky. She'd flown well into the
state, but contact was difficult. At 8:20 p.m. she advised them she would
land at Lunken. But she didn't show and controllers couldn't reestablish
contact. At 9:10 p.m., after repeated calls to her with no success, the
Lunken controllers declared her lost. The report says, "Being unable to
orientate herself on Cincinnati radio range she turned [north] in the
direction of Patterson Range," the air space around Patterson Army Air
Force base which today is Wright-Patterson Air Force Base near Dayton,
northeast of Cincinnati.

According to the report, she was in the midst of a huge rainstorm extending twelve thousand feet up. At 9:35 p.m., she contacted Patterson controllers, advising them "she was lost, low on gas," and giving them her position as best she could. "From [the radio] conversation all attempts were made to guide the plane into Patterson Field, but due to low visibility, low ceiling [the pervasiveness of the storm above her, obstructing sight and communications], fog and rain, all attempts...were futile."

Patterson was approximately ten miles northeast of Dayton, up the Mad River, which borders mostly on its northern edge. Katherine had come down low, apparently trying to see the terrain and also probably to be in position to land. When she'd first contacted Patterson, she reported seeing a "fan marker," a radio beacon used to guide planes on instruments to runways. Controllers guessed it was the beacon at Wilmington, a considerable distance south of the airfield. They relayed a new heading for her but Katherine "advised her instruments were faulty" and she was having difficulty doing what they asked. She was low on fuel, she said—had only ten gallons left. "She next reported [being] over a city... seeing [a] bridge, and a building with smokestacks."

Controllers thought it was Dayton, ten miles southwest of the field, and gave her a new heading. She "was told to look for Patterson Field [sic] revolving green and white beacon and was advised that spotlight was being used. Ship then reported...her [radio] signal was fading." She seemed to be circling in the area, going lower with each turn, losing more fuel.

They gave her still another heading, advising a 180 degree turn—a full half circle, meaning prior to the new heading she was going in the opposite direction from where the controllers wanted. They asked for her fuel level. She again said ten gallons left, according to the gauge, but said, in her estimation, she actually had twenty gallons left. Apparently, she did not trust her instruments. In the controllers' opinion, she was disoriented—not a good situation.

She had now descended lower than 1,400 feet, the altitude she was at when reporting she was flying over what the controllers thought was Dayton. With a suddenly stronger radio signal—probably because of an intermittent break in the weather—she advised she was turning her landing lights on. A tower operator, says the report, went outside in the rain to try and see her or hear the engine.

He could not.

At one point she said she saw "a rotating white light with a red stationary light over it." Possibly she thought that was the field but controllers did not know what it was. Apparently at this point she was flying very low, over farms. Rural residents several miles southwest of New Carlisle, Ohio, told investigators of hearing the plane flying low over their barns, very close to hitting the structures, the plane's engine sputtering and then "cutting out" just before the crash. An official Army Air Forces message the next day tersely reported, "Pilot lost, fuel exhausted, crashed attempting to find landing area." She hit the ground near a rural road and fence at 150 miles per hour, nine miles northwest of Patterson. Pictures show smoldering ruins in a wooded area, little left of the plane. It "burst into flame," said one of the residents. "I arrived at the crash about 2 minutes later and saw no sign of life."

Katherine died on impact. The fire amidst the rain destroyed almost everything at the scene—a tragic end to a storied life. One picture shows what looks like a bonfire, a broken tail off to the side of the bright mound, the only identifiable remains of what had happened.[1]

16

Shadows

t's hard to imagine the grief a husband like Dussaq might feel upon learning of his wife's tragic death. In René's case, the war had forcefully kept them apart. He had been reported dead, with the shock and heartache such news must have caused. At the time, he couldn't contact Katherine—wouldn't have anyway since he didn't know he was reported dead. He had not seen her for more than a year, maybe two. Now, expecting at long last to right the mistake along with the pain and sorrow it had brought and take her in his arms, he was met instead with the terrible news that he had arrived not to see her smiling face, but attend her funeral.

War is hell. Sometimes peace is worse.

That's what it looks like on the surface.

But perhaps it was not like that.

In 1951, a newspaper reporter quoted René as saying Katherine had died the very day he returned. "For months I had been listed as killed in action. She was told that I was safe on the day she crashed. I arrived home two hours later. That's life, I suppose."[1] He was remarried by the time of the interview, which might account for the seeming lack of emotion and matter-of-fact tone. But really, what else could he say? Few bare their soul in agony in a fleeting newspaper interview—especially someone as self-controlled and mentally strong as Dussaq.

However, at least in part, his recollection to the reporter appears wrong. An OSS communication, dated November 30, 1944—four days *after* the crash—indicates René was still en route to the U.S. when Katherine died. He had not arrived, it appears, the same day as the crash—but days after. Reacting for OSS to the tragedy, Sgt. Albert V. de L'Arbre, presumably in Washington headquarters, wrote in a now declassified memo[2] that Katherine's sister in D.C., Dorothy, who had already gone to Ohio by then to assist her brother Lindsay with funeral arrangements, had "asked us if it would be possible that a close friend of [René] meet him after he lands." A Red Cross representative "suggests that when we know the place and hour of arrival of Lt. Dussaq, we arrange for him to meet Mrs. Frey."

Mrs. Frey is identified in the memo as the wife of Dr. Henry W. Frey, of 55 Bow Street, Forrest Hills, Long Island, New York—a relative or friend of René and Katherine (it is not clear in the memo). René lists Frey on his 1943 OSS application as a "character witness" at whose Long Island residence he had stayed, presumably intermittently, since 1934. The OSS memo, a December 1 request by Dussaq for ten days official leave to attend Katherine's funeral (meaning it was that long before he requested it), and his later military separation papers saying he had arrived in the U.S. on December 2, 1944, seem to prove that it was almost a week after the crash that he, in fact, arrived in the U.S.[3] Was his statement to the reporter just a lapse of memory? The reporter's mistake, or hyperbole? In addition, interviews with several surviving members of Katherine's family suggest that after such a long and forced separation, the relationship between Katherine and René was not as good as one might expect.

To begin with, it is still not clear when, and even if, Katherine ever learned her husband was alive. One would expect that when René returned to England in late September she would have been notified, by the OSS or him, or both. If not, there was still roughly a month left before her death—time enough for her to learn the news. But he told the reporter in 1951 that she was informed he was alive on the day she died. If that is true, why had it taken so long? Was this, too, just a lapse of memory? What could have kept her for a full month from knowing her husband was alive and back? If it is true, was there more to René's mission in France than is divulged in the public records? Had he been detained and incommunicado in England because of the initial suspicion that he had deserted or been turned by the enemy? Had he been involved in something else in England that had kept him unannounced and incommunicado?

Whatever the answer to those questions, the story from Katherine's surviving family members lends support to Dussaq's reported quote that she didn't learn he was alive until the day she died. Nieces and children of the nieces to whom I've talked believe that it was on or close to the day she left Washington that she unexpectedly gave the safe deposit box key to her sister Dorothy with the sudden instructions to remove its contents if anything happened to her. What was in it? No one I've talked to knows. What was Katherine's concern? Again, no one knows.

But they all believe René got whatever was in the safe deposit box while Dorothy was out of town helping attend to funeral arrangements. Penny Eckert, Dorothy's daughter (and Katherine's niece), says her parents, now both deceased, did not like René. "There are two ideas I recall—one, that he was a spy (for whom I don't know), and the other, that he was somehow responsible for Katherine's crash (and how I don't know)."[4]

The crash speculation, as Penny indicates, seems unfounded. Dorothy, according to her daughter Penny, was a mathematics graduate from Columbia University—"brilliant at it"—and was working as a decoder for the wartime government at the time of the crash. In rushing off to Ohio to help her brother with funeral details, she either put off, or, in her grief and anguish, forgot about Katherine's request, and was later so distraught and "traumatized" about the lapse—allowing René, as several of them believe, to get to the safe deposit box first and empty it—

that she would not discuss what had happened with anybody, including family. "Since my mother couldn't talk about any of this, I only heard stuff in dribs and drabs," Penny, a linguistics professor at California's Stanford University, emailed me. "So there's a serious likelihood that my memories are garbled. But I definitely came away with the idea that [René] was bad news."[5]

Penny's father, Wallace, was, at the time of Katherine's death, an astronomer with a teaching position at Columbia. During the war, he "directed the Nautical Almanac at the Naval Observatory." So both parents had connections to the military, and, significantly, her mother probably worked for military intelligence under which decoding was usually carried out. But when I asked her if they might have basis beyond just not liking René to think he was a spy, she wrote back, "This is a glamorous idea, but way improbable. My father was on leave from his teaching position at Columbia...not a real member of the military. I'm sure I would have known if they'd had some kind of privileged information." Later, in response to a further question, she added, "Now that I think about it, the spy thing may not have even come from my parents...It easily could have been a speculation [amongst family members] in my generation. If you want something harder you have to deal with my uncle Apple."[6]

Uncle Apple, or "App" as he's also nicknamed, is Theodore "Ted" Applegate, Katherine's youngest brother, who, ninety-four when I contacted him, lived on remote Orcas Island, Washington, near the Canadian border. When Katherine died he was a young private in the army's medical corps at Ft. Lewis, Washington, and, according to a newspaper article from Walla Walla, Washington, where he, Katherine, and the other siblings had grown up, had attended the funeral and burial for her there. The article said, "A simple service was conducted...with an organist providing the music. Military personnel from the Walla Walla army air base served as pallbearers. Floral tributes were many. Mrs. Dussaq's brother, Maj. Lindsay Applegate of Wright Field, Ohio, accompanied the body west as military escort and her husband, Lieutenant Dussaq arrived by plane from the East coast [sic] in time for the rites."[7]

Lindsay, according to his surviving daughter Katherine—an Oregon teacher today and the fourth grader who was waiting expectantly for "Big Katherine" before the crash—was stationed at Wright Field near where Katherine went down. He may have been at the crash site, she writes, because he had remains of at least one of her scrapbooks and possibly knowledge about what might have happened prior to her fatal trip. But like his sister Dorothy, "he refused to talk about it," she wrote in an email to Ken Alder who shared it with me. And "it still haunts me... One day in the '70s I noticed that my father was burning something in the fireplace. Apparently it was what remained of at least one of my aunt's scrapbooks. I'd seen it as a kid—the edges of the pages were all charred—and not from our fireplace... I was very upset that he'd decided to destroy it, but I guess the painful memories had become too burdensome... Losing her was one of the worst things that ever happened to me."[8]

Lindsay is dead now, and whatever he knew about René and "Big Katherine" went with him. She was buried in Dayton City Cemetery outside Walla Walla, where a square gravestone with "Katherine Applegate Dussaq 1906–1944" remains. App eventually wrote me that as far as he knew, his older brother Lindsay, an engineer by trade, only blamed a faulty altimeter for the crash. "Until I read your letter," he wrote, "it had not occurred to me that there might be something 'fishy' concerning Katherine's death... If there is more to the story than that, I might ask, 'was the altimeter tampered with?'"

He continued, "Sometime prior to the plane crash, Katherine and I spent an evening together. She complained of having on occasions being followed—attributing that to Leonarde Keeler, who could easily have had it done. She said nothing of René's whereabouts or circumstance at that time." App wrote he had "met with the two of them prior to René's departure to Europe" and they seemed to have been on "very good terms at that time." After the funeral, René, Lindsay, Dorothy, and other family members "spent 2 or 3 days at my parents' home in Walla Walla, and he noticed no "low opinion with regard to René. Lindsay may have harbored some ill will, however, and spoken of it to his daughter... but he said nothing about René within my hearing. I found René to be an interesting, friendly, pleasant chap," although, he added, "we had no conversations in any depth."

However, there are indications of discord between René and the Applegate family in two post-crash documents I found. One was an "18 December 1944" letter in René's OSS file to a merchant in New York City. It says, "I have been notified by [OSS headquarters] that my check of $36.85 was returned by the bank due to the fact that my account has been stopped since the death of my wife. As soon as I make arrangements, I will be glad to forward the amount I owe."[9] The other is a "December 1944" Cook County, Illinois, probate court document showing Dussaq and the Applegates in a suit involving Katherine's "$20,000" estate.[10] It appears the family might have stopped his access to Katherine's bank account and that he was involved in fighting them for the money she had left in her estate—circumstances one would not expect to find if relations between Katherine, René and her family were good.

So what happened? Was the suspicion simply the result of a terrible loss some in Katherine's family could not accept at face value? Or had something happened in the long absence from each other that had pulled them apart or had at least threatened her? If so, what? Had she lost the love that seemed evident when she signed the happy portrait of herself "to my beloved René"? Had she met someone else? Had he? Was it a case of absence making the heart grow colder? Or was it all about her former husband Leonarde Keeler and the flame, even perhaps anger, he still had? We'll probably never know. Too much time has lapsed. The principals are dead, their secrets gone with them.

Truth is elusive, and in the absence of conclusive evidence, one must—and I choose to—give René the benefit of the doubt. Katherine's death was a crushing blow, unexpected and devastating—perhaps numbing to a man who had been through so much death and loss in the war and whose guiding principle was to meet head on whatever fearful, disruptive, and hurtful event he encountered. This situation had to have been one of the worst imaginable. Whatever truths lay behind it, what was left for him was a return to the war and devastation that had dominated so much of his life since he'd left Katherine.

PART 2

CLANDESTINE

17

The Basques

The period following his wife's death was probably a respite for Dussaq but not the end to his sorrow. How do you forget lost love? But at least it remained a glimmer in an otherwise troubling time. He was to help train Basque fighters to, among other missions, re-establish their homeland once the Allies invaded Franco's Spain, which it was assumed they would do. Dussaq's thoughts about Spain's politics are not known, but Franco was a Fascist dictator, similar to Hitler, whom Dussaq had been fighting. These Basques, an ancient people whose origins are unknown, had once reigned free and sovereign in the high PyRenées and lowlands separating France and Spain. But slowly, since the Middle Ages, their country had been enveloped and split by the two larger nations. Catholic and traditional, most Spanish Basques had fought against Franco—as had liberal, anti-fascist Americans in the "Lincoln Brigade."[1] Losing the war, many who survived were imprisoned, their families scattered and broken. Their unique language was banned, their culture forced underground. Now Dussaq and a handful of instructors were going to help them regain their country. The Basques were excited.

Since returning to duty Dussaq had been on a military fast track. Officially promoted to captain, he had been sent to parachute refresher training and was reunited there with Douglas Bazata, his good friend with whom he'd earlier trained as a Jedburgh and who had also heroically fought the Germans in Occupied France. They'd spent off-duty time together, Bazata writing years later, "After his beloved wife's death, I never saw him with another woman. He had only one aim—a free, self-directed Cuba"[2]

But this was the end of World War II and he was under strict orders. At first, he had been readied for a Far East assignment, specifically the India-Burma Theater. But war needs were rapidly changing as the Germans capitulated, and he was simultaneously considered for a secret Norway mission. By spring, his orders had been revised again, and he had been hastily jumped into the German Rhineland as part of the quickly-mustered Special Allied Airborne Reconnaissance Force (SAARF), a mission to protect concentration camp inmates and allied prisoners-of-war from last-ditch reprisals that were feared as the Nazis crumbled.

Given the horrors being uncovered in such camps, the assignment could not have been uplifting.

But SAARF was short lived and appears to have been successful. Now, in the late spring of 1945, René was some twenty-five miles southwest of Paris, just beyond the palace-rich gardens of Versailles, at what was known as the "Rothschild Castle," a large, former medieval monk's abbey bought in the 1800s by the powerful Rothschild banking family and refurbished into a neo-Gothic estate. Abandoned during the war, it was on the outskirts of Cernay-la-ville, a small town in the deeply wooded Rambouillet forest, a nature preserve. It featured arched, stone walkways and courtyards, exotic gardens with fountains and sculptures, and an adjacent blue lake. The setting was idyllic—just the place to forgive and forget. But this was still a secret operation with heavy war security. No one was to know what was going on at the cloistered abbey, especially Franco.

Officially, Spain was neutral and the Allies had to respect that. Unofficially, Franco favored the Axis, helping them in many ways. Consequently, Spain was a hotbed of spy activity. The OSS was at the forefront of the clandestine wars, clashing with Nazi agents and making secret deals with the Basque enemies of Franco. The Basques organized OSS-connected spy rings with their people in Spain, Occupied France, Latin America, and the Philippines. They also rescued downed Allied pilots, fleeing Jews, and others escaping the Nazis by guiding them over the rugged PyRenées to neutral Spain. They knew its secret passages. Their networks also smuggled saboteurs back into Occupied France. The payoff they hoped would involve U.S. aid and regaining their homeland, their independence. But it had to be kept secret. Officially, the training wasn't happening.

Some of the hand-picked Basques had arrived piecemeal into Paris by rail, traveling incognito. They had been met and transported to the abbey by disguised army trucks. Others had fought with the Maquis and were already in or around Paris, as were those chosen from the "Guernica Battalion," an army of Basques involved in Paris's liberation that had helped defeat one of the last Nazi strongholds in southwestern France— the four thousand soldier garrison at Gironde in the Bordeaux Region on the Atlantic Coast.[3]

Before any Spanish operations, the OSS planned to use the Basques in the coming occupation of Germany and, later, possibly against Japan, next to be conquered. "Because of their physical stamina" and "their personal desire to engage in hazardous missions," wrote an OSS official, the Basques "were considered particularly suited for operations [behind] the enemy's lines."[4] They were to be trained to be what today are called "Special Forces." It was envisioned that as many as one thousand Basques might eventually undergo the training, starting with small twenty-to thirty-men units.[5] It doesn't appear Dussaq commanded the mission, but who did is not mentioned in the few documents about the secret program I could find. Dussaq wrote tersely in 1947 about his participation: "Was

Operation Officer and instructor of a Company of former Spanish Civil War soldiers, including one general. Trained them in subversive activities, demolition, mine lifting, industrial sabotage, ambushing, assassination, radio communication, and all work pertaining to small unit tactics."[6]

French and Spanish documentation I found was equally sparse. It talks about the Basques receiving martial arts training—"jiu-jitsu" and judo. "The instructors were a motley crew," writes Mikel Rodriguez, a Spanish historian. They included a "British" named "Fairbanks, a legend in the martial arts world." I suspect that was W. E. Fairbairn, the former Shanghai police official notorious in martial arts and OSS circles for teaching lethal self-defense. If stories about him are true, despite his average size and unassuming appearance, he was one of the toughest hand-to-hand fighters the modern world has known.[7]

Among the trainees was Pablo de Beldarrain, a leading officer of the meager Basque armies in the civil war. Was this the "general" Dussaq wrote he instructed? I don't know.[8] Beldarrain's report does not name individuals. But it certainly concerns Dussaq—a picture of whom at the abbey with other instructors I received from Basque sources—and could, in at least one of its passages, be talking about him specifically.

"I am moved by a debt of gratitude to the instructors," wrote Beldarrain to Basque President Jose Antonio de Aguirre, in exile at the time in New York City. "Their love of freedom is as intense as ours." Skilled in teaching and "the military arts [they, like us] went without bed sheets and [washed] their own clothes." They "won the confidence of the *gudaris* [Basque for 'soldiers'] by using persuasive arguments, and recounting examples and factual incidents...With a real love and enthusiasm [they] went beyond fulfillment of their mission...They [were] good psychologists...subjecting us to classic tests to observe reactions...Each individual was taught to work in harmony with his companion, to accept responsibility, to learn self-control...and expand both physically and morally."

Their "captain-in-charge was not satisfied with just officers and good substitutes. No, his interest was concerned with what we could be" as leaders. "This forging of individual character was carried out in conjunction with instruction [about] the [15-man] patrol...the smallest army unit of effective action...We used the practice method, without undue theory, familiarizing ourselves with the weapons and becoming accustomed to all the sensations of the battle field, so that there would be no surprise at the moment of actual combat...In view of the personality of the instructors and the originality of the teaching methods...I sincerely believe the groundwork of our future military organization has been laid."[9]

Trainee Paco Lararreta was so inspired by what he learned that he wrote he felt like "Tarzan" willing to take on "anything. It was very powerful." He was ready to march out and begin fighting, he said. But suddenly, without warning, the training was halted. It was a Sunday, July 8, 1945. He remembered it vividly in an interview given to Professor Rodriguez years later. "The Americans were told that the unit was dissolved. No explanations were given." It was just over. "Even the uniforms were ordered burned in the castle courtyard to avoid leaving incriminating evidence."[10]

What had happened apparently was that high up, American officials had decided it would not be wise to invade and occupy Spain. President Franklin Roosevelt, under whom much of the Basque help had originated—prompted by OSS chief Donovan whom OSS records show favored the program—had died. The succeeding administration under President Truman had looked at the situation and pulled the plug. Not only was everyone tired of war, but they had enough on their hands already defeating and occupying Germany and Japan without adding Spain to the headache. They may also have sensed that Spanish cooperation soon would be needed in the Cold War against Russia, which had, however unofficially, begun.

Whatever the reason, stopping the program after such goodwill had been built up with the Basques, to whom he might have been distantly related,[11] was possibly the last straw for Dussaq. The photo at the castle sent to me shows him happily with other instructors and probably some of the trainees. He's sitting leisurely at the bottom of tree-shrouded stone steps somewhere on the lush abbey grounds. There's a cigarette in one of his hands and he's smiling contentedly at the camera. The others stand or sit variously around him and up the steps. They are not identified, but clearly there's a palpable bond among these men.

Regardless of Dussaq's reaction—embarrassment, anger, a betrayal he couldn't stop—the Basque training was his last assignment of the war. "Most of the demobilized *gudaris* returned to Spain," according to Prof. Rodriguez, to become part of a harassed and harried postwar Basque "region," dictated to and punished by Franco. Some Basques stayed in France, starting new lives. Others entered the legendary French Foreign Legion, probably fighting eventually in the Algerian and Indochinese wars of the 1950s. Some, writes Rodriguez, became the first instructors of the Basque separatist organization ETA, which eventually evolved into a skillful terrorist group waging a guerilla war against the government in Madrid.[12]

18

Radioactive

Of all the death-defying stunts Dussaq attempted in his life—airborne wing-walking, hand standing on top of the Empire State building, diving on dangerous sunken wrecks, and jumping alone as a spy into Nazi-infested France—this one was, in my opinion, the most audacious.

It was late June, 1946. René was part of the high-security atomic bomb tests being conducted by a massive joint Army-Navy task force off Bikini Atoll in the Pacific's Marshall Islands. In all seriousness, he wanted to stow away on a drone aircraft making tests that would be flown through the broiling, radioactive mushroom cloud. The test—dropping an atom bomb on a fleet of some seventy-plus ships to see the results—would constitute only the fourth known manmade nuclear blast ever. The atomic age was in its infancy. There was little known by the U.S. about nuclear explosions beyond what had been gleaned at "Trinity," the July 1945 test in the New Mexico desert, and the destroyed Japanese cities of Hiroshima and Nagasaki.

A *Newsweek* article reported on fears among the public and scientists of what the blast might cause: destruction of gravity, the oceans to vaporize into steam, their cracked floors swallowing anything remaining; earthquakes throughout the world that would spawn devastating tidal waves (tsunamis). "In San Francisco," said the magazine, "newspapers nearly panicked the crews of three Bikini-bound press and observer ships. They headlined a warning from Anatol J. Schneiderov, 'seismologist' at Johns Hopkins University, that the explosion would swamp every ship and leave no survivors. Hopkins University promptly announced that Schneiderov was only a student and—pointedly—'of Soviet origin,' and that his views were not those of the university."[1]

But Dussaq, commander of a photographic unit recording the tests, doesn't seem to have been concerned—at least not for the danger to himself that stowing away might present. Was he again testing his nerve, entering the holocaust simply to best his fear? Was it to make sure he did his job to the utmost and produced the best pictures?

Had he lost his mind?

■ ■ ■

Since leaving the Basques, Dussaq had not had a serious challenge—at least not according to what I've found. By July 18, barely two weeks after departing the "Rothschild Castle," OSS had granted him ten days leave in France to visit his family in relatively nearby Geneva.[2] He hadn't seen his father, it appears, since before the war when they'd met in Cuba, and also later traveled together on at least one ocean voyage when he supposedly was gathering information for his lectures.

It was time.

He was a different man now, married, widowed, certainly more mature through experience. He had proved, as he'd wanted to before joining the military, that he was the match in ability and courage of any natural-born American fighter. That goal had probably retreated in his mind. The war in Europe had raged chaotically for six long years. His family in Geneva, those still there, would certainly be glad and relieved to see him. While Switzerland was neutral in the conflict, it, like Spain, had been a beehive of spy activity, and most Swiss, one had to believe, were keenly aware of all the dying around them. Now with the war ending, it was probably an easy decision. His father, who doted on him, must have been ecstatic at the thought of seeing "Rajah" again.

As a Sufi, Emilien Dussaq was a pacifist. But he had advised his son to take the "bumpier" path and must have been acutely aware of the perils René had lately faced. His movement's late religious leader, Hazrat Inayat Khan,[3] had lost a daughter doing almost the same that René had in Occupied France—aiding and fighting with the resistance. Khan, revered among the faithful for bringing the Sufi movement to the West, had made Emilien Switzerland's Sufi leader. Khan's daughter, Noor, codenamed "Madelaine" by her SOE handlers, had been the first woman radio operator sent from Britain into Occupied France. Believed betrayed by a double agent, and with the Nazis hot on her trail, she had heroically declined a special rescue in order to keep London informed of vital information. But the transmitting eventually helped the Germans locate and arrest her. She resisted interrogation, most probably was tortured,[4] but never divulged any secrets. After repeated attempts to escape, she was sent to Germany and Dachau Concentration Camp where, on September 13, 1944—only days after René had returned from "Freelance"— she was executed with a bullet to the head.

How much of this Emilien knew is unknown. But he surely had learned she was missing, and because of Sufi brotherhood and his own sensibilities, he probably felt the loss almost as if Noor had been his own.

René's natural mother, Sara Matilde Pineiro, and Emilien were no longer married. Presumably she was in her native Argentina. A 1943 SOE file I have from when he was being vetted for Freelance says she was living in Buenos Aires. Inayat Khan's autobiography states she and Emilien were married in Paris in 1921—and divorced in Geneva the same year.[5] The marriage date seems in error. René was born in 1911 and his older brother, Maurice, five years before that. I doubt either was born out of wedlock. However, the divorce date could be right. The next year, 1922, was when Khan appointed Emilien General Secretary of the Sufi Movement in Geneva.

Religion may have played a part in their breakup. Her absence from Geneva now was probably no problem for René. According to Charlotte, he and his natural mother were estranged. "She was mean," said Charlotte, and had "once injured René's sister by throwing her down stairs. René did not like her"—so much so that he listed his stepmother as his real "mother" when he'd recently returned from France.[6]

In 1924, his father had become remarried to Marie Isabelle Lussy— known as "Maie" to the family. Her nationality, according to OSS documents, was "Swiss-Cuban." To Emilien, he wrote, she was a "great joy." All indications are they were happily married. One of René's two married sisters, Sara, nicknamed "Shanti"—Sanskrit for peace and tranquility—was still living in Geneva. (The other, Lydia, was in Brazil.) Like her father, Shanti was an official in Geneva's Sufi movement, probably aiding Emilien. If letters of hers to Charlotte are indication, she was well nicknamed. They are full of sympathy and Shanti-provided solutions, regardless of practicality, to almost every problem Charlotte presented her, however miniscule. "Generous and unselfish," René wrote about her years later. His aunt, Countess M. L. Pieri, his father's sister and another Sufi (she was married to a "count" who claimed royal ancestry), was also in Geneva.

His visit, if nothing else, would be a warm family reunion.

As René left for Geneva, he requested OSS put him back on "jump" status. Apparently he had been removed, which perturbed him. "With more than 150 jumps," wrote an OSS major arguing for the reinstatement, "he believes parachute jumping is an essential part of his work, and that he is willing and able to jump whenever ordered."[7] Throughout his life René had great pride in being airborne—more than being OSS, Jedburgh, or SOE. But it appears in this case he was also looking ahead to fighting Japanese in the Pacific, the part of the war still unresolved. The letter says that when he was recruited, OSS had promised he could maintain jump status. Although the war in the Pacific would be over before he could get there, his wish for reinstatement appears to have been granted. America's atom bomb, which would prematurely end the war before troops from Europe were required, was still being developed and was top secret. Neither he nor those in OSS Paris knew Japan would soon surrender.

Little of what he did in Geneva is on searchable records or otherwise attainable. All family members there at the time have long since died. I did find a picture of him in a Swiss newspaper's sports section. It showed him unusually thin but smiling proudly in summer khakis, sitting cross-legged with the Geneva rowing team, sixteen young men in striped tee-shirts and shorts, which, the newspaper informed, had just won a competition with the Lyon team, its long-time rival. The caption makes note that Dussaq is a "uniformed American paratroop commander" and "a rower from an older team" supporting his "compatriots."[8] He spent maybe two weeks in Switzerland and then returned to Washington.

On August 27—following the Japanese surrender—he was given "permission" to visit Havana, but ordered to "report" to the military attaché at the American Embassy there.[9] Presumably he was going to Cuba to see his older brother Maurice and probably other family members. But why the military contact? The war was over. Did he have a special mission? Was it was just a routine check in—the military keeping tabs on its asset? Bazata says he was Renéwing ties with clandestine elements—something I'll address later.

By September 13, if not before, Dussaq was back in Washington. That was the day, according to Richard Dunlop, a former OSS agent and author of *Donovan: America's Master Spy*, he was honored by President Truman "in recognition of Dussaq's heroism with the French Resistance. Truman was properly affable," notes Dunlop, "but later in the day he gave the go-ahead to...finish off the OSS."[10] Truman didn't like the spy agency. He thought it might get out of hand and become an "American Gestapo." It was finished, only to be reborn out of necessity as an interim group, and then as the much bigger Central Intelligence Agency (CIA) several years later. By early November, Dussaq would be honorably discharged into the reserves, and after a short visit in Chicago with his former treasure-hunting patron, Waldo Logan,[11] a member of Chicago's social elite, he was on his way back to Hollywood and a brief stint in a noted film.

O.S.S., an early 1946 movie starring Alan Ladd and Geraldine Fitzgerald, was not only critically acclaimed and a box office success, but also the first movie to feature the U.S. spy organization after the war.[12] Tough and suspenseful, shot in film noir style, the Paramount Pictures production was based on secret OSS files cleared by Bill Donovan himself, who was anxious to get the OSS story out and thereby secure his future in American intelligence. Perhaps that was why Dussaq got a bit part in it as a French artillery officer and did double duty as a technical advisor soon after arriving in movie land. The story followed an OSS team dropped into Germany to destroy a tunnel—much like missions in which René had participated. Paramount had ties to OSS, and Dussaq had previous stuntman experience.[13] It was an understandable match. I have a photo of Ladd and René sitting in director's chairs shaking hands on the set. Ladd, a short man, would have been dwarfed by Dussaq, had they been standing. As it was, the close up shows the handsome actor's hand engulfed in Dussaq's larger palm as the two smile at each other.

But Dussaq's budding acting career was cut short. As movie columnist Bob Thomas announced to newspaper readers nearly a month before the film's May 26, 1945, release date, "Capt. René Dussaq, advisor for Paramount's O.S.S., will help photograph the atom bomb tests."[14]

By that time, he had already left for the Pacific.

■ ■ ■

Operation Crossroads, conducted roughly from January to August 1946, was the largest postwar American military operation in the Pacific up to that time. Expendable ships from the American and defeated Japanese and German navies, including aircraft carriers and battleships, were positioned in the large Bikini lagoon with caged animals and instruments aboard—all ostensibly for the purpose of important research. What would an atomic bomb do to such a fleet and its live inhabitants?

In contrast to the Navy which provided ships used in the test, the Army Air Corps, to which Dussaq was now assigned, was tasked with most of the air needs of the operation. It provided crews and planes for transportation and supply to and from the U.S. mainland and between the other tiny Marshall Islands being used as bases for the tests. The Marshalls were infamous for the ferocious Battle of Tarawa, an early WWII victory against the Japanese. The army also provided most of the airborne testing for the two scheduled atomic explosions, including the B-29 that would drop the bomb for the first test, scheduled for July 1. A second test, on July 27, was to be of an underwater bomb which did not require an air drop. It would be electronically detonated on a submerged platform in the 180-foot deep lagoon.

Dussaq was part of what was called the army's "Air Photo Group," one of the specialized units in the task force organized for specific aspects of the testing—in this case, combat photography. Its mission was to take still photographs and motion pictures for the secret tests, and also for the less secret historical record. Most of its product was to be top secret—unavailable to the public. But some pictures and movies would be released. Special high-speed cameras had to be newly built from scratch and then fitted into the planes, including modified B-29s and B-17s. Dussaq had a lot of responsibilities. The high humidity of the islands caused fungus to grow in the cameras. He had to remedy that. He had to manage world-class photographers, including "primadonna" civilians. There would be countless, taxing rehearsals, and these were just the worst of his daily problems. He would later tell an interviewer he was "surprised" to be called back for the high priority mission.[15] The reason intimated was that he hesitated because of what it would require. But he seemed pleased. I can see the pride in his eyes as he shakes actor Ladd's hand in the photo on the *O.S.S.* set. Ladd is clasping *Dussaq's* palm—not the other way around. Dussaq, in uniform and paratrooper boots, was the real OSS agent—and knows it. Ladd was just playing one.

Crossroads, I suspect, was a challenge he welcomed.

The atomic bomb was America's greatest military secret in early 1945. The U.S., as far as is publicly known, was the only country that possessed "The Bomb." It was seen as the ultimate weapon, and one America would need as it moved closer to a Cold War against the Soviets.

It was an honor, even a privilege, to be selected for its testing. Dussaq's OSS background meant he possessed a key requirement. He'd already been vetted; i.e., he could be trusted with the secrets. This, I think, was key. He was part of the clandestine warrior fraternity, a military elite. His Hollywood experience also helped. To a general making the selections, seeing "Hollywood stuntman" on Dussaq's resume must have suggested that he knew something about film—which he did—a key skill for the Air Photo Group. He'd learned it working with John Craig. He was a "double-agent," so to speak—saboteur plus cameraman. He joined others similarly vetted, former secret agents and intelligence officers among them.

Craig, his old boss and mentor, was already involved. During the war, Craig had become a decorated intelligence officer and seasoned combat photographer. He had been one of those given clearance to document the crucial D-Day invasion, and, as head of a daring airborne combat photographic unit, had flown some thirty-five combat missions in the skies over Nazi-held Europe and Africa, including the famous low-level bombing raid on the Ploesti (Romania) oil fields, vital Nazi fuel sources. Footage he'd shot on that mission was reportedly later used in the acclaimed 1949 war movie *Twelve O'Clock High*. Craig was a lieutenant colonel by this time, awarded, among other decorations, a Distinguished Flying Cross (DFC), a top Army Air Corps decoration, and a Purple Heart for a wound received at the Remagen Bridge during the invasion of Germany.[16] Like Dussaq, he'd paid his dues. Craig may even have been influential in Dussaq's selection for the task force.

But they probably saw little of each other. Time was of the essence because of the July 1 deadline. There were few atomic bombs available for testing at the time, and the Russians would be there to see how they were doing. They would only have two shots. Each had to be perfect.

Thus Craig was by necessity separated from Dussaq. Craig was part of the larger contingent of the task force, including its headquarters, which was on Kwajalien atoll. It consisted of some 2,100 soldiers and most of the manned aircraft being used in the mission.

Dussaq, for his part, was 170 miles away on Eniwetok, one of the smaller atolls in the chain around the lagoon. It had a lesser contingent, approximately 450 men, and the few drone aircraft that would be used to fly through the dangerously radioactive cloud shortly after the explosions. Drones were relatively new in those days, although they'd been used and developed piecemeal since World War I. They were not the highly sophisticated lethal robots of today. These were converted B-17 bombers controlled from jeeps on the ground for take-offs and landings and from nearby airplanes when safely aloft and flying into the testing. It was uncertain whether the drones would even be able to perform their mission let alone survive in the broiling post-detonation cloud given the unknowns of nuclear explosions at that time.

Here is some of what the drones would encounter: as early as fifteen minutes following detonation, said to generate the heat of the sun, they would fly in from positions miles away and enter at various altitudes the thick mushrooming cloud, billowing ultimately to thirty thousand feet. "The intensity of radiation present in that boiling column of vapors would certainly prove fatal to personnel, even if the plane could survive the physical beating," wrote Dr. David Bradley, a scientist on scene.[17] Dussaq's own unit would produce a film about the drones, *The Phantom Air Fleet*, warning in its taut narration of the dangers of entering the cloud: "Seconds count. Ahead…the vast unknown. Charged air traveling at cyclonic velocities. Alpha, Beta, and Gamma particles in unpredictable quantities. Poisonous gases, many unknown to man…Here man himself dare not venture…He can only send the mechanical product of his ingenuity [the drones]…"[18]

Yet, for whatever reason, Dussaq decided he wanted to stowaway on one of these drone aircraft and fly through the hellish post-blast aftermath. In Dussaq's files I found a handwritten letter from a scientist whose scratchy signature I eventually determined was that of Dr. William

W. Runinson, a radio chemist involved in the task force, whom Dussaq apparently consulted on the matter. "As a result of our conversation at Eniwetok on June 4," wrote Runinson, "I have made some calculations on the radiation dose a man would take if he flew through the radioactive cloud at an altitude of 13,000 feet 15 minutes after the shot." At a speed of two hundred miles per hour, the dose "would be less than 10 roentgens, which is certainly safe." Contamination of the plane itself would only raise that [figure] "a couple of roentgen...So your plan for flying through the cloud is perfectly reasonable...However, there seems to be no chance that you will be permitted to do so. Dr. (Warner?) [Runinson's parenthesis and question mark] tells me orders against such exposure of personnel to radiation are so strong that if you flew through the cloud, even as a stowaway, not only would *you* be court martialed," but so would your bosses.[19]

Runinson's opinion on the radiation doses may have been correct, but it was only an opinion. Nobody had ever tried to fly through nuclear debris, and the possibility—indeed, probability—existed that Dussaq could have been harmed or even killed, if not in the cloud, then eventually by the damage done to his body.

Vice Admiral W. H. P. Blandy, commander of the joint task force, was already worried about stowaways and had ordered that the target fleet in the lagoon be searched by his police just prior to the test. "He considers the precaution necessary," wrote a reporter for Gannett News Service. "He has more than 40 letters in his files to prove that some people would like to expose themselves to the greatest destructive force ever developed." Among the five types of persons the admiral listed as possible perpetrators were "Obvious daredevils trying to prove they are afraid of nothing."[20]

Was this Dussaq's motivation—fearlessness beyond rationale? It's possible. But probably not exactly as the admiral phrased it. He wasn't a daredevil, but he might have felt sufficiently challenged in the exercise to want to excise the fear demon in his usual manner—by confronting it. And maybe there were legitimate professional concerns, like making sure the sophisticated, newly-constructed cameras, unvetted by live fire, did their job in case of a breakdown. His reputation was at stake.

No one will ever know his motivation. The answer died with him. Further, it's a possibility he actually did stow away. His second wife Charlotte told me he did.

"He got on a drone unbeknownst to everybody," she said.

"Nobody knew he was on it?" I asked.

"No. He got on it and took the trip."

"This was a drone used in the test—when the atom bomb was used?"

Yes, she insisted.

What happened?

"Well, he got back. He was fine. Nothing happened…When we were married…He said, 'You don't have to worry about children…because of my tremendous exposure to all the radiation…'"

Maybe the story he told simply evolved into that? Maybe his statement indicating sterility was just a joke given his proximity during the tests? But wouldn't she know that? And an Associated Press story I found gives her belief credence—at least that he actually tried to board a drone.

Appearing in newspapers on July 19, two weeks after the first test, the story told of a number of scientists and soldiers who requested to stay close to the blasts—including Runinson—but were denied by Admiral Blandy. "Topping all in daring," it says, "was Capt. René Dussaq, a deep sea diver who wound up as a parachute trooper…It was disclosed today that Dussaq was so determined to ride a Flying Fortress drone through the atomic cloud July 1 that his commanding officer assigned military police to watch his movements. It was feared that Dussaq would try to stow away on one of the bombers, which were flown by remote control. He was found in the drone parking area an hour before the take-off and was ordered away."[21]

Did he return? Dussaq was a clandestine master. Like a burglar who gives a barnyard dog a bone while slipping over the fence, he knew all manner of ways to get past military police.

Did he do it at Bikini?

Whatever happened it had no lasting repercussion. By the time the secret photos and films his unit had made were ready to be taken back to the states, he had been entrusted to personally courier them via air—with a parachute on his back, according to Charlotte, in case the plane encountered trouble. In July 1947, he was informed by Major General Edward F. Witsell, adjutant general in the War Department, that he had been awarded an Army Commendation Ribbon for his "meritorious service" during the tests. The citation lauded his "exceptional professional knowledge and leadership" and said he'd "contributed greatly to the outstanding success" of the mission.

By then he was out of the Army again and back in Hollywood.

19

"Juanita"

Dussaq's experience at the Bikini tests apparently left him thinking he might become a movie producer. That's the occupation he listed on his separation papers as he left active service from Fort Meade, Maryland, on October 29, 1946. He had produced two army films which he'd escorted on planes to government movie labs in St. Louis, Missouri, reportedly with the safeguard parachute at the ready.[1] He'd also listed a Hollywood apartment at 1801 Tamarind Avenue as his new address. Google maps today place the apartment building in "the old Hollywood Studio District." It was conveniently near Sunset and Hollywood Boulevards, Paramount and Columbia Studios (among others), the Brown Derby restaurant, and Grauman's Chinese Theater—all bustling Hollywood landmarks in the post-war 1940s.

But he never became a producer—perhaps because an important personal event intervened.

Through his speaker's bureau agent, Harold Peat, his arrival back in Los Angeles was preceded by a hasty request from Peat's wife, Louisa, the literary half of the agency. She asked that one of the agency's Hollywood contacts arrange a welcoming dinner-date for René. Aging Mrs. Peat, it appears, had a platonic fondness for Dussaq—if she wasn't simply making sure a prized agency asset was helped, thereby keeping him happy. Her contact was the sister of Charlotte Clary, an aspiring young actress and budding screen coach at Paramount. Charlotte was destined to become Dussaq's second wife. But at the time of the request, she told me, she had no interest whatsoever in a blind date. However her sister was persistent and pleaded with Charlotte to help out.

Charlotte finally agreed.

"It actually began quite well," she said of the date. The new arrival (René)—whom an international reporter in 1951 would describe as "almost a double for Errol Flynn,"[2] the handsome reigning Hollywood heartthrob at the time—made her glad she'd accepted. He was quite charming—until, she said, he declared "'all old people should be done away with.' I thought of my grandmother and said 'What are you talking about!' I didn't like his attitude."[3]

But the displeasure soon dissipated and had no lasting effect. Barely a month later, on December 7, 1946—the coincidental anniversary of the bombing of Pearl Harbor and America's entrance into World War II—the couple, after a whirlwind courtship, eloped up the California coast to Santa Barbara and were quietly married at the city's Moorish style court house, a public service the classically stone and arched building was well known for in Hollywood.

Interestingly, Dussaq's new wife had marked similarities to Kay, his first wife, dead now only two years. Like Kay, Charlotte was a blond beauty, smart and accomplished. Physically, the two women could have been related, both looking like Hollywood starlets: tall (for women), slim and shapely. Charlotte had a degree in English and dramatic arts from Occidental College, a Los Angeles liberal arts school. She'd been a top talent in plays there and attended graduate school at Stanford University, one of the country's best. Both women were from Washington State,

Charlotte from Spokane, north of Kay's Walla Walla. One difference, however, seems to have been that Charlotte wasn't as outwardly ambitious or publicly known and flamboyant as Kay. Her accomplishments were behind the scenes. Among the famous she would eventually coach for the silver screen were pop singer Rosemary Clooney and rock and roll icon Elvis Presley.

The newlyweds set up house in Dussaq's Hollywood apartment. While René's producing aspirations—if he actually ever really had any— never bore fruit, he did continue the acting he'd started before Bikini. Perhaps with Charlotte's insider help, he landed bit parts in two Paramount-produced Bob Hope comedies. He played a police officer in *Where There's Life*, also starring William Bendix, and a restaurant maitre d' in the Academy Award-nominated *Road to Rio*, one of five successful *Road* movies teaming Hope with Bing Crosby and Dorothy Lamour.

These were good, successful movies.

In the meantime, he continued his public speaking on politics, agented through Peat. If one of his speeches I found in his home files is any indication, he would have been welcome at today's right-wing political rallies. It exalts the Constitution and God, hits the Left and communists as destroyers of liberty and wellbeing, and, summoning George Washington's 1796 farewell address, warns, "Never permit the situation to arise...in which any one department of the government can assume unto itself so much power and responsibility and functioning that it threatens the independence of the other two departments of government."

But none of it—even apparently combined with Charlotte's salary— was enough to pay all the bills. Whatever money René had accumulated, said Charlotte, he'd entrusted to Waldo Logan, his millionaire treasure-hunting backer, to invest. Wealthy Logan, who, penniless in 1957, would eventually commit suicide in a Miami hotel room, "made one bad investment after another," mostly on elusive treasure hunts. "One day René got a phone call," recalled Charlotte. "When he hung up, he just turned and said, 'Guess what? I'm broke!'" It didn't seem to faze him. This was also around the time he was negotiating with CBS Radio over his life story which, if he hadn't nixed it, could have helped financially. But apparently fortune—like fame—wasn't that important to him.

Consequently, the newlyweds left the expensive Hollywood apartment and moved in with a friend (and his wife) whom René had met on the lecture circuit. Sydney R. Montague was a former Royal Canadian Mounted Policeman turned explorer, author, and speaker. He'd ventured to the Arctic Circle and written, *I Lived With The Eskimos*. He'd written an insider book about the Mounties in *Riders in Scarlet* and detailed more of his pathfinder travels in *North to Adventure*. He was Dussaq's type of man: bold, inquisitive, "a soldier of fortune," as he was often billed at lectures. He and René sometimes spoke on the same programs. "Monty" and his wife Hazel had a modest house on Price Street in Los Angeles's well-to-do (then) Griffith Park-Los Feliz area. They welcomed the newlyweds in what, with shared rent, was probably a beneficial arrangement for all.

On December 28, 1947, just a year after their marriage, the couple was blessed with the birth of a boy. They named him Maurice Montague Dussaq, the middle name honoring "Monty," with whom they shared the house. For the first time in a long while, Dussaq, it appeared, couldn't just up and leave. There was no war and he was married with a baby and newfound responsibility. It was time to settle down and be a good husband and father. He decided to take a normal job. One of his first employments out of college had been selling insurance in Cuba. He had done well. Selling is largely a game of personality. He had the charisma, determination, and organization. He took a job as a salesman with New York Life in Los Angeles that, by the beginning of 1948, enabled him to win a job with Prudential, one of America's oldest and most respected insurance companies.

"He was very versed in different languages," remembered Rick Weber, a Prudential colleague who later apprenticed under him. "He told Juanita [the nickname René had given Charlotte] I'm going to make 4,000 cold calls, or some unbelievable number knocking on Beverly Hills doors. This is how he was going to get going in the business. She said

René A. Dussaq as a young adventurer, probably in Cuba. His father was a Cuban diplomat. His well-to-do family was involved in travel enterprises there. He spent summers on the island, went to law school at Havana University, and was a Cuban tennis star. He was involved in the 1930s Machado Revolution, which appears to have launched his clandestine life. *Courtesy Dussaq Family Collection*

Dussaq (dark suit) diving for sunken treasure off the Dominican Republic in 1938. With him (white suit) is explorer-adventurer John Craig, head of the expedition, and a crewman from their vessel. They hoped to locate twenty million dollars in gold, silver, and jewels lost on Spanish galleons sunk in storms in 1642. *Courtesy Dussaq Family Collection*

A real life version of the 1950s television program *I Led Three Lives*, Dussaq worked as a successful Prudential life insurance agent in Los Angeles while secretly infiltrating communist cells in Hollywood as an F.B.I. undercover agent. He also continued speaking before civic groups. It's not clear, however, who he was really working for as subsequent events called his true motives into question. *Courtesy Dussaq Family Collection*

Secret diaries of highly connected clandestine Douglas Bazata detail Dussaq's alleged involvement in the John F. Kennedy assassination. Bazata, also an OSS Jedburgh, was a close friend of Dussaq. Their relationship went back to the 1930s in Cuba and continued in the Cold War. Pictured is an identification card used by Bazata while conducting clandestine activities in Europe in the 1950s. *Courtesy Douglas Bazata*

An OSS assassin who continued such activities for spy agencies after the war, Bazata was also an acclaimed artist, one of his covers. This self-portrait depicts his sinister side. Dussaq, whom he considered a mentor in many respects, was one of the few persons to whom the tough Bazata deferred. *Courtesy Robin T. Kondrk*

Bazata was friends with Salvador Dali, the surrealist painter. This picture of the two in New York City, December 1963, ran with Bazata's *New York Times* obituary. That date is only weeks after the JFK assassination when Bazata claimed he was in Europe. Was he there too? Strangely, the picture has vanished from the Internet. *Courtesy New York Times*

Dussaq, wearing a crew cut and tanned, in the backyard of his Encino, California home. It's 1962, a year before the assassination. His son is to his right, two nephews to his left. Although in his fifties, he was still in top shape and urged the same of others. He'd been an acrobat, Olympic coxswain, and Cuban national tennis champion. Sometimes he requested able guests to speed climb a rope hanging in the backyard. Physical culture was a mainstay in his life, as it had been for his Sufi father.
Courtesy Dussaq Family Collection

While undercover in France, Dussaq assumed many false identities. This is the photo accompanying a June 1944 "Carte D' Identite" for "Alexandree René Lacoste...professor from Saint-Santin-Cantales." Erudite, master of many languages, including French, he had little trouble selling the role. If caught, he would have been executed. But the greater the danger, said a friend, the larger his smile. *Courtesy Dussaq Family Collection*

Dussaq, possibly in France with a Maquisard. Most were untrained. He taught them how to fight in small numbers, ambush Germans, use the Bazooka, and assassinate key personnel. He was caught but escaped, killing his Gestapo torturer. In a monumental bluff, he talked a five hundred-man Nazi garrison into surrendering. *Courtesy Dussaq Family Collection*

At the end of the war, Dussaq and a handful of OSS fighters were picked to secretly train Basque nationalists outside Paris. The Basques planned to fight for their independence from Spain. Dussaq sprawls at the base of the steps, cigarette in hand. Famous hand-to-hand fighting expert William E. Fairbairn sits at the top. The mission was suddenly halted for diplomatic reasons—perhaps this was the beginning of Dussaq's souring on U.S. politics. *Courtesy Guillermo Tabernilla, Sancho de Beurko Association*

Following the war, and after considering a job in Cuba, Dussaq returned to Hollywood where he began a movie career, starting as advisor to the acclaimed 1946 movie *O.S.S.* It starred Allan Ladd, seen here shaking hands with a confident Dussaq. Ladd was playing a part. Dussaq had lived it.
Courtesy Dussaq Family Collection

The budding actor. He appeared in several successful films, two of them Bob Hope–Bing Crosby "Road" movies. But he was called back into the military.
Courtesy Dussaq Family Collection

Ordered to help film the historic 1946 Pacific Bikini Atoll atom bomb tests, Dussaq may have outdone his own fearlessness. Evidence indicates he stowed away on a pilotless drone aircraft to get exclusive pictures inside the broiling, radioactive mushroom cloud. *Courtesy Dussaq Family Collection*

Two years after the tragic death of his first wife, René married Charlotte "Juanita" Clary, a former actress and, by then, screen coach at Paramount where she tutored such notables as Rosemary Clooney and Elvis Presley. They would have a son and remain married until his death in 1996.
Courtesy Dussaq Family Collection

As World War II brewed, Dussaq parlayed his adventures into becoming a top-rated public speaker represented by the same New York agent as comedians George Burns and Gracie Allen, Nobel Prize laureate novelist Thomas Mann, and poet Ogden Nash. As war commenced, his lectures changed to politics and America's dubious (in his opinion) treatment of Latin America. *Courtesy Dussaq Family Collection*

The Brilliant Young Argentinian
Interpreter of Latin America to Its Northern Neighbor

RENÉ DUSSAQ

"A South American's View of South America"

"No writer of fiction has invented more exciting characters," a Hollywood producer wrote about René and his first wife, Katherine Applegate. She was gutsy, inventive, a WASP pilot during World War II, and a statuesque beauty Chicago newspapers called "Wonder Woman." She died mysteriously ferrying a warplane possibly to meet René after the OSS had declared him dead. The inscription on the photo reads, "To my beloved Rene." But did it really end that way? *Courtesy Dussaq Family Collection*

Fearless and talented, Dussaq, once accepted by the Army, rose quickly, from private to paratroop officer to OSS Jedburgh, a member of America's first special forces. Besides wanting to get into the fighting, his object was to show that an Argentine-Cuban could perform as well as any homegrown American. *Courtesy Texas Women's University Library*

Dussaq was proudest of being a paratrooper. At age eighty-three, he jumped from an airplane in commemoration of the D-Day landings in France. As a stuntman and soldier, he'd wing-walked, fought sharks and octopuses, and hand-walked on top of the Empire State Building. *Courtesy Dussaq Family Collection*

A portrait of Dussaq by British SOE artists before he parachuted into Occupied France. He was trained as a saboteur, assassin, weapons expert, and organizer of the Maquis (the French Underground). When he left, he'd become the legendary "Capt. Bazooka," revered and decorated by the French as well as the U.S. After the war, he brought those skills home and continued in clandestine work. *Courtesy British National Archives*

July 1971., McLean,,,

Baz:
    This will confirm that area of our mutual records pertaining to
the assassination of President John F. Kennedy in Dallas, Texas on
November 22, 1963....

    You referred to this assassination as 'The Execution'; noting always
that your source of information was an anonymous 'Paul'; whom you obviously
knew extremely well. You also referred to this tragedy as 'Operation
Hydra-K'....
    In all four herein noted cases-dates: I passed the word along as you
and your Paul requested.

    You wrote to me in either very very late 1959 or the earliest days of
1960: to Teheran: my then current station.... I, as noted, passed the word:
so notifying you by mail to Johannisberg-Germany: chez les Mumms...
    Next: we met at the downtown Prunier for Oysters on Christmas Eve.,
where again you made this violence known to me. Again I passed the word.
And wrote confirmation to you at Brat's/Madelaine's....
    Our third such correspondence came from you to me while stationed in
Saigon.... You seemed 'alarmed' that official contact to you was very
bizarre... I did as you asked: so writing to you chez Brat/Madelaine....
    The last exchange took place via a letter (coded as agreed) from you to
me while still in Saigon... This was about mid-July of 1963.... In this
note you mentioned a 'fixed' date.... Throut these four notices: the plans
were altered considerably: but number four gave out a final solution to
the plan 'Hydra-K' of your Paul....

    Of course, I specifically recall this fourth note; as it coincided with
the peaking of the task assigned me here in Saigon.... I therefor invited
you to come out 'earliest'......for full discussions: possibly with superior
participation?   You agreed!

    That was it until we met again in Paris; January of 1964...when 'Both!'
slayings had been accomplished.... The lengthy parallels of our careers
struck me harder than ever befor...... You will certainly recall our most
vivid conversations at that time!
    You will well recall, also, our concern for each other!

                    Sincerely:

                              Luigi ....

Letter from CIA agent Lou Conein to Douglas Bazata about Operation Hydra-K.
Courtesy Douglas Bazata

'You're nuts,' and nearly packed her suitcase and left. But he went out and did it. And from those cold calls he secured 10 sales, about $4,000 in premium and $2,000 in commission, which was huge money in those days."

From that he built a clientele based on referrals, said Weber. Becoming a top LA Prudential agent, René would enter the "Million Dollar Rountable," an exclusive club of ranked sellers and eventually become manager of his own agency for the company. He taught the "KISS" principle, said Weber, "Keep It Simple Stupid," and was not above "stomping" on another agent's foot to prevent losing a sale. He did just that, said Weber when, the deal almost sealed, an agent with them started to lift from his briefcase a complicated price chart. Surreptitiously Dussaq's foot hit him. "It must have hurt like hell. But [René] just leaned back in his chair like nothing had happened and said, 'Oh, it's something like 5 or 6 cents on the dollar.' We would have lost it if we'd shown them that chart."

In 1949, Polly Pope, a reporter for the Beverly Hills edition of the Los Angeles *Independent,* wrote about René: "Outside of the air of intrigue that surrounds him, Dussaq is a friendly, frank man with wanderlust."[4] She saw the mystery and adventurer in him but perceived it fading. He seemed to be moving toward conventional domesticity. By 1950, he and Charlotte had enough money to buy a nice but small house in the exclusive Encino area[5] near famed Ventura Boulevard, the main San Fernando Valley artery running ribbon-like at the base of the Santa Monica Mountains. As part of his job, he gave speeches to the local Rotary, Chamber of Commerce, and various women's clubs. It appeared he'd finally abandoned his clandestine ways.

But looks are often deceiving.

20

Counterspy

n the early 1950s, one of America's hit television shows was *I Led Three Lives*, a half-hour Cold War drama staring Richard Carlson. The show was based on the schizophrenic spy experiences of Herbert A. Philbrick, a Boston salesman who in the early 1940s became aware of communist subversion of a youth council he chaired. He subsequently volunteered to secretly join the party as a counterspy for the FBI, and did so until 1949, while keeping the clandestine activity hidden from his family, friends, coworkers and, of course, the communist deceivers he was deceiving.

It was dangerous.

As *Conelrad Adjacent*, a website devoted to Cold War memorabilia describes it, the show was "a nonstop paranoid fever dream" that delivered edge-of-the-seat suspense. It ran for 119 episodes, from October 1953 to January 1956. Counterspy Philbrick, constantly afraid of being unmasked, was always a hair's-breadth away from sudden discovery—and his possible undoing by the communists, American traitors portrayed as squinty-eyed villains, relentlessly suspicious, rude, and ruthless.

Even before the show premiered, Dussaq, a salesman like Philbrick, was living the same paranoid life. Only his secret activity wasn't scripted. It was for real—just as authentic as Philbrick had experienced it. However, it doesn't appear Dussaq was as frenetically afflicted as his TV counterpart. In fact, he probably welcomed the fear and danger, smiling ever more broadly as he liked to do, the worse things became. Domestic routine just didn't offer the excitement to which he'd been accustomed and probably needed. Charlotte told me he hated selling insurance.[1] Like Philbrick, he led his counterspy life in secrecy—just as he had his missions in the OSS. He did not tell his friends or family (at least while it was happening), although Charlotte would eventually find out by accident.

These were unsettling days in American politics, especially in left-leaning Hollywood. The Soviet Union, a U.S. ally in World War II, had been exposed as a tyrannical power hoping to spread communism ruthlessly throughout the world. It established an "Iron Curtain" of police and physical barriers across Eastern Europe to prevent inhabitants under communist rule from escaping. It acquired the atomic bomb, the ultimate weapon at the time, with the help of traitorous American spies. U.S. code breaking operations (among other sources) have revealed that Soviet dictator Joseph Stalin had "moles" hidden throughout American society, especially in the government and military. These spies were working to undermine America—a fear only suspected at that time because of the lack of hard, public evidence.[2] Who, how many, and where were these communists? Fear reigned. How do you fight an unseen enemy? How do you defend against a bomb that destroys cities? Politicians demanded investigations to root out the traitors. The Left, in opposition, called such efforts "witch hunts" and condemned them as violations of liberty and rights.

Exactly when and how René began as a counterspy is hard to determine. He himself left only traces of evidence.[3] Prying information from the CIA, FBI, and military—the likeliest agencies with pertinent files—is hard; in some cases, impossible. They resist revealing their secrets, even if the reason for secrecy is bogus, or has vanished. Aiding them is a maze of bureaucrats, official procedures, legitimate and illegitimate concerns, and long delays brought on in part by backlogs from mounting inquiries. But what I've received so far from Freedom of Information Act (FOIA) requests shows that at least by 1950, Dussaq, acting for the FBI, was infiltrating communist groups in Hollywood and Mexico, if not elsewhere.

One can see his drift back into the clandestine as early as May 1947 when, as an Army reservist—and despite his rise at Prudential—he applied for extension courses in "airborne" specialties, typically including night jumps, assassination techniques, and ambush.[4] To his dismay, the course wasn't available. Further, in 1949, he listed "espionage" and "saboteur" as his army jobs of choice "in event of emergency."[5] FBI documents show the bureau's Washington headquarters had "miscellaneous papers" about Dussaq back to at least 1949, including a November 3, 1949 "memorandum" about his past. The "miscellaneous papers" were inexplicably requested by the Pentagon, and the "memorandum" was marked "forward to CIA."[6]

Was he at this time connected to the CIA into which the OSS had morphed?

Had he never really left the clandestine services?

Whatever the answers, the FBI's Los Angeles office indicates its first contact with René came prior to March 28, 1950, the date of a memo when agents wrote of interviewing him "in connection with other official matters." What were those matters? Why was he being questioned initially? The memo doesn't say. However, during the interview he volunteered that "in connection with" his job at Prudential, he "had occasion to meet several persons in the moving picture industry" whom he believed "may be members of the Communist Party." He and his wife's Hollywood connections provided possible ties to communists too. However he had come into contact with communists, he informed the agents about his OSS history, said he'd lived in Paraguay—which I'd never heard before—and divulged that on December 7, 1941, the day the Japanese attacked Pearl Harbor, he was on a train, "traveling across the country," and had been interviewed by the FBI that day "on several occasions...at various train stops."

What had that been about? The two-page memo doesn't say. It's addressed to "Director, FBI"—meaning bureau head J. Edgar Hoover in Washington—and concludes that on the basis of what Dussaq had volunteered, they were investigating him, probably a routine action, before deciding their next move.[7]

By mid-April the FBI had unearthed more of René's history, including another piece of information I had not heard before. In conjunction with his 1940 statement about staying at "Nazi headquarters" in Chile, they revealed that he had also at that time been a "representative" for a pro-German news service in Havana.[8] That shaded a bit the idea that he'd only been joking—what he'd told the OSS. It also connected him to Cuba at a time when he had not made that connection well known. But he'd cut the tie, they noted, shortly after Pearl Harbor. Interestingly, while their investigation appears thorough, they'd gotten his arrival in America wrong. René, conclusive evidence shows, had landed here in early 1933. But the FBI had him arriving a year later—in February 1934. That meant they had likely missed his very early Hollywood experience and the crash down the Mulholland cliff that had killed Daisy Moreno.

Obviously, he had not told them.

But apparently they were satisfied. By September 1950, after the start of the Korean War and worry about communism in the U.S. had heightened because of the hostilities, they clearly were advising, if not running, René in his Hollywood counter-espionage. "He has been meeting with [a] group [of communists] on an average of two or three times a week," says a September 21 memo about him addressed to "Director, FBI" from "SAC, Los Angeles." The memo identifies the cell as the "Factionalist Sabotage Group," which, according to several sources, including the FBI, appeared to consist of Hollywood leftists and former Abraham Lincoln Brigade veterans who fought against the fascists in the Spanish Civil War.[9] Its main purpose, according to documents, was sabotage, especially if the

Korean War enlarged into a bigger conflict involving Soviet Russia and/
or Communist China.

"The majority of [its] meetings are of a social nature and do not
pertain to the work [sabotage] that is planned by this organization," says
the September memo. They sing, drink and dance. But there "have been
occasions when [Dussaq] has discussed actual methods of sabotage with
some of these people, and he has been told by two different members...that they have a place for him...'when the time comes.'" The
place would be as a "leader...because Dussaq is a captain in the U.S.
Army Reserve, was a paratrooper and saboteur...and has had thorough
training and experience in actual sabotage." From "other sources available to this office [probably additional FBI spies in the group who were
unknown to René], it is known that the group has a high regard for
Dussaq."

Around the time that the September memo was written, a group
leader asked René to go to Mexico and meet higher group leadership,
including a woman who oversaw their activities from across the border.
He accepted the invitation, spending perhaps two months there, maybe
more. What he did on the trip is only touched on in the FBI documents
and consequently is basically a mystery. But a December 20, 1950, memo
in the batch indicates that someone in the group accused him of being
an FBI informant. They said he was at their meetings "too often" and
wondered why someone of his military capabilities hadn't been called up
for the war, which Dussaq himself had told them was a possibility.

The unnamed woman leader, however—identified as being "in
Cuernavaca, Mexico" by a source who appears to be another unnamed
counterspy—took his side. He must have charmed her. "[René] is trying
to do for the people anything that will help them," the memo says she
argued. Those against him she labeled "traitors." Specifically, one accuser
was "selfish, ungenerous and arrogant...interested only in his own
welfare," she charged. Appearing typically unfazed, René told the FBI
that the suspicion was merely jealousy by one of the group's members
who resented his leadership skills, especially his ability to speak before

people. He said he'd smoothed things over, according to the FBI memo. The rest of the group, as well as the FBI, seemed satisfied.

It was during his Mexican visit, said Charlotte, that she learned he was a counterspy. In later FBI documents (to be discussed in an upcoming chapter), René says his only worry while away was for his family's safety. He feared his wife and baby might be harmed if things went wrong in his absence. He asked the FBI to protect them. One day Charlotte got a visit at Paramount—from two "very nice gentlemen," she said. They turned out to be FBI agents and told her, "There was nothing to worry about." Worry? "I had no worries." They told her René was in Mexico and "it's all right." They had a strong presence there with a station in Mexico City and "he's well protected'... Everything they said indicated he was doing something horribly dangerous and terrifying," she said. "They should have left well enough alone" and not told her.

Charlotte's story raises questions. What excuses had René used to explain his long absence? By the time that question had become pertinent to me, Charlotte had died. I couldn't ask her. And what had he told Prudential to explain his absence? I've heard the company, formed in New Jersey in 1875, has been a cover for clandestine activities at least since World War II.[10] A Prudential coworker of Dussaq, Walter E. Puth Jr., whom other coworkers say was closest to him in later years, told me René told him the agency's manager knew about his spying and covered for him. "The manager knew what was going on but nobody else did. He had instructions that whenever anyone called [for René, the manager would] take the phone and make excuses." It wasn't hard, said Puth. Agents "work all kinds of hours and could be anywhere at any time."

I could not talk to the manager. Puth said he died "years ago." He had a name as common as John Smith so I wasn't able to locate his family, although I spent time looking. Contacting Prudential didn't help. The company guards its records like the CIA guard theirs. It refused to let me see anything in company files regarding Dussaq, let alone the manager—if, in fact, they still have either man's records.[11] However, while in Mexico, René himself wasn't so secretive that he wouldn't reveal at least his whereabouts to his older brother.

On November 4, Charlotte got a letter from Maurice in Havana saying that on Maurice's birthday, September 24, 1950, he'd "received a cable from 'Rajah somewhere in Mexico but no more news.'" He suspected René was undercover since he'd received earlier word from him that he expected to be called back into the army to "[train] recruits in guerrilla warfare." Their mother-in-law, Maie, had just died and Maurice was worried about their father. Emilien "is now 68," he wrote "and notwithstanding his great moral strength, he has been deeply affected." In addition, Emilien had "begun to worry again about Rajah." Maurice asked Charlotte to send him any news she could about René. "If the information must be kept confidential I shall not divulge it to anybody but" will use it to "invent some story for Father."

Apparently she wrote directly to Emilien because on November 21 Charlotte received a thank you letter from him. "Jaunita Darling," her father-in-law wrote, "Great many thanks for your kind letter dated Nov 8th...I was rather anxious about [René]. The last news I had was that he had been operated on [and] the scar...was 8 inches long." Emilien assumed it was because of back problems from the 1933 Molholland crash, but "there had been no mention," he wrote, "of what had been removed." He'd written René several times but had received no answer. He then wrote Maurice "to get in touch with you—and your wonderful letter came."

Later, there would be controversy about what Dussaq did undercover in Mexico and possibly elsewhere—charges that he'd performed "strongarm" missions and witnessed FBI agents "man-handling" a communist "sheet metal worker."[12] Had there been violence? The medical operation Emilien talks about comes out of the blue. It's a complete mystery. Had René been injured south of the border? Had he been elsewhere? Charlotte did not mention anything like that in our interviews, and as far as the record shows, he'd had no back problems since recuperating from the 1933 crash—nor had he had any other physical problems beyond those injuries that occurred during World War II, which as far as I could determine were not serious. He was certainly passing his Army physicals or they wouldn't have kept him in the reserves.

So any surgery was a puzzle. What had happened? Was his father simply wrong? Had Emilien somehow gotten bad information? Or had more gone on in Mexico, or elsewhere, than Charlotte or even, possibly, the FBI knew?

That mystery not withstanding, Dussaq had been forthright in telling members of the Factionalist Sabotage Group that he might be called back to the Army. He was—probably at his own request. It happened while he was in Mexico. The Los Angeles FBI, not wanting to lose its counterspy, pulled strings in Washington, according to its documents, and got the recall delayed about a month—probably long enough for Dussaq to finish his secret mission, whatever it was.

In mid-November, Charlotte got a letter from René.[13] "Hello Juanita," it began. "Did you think I had dropped dead?" It sounded like their first communication since he'd left. He was on his way to the bachelor officers quarters (BOQ) at Alameda Naval Air Station near San Francisco. He had been appointed, presumably through the Army's arrangement with the school, an assistant professor of Military Science and Tactics at the University of California, Berkeley. He makes no mention of Mexico or anything he'd done while gone. From the tone and information in the letter there doesn't appear to have been a need for explanation. Either they had already worked it out or he was presuming a lot on her part. He gave her his new address and asked how she was "holding out!" He'd be receiving money "around the 10th of December," he said, and would "immediately" send a check.

"I assume, Darling, that you are continuing to work as hard as usual." He complimented her on her ability to "run successfully both your career and your home" and lamented, tongue in cheek, that he'd had to leave without fixing the yard. "I can visualize the weeds growing bigger and better by the day and being a constant reminder to you that I did not carry out my original plan." He'd try to make it home at the end of December but couldn't be sure. "If I knew what the Chinese, Russians, U.S. and Reds had in mind, I could be more specific."

Whether or not he was still an FBI counterspy is unclear.

"Prior to his depature" from civilian life, says a December 20 memorandum to "Director, FBI" from "SAC, Los Angeles," "Dussaq contacted (name redacted) of the Factionalist Sabotage Group, relative to any instructions [they] may have for him." He was told that if, in his new capacity as an active army officer, "he were questioned about his association...with the group [he] was to say [it] was purely social." He "enjoyed the...drinking, dancing and singing." He was never to indicate he knew anything about the group's "real purpose."

If the war "spread or...became more violent," he was told, members like himself "would be...badly needed." His "A-bomb" work on "Bikini" was especially prized. "My God," the memo says they told him, "that would be wonderful because you would then be able to obtain work in San Francisco where they [presumably the U.S.] have their A-bomb setup." So, "by all means," he was told, "keep in contact." He was advised to send postcards signed with the codename "Duke." The Factionalist Group had "people" in the San Francisco area, they advised him, and if and "when a contact was made it would be necessary to be very discreet and circumspect. Every precaution should be made to see that they did not jeopardize their association [with the group] by a careless move."

Little is known of the "Factionalist Sabotage Group." The FBI has sent me nothing about it beyond what I've divulged. But FBI releases to others under the Freedom of Information Act appear to offer answers.

For instance, FBI files on folksinger Woody Guthrie, a Leftist icon believed by the bureau to have been a communist, say he met with the same group at roughly the same time as Dussaq. Guthrie, says the file, "resided at the home of (censored name) of Los Angeles, California...an individual who has also been identified as a member of...the Factionalist Sabotage Group." The house was a large, multi-roomed place in the Silver Lakes area. The group consisted of "approximately thirty men and women, some veterans of the Abraham Lincoln Brigade and expelled Communist Party members...According to [redacted], this group has a headquarters in Mexico City, Mexico," and has a woman member who "left Los Angeles in December 1949 to work in this headquarters" in "Cuernavaca, Mexico." The "ultimate purpose of this group is sabotage against the United States during war with Russia." Group members have outlined to the FBI's source "group policy in recruitment, method of operation, publications, finances, and has advised the informant that [the group] has a direct contact with the 'Comintern' [the Communist Party's Soviet-based ruling body]."[14]

Sounds like Dussaq's group to me.

In addition, Dussaq's nephew, Dr. Francois W. Sauer, a physician, who lived in Mexico, recalls René, many years later, telling him of smuggling weapons to a communist group in Cuernavaca. "What I understand is he was working for the benefit of the U.S.," Sauer told me. "In order to infiltrate a communist group in Cuernavaca," about a half hour's drive south from Mexico City, "he was providing them with guns. He was bringing them across the border."

René wasn't telling him this, said Sauer, to boast or make himself "look good. He never did that. I had lost my father, which was a big problem for me, a confidence problem, and he was showing me how to overcome such adversity by finding opportunity and taking advantage of it. It was like when he captured the Germans in France. He had a local tailor make a small US flag. They put it on a car, presented themselves as the advance of the US army, and captured a town."

As an example, said Sauer, Dussaq used the adversity of having to smuggle the weapons across the border. He had to do this to demonstrate to the communist group that he was one of them. So how did he do it? "At that time, the border wasn't covered night and day. You were able to have your car inspected as you went over in the night. Then you could come back in the morning and return without another inspection. They'd already checked you. I was a young man listening to this veteran, my trusted uncle. I didn't question him but it was fascinating to hear about such nonsense at the border. His council helped me."

Further, Sauer, who, in the acknowledgements for his book, *Relearn, Evolve, and Adapt*, credits his uncle with being "a very important mentor for me," said René told him they'd had to "put down" a union member while in Mexico. "He told me that on one occasion they did that. He used that phrase, 'put down'. He didn't give me any details but they created an 'accident' for that person." When I asked Sauer for details, he didn't have any. "He wasn't telling me about the incident beyond that it happened. It was just, 'When I was in adversity, here's what I did.'"

What else had Dussaq done in Mexico? And for whom?

Running guns and "putting down" a union member seems extreme for his role as a counterspy.

21

Red Scare

"I guess you were right," René wrote to his wife from Alameda as he readied for his third tour as a regular Army officer. "I really enjoy fighting. I seem to thrive on it. I am in the best of moods and getting again in the best of physical shape."[1]

He signed it "Bazooka."

The letter is one of the first in a collection of more than 150 the two wrote to each other mostly during the Korean War years, 1950 to 1953, when he was stationed on the East German border adjacent to the Soviet's "Iron Curtain." Charlotte gave them to me before her death. They provide a needed first-person glimpse of his personality and thinking, at least at this time in his life. Letter writing, especially to one's wife, might sometimes be an exercise in trying to look good to number one. But the sheer volume of communication surely has truth in it, and, as such, the letters provide a window to Dussaq's personality. As a whole, the letters paint a portrait bordering on intimate, although he still remains guarded and mysterious. In terms of the big question—could Dussaq, incredibly, have been involved in the JFK assassination—they show him emerging, as a result of his overseas experience, a more cynical and less patriotic American.

It didn't start that way.

His first assignment was as an assistant professor of military science in the University of California, Berkeley's Reserve Officer Training Program (ROTC) program, a non-combat billet he seems to have gracefully accepted and for which he was demonstrably suited. "He left an indelible picture in my mind when I first met him as a freshman in 1950," wrote a former ROTC cadet years later. "He cut quite a swath...with that mustache, a slight graying at the temples, a swagger stick, cavalry britches, polished boots."[2] A *San Francisco Chronicle* reporter added, "He is literally one of UC's brightest ornaments. He wears three rows of ribbons, including the Purple Heart, Silver Star, and the Army's second highest honor," the DSC.[3] "The only thing I missed," Dussaq quipped, "was the good conduct medal," adding, "I was very fortunate. Normally men of action are not very intelligent and intelligent men are timid. I just happened to combine the right qualities."[4]

While the standard in ROTC was to teach "logistics, statistics" and "mechanics" pertaining "to regiment, division and army" levels, he wrote Charlotte, he frequently deviated and emphasized "courage, loyalty, leadership, confidence, strength, determination, patriotism and aggressiveness...I feel guilty" about it, but wanted "those poor boys" to know how to handle "leading a small group of...men up a hill, across a river, around a bush, in mud, in sickness, in fear, in confusion, with an enemy hitting them from all sides!"[5]

Sanctioned or not, it was classic combat preparation.

Championing honor before survival, he wrote, "There are many [who believe] it is better to save lives than face...They [only think of life's] physical aspect. 'Face' [to them] does not represent pride, dignity, honor [or] conviction" but "conceit, vanity [and] arrogance." They "consider...survival more important than moral or spiritual" wellbeing. "I do not believe that one can ever be disassociated from the other without both perishing in the end."[6] He liked the individualistic, anti-establishment philosophy of Mortimer Adler, popular (at that time) founder of the self-educating "Great Books" series. Adler disagreed with modern pragmatists, most in academia, who said the old truths were no longer relevant and should be discarded. He attacked Darwinism, and argued against modernists, for instance, asserting that God, good, and evil were unchanging and immutable. *Time* magazine featured Adler on its May 17, 1952 cover, and René urged Charlotte to read the article about the feisty iconoclast.[7]

He was a tough teacher, Dussaq wrote years after leaving Berkeley. He wasn't trying to win a popularity contest. The lessons he attempted to teach were at a "deeper level"—"mental development…inquisitiveness…perception and retention…analysis" and "logical thinking." Most accomplishment is painful, he wrote. One must want it, be uncomfortable in the process, and not deviate from the objective. Mental growth is essential to a useful life. The "easy way" seldom yields good results. One must fight for success regardless of the opposition, ie, persevere. Mental growth is "achieved painfully, often slowly but demonstrably, step by step."[8]

His students loved him.

"I have just come from a lecture in military science which I'll not soon forget," a cadet wrote Dussaq's superior officer in early 1952. The student wasn't sure of the spelling of René's name, "but I am sure that is hardly of any importance where the man is concerned. He is the finest man I have ever heard speak, in R.O.T.C. or in any of my other university classes. He spoke to us and made us realize what we are and what it means to be in the Army of the United States. I have had the flag waved at me…and been inflicted with hours of meaningless lip service, but here was a man who has inspired our small class of some 15 students to leave…in silence and thought, considering the deep personal shame and pride somehow strangely co-mingled." The shame isn't explained but perhaps meant regret at not knowing earlier what they had just learned. "I want to pay thanks to [Dussaq] who has taught me how to feel the pride and vigor of being a man."[9]

In June 1952, an entire class lauded him to his commander, "The undersigned...wish to express their appreciation and admiration for 'Captain Dussaq.'" His "constant emphasis and example of self-discipline, dignity, and military bearing have contributed immeasurably to high class morale, enthusiasm, and esprit de corps. Furthermore, the manner of presentation of the course material encouraged a more intimate appreciation of the problems which confront company officers as well as a fuller consciousness of the responsibilities of army service."[10] He was given a letter of commendation by one of the high-ranking officers on the ROTC staff.[11]

So it is strange that he was abruptly dismissed without explanation from teaching at the beginning of the 1952 summer semester. A curt letter from the university, dated July 1, 1952, informed him simply that he would not be retained. A dig into school records yield only "Army orders" as the reason.[12] He had already gotten whiffs of the decision several months earlier. "I learned, today, by accident," he wrote Charlotte on March 4, "that a replacement for my position at the university" was being sought. He suspected somebody didn't like him. "Although I can find no one in authority who will tell me openly that this transfer was requested because I stepped on too many toes, I have a strong feeling [that is the case] and a few facts backing it."[13]

He was not more explicit. But I suspect his straightforwardness, even his challenging of those he disagreed with, might have been involved, to wit.

By this time, the "Red Scare" from Washington was raging. Democrat President Harry Truman—spurred by convictions of Russian atomic spies the Rosenbergs,[14] Alger Hiss, high-ranking State Department official accused of espionage and found guilty of perjury,[15] and the communist takeover of China—ordered that loyalty oaths be required of suspected communists in the federal government. California mandated its own loyalty oath, particularly in its university system, where communists were believed to have strong and rampant influence. At the time Dussaq learned of his replacement, UC system authorities were outright dismissing professors they suspected of subversion or who wouldn't sign the oath.

From the beginning of my research, I had heard a pertinent story about René: despite his work as an FBI counterspy, and his demonstrated patriotism, he couldn't be pigeon-holed politically. If anything, he was a strict constitutionalist, said Charlotte, especially strong on individual rights and protection of the little guy—or "little" country, as it were. He did not like U.S. exploitation of Cuba, his adopted home. Supposedly, when one of the communist-hunting committees came into his sphere—the story tellers do not know precisely when or where, but indicate it was most likely in California—he put on his Army uniform, ribbons, and medals and conspicuously attended the hearing and berated the inquisitors. "He got in trouble with the House Un-American Activities Committee," John Maloney, a journalist and public relations executive writing a book on OSS Jedburghs, told me.

Maloney interviewed Dussaq years before his (René's) death. He couldn't remember specifics, even exactly what committee it was. "Possibly" it was "because of his Cuban activities...that type of thing."[16]

Was this why René's teaching contract wasn't Renéwed?

Was it because of the Red Scare?

Had they found a communist proclivity in him?

I've combed every resource available, literally hundreds of volumes about the hearings collected and archived at the University of California, Los Angeles, and elsewhere. Archivists at the National Archives in Washington, D.C. and at College Park, Maryland have searched for me as well. None can find his name listed anywhere in anti-communist committee records. The best guess is he showed up unofficially and therefore was not listed in official proceedings.

Then again the story might be bogus, part of the legend of Dussaq, started because of other larger-than-life things he did, like hand walking near the top of the Empire State building or single-handedly capturing all those German soldiers.

Charlotte told me, "He got in trouble [at Berkeley] for saying that our boys were not prepared for World War II, or trained well, and that the Germans were much better trained. They said he wasn't a patriot."

I can't confirm or deny it.

22

Letters

Before he left Berkeley, Dussaq attended what he called the "Peace Treaty meetings." Precisely what they were isn't specified in a September 11, 1951, letter to Charlotte in which they are mentioned. But they probably were for what became known as "The Peace Treaty of San Francisco," the final treaty between Japan and the Allied Powers in World War II. The treaty was signed by forty-eight nations in San Francisco, near Berkeley, on September 8, 1951. It officially ended World War II, six years after the fighting had ceased, and gave compensation to civilians and Allied prisoners of war who had suffered war crimes at the hands of the Japanese. The Russians attending the conference protested the treaty. It did not give them territory promised at Yalta. Newly-created Communist China, aiding North Korea in the growing Korean War, was not invited. The specter of world communism caused international conflict and disagreement.

Dussaq wrote: "It is remarkable how men of great intellect and knowledge of parliamentary law, as most of the delegates were, could go on arguing the letter of the law without ever as much as touching on the spirit of man... Yet, it is the spirit of man that prompts him to go to war. Law is man made. It permits man therefore to break it or to interpret it as his spirit dictates. If his spirit has greed, selfishness or plain physical fear, so will it construe the law in an effort to assuage or quiet momentarily these feelings. To argue the legality of this treaty is as futile as arguing the right of cancer to kill your grandmother. Since when can we expect legality to take the place of good will in man's heart? Of man's heart I saw nothing at this conference, of man's intellect I saw much. I expect to see little of peace and much of war."[1]

Dussaq wasn't moved by all the phony and insincere pronouncements by politicians. His father had participated in the forming of the League of Nations, and he saw what that effort had wrought. Most people act in their own interests—not in the interests of others—politicians the most. He was becoming more aware of that.

But now he was a soldier, not a politician. And that's what he wanted to be.

■ ■ ■

By July 23, 1952, René had completed a four-week infantry refresher course at Ft. Benning, Georgia. And after scheduling his flashy 1948 Buick convertible for shipping slightly later, he was on his way by ocean liner from New York to Germany as an intelligence officer assigned to the relatively newly-formed 532nd Military Intelligence Service Battalion. The battalion was an organization basically of U.S. spies, headquartered at Patch Barracks, Vaihingen, eight miles southwest of Stuttgart, Germany, an Allied hub near the Iron Curtain.

Dussaq was part of a buildup of American forces in Europe to counter the increasingly malevolent Soviets who, as occupiers, were ruling Eastern Europe with an iron fist. The "Black Horses," as the 532nd soldiers were nicknamed, were responsible for supplying intelligence to the armored units patrolling the Iron Curtain border of barbed-wire, electrified barriers, and manned watch towers separating East and West in Germany's southern mountains. He was "most depressed by the general atmosphere" of the place, he wrote "Juanita," using his pet name for Charlotte, after arriving in Stuttgart. "I am sure my beloved that you would not like it anymore than I do. My work presents...certain possibilities. I will have to wait for a couple of months before I know for sure whether they mean what they told me [the possibilities otherwise not defined—and probably secret]." He missed her "terribly," he added. Stuttgart "is only 350 miles from Geneva. I hope before I get too involved [in his job] to have a chance to visit Dad for a couple of days."[2]

He got the chance a few days later. "Beloved," he wrote, "I left Stuttgart by train and arrived in Geneva 10 hours later." He spent the weekend "with Dad, Shanti [his sister and her family]. I had forgotten how beautiful Switzerland was. Viewed from the train, it is like a succession of picture post cards." He wished she was with him to enjoy it. "You are the only one I have ever needed to be completely happy. I love you for the same reason I love myself...Whenever I think of myself I think of you and whenever I think of you I think of myself." But "outside the scenery," he found little "we cannot find anywhere else...with the possible exception of the anxiety you experience when you have to go to the can and don't know how far you must travel before finding one. [But] there is an equally rewarding experience when you flush the toilet and it works!"[3]

Not exactly romantic—but real, apparently his preference.

He took a crash German language refresher course and found a makeshift gym where he could exercise. By early October he had been assigned to the battalion's 529th Military Intelligence Service Platoon adjacent to the East German border at Fulda, a medieval but strategically important town some sixty-five miles northeast of Frankfurt, the main American headquarters in the region. Fulda was key to U.S. defenses against the Soviets. It sat on a river valley that American planners believed would be the likely path of a surprise Soviet tank invasion— should that holocaust be unleashed. With its ancient churches and castles, a railroad station, and small, rundown commercial area, it was on a swath of flat land between mountain ranges that extended through both borders. The area was called the "Fulda Gap" —an escape route Napoleon had used. Tanks rolled best over flat ground. The gap was the enemy's ace—a corridor to the prime target of Frankfurt, where American forces where concentrated. Dussaq was at the tip of the spear, so to speak, staring into the crosshairs—a position he probably liked.

But he played it down.

"It's a stone's throw...from the border of the Russian Zone," he wrote Charlotte. "Please, my darling, do not let this bit of information disturb you. There is absolutely nothing hazardous in the type of operations we shall conduct, just routine work."[4]

In fact, even without an invasion, he'd be patrolling the area within shooting distance of the trigger-happy enemy guards, making daily reconnaissance trips and interrogating escapees who were not only good sources of intelligence about the Soviets but possible double agents and therefore threats. Sometimes he'd sneak over the border himself for dangerous clandestine fact-gathering and other secret missions. It wasn't Occupied France but if he were caught it was comparable. The Russians were as brutal as the Nazis.

"There might be a bit of delay...in the mail," he concluded. "But do not let it worry you. With this assignment, I doubt whether I'll have a chance to visit the family often, maybe once in a while."[5]

Around the same time, Charlotte sent him basically a love letter. She felt guilty over having gotten angry at little Maurice for wetting the bed and missed René "terribly"—which, she confessed, probably provoked her outburst. But she'd done penance for the "temper tantrum" towards little Maurice, and even found solace for her loneliness without René by cleaning leaves from the back porch and yard. "Being physically tired is a nice feeling. I don't know why I don't try it more often."[6]

Charlotte ended with what she considered "exciting" news from her job at Paramount. Two of her students were tested for "love interest leads in a new MGM pic [sic]. The idea is to have two unknowns surrounded by Broadway stars—examples Tallulah Bankhead, Rex Harrison [and]

Lilli Palmer…It would be such a marvelous opportunity for them. We worked on the scenes last week [but] the competition has been terrific…MGM [apparently in contract with Paramount for the picture] would prefer to use their own people…I'll keep you informed…"[7]

By October 6, René was already in the field.

"As you know this is a sort of job for which I am well cut out. I have an opportunity to learn quite a bit." And although, because of Charlotte, he wrote he was experiencing loneliness really "for the first time," the work helped "make the time pass."[8]

However, he added that his commanders, in his eyes, were sorely lacking.

Explaining that he had spent time at 7th Army headquarters in Frankfurt, he wrote, "I'll be damned if I can understand how…we can win wars with so many high ranking jackasses … [They] apply whatever intelligence they have to figuring ways and means to make their own miserable little existence as pleasant as possible and the hell with the idea of devotion to duty and service. When it comes to promotion, Bingo, dances, bowling, chasing…they really wake up. I do not know why I should even mention this. I certainly have lived long enough to know that a uniform does not change human nature, and never will. Anyway beloved I am really pleased to have been put in the field where the sins of human nature are at least not so blatantly exhibited."[9]

To a problem Charlotte was having with little Maurice, he counseled (and I paraphrase somewhat): "Glad you are standing up to Maurice. You must be consistent. Imagine what would happen if I returned and saw him lacking respect for you or disobeying? That would be most unpleasant. You have an opportunity to teach him while he is pliable, or I might have to teach him head on. And believe me, Beloved, I have a very hard head."[10] As if in response, she wrote, "You are very much a part of little Maurice's thinking. Whenever he is hurt, he tries hard not to cry—'like Daddy told me'—so he can tell me how he's controlling himself."[11]

On October 9, he described his meager living conditions:

"My room is fairly similar to the one I had at the naval air station at Alameda except that it is half its size and has no shower or toilet. There is practically no one living here—just a few transient officers who just stay overnight...Around here, unless a man works, there is little he could do...I guess he could get drunk in solitary splendor, but if he did he would not last very long at this kind of work."[12]

Soon, he'd made a friend, he wrote—not a native born American, but one naturalized like himself; a Russian American "educated in China and Manchuria" which, by then (1952) had consolidated into a rabid enemy of the U.S. (Such persons were sought by American intelligence because of their knowledge of the enemy—but always with the threat of unsuspectingly recruiting a double agent.) "He and I took to each other immediately. We agree as to the methods of operations" as well as the incompetency within their leadership. "For the past year," the friend told René, he had been "very much hamstrung by various directives issued by higher headquarters. It is the same old story. In the field, you have very conscientious, devoted, honest craftsmen thinking only of the objec- tive...being directed by high level personnel who are prone to forget that there should be more to high rank than just privileges and politics."[13]

He enclosed two small black and white pictures of Stuttgart in the letter. One showed a pleasant city photographed from overlooking hills. The other was of Stuttgart's train station. On the back of the train station photo he wrote, "View from my hotel room. Unfortunately it overlooked garbage cans in the service entrance. Garbage cans are the same the world over."

Dussaq was not happy in Germany, which other letters would con- firm.

His basic attitude towards the U.S. and its military was changing.

Fulda was depressing, he wrote in late October, a whistle stop as he described it, plagued with nasty, incorrigible weather. "I do not believe that the sun itself has dared show itself more than 10 minutes during the 4 weeks since my arrival. It's wet and humid. It rains intermittently and timidly." Fortunately, he wrote, as one of the unit's officers, others do the "dirty work" and "I reward them with an evaluation and criticism with all the dignified assurance of a man who knows all the answers not only of the world itself but of life in general!"[14]

René prided himself on self-control. But will power alone wasn't enough, he wrote. It might yield some success—"but ulcers too!" The real key to self control was harnessing of "emotion," the core ingredient which makes "an individual ... act or react like an ass in the first place." Proving his point several letter lines later—as well as his ability to still laugh at himself—he concluded his incite with, "Ho hum, Sweetheart, I have succeeded in putting myself to sleep."

René's work was secret so he couldn't give many details. But these he could: the streets in Fulda were cobblestone or dirt. The platoon operated "from a "requisitioned" private house located on the village's outskirts. "We are responsible for other smaller units which operate from nearby villages." To physically contact all of them required trips as far as 250 miles total. "By American standards most of the roads...are very bad—narrow, muddy and bumpy" especially punishing in the open-air jeeps they used. He drove his Buick only to and from work,[15] and because of the punishment it suffered, was sorry he'd brought it over.

The platoon worked within Fourteenth Cavalry Regiment territory. The Fourteenth was the army unit tasked with being first responders to an attack through the gap. Its soldiers patrolled the border in "armored cars." They manned "stationary observation" posts twenty-four hours a day, seven days a week—no respite. The regiment's headquarters, where his own living quarters were, had a movie theater, library, gymnasium ("very inadequate") and officer's club which "most of the time was deserted." Most of the officers he served with were young and regular army who, he wrote, found "the greatest merit" in being lucky enough not to be in Korea, where the fighting was hot. They were in the Army basically for "financial security"—a view point, now that he was realizing certain "realities," he was finding less offensive.

"There was a time not long ago when I thought that patriotism and service to one's country were strong incentives." Today, he wrote, such sentiments seem "hollow...I have become so disappointed in Eisenhower," the World War II military leader who at that time (1952) was running for president as an anti-communist Republican. The exact reason for his disappointment is not stated. But in an earlier letter he had written, "For what I have read in the papers…Truman [Democrat], Stevenson [Democrat], Eisenhower, Taft [Republican]…are not exactly throwing flowers at each other. In light of what we are facing here at the border and in Korea, their verbal exchanges, accusations and insults, half-truths and empty assurances are nothing short of disgusting. But I guess that these fine men are caught in a political maelstrom that makes them lose all sense of personal…integrity. When you are in a free for all without a referee to warn you that you are fouling, and with a mob yelling for victory and blood, your conscience becomes so inaudible and your ego so exalted that anything and everything the opponent does is wrong."[16]

Eisenhower would win the coming election. He ended his political discussion thusly: "I wonder if [Eisenhower] too has become disappointed in himself. He alone could know and certainly he would and could never tell. Well I expected a saint and I see only a man made not in the image of God, but in the image of man."[17]

America's "grandfatherly" Eisenhower was far less to Dussaq.

On October 26, "Juanita" responded: "I like the sound of your Russian friend. I know I would like him." She asked how his Buick was holding up, and informed him she had shown his "special agent" card to Preston Sturges, the award-winning director and screenwriter known for his comedies. "He was very amused. He also gave me a brief lesson on the pronunciation of René`. Said it should [have accents on both e's—"Ree-knee"]. I've been working on it. He has written a new play that he plans to open around the first of the year. He wants to talk to me about the casting of it. The story sounds very good…We tested Joan Taylor Friday…She got closer to the character than I thought she would—but whether it is close enough is another thing…Also tested two other girls…the second is a star if ever I've seen one—a beautiful figure and the face of Vivian Leigh and Jean Simmons. But it doesn't end there. She has great sensitivity and can be an excellent actress. In fact, for an inexperienced girl, I've never seen such a performance."[18]

The actress was seventeen-year-old Marla English, who had won a San Diego beauty pageant thus coming to the attention of Paramount talent executives. "The word had gotten around the lot and though we had a closed set, the place was black with people. They must have crawled in through the walls! If she doesn't come through on film there will be a lot of disappointed people."[19]

(In fact, she did come through, rising as a young actress at Paramount in primarily B movies until 1955, when she landed a coveted starring role opposite Spencer Tracy only to reject it and, in a surprise [at the time], subsequently quit Hollywood forever.)[20]

Charlotte concluded, "Maurice just got back from Sunday school— we have our moments but on the whole we're getting along quite well. He is getting so big! It would amuse you—every time he sees the Western cowboy heroes being brave and winning fights on TV, he compares them to you and they always come in a poor second. And, you know, he's right."[21]

In early November René went to Switzerland again. "I have just returned from a weekend in Geneva," he wrote on the tenth. He'd driven the Buick and made the five hundred miles in thirteen hours fighting two distinct snow storms. "I hope my visit gave some pleasure to Father, Shanti and Werner [his sister and her husband]—more pleasure than it gave me. They live in a mental and emotional world which is so different from mine that although they are wonderful people, I find myself saying and doing things in which I really do not believe. They seem to love me for what, in fact, I am not and they wish things for me which I do not want, and all through this routine I put on an act which both tires and depresses me."[22]

There's no question René had gone from unequivocal adulation of his father to something different. He's not clear in the letter what that new feeling was or how it had come about. But he tells Charlotte she was the unique wife (of the two) in his life— something she undoubtedly (aware of the earlier more flamboyant Katherine) enjoyed hearing: "My beloved Juanita, you are the only one with whom I have ever known happiness and peace of heart. I enjoy so much your letters and all the happenings you describe. It makes me feel as if I were home with you sitting at our little bar, having a few drinks and talking about what took

place during the day.... You are so honest and sincere in your work...suc-
cessful...too!"[23]

Apparently Charlotte had been offered a directing job at the studio
but had turned it down. René agreed with her decision—"although," he
parsed, "it might not be for the same reason. You wrote that...if you
accepted you would be nowhere—one picture to your credit, no job in
the talent department, and the only woman in the business. That, of
course, was a good explanation...However, putting aside all practical
reasons...If you had accepted you would not have been true to yourself!...Your heart is in developing talent. Your happiness is in launching
young actors and actresses on the road to success. You train them first,
then test them. [That is how] your purpose is fulfilled. By doing so you
have been true to what is the desire of your heart..."[24]

At the end of the letter, he added a P.S. "Please tell Toro [Spanish for
"bull" and little Maurice's nickname] not to think of me as a cowboy—
I like the Argentine word 'Gaucho' better!! Ola!!"

By late November loneliness and work—and possibly something
else—were grating on René.

"It's been many days since I have had a chance to sit down and
[write]. We have been quite busy and in this [spy] game where you do not
let your right hand know what the left hand is doing, you never know
what the next hour has in store for you." He was "hitting bottom" with
feelings of "discouragement and futility"—what he labeled "life's dark-
est moments." He does not disclose exactly what was eating him. More
trouble with higherups? Something worse? Whatever it was, he wrote,
"Do I have a solution? I do not!" The only thing that helped was thinking of her. But "I am goddamned frustrated." He hoped that their
reunion, being planned for the spring, would make things better.[25]

"Even my work has a tendency to bore me. I do not find it anything
particularly challenging or exciting...My associates think that I have ice
water in my veins—little do they know that in comparison to my love for
you nothing is important to me." "It was quite easy," he wrote, "to
approach their so-called monumental problems with a shrug of the

shoulders." He wanted her to come there immediately. "Yet I real-ize...that...would condemn you to a most uninteresting life and uncom-fortable to a disagreeable degree. The climate is as bad as I have ever seen—cold and wet. My work would hardly permit me to see you." She "would live in an apartment house some 40 miles from here...Army wives seem to accept these conditions...And by the looks and mentality of most of them they could hardly expect more. I shudder at the thought of your having to associate with these idle, gossipy parasites who seem to have in common a remarkable state of arrested development..."

"I detest army social life. It is true that I have participated in it so little that I may be hasty or unfair in my criticism...I am so accustomed to work and to be alone that I can easily avoid all social activities however it might not be as easy for you...Maybe I am painting the picture too black...It was not very long ago that I used to toss around such words as patriotism, dedication to the preservation of the American way of life, duty to one's country...And although, even today, I still recognize the merit of these feelings, I could no longer orate about them...I am far more concerned about my life with you than I am about the fate of our little civilization." However, he cautioned, don't be "alarmed...Although my heart is not in [the job], my mind is."[26]

Charlotte answered with sympathy and more Hollywood news. "It must be strange [playing a part] that no longer interests you...Tested Guy Mitchell," a pop singer who eventually would top the charts with songs like *Singing the Blues* and *Heartaches by the Numbers*. "Have never had more fun. This boy is really something. I've never seen so much energy all rolled into one person. He's like a big, loveable St. Bernard—not much to look at but so much talent...Hope they sign him...would love to see Guy teamed with Rosemary Clooney" with whom he'd made several big records. She'd tested an actress for a James Cagney drama, *A Lion in the Streets*, and had dinner with "the Loews," who owned the national theater chain. "Went with them to see Harpo Marx in *Yellow Jacket*. I met Harpo after the show. He's a charming person. But the Loew family! Such wealth! I found it all quite tiring and was happy to come home to our little house and Maurice. The more time I spend with other people, the more I appreciate us!"[27]

He felt the same. Following another trip to Geneva, he wrote: "Stayed with the family. It is kind of pathetic the love and admiration they have for me. Their capacity for 'idealizing' is amazing...It does take me a little effort to accept it." He was going to Nuremberg for two weeks of schooling on the Soviet Army, he lamented. It would mean he'd miss her letters. "The weather," he wrote, "has turned sharply cold. Ice covers the streets and snow covers the border." He was having trouble motivating his troops. Whoever a person is, stuntman or dancer, black or white, rich or poor, they're all essentially the same. "I feel like I'm listening to a broken record. It's all so familiar." Yet, as seemingly malleable as his soldiers thus were, he couldn't get them to exercise. "I never fail to get an audience when I work out in the gym. But I will be damned if I can ever encourage anyone to lift as much as a finger to better their own health." Apropos, he asked, "is Toro doing his push-ups, chin ups, and knee bends regularly—I bet he is not! What about his hair—is it cut really short and manly?"[28]

Weeks later René scored highest in his Nuremberg class's final exam, "98 out of a possible 100...There were 223 questions...I missed 3 ½...I studied every night until 3 a.m." It was the severest "siege of mental gymnastics I can recall...I confess I reached the very maximum capacity of my brain. If there had been one more thing or thought to remember...I could not have done it." His family in Geneva was going to France for the holidays but he was staying in Fulda "by myself." The song *White Christmas* "might be a wonderful dream in California," he wrote, "but here I assure you it is a...nightmare." Driving back from Nuremberg "I had to put chains on the wheels which were hubcap deep in slush while I was up to my navel in mud and snow, my hands frozen and bleeding from trying to fasten those chains. What do you think they were playing on my car radio? Yes Darling... *White Christmas*." He doesn't divulge his reaction except to write, "Damn it, I had to take it out on something!!"[29]

On New Years Eve (1952) he got drunk, "So much so that frankly I do not recall that fateful [midnight] moment. It is lucky my quarters are just across the street from the officers club. Somehow I must have managed to reach my bed. I have definite proof ... because at 7 a.m. this morning I opened my four eyes (two to each of my heads), fell out of bed fully dressed and reported to duty hoping desperately that a major war [had not broken] out.... I spent the whole day flying a border patrol. It was the first time in my [piloting] experience that the only way I felt the plane was level was by putting it in violent tail spins. I would not actually [have believed] it if it were not for my flying companion...a Negro [who] at the end of the day looked as if he [was almost white]...Am leaving tomorrow for Munich."[30]

Charlotte had spent a "beautiful" New Years at the Rose Bowl game, she wrote back, unintentionally rubbing it in. "It's June in January...Wonderful California...79 degrees...and clear as a bell."[31] She was excited to be getting passports for herself and little Maurice in anticipation of traveling to Europe and seeing him soon.

But things stayed cold in Germany.

In Munich, at an eight-day policy conference, he'd been reprimanded for bringing his pistol and carbine, which he thought should always be at his side. "You should have seen what commotion this caused...They have some 200 officers from all parts of Germany...The commander of the conference informed me that they had no facilities to guard my combat equipment," adding that he should have left them at base. "This commander was not, however, in a position to assure me that the Russians would be kind enough to give us warning [of an invasion] so as to permit us to return...home...for the purpose of equipping ourselves...It is remarkable how little we learn...There was such a big ado about our forces being caught with our pants down at Pearl Harbor, and yet today one can [see what] led to [that] debacle."[32]

Even Dussaq's humor was dark: the drive to Munich had been an all-nighter in bad weather. Along the night-obscured roadside he'd seen a figure carrying a bundle. "I assumed she was a country woman going to some city to work to support her children." He offered a ride. As they drove in the darkness "she asked me about America and my trip across the ocean…then her conversation turned personal." Dawn was breaking and for the first time he saw "she was no country woman…but a horrible looking third rate, beat up prostitute plying her trade. I informed her that I was a happily married man and quite faithful—whereupon she howled with toothless laughter… 'I could not possibly be married,' she said, 'since I did not wear a ring," nor, she reasoned, would a married man be driving at night. He stopped the car, "took one more look at her [and] became irrevocably convinced that utter faithfulness was in order." He told her to get out. "And so came the end of what I will remember as: 'Death warmed over hitchhikes to Romance!'"[33]

It was a risky story to be telling one's lonely wife, humorous or not. But Charlotte didn't react, so excited was she about their coming reunion. In his next letter, however, dampening things a bit, he explained that he was expecting a special secret assignment "which would preclude all possibilities of a leave until the end of May." He felt, therefore, it would be better if she delayed her trip and came instead around the first of June. He also wanted her to stay not with him in Germany but in Geneva with his family. Switzerland offered more for her to do and she'd be happier there given the meager amenities in Fulda. He would ask for a leave when she arrived so they could travel around Europe together and after that he'd visit her on weekends.[34]

Delayed from her earlier anticipation, Charlotte began to worry about expenses. No need, René advised. The pleasure would be worth the price. In addition, "I manage quite easily to save as much as $50 or $60 every month [a good amount in those days]…I was born with a miserly soul and exceedingly inexpensive tastes…The worst that can happen is that I might have to go to work as soon as I get out of the army and I am quite sure I could survive such an ordeal! You have worked hard all your life and it is about time I should attempt to imitate you."[35]

His "wonderful letters" did the job, she wrote after several exchanges. She'd gone over all their finances and her mind was "considerably eased." She even had a potential renter for the house during the summer months she and little Maurice would be gone. It was Mary Murphy, a friend and actress who "just signed to play opposite Marlon Brando in his next picture," which turned out to be *The Wild One*, a hugely successful and iconic 1953 outlaw biker film.[36]

But a problem soon arose over travel arrangements. They were being handled by René's older brother Maurice, head of Dussaq & Toral, S.A., a major Cuban travel company. The exact problem is unclear. But it appears to have been about whom in the family, also traveling to Europe, she'd be rooming with on the voyage.

René was not sympathetic.

"Poor little sweetheart," he wrote back sarcastically to her complaints. "Life is certainly tough all over. Even prospective vacations become a sort of Cold War [with you]...I bet Mr. Limon, passenger manager of the Holland American Line would love your remark, quote, 'I would rather be caught dead than on the Holland-American Line.'...Well, Baby, before we all drown in a tea pot tempest, I suggest you drop a line to Maurice and tell him that circumstances beyond our control will make it impossible to travel with Nelly—you need not enumerate the 6 circumstances...It's actually very simple—There I go again oversimplifying the most monumental problems. Anyway Beloved, just take a hot glass of milk and relax. Come by plane and everything will be alright—that is, provided you do not miss your plane connections!!...By the way, are you having your period?"[37]

His tough response worked. "Just what the doctor ordered," she replied. He'd made "mole hills out of her mountains" and "re-awakened my dormant sense of humor."[38]

She was laughing at herself.

But not for long.

By late February government snooping in Encino had her verging on paranoia.

"This must be quite an assignment you're on!" she wrote. "Two army intelligence men were in the neighborhood this last week. Of course they didn't come here and apparently didn't have much luck elsewhere—the only [neighbor] at home was Mrs. Osborne...and she told them quite truthfully she didn't know you at all. They'll probably come back another day. I know it's silly but quite suddenly this mission of yours seems to take on all kinds of sinister aspects. And since [their visit] I find myself giving myself little reassuring talks about your ability to take care of yourself and any assignment—no matter how dangerous."[39]

What the Army snoopers were doing is a mystery. I've queried all pertinent agencies, including the Counter Intelligence Corps (CIC),[40] now defunct, but at the time a very powerful military anti-spy organization, which Dussaq's records show handled security in his unit. All deny any records about Dussaq, which could mean they only have him under codename or otherwise disguised. They could also just be lying, or the aging records simply could have been routinely destroyed after a man-dated time limit. The organization was one of the most secret in the military. Was it just a routine investigation, a periodic checkup mandated by rules? Unlikely. He'd already been vetted before he went back on active duty. It seems more likely this was the beginning of a problem that, in fact, would eventually get his security clearance revoked and end his tour in Germany—if not in the active military forever.

But as far as the letters reveal, he doesn't respond to her fears—unless, of course, those letters were purged or somehow otherwise extracted from the many I got. Then, in early March, he sent a note that he'd "been continually on the road" for ten days and was "on my way to Kronberg," an ancient town approximately seventy-seven miles west of Fulda. Without details, but possibly reacting to adverse events, he wrote sarcastically, "As suddenly as I precipitated myself in one of my dark moods, I have pulled myself out of it. It had been such a long time since I had felt really depressed that I really enjoyed every bit of it!! (I hope you did too!)"[41]

By March 17, his problems with the Army were mounting again.

"I have been spoiled by my past experiences which I could not discuss with my present superiors for the simple reason that they would lack the capacity to use them to [accomplish] our mission. And so once in a while someone gets caught, or killed or beaten up when in reality it could have been easily avoided." He'd earlier had input into operational plans but now, "I have less authority as a captain than I had as a corporal during the war…The motto of our Great Fighting Force seems to be…look good at inspection. If it moves, salute it. If it doesn't move, pick it up. And if you can't pick it up, paint it!" In other words, they were mired in ineptitude. He blamed their "low performance" on a lack of sustained combat. "Yesterday a [captain friend] who asked to be recalled to active duty last year after being out of the army since 1947 told me: 'It took me 3 months of active duty to remember why I had gotten out of this goddamned army the first time!!'" He noted the death of Soviet dictator Joseph Stalin (March 5) and added, "I can well imagine the grief that many millions of Russians must have after losing Stalin."[42]

It was strange sympathy from one suffering the Cold War and daily fighting the Soviets.

Throughout April his disdain for the Army got worse. "Our military operations are so poorly organized and executed that it's difficult to refer to them intelligently…We play at everything. The only thing we don't play at is being Jackasses—that they do quite well naturally."[43]

In May he made trips to Geneva and Munich. The first was to see his father, who was sick and died early in June. He took the death seemingly in stride. His father missed his departed wife and apparently believed death would reunite them. "You know, Beloved, that I knew Father fairly well and understood him too. When people were supposedly paying him respect (or satisfying their morbid curiosity—I don't know which!) viewing his body, I watched his face and the faces of these other people and I am convinced that he was the only one who was having a good time! He and I had talked quite a bit about this moment on my last visit…and we had many good laughs. Well Beloved, you know what is said: He who laughs last laughs best. Believe Darling he certainly laughed last and laughed best." His thoughts were only of her, he concluded, and how lucky he was to have her as his wife.[44]

Charlotte and little Toro arrived July 10. They stayed through early September. He met them in Paris where, for nearly a week, they stayed at the elegant Hotel Continental (today's Westen Paris), the city's largest hotel, occupying an entire block, home in the past to, among other celebrities, the Russian Grand Dukes when they were in Paris. It must have been a wonderful few days. Then he drove them "leisurely" to Geneva, through soaring mountains and tranquil meadows, where, for the first time, Charlotte met his sister Shanti and her family. "She is not as selfish or calloused as I," he had written her when his father had died. "She is so looking forward to [your visit]. It will be a wonderful deterrent to her pain. She is such a generous and unselfish girl and so devoted to us all. I am sure you will love her very much."[45]

Then shock.

She'd barely left when, in late October, he was suddenly informed that his security clearance had been cancelled and that he'd been reassigned to a battalion in Vaihingen until he could be shipped home.

What had happened?

The fateful orders don't say more than that he is relieved of his assignment and is to await transit from Bremerhaven, the German port on the North Sea. Dussaq doesn't discuss the situation except to write that he's through with this "army of Boy Scouts" and has accepted early release which was being offered throughout the Army's officer corps presumably because of the Korean War armistice late in July. He's already thinking of what he will do post Army and has been offered a position as "liaison with a chain of ice cream stores in Cuba"—a strange choice for a man of his talents—except for the location.

Cuba, at least according to his Jedburgh friend Bazata, had by this time become a central focus in his clandestine life.

23

Accusations

Dussaq couldn't wait to get out of Germany.

"Whoopee!!!" he wrote Charlotte on October 26, 1953. "Am reporting to the port of embarkation, Bremerhaven...The ship will leave on the 24th or 25th (of November). And if all goes well, which is unlikely on an army transport, we should get in New York some nine (9) days later. You see, my beloved, it is not exactly the New Amsterdam [a luxury liner]! But even if I had to row for it I would not mind!"

On the surface, the Army showed little concern about his security clearance problem. He was given an honorable discharge and retained his rank of captain in the reserves. When I filed Freedom of Information Act requests to the Army for pertinent records about the problem, I was told none existed. There might have been some years earlier, but records dating prior to 1959 were destroyed in compliance with federal law allowing for agency house cleaning.[1]

They had destroyed them—or so they said.

So much for that route.

Authorized or not, evidence indicates he'd kept, upon exit, his .32 Colt automatic pistol issue. Friends visiting his house in later years have reported seeing it and other Army issue weapons. I have correspondence by Dusssaq indicating the same. His discharge papers show he was given $647.57 in back pay.[2] Before sailing, he made a final visit to Geneva, which was probably when and where he sold his Buick, arranging to have the money sent back to his account in Los Angeles.

In New York, he had the opportunity to interview for an agent's job with New York Life, a company he apparently had worked for earlier. It is one of the nation's oldest and largest insurance companies. His father-in-law, Harry S. Clary, who worked for New York Life in Los Angeles, arranged the interview, indicating in a letter to René about the interview that he might be aware of René's security problem. "I feel sure you are making the best of your situation and hope that these letters from home will cheer and encourage you to bear with good will the problems you face until such time as you…return to your family"[3]

But it doesn't appear René kept the New York Life appointment. That's the impression given in a letter to Charlotte.[4] He had written his old boss, Jack White, at Prudential in Los Angeles, about his pending NY Life interview. White had promptly cabled back that Prudential would match or better any offer. That, it turned out, seems to have been what René wanted to hear. There was no further mention by him about Cuba or his ice cream venture there except to tell Charlotte that a friend was contemplating going to the island for Christmas.[5]

Cuba would remain a mystery in his agenda.

■ ■ ■

Dussaq had spent nearly three years away and there's little question he returned to Los Angeles a changed man, soured on the Army and U.S. politics in general—even more than he had been in his younger days of pro-Latin America, anti-imperialist speeches. But exactly how that change manifested itself in his daily life is unclear—except perhaps to

Charlotte who, no longer alive, cannot shed any light. He was not publicly vocal about the change. To the contrary, he kept it to himself.
Instead, he rejoined Prudential in Los Angeles as a returning star agent
whom the company volunteered periodically as a community speaker
when they saw it in their interest. He still enjoyed the podium—as audiences still enjoyed him. And in April 1954, only a few months after
returning and settling in, he notified the FBI of his problem in Germany.
As a result, it eventually became clear that the reason for the security
denial was that he was accused of being a communist.

Why he'd want to inform the FBI of the military's suspicions about
him is a question. Was he looking for redemption that maybe he felt the
bureau could give? Had he new clandestine plans because of what had
happened overseas and he needed Renéwed liason with the FBI? Was
there more mystery to what had happened to him in Germany than is on
the available public record? Probably so. Whatever the answer, the
bureau's response, was not sympathetic. It launched an investigation.

"In April…Dussaq [advised] that he had just received his discharge,"
says a September 21, 1954 "urgent" memo from the LA FBI office to
Washington. The memo appears to be for the purpose of filling in background for headquarter decision makers. "He further stated that in the
fall…he was advised by army officials that his security clearance was
being withdrawn. According to Dussaq, no explanation was given…He
stated that he contacted the CIC [the army's FBI, so to speak, which was
handling the investigation] in an effort to determine why…It was deemed
advisable to ascertain why the army had withdrawn his security clearance and especially to ascertain if the army had any derogatory information or information reflecting on the loyalty of Dussaq."[6]

Even FBI director J. Edgar Hoover got involved. "What is this all
about?" he scribbled on the urgent message. "I never heard of this character."

In fact, he had—when Dussaq had been spying on the Factionalist
Sabotage Group prior to leaving for Germany. The LA office had kept
Hoover informed, as they would remind him in subsequent memos.[7]
Apparently he'd either forgotten or, because of what the investigation

revealed, he wanted it to appear so. Because by the time he'd scribbled the note, the results of the lengthy investigation were in (perhaps the reason for the review at this time). They were not complimentary to Dussaq or the bureau.

The investigation said that as a result of CIC records obtained from Ft. Holabird, Maryland, it was learned "that on or about November 10, 1952, Captain René Dussaq, executive officer…revealed in confidence to [the person making the charges, whose name is redacted in the files sent to me] that he, Dussaq, was a member of the Communist Party of America in the state of California…[Dussaq told the unnamed informant] that he joined the Party on orders from the Federal Bureau of Investigation. The cell [to] which Capt. Dussaq belonged was known as the Sabotage Cell." Further, alleged the accuser, Dussaq said "he personally met and discussed" his activities with "J. Edgar Hoover."

While the two returned from business in Frankfurt, recounted the accuser, he had asked Dussaq if he "was still a member of the Communist Party. Dussaq replied in the affirmative" —an explosive accusation, according to the memo writer. Additionally, he "told me…that he had witnessed…an interrogation by the FBI of a Communist Party member in the United States, during which the Communist, a sheet metal worker, was manhandled. When I stated that U.S. Intelligence Agencies do not manhandle suspects or ever used methods of duress, Capt. Dussaq laughed and said that they did, pointing out that they have methods which do not leave marks or traces. He [Dussaq] continued that after this incident, the sheet metal worker, after being beaten bodily, stated, 'I may be wrong in your eyes, but history will vindicate me.'" Dussaq also said his wife was under twenty-four-hour FBI guard. [8]

The CIC report immediately angered FBI chiefs in Washington. They did not like, true or false, that there were official military reports that a U.S. Army officer, Dussaq, had claimed that the FBI had made him join the Communist Party, nor that he had witnessed an FBI beating, a problem on various ethical and political fronts which they vehemently disavowed— as they did that he had ever met with Hoover. Hoover, himself, in the documents, seems personally affronted—a fact that likely heightened animosity towards Dussaq amongst the powerful director's Washington aides. Finally, Dussaq had agreed never to disclose his FBI activities to anyone. The fact that he was alleged to have done so was, to them, an intolerable breach of confidence.

On October 4, after considerable communication back and forth with FBI headquarters in Washington on the problem, the Los Angeles bureau was instructed to "immediately contact Dussaq and advise him in no uncertain terms that the Bureau will not tolerate his making false statements involving the Federal Bureau of Investigation." He was to be "advised to immediately cease...claiming he is personally acquainted with the Director" and to "refrain from making false statements [redacted] and...alleging misconduct on the part of Bureau Agents in conducting interviews with Communist Party members." He was to "be asked to explain in detail why he made the...false statements" and if he indicated "a desire to set the record straight by denying the truth of his statements...the Bureau" would "accept a signed statement from him reflecting his denial."[9]

On October 14, apparently presented with the findings, he responded.

"I, René Dussaq, desire to make the following voluntary statement," he wrote in the presence of Agent Vincent W. Hughes, identified as a "witness" on his statement. "I understand that statements have been attributed to me which are not accurate and this is my opportunity to clarify any mistaken conceptions which may have arisen from any remarks."

Although not told, he surmised that the charges against him had been made by his former commanding officer, Capt. Rudolph W. Kogan, head of the 529th Intelligence Platoon, of which, by the time he left Germany, he was executive officer; i.e., second in command. Kogan, he said, was "very anxious" to "develop his position" as CO of the unit by using "covert activities." Dussaq therefore offered his experiences from WWII and earlier conflicts and "likewise related incidents of associating with persons in the Los Angeles area who were former members of the Communist Party and my subsequent trip to Mexico...I felt that since we were engaged in work of a confidential nature...on behalf of the

United States Government that I could feel free to speak to my commanding officer ... without fear that the confidential nature of these assignments would be broken." He was only doing so, he stressed, to help "the armed forces of the United States."[10]

He denied making any "false statements." Specifically, "At no time did I say I actually joined the Communist Party. I did state...that I associated with...Communists with the knowledge of the [FBI] in order to carry out my assignment." He acknowledged traveling to Mexico with communists "but I never used the term 'strong-arm' mission in connection with my trip...I did not state that I had ever witnessed [a manhandling]. However, I do recall an occasion when I was talking to Captain Kogan and deploring the fact people who claim to be for democracy do not show the same zeal and intensity as people who are Communists, and I related to him an incident when I had a discussion with a man who I believe was named George Haggerty, who was part of the group with which I associated in Los Angeles. Haggerty, who I believe was a sheet metal worker, once made the remark to me that he did not care if he were picked up by the Police or the [FBI] and was beaten to the verge of death that he would not lose his loyalty to Communism and that history would vindicate him in his decision."[11]

Haggerty, it appears, is the same George Haggerty (aka George Nelson and some other names) identified in FBI files as a leader of the Los Angeles sabotage cell Dussaq had infiltrated before leaving for Germany. He "definitely outlined potential sabotage plans," say the documents about Haggerty.[12] The website *Abraham Lincoln Brigade Archives* identifies Haggerty as a "steel worker" and "coal miner" from Wilkes Barre, Pennsylvania, born in 1911, who fought in various units in Spain during its civil war and returned to the U.S. in 1938.[13] A book about the brigade, *The Good Fight Continues*, says that in November 1944, while employed as a sheet metal worker at the Naval Ordinance Testing Station, Inyokern, California (China Lake), Haggerty was "arrested for security reasons" as part of a government purge of "antifascists."[14]

Was Haggerty the union member René told his nephew, Francois, he had "put down"? Was "put down" really just a beating; an embellishment or exaggeration? Had Francois misinterpreted the remark? Or was Francois correct and René was now giving only a positive picture?

Only Dussaq himself knew. But the questions are legitimate.

About the accusation that Dussaq had said his wife was under twenty-four-hour FBI guard, Dussaq denied it. "However, I recall making a statement to the...effect: that when I went to Mexico, my primary concern was the safety of my family...I told Kogan that the agents had assured me that there was little chance that anyone would attempt to intimidate my family and...if it gave me a greater feeling of security...the agents would contact my wife on several occasions"—which they did. Like the other charges, he wrote, this one seemed to him an "embellishment" by Kogan whom he found to be "a very high-strung, nervous individual...anxious to do a good job" but with "a very vivid imagination" who "could never stand to have his authority questioned"—which, Dussaq wrote, he had frequently done.

Kogan, who had risen to the rank of colonel in the army, according to research, appears to have died and thus is unable to comment further.[15]

Dussaq concluded his statement by calling attention to his distinguished military record, especially in World War II, and the fact that he'd helped the bureau in its investigation of the Sabotage cell. But despite the statement—and a tepid attempt by the Los Angeles bureau to vouch for him—FBI headquarters in Washington basically disowned him. It brought up the old charges of his family possibly being pro-Axis and the apparent joke he'd made when arriving in Chile that his address would be "Nazi headquarters." The FBI said it had additional documents showing Dussaq's "exaggerated self-importance and lack of discretion,"[16] and therefore denied his request to use FBI information to absolve the matter with the army. "You are instructed to advise Dussaq that the Bureau cannot give him clearance to advise military authorities or anyone regarding his past," says an October 27, 1954 instruction to the Los Angeles office from Hoover himself. "It is to be pointed out to Dussaq that the present situation has been brought about by his failure to comply with the previous request."[17]

The rest of the message is redacted.

In view of this FBI abandonment, and earlier accusations when he was on the speaker's circuit, the question remains: Was Dussaq, in fact, a communist? Had he actually been more intricately involved in double and even triple spying than the FBI had known when he had worked for the bureau against the Factionalist Sabotage Group? His trouble in Germany and subsequently with the FBI appears more puzzling than it first did on the surface.

Was there more going on in Dussaq's clandestine life than had so far been revealed?

PART 3

HYDRA-K

24

Secret Diaries

HAVANA HARBOR, LATE 1920s[1]

The night bay was choppy. It was secluded in this part of the sprawling harbor, easy to navigate without calling attention. The small launch moved quickly over the waves, a shadow in the tropical moonlight. "Baz" was with "Hamburg," the German-born boatswain and fellow mate on their mother ship—a U.S. passenger liner regularly departing down and off the East Coast of America, from New York through the Panama Canal and up to San Francisco.

The ship's Caribbean leg was a highlight. It docked at several of the island ports, Havana being the largest. While departed passengers reveled in the city's after-hour delights, Baz and his older chief were smuggling liquor, perfume, drugs, and cigarettes—"Lucky Strikes" among the most prized—to the island's underworld. In exchange they'd get ready cash and Cuban contraband they would sell elsewhere. It was a lucrative, if outlawed, enterprise, well worth the risk.

Douglas Bazata was only fifteen or sixteen, but large and older looking—a lean six-foot-one, 190 pounds, powerfully built. He had bruising fists and a penchant to use them. His father, a New Jersey minister and storied Southern California athlete, had taught him to box, and he'd been blessed with a lightning-fast jab. He was also good with weapons. He'd already killed his first man with one when the ship's captain, noting his prowess, had put him in charge of prisoners, mostly stowaways. A prisoner he was guarding had attacked him from behind. He'd beaten the man to death with a lead-filled bull's "prick" he'd been issued for the job and dumped the body overboard.

"Lost at sea," they'd written on the report.

This was Bazata's "shakedown" cruise, his first of many, eventually launching his career as a successful clandestine. He'd also been recognized for "valuable attributes" by the ship's military detachment. Seeing his potential, they'd quickly recruited him as an undercover informant. The ship carried U.S. mail, which justified the detachment's presence. In truth, its real purpose was gathering intelligence throughout the Caribbean and Central America, where revolutions were rife. Among Bazata's unofficial ship's duties, pimped by its wily purser, was providing "sad sex to old ladies." The money was terrific and occasionally worth the tryst. But tonight's enterprise was what he enjoyed most—what he called "spy trade." He loved the sneak, the unknown, the danger and quick-witted action. Adventure was why he'd gotten his dad, who knew he couldn't be dissuaded, to sign him on despite his age.

They slowed the launch, turned inland, and cruised into a covered slip. It was then that he first encountered the person he would later say was the most impactual and impressive he'd ever known—his future mentor. The stranger appeared to him no older than himself, maybe even younger—Latin-looking, handsome, an air of confidence in his manner. Baz assumed he was Cuban, probably from one of the wealthy landed families. He had the look and style. The young stranger stepped quietly from the dock's shadows. "He seemed about my size and age," writes Bazata, "perhaps a little thinner. He eyed me coldly but smiling. He spoke elegant English."

Their young greeter acknowledged the brooding Hamburg but inquired about Bazata. He was new. Who was he? Could he be trusted? The German, who had earlier cautioned Bazata that he'd do the talking, got impatient. "He's my cousin," he lied, as if that should end it. He wanted to get in and out quickly. It was the safest way. But their questioner wasn't satisfied. "I don't know if he was a guard, observer, or high in the organization, but he wasn't buying it. He looked at us coolly, always smiling. We'd have to go see 'The Mule,' he said—the local boss."

Hamburg had no retort.

They followed.

■ ■ ■

The above is a reconstruction from fragmentary accounts by Bazata of how he was first introduced to René Dussaq—the confident young man on the dock. It is a composite picture from secret diaries written by Bazata, who went on to become a world-class spy and underground operative. He gave me, before his death in 1999, more than forty of the ledger-like notebooks which he'd penned roughly between 1969 and 1989.[2] They show a different side of René than I'd previously encountered—very different. And if what Bazata writes in them is true—and there is reason to believe it is—then a new, darker side of the mysterious Dussaq is a possibility.

As I've written earlier, Bazata and Dussaq knew each other in the OSS. That's documented, but a relationship before and after those war years is not in the public record. There is circumstantial evidence for it. However, as far as I've been able to determine, personal details are solely in Bazata's diaries—and again, with good reason. What the diaries reveal is explosive—not something that would be public. In threads throughout his secret writings, Bazata details a longtime friendship with Dussaq. He claims that (1) because of Dussaq's fervent belief in the right of individuals to determine their own destiny, and (2) because of U.S. dominance and exploitation of Cuba, his long-time friend was a primary organizer and plotter of the assassination of President John F. Kennedy. Bazata further claims that Dussaq was one of the shooters who killed Kennedy in Dallas, November 22, 1963.

The assassination, most who have studied it agree, is still an unsolved mystery. Dussaq, himself a clandestine, is also, in many ways, a mystery. For those reasons alone the diaries are important.

But Bazata, too, is reason to take them seriously.

Although controversial[3]—and what spy isn't?—Bazata, by his own admission,[4] was an OSS and Cold War assassin. He knew well that violent, secret underworld. A top marksman and weapons expert, he ended World War II as an Army major. He was awarded the Distinguished Service Cross (DSC) for heroism, nominated for the Silver Star, and earned four Purple Hearts, among other honors. Following the war, he spent nearly three decades in Europe as a freelance operative for the CIA, France, and other important countries' spy agencies, performing secret missions often behind the Iron Curtain, including into the Soviet Union.

Bazata was a clandestine's clandestine— a keeper and maker of the secrets. As a good friend of the late William Colby, former CIA director with whom he served in the Jedburghs, he returned to the U.S. after staying with Colby in Vietnam during the Vietnam War, and served in the 1980s as an assistant to Secretary of the Navy John Lehman in the Reagan Administration. As one of the original cadre of thirty-eight Jedburghs, he was an American Special Forces pioneer.[5]

Bazata is credible, especially in secret matters, certainly as credible as most of those who have claimed secret or deduced knowledge of JFK's assassination. Check Amazon for the plethora of books and articles speculating about the killing. He should not—especially among so many lessor experienced speculators—be dismissed.

So let Bazata tell it.

■ ■ ■

In a diary written in 1970—only seven years after JFK's assassination—Bazata begins, "This is a history of the liaison of 2 men across 50 years of clandestiny...It culminated in the death of John F. Kennedy [although, he adds, Kennedy wasn't the first president targeted.][6] It is not a belated 'confession' or spate of 'remorse' or spiteful tale. It is not told for money...It is revealed because this 'telling' is part of the gigantic [assassination] plan [bringing it] to a 'near' finish. It remains for [America to change and thus] finish it."[7]

Dussaq, writes Bazata, hatched his plot ultimately to make America aware of its leaders' manipulation of smaller countries, and the price he believed would have to be paid because of that waywardness. Further, he delegated Bazata, when the time was right—after the assassination's shock had dissipated—to tell the public the truth about what had happened in hopes America's leaders would change and allow sovereign nations like Cuba to decide their own fate rather than have America decide it for them.

Throughout the diaries, Bazata, to protect his friend, calls Dussaq "Peter" or "Paul," mostly "Paul." It's a play on the Biblical transformation of Saul to Paul, which occurs soon in their relationship. But there is no doubt in my mind who Bazata means. Occasionally he slips, naming Dussaq outright. Regardless, there are so many indicators in the story pointing directly to Dussaq that "Peter" or "Paul" could be no other. The plotter-shooter in Bazata's diaries was born in Argentina, grew up in Switzerland and spoke many languages. He was an ex-Hollywood stuntman, had a bad back, was naturalized in 1942, and lost his wife tragically during the war in a military aircraft accident. He even carried a picture of his father's bicep, as Dussaq did.[8] Plus, again, Dussaq is inadvertently named sometimes. The odds that Bazata is writing about someone other than Dussaq are astronomical.

"Long have I kept Paul's story in my heart," writes Bazata. "Paul never spoke to me from bragging or compulsion. He spoke in tears and hope...He chose me to [tell the story]...You either believe me or you don't. I care not one fig either way. I merely set down here a story 50 years in the making. It is all totally true...I change only the names of those I love [Dussaq and other clandestine brothers involved] and those I fear. Yes fear. I have survived these past 50 years through skill and never talking. Not once [through] tortures, doubts, temptation, sleepless nights over this...Now I'm going to lose my privacy." He felt compelled. "The nuts will come out..."[9]

Only they never did. Bazata never allowed what he'd written to be published. Why is a matter of speculation. Perhaps the fear became too real and halted him? Perhaps, as the story will show, his attempts to leak it out piecemeal to friends were ignored or shunned which gave him pause and he retreated. Perhaps publishers didn't believe him, or didn't want to believe him. No question the diaries are not only explosive but in need of editing. They are hard to read—several thousand handwritten pages in all—often coded, jumping from thread to thread on different pages. And from page to page out of numbered sequence, requiring the reader to go to different parts of a notebook, and/or turn the notebook upside-down to continue reading. Sentences are unfinished. Different handwriting and script styles are used, even different sizes of letters which is jarring to the flow of the sentences and their meaning. All this presents a problem to anyone not willing to fight with what is written until it becomes clear.

But once deciphered, the JFK passages jibe with much that is known.

There are gaps in Bazata's knowledge. "Tho I knew Peter/Paul most profoundly, I know almost nothing of prolonged periods [in his life], vast areas of surely much activity. We [clandestines] never confided in anyone, ever—including each other, never probed each other, never asked a personal question. We just let it issue forth as the talker wished and decided. We trusted each other. We were brothers to the fullest."[10]

They shared the strong bond of fear and danger.

I don't think Bazata wanted anyone else, not sanctioned, to read the diaries, and was still debating within himself when he died whether to go public or not. The reason he gave me access, in my opinion, was that he'd recently had a stroke, which had weakened in his mind the long-time code of silence he'd always lived by. He gave me the diaries almost nonchalantly, as if to say, "Go ahead if you want. Look through them. Take them..." He didn't seem to care. I had approached him on another subject[11] and was later completely surprised with what I found.

Near death, had he lost the fear and wanted me to discover what was in them?

Is it all a lie, made up? But for what? He didn't ask for money or even credit. Perhaps this was his last, tired attempt to set the record straight.

You be the judge.[12]

25

"Little Time for Whiners"

The meeting with "The Mule" went well.[1] Afterwards, Dussaq handed Bazata a note. It had the name of a coffee bar and address scrawled on it—and Dussaq's Havana telephone number. He suggested they meet. Their similar age and size, Bazata figured, caused the invitation. He was impressed with the young smuggler and agreed.

Two months and several cruises to Havana later, they were "quick friends, sipping rums with lime filler" at the city's best sidewalk cafes. Dussaq was always alone, although acknowledged, Bazata noted, with respectful nods by "people of standing" at tables near them or greetings by passersby. Once, a beautiful girl stopped Dussaq on the street when they were together and whispered something in his ear. He turned to introduce Bazata but, to Bazata's chagrin, she was already off when they turned back. All he got was a wistful Dussaq smile.

Bazata found they had much in common. "We had little time for whiners or the self-indulgent. We were both compulsive supporters of

the truly suffering—the dominated, the oppressed, the victimized"—
especially those Dussaq characterized as prevented from exercising their
God-given free will. "He was very sophisticated—but made of pure
steel," both traits which Bazata admired.

Sometimes, when schedules permitted, they had dinner together and
talked well into the night.[2] "He introduced me to his aim of a free
Cuba...Paul was totally devoted to eliminating outside meddling and
Cuban (puppet) dictators—the castration, the emasculation, the domination of his country." This too appealed to Bazata, a rebel and iconoclast
himself, often at odds with authorities since he was a child.

"Paul was totally selfless," almost "mystic" in his beliefs and arguments. "As brothers, we made revelations to each other...including who
we had killed. We were joyfully astonished to learn we slew none for
vengeance or anger, satisfaction or orgasm...We both quietly aimed only
at eliminating evil."

This would become a constant refrain in Bazata's diary writings of
his "hits" and contracted assassinations—perhaps justification for such
a self-troubling profession. He didn't kill for gain or satisfaction—never
with passion. He was in the business basically to rid the world of bullies,
predators, and those who otherwise hurt others and should be purged.
Killing for hire or by order was always cold and emotionless for a professional executioner. He called it "weeding."

Sometimes, before their friendly get-togethers, Bazata would deliver,
as part of the contraband exchange, special hand-carried parcels about
which he knew nothing beyond that it had to be guarded and passed on.
He wondered what was inside. Was it political? Was it espionage? He
knew it had priority because he was given carte blanche when he had it
and told not to worry about returning on time or military schedules until
it had been delivered.

He was covered.

"We never asked questions...always respected each other's secrecy,"
he said about Dussaq. "I really didn't know much [about him person-
ally]...He drew his cat line as cats will do...He seemed far above me in
many ways."

Eventually, Bazata left the passenger liners—and thus his newfound friend. He went to Syracuse University, played football, and ran high-hurdles in track, but was kicked off the team for, it was alleged, stealing a car and joy-riding in it.

He didn't care. He was through with school anyway. It was the Depression. He wanted adventure. He started riding boxcars. The diaries record a particularly tense killing by Bazata of several menacing hobos. They thought they had an easy mark in a relatively well dressed young man carrying an expensive-looking bag. They attacked him in a speeding boxcar. What they didn't know was that he kept a lead pipe in that nice jacket. He clubbed the first attacker to death and hurled the second out an open door where he slammed into a telephone pole whizzing by. The third was left whimpering in a corner of the boxcar fearful of what he was about to receive.[3]

Bazata traveled on to become a cowboy in Colorado, a saloon bouncer and "Friday Night" prize fighter, taking on all comers in Wyoming, and a rough and tumble lumberjack in Washington State.

He and Dussaq were geographically separated but would soon, according to Bazata, reunite.

26

Hitman

HAVANA, LATE 1933

Bazata rested quietly as the others filed out. He was a U.S. Marine now, a private serving on the USS Wyoming, a World War I battle-ship stripped of much of its armament plying the Caribbean, watching out for U.S. interests. He was the ship's boxing champ, top marksman, and still smuggling—only now it wasn't from cushy passenger launches. It was from a U.S. Navy ship. While most of the sailors and Marines joined topside to watch movies under balmy early evening skies, he'd sneak aft to a vacant gun port, climb through it, and swim ashore with his protected contraband.

But tonight was different. He'd been given his first mission as a Marine "hitman," as he labeled it. It was an assassination. He was both excited and apprehensive. "I was a kid with kid can-do mentality." This was an opportunity. He didn't want to screw it up.

Seeing him subdue a berserk Marine—probably more—an officer had invited him to a private conversation. After small talk about his abilities, the officer had gotten to the point.

Had he ever killed anyone?

It was a tough question. Would the answer get him in trouble?

No, assured the officer. It was between the two of them—only.

Okay...a few...all in self-defense, he quickly added, still not sure of his position.

The officer smiled, and then made a proposition: "Douglas, we've a special job for you. We feel that only you can do this...Kill Batista...We have confidence in you, Douglas...Will you do it for your country?"

Batista was Fulgencio Batista, the Cuban dictator ousted by Fidel Castro in 1959. But in 1933, Batista was only a Cuban army sergeant and mustering leader of a revolt against U.S. puppet-dictator Gerardo "The Butcher" Machado.[1] Bazata, as did most Marines, knew who Batista was. Island insurrection was why they were there. But his loyalty, at that time, was more to his buddies than the flag. "My country? Hell," he wrote. "My country was Joe Buckley [his gunny sergeant], 'Moo-moo The Mortician' [because he never smiled] Craig, Red O'Neil, Jeff Jeffries [fellow boxers] and Johnny Goosman," a light-weight who, pound-for-pound, he regarded as the best fighter besides himself. "You want me to hit that little dwarf, 'Fatso Batso'? You kidding?"

He accepted.

Now, as the silence below became palpable and he felt safe, he rolled from his bunk and made his way stealthily and cautiously aft to the vacant gun port where he quickly stripped. He had with him a loaded .45 pistol. He stuffed it, along with his meager clothes, packs of Lucky Strikes, and cash he'd been given, into a special watertight cap, and strapped it securely on his head, buckling it below his chin. Moving snake-like through the open port, he dropped down a knotted rope and slipped into the water. It was a fairly long way to shore but he was an excellent swimmer.

The plan was for him to get into town from the wharf the way he usually did—giving a pack or two of cigarettes to a cabbie. He knew most of them. American cigarettes were as good as money—especially Luckies—and worth much more than the three or four cents per pack he paid on the ship. He had been given enough cash for several days and emergencies. He was told where Batista would be the next day— in a restaurant—but that was about all. He knew the town and the officer giving him his orders said he'd be better off handling details on his own.

He liked it that way.

Drying off and dressing on the dock he felt good. He was sure no one had seen him. The landing spot was, as usual, dark and remote. Suddenly a noise startled him. It seemed to come from the shadowy side of what he knew was a dock building behind him, too dark to see well. Had he been spotted? Was it the police? Cuban military? Rebels? He "felt his heart jump a few beats to full alertness—an apprehensively exposed deer," he wrote. But when he heard the coming greeting, he instantly knew who it was. "There was no mistaking the voice...Peter!"[2]

But how?

He and Dussaq had Renéwed their friendship when Bazata had begun returning to Cuban waters. When he was still working on passenger liners, he writes, Dussaq had helped him move prostitutes from Panama—no more details in the diaries—and had actually traveled incognito and partied with him on one of the ships. They'd probably already dined together recently. But he'd told no one about tonight's mission—certainly not Dussaq, a civilian—at least that's what he thought Dussaq was. He'd been warned. Assassination was not in any treaties. If he was caught, the Marines would deny all knowledge of it.

He was on his own.

Dussaq emerged from the shadowy darkness calm and smiling—and "frighteningly" clear—"Don't try to kill Batista," he said, shocking Bazata with his knowledge. "How'd he find out"—and exactly the day "after that nice, plump lieutenant asked me?" Bazata didn't know what to say. His eyes darted. He stammered a hello. "Gotta listen, pay attention," he thought to himself. He felt vulnerable, confused—a tough guy suddenly not so tough.

"Your own men [betrayed] you," said Dussaq. "We need to talk."

He indicated the road behind him. Bazata peered and saw "a small black car...silent...ominous." René reassured him. "Douglas, I know no one can frighten you. But I imagine you are perplexed and wish explanation. Be certain I am your closest brother. I am here to clarify certain items, but only as your friend..."

Bazata calmed somewhat "but kept my alertness." The two walked to the car, entered and drove off. Dussaq, "relaxed" and maintaining the "smile...kept silent as we drove on the far side of Havana...He knew I was logging every point of mark, trying to memorize our route, direction, distance, destination."

They pulled into a small "refreshment" stand. It was empty except for the proprietor. Bazata, feeling he was safe—at least for the moment—relaxed somewhat. Dussaq suggested coffee and "a fluffy type of churros." It tasted wonderful. He relaxed more. Maybe things were not so bad after all.

Dussaq quickly brought him back to reality. He produced a document and handed it to him. Shock! It was the plan he was there for—assassination of Batista—the entire plan, from creation to his recruitment. He read it incredulously. "You're a patsy," said Dussaq, anticipating his reaction. Those who sent him—whom he had respected and put so much trust in—didn't expect him to succeed. It was basically a set up. They expected him to get killed and thus cause an incident that would allow them to come in and take over. That's why they left the planning to him. If, however, he somehow succeeded, that would be okay too. They'd be rid of Batista, a thorn in the U.S. side.

It was a bitter pill.

But how, he wondered, how did René know?

Informants on the ship, answered Dussaq. They, Dussaq's people, weren't stupid. They'd been doing this a long time.

"They?" thought Bazata. Who was this guy he'd known for years? Then he realized fully the pickle he was in. "The gravity of my situation hit me. Here I was a 22-year-old...bungling, lowly hit man...facing an [approximately] 22-year-old...profound exponent of espionage." Dussaq was brilliant, mysterious. He hadn't really known him. "I was at his mercy;" "confused...angry." But Dussaq didn't take advantage. On the contrary, he told Bazata, "don't take this personally. It's not a setback or defeat. Consider it part of this [dirty] arena you've entered [espionage—clandestiny]; consider it a lesson...and," producing another document, "a great piece of luck."

He handed it to Bazata. "You were duped by bumbling idiots...Killing Batista will solve nothing. It just vacates the palace. Another puppet will replace him. We must solve this ourselves. [Your people must not.] I ask you to forgo this [mission]. We have become brothers. I want to work with you...Had it been anyone else, I would have killed him."

Bazata believed him. Outlined on the new paper was an alternative plan. Bazata would go to the restaurant the next day as planned on the ship. But instead of Batista being there, a double, looking like him, would be eating. Bazata would fire blanks. The double, with blood and such arranged, would appear to have been killed. Bazata would quickly be arrested by "our people" and hauled away—but escape shortly in what would appear a daring break, his pursuers also shooting blanks. He'd return to the ship a hushed hero. Later, when the fact of the double was announced in Cuba, his superiors could not fault him for not knowing—he'd done his job—and would be sure to bury the plan to protect themselves.

"I went through the entire dizzy proposal," writes Bazata. "It was a scary scene—my first in the dread-horrors of...clandestiny...I was all alone in a violent sea of sharks—deadly pros... My mind whirled...Who really was René?...A revolutionary?...Was I now a double patsy?" Was this yet another turn in this evil process? "You've no concerns at all from us," Dussaq assured him, reading his doubts. He went through the plan again...I couldn't believe a counter-plot—not by René." As Dussaq talked, "I shook myself from my kid dreams." "Did I not come to *you*,"

Dussaq reiterated. That wasn't a requirement. "I could have just as easily killed you on the dock. We are brothers. This is the solution, Douglas—the solution for both of us."

Bazata nodded, still not sure.

■ ■ ■

They drove to a safe house. "It was plain, void of personality, very
clean and completely practical—no plants, crucifixes, or sign that anyone
lived there." It gave him a "chill"—except "two absolute beauties" were
waiting to attend to his needs. "This is your house," said Dussaq. "Ask
the girls for anything you desire."

He couldn't argue with that.

After settling, Dussaq explained precisely how the next day's sting
would proceed. "At exactly 1700 hours [5 p.m.], a dark blue Chevrolet
sedan will come for you. The driver will not leave the car. Kindly take a
seat in the rear. Say 'Antonio, I am ready'—only that. He will respond,
'Thank you, Señor LeBeau.'[3] Should the driver's communication be any
different I suggest you return to the house and await word at nightfall."
They "embraced Latin fashion." writes Bazata. Dussaq left.

"I sat down to take stock, feeling drained and empty, [mulling] this
extensive mystery. There was no fun or thrill or excitement to espionage."
One of the girls—with "a dazzling smile" and "lush hair"—approached
him. "'Would Señor LeBeau have wishes, perhaps a nap should the senor
be fatigued? I couldn't miss her ample charms and even though I'd been at
sea I steeled me and kept a dignified distance. Was I emulating Dussaq—
no longer the rough, tough marine, but the proper gentleman? I was never
a gentleman. But I was polite to the polite. I kicked me and had to chuckle.
At least my humor held."

He fell asleep "instantly" and "like a rock. Was it a case of escape?
Perhaps…I was damn weary" and still not totally sure about what he
should do. But he was awakened the next morning by "an angel"—"Aye,
and to think I never saw those two gals again." They had a "tall, cold
drink" waiting for him and "a tray of assorted clams, shrimp, mussels

and fish. I devoured them." And after a post-breakfast bath and two cups of "that marvelous coffee," he was feeling much better—and much surer of the course he'd taken.

■ ■ ■

The Chevrolet arrived precisely at 1700. Code phrases were exchanged "and off we went." Dussaq "was in full control," mused Bazata as they drove through the late-day Havana streets. He and René were much alike—both "physically extremely strong...both without fear"—although now, he had to admit, the pangs were returning. René, however, always "seemed so calm, so void of all fear...never plagued by doubts." Too late now. What would be would be.

"Antonio" dropped Bazata at a "corner café," several blocks from the restaurant, where a contact—a soldier, he'd been briefed—would be waiting.[4] As they sipped coffee, the "soldier handed me four blanks. I gave him my live rounds. Meanwhile, the soldier "accosted every passing female—'Señor, look at that ass—Look at that one!' I nodded assent." He certainly "loved life—at least his life. And why not? So many scant skirts and high heels. Yes, I'd known a few over the past weeks. Havana was open, free. It was fun."

But he was now only partially interested in "waggles."

The job at hand was paramount.

At "exactly 17:45, as agreed, Soldier Boy stood and said, 'Señor LeBeau, may I escort you down the street.'" Bazata rose. This was it. They were three blocks away. As they walked, his escort kept pointing out sexy women and "shooing" away pesky beggar boys. "Never give them what they want," he advised. "They'll swarm you."

Now it got crazy—Keystone Cop-ish.[5]

The soldier, apparently oblivious to discretion—something Bazata would become known for in years to come—walked boldly into the restaurant and right up to the table where the double sat hidden behind a newspaper. "I could not see his face as his back was to me," writes Bazata. Clicking his heels, the soldier announced, "Señor LeBeau. This is the place" and pointed to the seat Bazata should take opposite the double—who did not turn from the newspaper but surely heard it all. His escort's lack of concealment apparently amused Bazata, who smiled and thanked him appreciatively as the smaller man saluted and left.

But the double wasn't laughing. "The fool, the silly ass," he growled, still hunkering behind the newspaper, "He might as well have been waving a flag"—a comment that didn't sit well with Bazata, who apparently had grown fond of his quirky contact. "I already didn't like [the double] and determined to shoot [near] his head [to] give him the loudest blast and concussion I could." To make matters worse, the double shoved a part of the paper across the table to Bazata instructing him to check out page seven. No explanation—just check it out. Bazata, for the life of him, couldn't find anything pertinent, nor was he in the mood for such orders or distraction. "Now I really disliked the bastard. Too bad he wasn't Batista. I would have enjoyed plugging him."

A waiter came and Bazata finally saw the double's face. He was impressed—at least in the likeness to Batista. A dead ringer. They ordered drinks and Bazata stealthy removed the .45 from inside his shirt and readied it below the table and against his leg with his right hand—his firing hand—and drank awkwardly with his left, anxiously anticipating the signal from the double to fire. "I said to me, kid, you're NOT nervous. This is going to be easy. Keep calm."

He took a deep breath and searched for the police who were supposed to arrest him. "I saw none. Nowhere! I even looked upward on the ceiling, embarrassed that I was so worried, and [still] despising [the double]."

Where were they?

At last the double discarded the newspaper—his signal to fire. "Astonishingly, I noted that his glass was empty. He must have been drinking behind the sports page. How could I notice such crap at such a time!"

Okay, police or no police, this was it.

"I let go a round...well over his head. The noise in the [room] was so awesome everyone froze, including [Double] who was supposed to fall dead...It seemed an eternity, but at last he fell forward, his forehead thudding loudly on the white marble table top...I looked about. No cops. No nothing! Then everyone seemed to roar. They all seemed to be rushing me."

He fired in the air. The mob stopped. "Where the hell are those damn cops!" He pointed the .45 at the poised onlookers. "Stand back you fucking greaseballs or I'll blast all of you!" The brandishing pistol momentarily cowed them.

"Still no cops. Jesus!"

They rushed him.

"I let go another round at the ceiling, screaming a warning in my best New Jersey accent. The blast halted them again. A hurled bottle went sailing by him, smashing nearby. He jumped up on a wall seat, gesturing wildly, and fired point blank at the rushers. "They fell back like dominoes...one guy yelling like a stuck pig...He hit the tile floor in a swoon." The wadding in the blank, Bazata figured, must have grazed him.

He writes he fired another shot—but he was already out of blanks—at least by the numbers he gives. Two policemen finally arrived. "Foolishly, I yelled, 'Let them through!'" Luckily it was in English. We were on our way."

He checked his watch. It was 17:50. The entire episode from leaving the "corner café" to being "arrested" had taken only five minutes![6]

■ ■ ■

They whisked him away in a car. But instead of the police station, he was taken back to the safe house where a group of men, including Dussaq, were waiting. "Well done, Douglas. Perfect," complimented René. Bazata showered and shaved. They had a dinner waiting for him.

At midnight he was driven to the dock where he stripped and swam back to the ship, where the knotted rope was still hanging just as he'd left it. Creeping into his bunk, friends jumped him. "Where have you been? Luckily no one came looking." He swam in "to get laid," he told them, and they all decided they'd do it too, which he encouraged.

Good for his business.

He "never heard a word from the brass," he writes—and just as well. He'd learned on his excursion just how dangerous his chosen work could be. And that even those supposedly on his side would sell him down the river for little more than a notion. They were manipulators, users. They played a game of vipers and one had to look out for oneself—look out very carefully.

No one else would.

But he'd always trust Dussaq. "I owed him my life and would thank him many times."[7]

27

A Seed Is Planted

If Bazata had more contact with Dussaq in Cuba he doesn't reveal it. He was honorably discharged from the Marines in April 1937, having been both the Corps' "unofficial" heavyweight boxing champion, as he describes it, and a member of its elite world champion rifle team, which dominated competition in those late-Depression days. "The Marines were tough," he writes. "I loved it." But he was a private and "got into too many [unofficial] fist fights."

These were jobless days for most, unless one was in Washington, where money and favors flowed. That's where he eventually went. With World War II brewing, he wanted to continue in "clandestiny." It could be lucrative. He now had experience. He knew he could do it. But he couldn't tell prospective hirers about capers like Batista. "[He'd] learned to keep a secret," the *Washington Post* titled an article about him in its Sunday magazine years later.[1] So he decided to go into business for himself.

After various jobs, he landed one with Hoover Vacuum selling and servicing their new "streamlined" model. It was a much sought-after item. His territory was Washington's Embassy Row along ritzy Massachusetts Avenue. It was perfect. After making a friend in an embassy, "I'd tell him [or her], well, you got your Hoover, you ought to be able to pick up a lot of CRUMBS," the *Post* quotes him explaining.[2] In that way he got information from one embassy and sold the "crumb" to another—at "$50 a shot"—a good sum in those days. He doesn't give specifics about the intelligence he got but writes he became quite successful. Eventually he owned several "flashy new cars" and had an expensive D.C. residence.

One day, entering LaSalle DuBois restaurant, one of the city's newest and most fashionable, he spotted Dussaq "eating alone. I wasn't. We looked straight at each other with no signs of recognition tho [sic] each knew the other instantly and each was delighted."[3] Apparently secrecy was still operative. Bazata was with a lady. "I decided against a note." He explained to his female companion that near a certain table he was going to use "what might appear to be ridiculous language. Knowing me, she smiled." Subsequently pausing within earshot of Dussaq, he said loudly, "Very good, honey. I'll ring Teddy to hold the round table at the Mayflower [his residence] from 1800 [6 p.m.] on...[Dussaq] was there at 6:05."

But, strangely, Dussaq had changed. Instead of speaking English with a British accent—like a European might learn it—and as Bazata remembered it—Dussaq now had a "strong Latin accent.[4] We chatted as of yore. No questions. Today [meaning 1976, when he wrote it in the diary], some 35 years after that 'change'...I still do not know why, have not the slightest idea. I never asked and [Dussaq] never volunteered to reveal or hint why. [But] it is of no importance. What is important was the fine fact that we rekindled our union at once. René was now more Argentine and Swiss than just Cuban."

They quickly caught up. Dussaq had tried to enlist in the Army, writes Bazata, but "because of a severe back injury" had been rejected. The injury, he writes, had occurred in Texas as René had wing-walked on a plane "in 1931 or 1932...He wore no chute." After an undisclosed problem during the stunt, the pilot—his "courageous, skilled" wife—had "crashed the plane into a small, thick grove of trees." He'd broken his back and his "gallant" wife had been "severely injured."

This was either a mixup in Bazata's memory about the truth of René's back injury—the Los Angeles car crash resulting in Daisy Moreno's death—or a disguise of it by Dussaq.[5]

Dussaq had a "flat in DC," notes Bazata. Was this perhaps the residence he shared with his first wife, Katherine? If so, Bazata doesn't indicate it, nor does he indicate that Dussaq was married. He "was always alone," Bazata writes of his refound friend. They began meeting regularly over drinks—again, always alone. (Had such surreptitious meetings perhaps been the genesis of what might have become Katherine's later suspicion of him?) Both had keen interest in intelligence. But while Bazata's interest was for little more than "fun" and profit, Dussaq's, he writes, was ideologically driven and impressively connected.

"René was [now] totally aimed at the disposal of Batista." Since Bazata's near disastrous assignment to kill the Cuban sergeant, he'd promoted himself to colonel and, by 1940, would be elected Cuban president. Dussaq was now openly against his former revolutionary ally and the "juggling of all [such] evil puppets" by companies, mostly American, which had "bled rich, innocent Cuba for so very long." He had actually participated in a failed plot to assassinate his former ally and informed Bazata there already existed a "plan" to oust Batista once a successor had risen. "We have some fine lads moving up."[6]

Dussaq, Bazata surmised, was involved in his own spy operations involving "many" countries, especially Europe and Latin America. This was partly because of his Latin heritage but also because of the coming war, which they discussed incessantly. Dussaq was against the fascists in Germany, Japan, and Italy—as evidenced partly by his attempt to enlist—but they both believed U.S. politicians, especially President Franklin D. Roosevelt, were manipulating America into the conflict. "Should we have executed FDR?" he writes that Dussaq asked. "Is it too late? Could we still do it?" Bazata "felt these questions were posed [more] to elicit a response [than actual action]. I replied, '[René], you know I have almost no confidence in the Power Boys [the FDR Administration].'" They are "self-pushing, brassy politicians." But "an adoring public knows little of the true FDR" so any such action would be fruitless and counter-productive, not to mention hazardous. But "perhaps we can keep America out?"[7]

Dussaq "laughed." No chance. The war will be worldwide. America will be in it soon. It already is secretly.[8] And when she enters there will be a "patriotic surge" and an avalanche of "war propaganda." The U.S. would be all in, including him and Bazata, hopefully sooner rather than later, said Dussaq. And when the war was over and won by the Allies, which Dussaq predicted would happen, the U.S. would be the mightiest power on earth and would go the way of other great powers before them "devoured by that Queen of Fate and Time and Anti-Evolution, destined for nuclear everything, Xeroxed, computerized, sterilized, becoming a land of inhumanity, keeping only man's basic greeds"—just as had happened prior in "Egypt, Greece, Rome, France, England, The Netherlands, Portugal and Spain." Dussaq even forecasted, writes Bazata, that when the war ended, "the American general of all the forces will become president...in such a hysterical ambiance of sainthood and fatherhood" that he would be "untouchable."[9]

Writing this in the 1970s, Bazata had the benefit of hindsight. "Xerox" and "nuclear" were not well-known terms prior to World War II. Dussaq using them before the war makes him seem prescient. Similarly, Supreme Allied Commander Gen. Dwight Eisenhower, who basically ran the war in Europe, did become president. As far as Bazata was concerned, Dussaq, with such vision, was brilliant. "I remained a today guy, a get-things-done-now guy. René was 'The Prophet,' 'the genius.' He saw it all as clearly as the sky or sea or mountain." It was almost enough to make Bazata feel deficient. "I was so gripped by René that I never considered embellishments as was my custom with others." Dussaq, he writes—who he says was an optimist as opposed to his own "pessimism"—was already planning the liberation of Cuba after the coming conflict ended.

As a result of their discussions, Bazata says he decided to start an espionage group he calls variously in the diaries "La Table" and the "Co-Op." It would be an expansion of what he'd begun with his operations along Embassy Row. After the war, as Bazata became a Cold War operative in Europe, the Co-Op would grow, he relates, into a clandestine special operations group with some twelve secret members, tough and skilled, loosely organized and hired through Bazata by various country's intelligence agencies, including America's CIA. They would do particularly difficult and dangerous jobs like rescuing a captured French officer from Algerian rebels, performing political and military assassinations, and safely escorting and depositing spies into the Soviet Union and extricating them and others who had to get out fast.

But that would come later. At this point, the Co-Op was just in its beginning stages with Dussaq its first recruited new member, writes Bazata, although René cautioned him that he had other priorities and might have to leave the group. For the time being, however, Dussaq suggested they study the successful espionage operations of several countries, mainly the Soviet Union, which had thoroughly infiltrated the American government,[10] and that of Great Britain "to learn precisely how they controlled America and thus the world." To this end, he writes, Dussaq, perhaps involving intermediaries, introduced him to espionage heavyweight British spymaster William Stephenson, who would become known as the legendary "Intrepid"—from his wartime code name—and "Wild Bill" Donovan, who would create and head the OSS into which both Dussaq and Bazata would soon be accepted. "René was deeply embedded with Stephenson and Donovan...inserting himself into America's and Britain's deepest plotting circles."[11]

It is said that Stephenson and Donovan met during World War I where Donovan, an infantry officer, was awarded America's highest tribute for valor, the Medal of Honor, and Stephenson distinguished himself as a decorated fighter pilot. As the war against the Nazis mounted in Europe—but before Pearl Harbor—Great Britain found itself almost alone in opposition to the Germans and in desperate need of aid. Stephenson was dispatched to Washington to coax FDR into giving England vital war supplies. FDR was sympathetic but faced an isolationist-prone citizenry. Lend-lease became the surreptitious answer. It allowed America to ship weapons and other needed items to the besieged nation in return for the use of Great Britain's Atlantic and Caribbean bases. Americans would tolerate a reciprocal deal, especially to an underdog.

While in Washington, Stephenson and Donovan got together and what would become the OSS was born under Stephenson's tutelage. There is still controversy over whether or not Donovan was a British agent.[12] This Stephenson-Roosevelt drama, it seems, was occurring at roughly the same time Dussaq and Bazata were meeting, although exact dates are impossible to determine. During the war—if not before, as Bazata writes in the diaries—both he and Dussaq would become personally involved with Donovan; Bazata as an OSS assassin taking orders directly from the OSS director,[13] and Dussaq earning the unique distinction of being the sole OSS operative tapped by Donovan to receive personal recognition by President Harry Truman.[14] So a connection here cannot be dismissed.

How long this prewar liaison between Dussaq and Bazata continued, Bazata doesn't say. But for the first time in their relationship, he writes, a Kennedy was mentioned—not JFK, the future U.S. president, but his father, Joseph, who at that time was the U.S. ambassador to England.

Joe Kennedy, a stock-market-made millionaire and son of a popular Boston politician, was a lifelong Democrat with presidential aspirations. As a leader of Boston's heavily-Democratic Irish community, FDR had appointed him head of several national commissions, and in 1938 sent him to England as ambassador. But as war clouds gathered, he was at odds with the general anti-German position of both America and Great Britain, as were many Irishmen who had suffered after centuries of British domination. He supported British Prime Minister Neville Chamberlain's unpopular appeasement policies toward the Nazis, sought personal meetings with German dictator Adolph Hitler without State Department approval, greatly angering his superiors. He was also against giving aid to the threatened island nation. He stated publicly that England's struggle was only to save its far-flung empire, infuriating the British populace.[15]

Such opposition to official U.S. policy—not to mention the sentiments of most in the free world—incensed President Roosevelt, who demanded and received Kennedy's resignation in late 1940.

Joe Kennedy was disliked by Dussaq too, writes Bazata. He saw the Kennedy patriarch as "vengeful … controlling…embryonic spiritually" and "a lip-service-paying Catholic." Bazata continued that "Over and over, René said this is the coming [American] dictator." Only "the war saves us temporarily from total takeover by Joe…Hitler is difficult to forecast [because] he doesn't know himself." But Joe is easier. He knows exactly what he wants—"world domination with a castle headquarters in Ireland and a 'direct phone' to an uneasy Pope"—and Dussaq was a Catholic, at least by birth. Joe "is too old…too dirty violent for our times." But he will buy his way to the top and "use his sons…the K-clan…to make…our times…after his fashion."

Why don't you "hit Joe?" Bazata asked Dussaq.

"Never!" he says Dussaq answered. "He almost raised his voice. 'Never, never! For this Big-horn [Joe Kennedy] is also our savior. He is of us [that which is wrong in America] and…exactly what we require to bring it all to a head. I welcome him heartily—tho [sic] with no joy.'" Joe Kennedy would provide the way for America to be shown its folly. "And I watch his boys…Joe is ungallant and thinks his girls lower. They [the girls] do not have the ability to do it—win the power he seeks. He must focus on his sons…He will not risk [losing the prize] but manipulate, contrive, lie and buy…until the ground work is built solidly and his boys are fully prepared." Then he will make his move. "If not for this coming war, it would be happening now. Beware America. Beware world."[16]

Bazata's recounting of Dussaq's discussion of Joe Kennedy may be tainted by his own experience and prejudice. He had a personal reason to dislike the patriarch. In 1937, out of the Marines and looking for a job in security, he was able, probably through his pastor father's influence, to get a recommendation from New York Senator Royal S. Copland to Joe Kennedy, at that time head of the U.S. Maritime Commission, a newly-created board regulating ship building. With his naval experience, Bazata was applying for the position of "investigator." Copland wholeheartedly endorsed Bazata but Kennedy turned him down, writing Copland that "regretfully" only civil servants were eligible.[17] In the diaries, Bazata gives his version of the turndown. "He asked me, 'What's your religion?' I said, 'Protestant.' He said, 'Get out!' I was young then. I wanted to kill him. When I became a wiser pro, I realized not now. Kill him later."[18]

Sometime during these private conversations, Dussaq told Bazata about a U.S. intelligence organization about to start. "In a matter of weeks our Keystone Cops spy outfit [the OSS] will be formed and I will join you in it in a year or so."[19]

And so he would.

28

Incubation

FRANCE, LATE 1944

A round the end of August or beginning of September, Bazata joined Dussaq at a "tiny" airfield outside Amberieu, a small but important railway junction in the southeast part of the country. It was near the Swiss and Italian borders.[1] The field, probably what is known today as French Airbase 278, had recently been vacated by Germans fleeing Allied armies advancing rapidly through France toward Germany. Gen. George S. Patton, the most feared commander in Europe, was leading the thrust that had just enabled the liberation of Paris.

Both Dussaq and Bazata were "commandos" helping the Maquis to aid the Allied advance, begun mightily almost three months earlier with the massive June 6 D-Day invasion. By now, a second, smaller Allied invasion had landed on France's Mediterranean shore and was advancing north towards Paris. Since late May, Dussaq had been fighting as part of Freelance, the small British SOE team operating in France's south central region—one of many similar teams operating throughout Occupied France. Bazata, who had arrived later, headed a Jedburgh team, "Cedric," fighting and spying north of Amberieu up near the German border. The two had been involved in almost nonstop action since parachuting into Occupied France, and once together again at this reunion, would embark on a mysterious "five-day mission" into Italy.

Since separating during Jedburgh training in 1943, each had lived through adventures enough for any blockbuster movie or thriller novel. Dussaq, as part of the small band of English and French resisters comprising "Freelance," had daily harassed and blocked enemy units, often large, trying to push north to defend against the advancing Allies. In the process, they'd killed many Germans. They also lost many of their own. At one point, Dussaq, in his fearless way, had almost single-handedly caused a heavily-defended German garrison to surrender without a shot being fired by bluffing that he was an advance element of a nearing American force.

Bazata, terribly injured in the thigh by a slicing parachute wire when he'd jumped into France, had nevertheless managed to help lead the small contingent of SOE and Maquis he had joined after self-doctoring his wound. What he experienced with the wound alone had been incredible. His leg had swelled to twice its size. He'd had to operate on himself, staying conscious without anesthesia as he'd cleaned, sewn, and packed the wound.[2] Nevertheless, he was in the field, his leg wrapped like a bloody mummy, and fighting only days later. He and his group, like Dussaq's, had delayed, and wherever possible, destroyed, German units and weapons moving north to battle the Allies. This was guts-ball fighting. At one point, in possession of crucial information needed by the Allied armies, he and the SOE Brit with whom he was working—George Millar, later the author of the bestselling *Maquis*—commandeered a motorcycle and virtually flew at times because of their high speed, through miles of German-defended bridges and checkpoints to deliver the intelligence. They had miraculously survived hails of bullets and road blocks hastily constructed to stop them by angry and surprised Germans.[3]

This meeting at Amberieu, it appears, would be the first for the two in many months—if not longer.

Following America's entry into the war in December 1941, the two, writes Bazata, had kept in touch as best they could when their schedules and whereabouts permitted. Bazata had enlisted in the Army rather than Marines because Dussaq had told him America's new big intelligence agency would be an Army show. He'd been offered a Marine officer's commission by the corps, but turned it down. The Marines, in his judgment, didn't offer the best chance to be a spy-commando. He was so impressive at Army basic training at Ft. Meade, Maryland, that the *Washington Post*, in a rare story about a recruit, featured his weapons prowess. "Eyes popped" it said, as he coolly registered "198 hits out of 200 possible" on a range target, thirty-five of them bull's-eyes. "Alvin C. York couldn't have done better."[4]

By mid-1942, the Army, recognizing his talents, had commissioned Bazata a lieutenant and made him a weapons and tactics instructor at Ft. Benning, Georgia. He'd hoped to see action immediately but instead was ordered to teach combat skills to officers, many of whom outranked him—which must have amused him. Bazata was not only big and bold enough to intimidate superiors, but had a wry disdain for unproven authority, especially if possessed by those who had not personally earned his respect. He was known to brazenly address colonels as "Sugar," and, as a recruit, had reported at a predawn muster in pajamas, his duffle bag stuffed with pillows. And he'd gotten away with it![5]

In the meantime, Dussaq had enjoyed his own rapid rise. In a matter of months, he'd gone from enlisted grunt, to company staff lieutenant, to paratroop instructor. And by mid-1943, he was, "from time to time," according to Bazata, teaching jump skills at Ft. Benning, where the two would get together. Prior to Dussaq's enlistment, they had seen each other almost "weekly." Dussaq then was still living in nearby Washington, D.C., according to Bazata. Once he began appearing at Benning, however, Bazata notes that he was "surprised" to learn his foreign friend had been naturalized as an American citizen. He was convinced René had done so with the aid of "phony, forged, or arranged" papers, probably, he speculated, with help from the Cuban government, among other clandestine connections.[6]

One reason for Bazata's suspicions—beyond what he'd previously surmised about Dussaq—was a conversation he had with a Marine general at Quantico, Viginia, the noted Marine training base. Apparently the Army required that he attend the staff and command school there— which he did, acquitting himself nicely. The general had been one of his superiors, a captain then, when Bazata had served under him in the Caribbean. The two were at the officer's club discussing Cuba when the general suddenly asked if Bazata knew an operative codenamed "XYZ,"[7] whom Bazata indicates was Dussaq. "No sir, not by that name," he answered. "The general looked long and intently" at him "finally order- ing another gin and tonic and saying, 'You deserve this. You've earned it. Yes, you'll go far'...I told this to René...who was not amused, remarking, 'Privacy isn't easy to come by.'"[8]

Such mysteries, however, did not concern Bazata. He was only glad to see his friend at Benning and spend time philosophizing with him.

"By 1942, I'd decided our system was amiss," he writes. The war was being fought for "secret gain...not security." Innocents, he was con- vinced, were being slaughtered by personal and national greed. But he didn't know what he could do about it, nor did he really care. But René, he says, offered clarity and direction. America was on a wrong course alright. It was "a meddling dominating bully," he quotes Dussaq. The problem, said René, was "as a nation, she's never been dominated her- self...Oh she's been dominated by England [presumably in pre-revolu- tionary days]" and now [in World War II] covertly by "Britain, Russia, the media and politicians." But she's not been occupied, tasted the lash, bowed before the oppressor. "This is her greatest weakness...Whereas my [Bazata's] pastor father taught [spiritual change] via the Bible," Dussaq said America could only be saved by "a few punches in the nose, a smart kick in the balls, and an occasional bullet in the head—neat, clean and decisive."

Bazata liked the assessment and was impressed with Dussaq's fire.

"René, you use the words of Christ," he told his friend. "You are like a preacher." Dussaq agreed. "I repeat [Christ's words]...as I learned them...And I obey...[But] I don't speak of all the nobilities of Christianity—love, forgiveness, tolerance, etc...I do far less, for I am limited in talent to only one [nobility]—freedom...to know one's self...one's brother." His quest, he told Bazata, was "to be heard, to instill in others a voice that must rise above the mass of voices...for one deathly silent moment." Then the people will "awaken" and "behold the way to freedom!"[9]

In other words, the masses must be shocked into change—as with an assassination.

Although skeptical that anything could be done to change the situation in America, Bazata writes that he believed Dussaq's views wise and heartfelt. His praise for his friend in the diaries is effusive. Dussaq was "brilliant...thorough...erudite." And Bazata appreciated his sudden candor. "We opened up to each other...We both were totally against evil...We grew closer than ever."[10]

This growth continued as they were accepted into OSS and became elite Jedburghs. They had long discussions about their fathers, both very religious men, both deeply loved and admired by each. Because of their own experience they found the OSS's emphasis on cloak-and-dagger amateurish. Aware their superiors were watching them, they had fun playing jokes on paid OSS informers like waiters and taxi drivers— so "obviously spying" on them during their training "that it was laughable." For instance, Dussaq, in a taxi backseat, would say to Bazata, "'Tell 'em about the time you killed those mobsters at sea.' I would say, 'Oh, they weren't mobsters.' It would build from there." The informers would go back to their OSS handlers "and say, 'Boy, that guy's a killer.'"[11]

Bazata, by his own admission, *was* a killer—up until the war, of course, primarily in "self-defense." He had hoped the backseat banter would get him an assignment to assassinate top Nazis like Rommel, Goebbels, or even Hitler himself—an idea he said he seriously proposed to OSS only to be met with stunned silence. "They must have thought I was insane...or a crank...It would have been quite easy...One man, one bullet... You can protect against nuts and crazies. There is no protection at all against the professional..."[12]

As it was, the banter backfired, and he was to become an "official" OSS assassin, christened, he writes, by OSS chief Donovan himself. But his job included executing the talkers and double-crossers on his own side, and getting orders, among other "horrifying" jobs, to first hinder Patton's advance at the German border, and after the war in collaboration with a Soviet assassin, to *kill* Patton—the story of which is detailed, along with the mystery of Patton's strange death, in my 2008 book, *Target: Patton: The Plot to Assassinate Gen. George S. Patton*. But that tragedy would come later. Right now—in late 1943—Bazata was still in the states, not yet involved in such intrigues, participating in initial OSS training in Washington, D.C. along with Dussaq.

One night, he writes, they got into a barroom brawl in what appears to have been either the D.C. or the New York City area. "René was very strong...Dark, handsome...I was slightly taller, extremely quick and strong...I was all fists, eye-gouging, knees to balls" and broke two chairs "on heads...mostly sailors in whites. René was occupied the entire time strong-arm wrestling...like a python. I was actually shocked and came over and kicked [his opponent] silly. René stood up, saying politely, 'Merci mon ami.' We exited." Outside, Bazata asked, "What the hell were you doing?" "Me?" René retorted, "I had their leader." "Balls!" said Bazata. "'You were like an Oxford guy dueling in Buenos Aires!' That's the way we were. René: slow methodical, strong, thorough; Me, quick, a bit too sly, impatient to get to the point and get it over...We were a well-balanced pair."[13]

Finishing basic OSS training in late 1943—and after Dussaq controversially hand walked for cameras on a windy ledge atop the towering Empire State Building—they shipped out together for Britain on the Cunard luxury liner *Queen Elizabeth*, which was recommissioned as a troop transport. While Dussaq had successfully convinced OSS investigators he wasn't a Nazi, the captain of the ship, packed with eighteen thousand soldiers (Bazata's figure) wasn't taking any chances. He'd given an order that all direction-finding equipment be turned in. Dussaq, however—to Bazata's amusement—wasn't to be denied. He'd kept a "sextant." When, at a briefing, the captain told pilots assembled on deck, "Sorry but I cannot tell you where we are," Dussaq leapt forward taking the startled skippers's baton, saying "I can!" He pinpointed their position off Scotland, for which, writes Bazata, they "at once" put him in the brig "certain they'd caught a spy for Herr Hitler." Refusing to give any more information than "name, rank and serial number," Dussaq, he says, was sent back to the U.S. upon reaching port. "We didn't see him for 4 months."[14]

This was and, if true, still is a questionable situation in Dussaq's mysterious life. Why would he be gone so long? It's understandable that the British ship captain might have overreacted and imprisoned Dussaq. But why, after being sent back to America, was he kept incommunicado for so many months? OSS surely would have stepped in and quickly sent him back. They needed him—unless the arrest and delay was by design; i.e., the OSS or someone else wanted him back in the U.S. for other reasons.

There's a curious item in Dussaq's movements just prior to joining the OSS. According to FBI documents, he passed through immigration at Miami, Florida, on July 30, 1943, "advising" officials that he was a member "of the United States Army" and that his destination was the War Department, Washington, D.C."[15]

What was he doing in Miami at that time? Why would he be heading to the War Department, which ran the war? He was a junior officer supposedly involved in basic training.

Why had he entered through Miami? Had he been to Cuba? If so, why is that not in his military record? What would he have been doing there?

Was this one of Dussaq's secret doings Bazata suspected?

More mystery. It never bothered Bazata. His life was full of secrets. And now—late 1944—he and his friend, separated since Jedburgh training, were reuniting again outside Amberieu. "It was a very strange meeting," Bazata writes of it. He had "put off" his SOE colleague, Millar, and "a certain commie leader" to meet Dussaq—meaning, apparently, Millar, technically in charge, didn't know. "René was present on another mission"—undisclosed. Nor are any details of their subsequent "5-day job" in Italy given. Rather, Bazata describes only what happened after the "job" as he and his "chauffeur Berger"—not otherwise identified—drove Dussaq to Dijon, presumably on his way to Paris, from where, as records state, he would return to England.[16]

If they had not liked the politics of the war before, they now agreed that the conflict they had been fighting was an unmitigated disaster—"a crime by greedy bastards, evil and stupid to a man," badly fought, causing the needless deaths of many and with a bad outcome for most. They talked of how Patton had been held back when he probably could have ended the war in 1944,[17] and how half of Europe, after domination by the Nazis, had been handed over to the Soviets by Roosevelt and Churchill and thus thrown back under another power's domination. "We were both fervent Gaullists [admirers of exiled French leader Gen. Charles DeGaulle, who believed only France should determine its own future]. I suspected René was working for DeGaulle." They believed the wrong people and governments would profit from the war. Enslavement of Eastern Europe, an evil "world government," and "persecution" of non-Nazi Germans were discussed. "We idiots reward monsters," he quotes Dussaq, about the postwar situation. He was now more than ever determined to free Cuba.

Dussaq, writes Bazata, was in his fervor a mix of 1850s abolitionist John Brown, who believed in violence to end slavery, and Civil War President Abraham Lincoln, who used "impeccable logic" for the same cause. "Both died violently…Both…realized…spilling their blood" might be necessary. Dussaq apparently was ready to die for the cause.

As the two drove to Dijon, they "sang John Brown's Body [Lies A-molderin' in the Grave]—to the consternation of [chauffeur] Berger."[18]

The dye for bigger things, indicates Bazata, was being cast.

■ ■ ■

When the two next met—a few months later in England in early 1945—it's doubtful there was any singing. Dussaq's first wife, Katherine, had tragically died. The war was heading quickly towards its furious conclusion. The two assassins finished training and then performed last ditch secret missions; Bazata in Belgium and Denmark, Dussaq in Germany and France.

The end of the war in Europe saw both return to Washington, D.C. where, as OSS was breaking up eventually to re-emerge as the CIA, they lived briefly together at "the Statler Hotel...René found a bug [listening device]" in their room. "We left it" and "loaded it" with lies, writes Bazata. When the Japanese surrendered, Bazata, nominated for the Silver Star, and holder of the DSC (as was Dussaq) went back to Europe, where he felt he could best continue in "clandestiny" and build his fledgling, secret Co-Op.

Dussaq, he confirms—and as records show—went right to Cuba, where he was "stunned by the graft, corruption, gangsterism" and "brutality." He subsequently let Bazata know "the time had come" for him to leave the Co-Op. He was sorry but he had pressing things to do. They kept in touch, writes Bazata, for a year or two, especially concerning intelligence. But basically Dussaq eventually disappeared. "He...went Southwest [to] Cuba—Mexico—Guatemala..." Bazata wasn't sure.

It was what he called an "incubation time."

29

"Will You Join Us, LeBeau?"

I've got my man," said Dussaq. He was excited. "Yes, at long last— after all these years—I've got the star—Cuba's star—our leading man."

Bazata, basically clueless, responded with approval. He'd not heard of Fidel Castro. But he wanted to show solidarity with his friend with whom he'd kept in periodic contact over the years.

It was late 1952.[1] He and Dussaq were somewhere in Germany where René, it is known, was serving with U.S. Army intelligence and Bazata was covertly a freelance-for-hire commando and spy, leader of his growing Co-Op, while maintaining cover as a vineyard manager in Germany for G. H. Mumm, maker of the famous Mumm champagne.

"Fidel Castro!" repeated Dussaq, adding that he'd picked Castro from among other possible Cuban saviours to support. "Isn't it perfect— to have the name Fidel—like your Semper Fidelis," "Always Faithful," the motto of the marines, whom Bazata still revered. "He's young, 25 or so...already seasoned and proven..."[2]

Although he didn't know Castro, Bazata welcomed Dussaq's excitement. Since the war, as they'd met intermittently, he'd not often seen his friend smile so broadly. Dussaq, he writes, had been through trying times. For one, he had been involved in a secret, failed plot to kill Fulgencio Batista, his former ally in the Machado Revolution. Batista was Bazata's nemesis when he and Dussaq had first met. Batista, a sergeant then, had gone from that bloody 1930s insurrection to rule Cuba through most of World War II. In danger of being voted out, he'd reluctantly exited the island nation for Florida in 1944 before returning in 1947, re-entering Cuban politics as an elected official, and seizing power by force again in a March 1952 coup.

Dussaq, writes Bazata, had managed bizarrely to remain in Batista's trusted circle—even after secretly trying to kill him and still being opposed to him.

It was a tricky, tension filled dance.

"René had much contact with Batista during those years, supposedly as an 'in man'...By 1949, he was certain of the dictator's plans." He didn't like them. Batista, like all Cuban dictators before him, was corrupt, a wily pawn of exploitive foreign governments, especially America, and more recently, America's Mafia. The Mafia loved the unrestricted, freewheeling openness of Cuban society and the willingness of the Batista regime to cooperate in return for a healthy piece of the action. "René knew well all Batista's henchmen and, as always, had remained the very low-key mystery man. He was already deeply [in penetration] of British, French, US, Cuban, Swiss...Russian, Czech, Mexican and Guatemalan Intelligence, quite possibly others...He would try to get me involved [in sabotaging the dictator]. 'Lebeau,' he would say. 'This is my life...consider participation, part or full time. We need you.'" But Bazata always refused. While he sympathized, he told Dussaq he had his own pressing concerns. But he was impressed with Dussaq's methods, which kept him interested. "In all my [clandestine] experiences, I never knew one man so gifted at soft-strong penetration."[3]

But whatever else Dussaq had attemped for Cuba apparently had failed.

"It didn't work," Bazata quotes Dussaq saying repeatedly when, he says, the two met in Washington, D.C., around 1950. "'Not this time, maybe next.'"He was gaunt, more silent than I'd ever seen him. He tried to smile, make small talk. But that fizzled...After his beloved wife's death, I never saw him [in the intermittent meetings] with a woman, not one time. Nor did he speak of any woman, save now and then some friend or flirt of mine...But then I rarely saw him with a man. He was the loneliest of loners. He had one aim only—a free and open, self-directed Cuba. 'One day,' he kept stressing, 'yes, one day Cuba will be free.' That was his life."[4]

Throughout the diaries, he never mentions Dussaq's second wife, Charlotte, whom Dussaq married in 1946.

Perhaps—if Bazata's recounting here is true—what had happened to Eduardo Chibas factored into Dussaq's postwar gloom.

Chibas, a mid-1940s political star in Cuba, had been a revolutionary contemporary of Dussaq's during the Machado strife. He had been one of the revolt's many youthful leaders. Following the rebellion, he'd entered politics, becoming famous for his crusade against government corruption and collusion with foreign governments. He'd demanded sovereignty. In 1947, Chibas had formed his own political party—the Orthodox Party. Its chief tenets were Cuban identity and independence. Chibas had taken his fight to the radio airwaves, conducting a weekly broadcast that, in the early postwar period, became the most listened-to political show on the island. But in 1951, embroiled in a dispute with the government—the one Batista would shortly overthrow—he'd apparently shot himself in the stomach at the end of the broadcast, presumably to bring attention to his charges which the government was ignoring or denying while simultaneously attacking Chibas. He died several days later from the wound.

"René and I knew 'Eddy' [sic]," writes Bazata. "He was from a wealthy family like René. They knew each other socially [as well as politically]. René had high hopes for him [to help free Cuba]." Bazata and

Dussaq wondered if Chibas had been murdered. It had been a strange death. The unexpected shooting had occurred dramatically in studio at the broadcast's conclusion. Chibas, it's been reported, mistakenly believed he was still on air, and had delivered an impassioned political speech immediately before the shooting. But, unknown to him, according to the reports, the program engineer had already disconnected his microphone.[5] Why? Questions remained—at least for Dussaq and Bazata. Officially, the government he opposed ruled the death a suicide.

Chibas very well could have been a link between Castro and Dussaq.

Castro, too, was from a wealthy family. His father, a Spaniard from Galicia, had come to Cuba as a Spanish soldier to fight in the Spanish American War. He'd stayed and become a relatively prosperous farmer-manager for, according to Castro, first U.S.-run United Fruit, and then himself. His crop was sugar cane. Thus Castro had gone to good schools in Cuba, including two run by Jesuits—members of a Catholic order founded by a sixteenth century Basque warrior-turned-priest, Ignatius Loyola—where, Castro writes, he learned discipline. Smart, a bit of a hothead, ambitious, and courageous, Castro had become—like many of the well-to-do youths of early twentieth century Cuba—a reactionary drawn to violence and sabotage to effect change. He had joined Chibas's Orthodox Party and participated in foreign revolutions in the Dominican Republic and Columbia—just as Dussaq, it appears, had in Guatemala and possibly other Latin American countries. He'd become noted in Cuba as a fearless fighter—a trait that would have appealed to Dussaq. Although Left of Chibas, sometimes argumentatively so, Castro was a pallbearer and part of the honor guard at Chibas's funeral. It was Chibas's death and Batista's 1952 coup, writes Castro, which launched him into secret planning for his coming Cuban revolution.[6]

But Bazata provides no connections. He probably didn't know what they were. He only writes that Dussaq picked Castro from other possible candidates and was a shadowy figure backing him. Castro himself says in his book, *My Life,* that he depended on unnamed "people" in the Orthodox Party for intelligence on Batista.[7] Dussaq could have been one of those. Castro also certainly would have welcomed a man like Dussaq for what he knew about war—and had accomplished in combat. He had to build an army for his coming revolution, which Dussaq had already done in France, with the Maquis. He was adept at everything Castro would need in the future fight—weapons, assassination, sabotage, and intelligence.

Bazata writes that it was during Dussaq's post-war funk that he came to know his friend better than he ever had before. "I tried to cheer him up, get him away from…this frightening phobia [of freeing Cuba]. He [René] laughed, 'Doug, don't ever worry about me. I will not crack up and it [a free Cuba] will be…We would have dinner'…He was always polite, gallant and interested…We attended sports events and the theater. He was attentive with after-event comments both perceptive and droll. He had a very great sense of humour [sic]. It was then that I learned most about him, for during the 'humours' [sic] he would tell story after story long into the night and into the morning," revealing himself more than Bazata had seen before.

However Castro and Dussaq might have connected, Bazata indicates their contact and communication was mostly indirect, through intermediaries. In all cases, he indicates secrecy, including code names and surreptitious meetings, was maintained. Most of whatever contact they had, Bazata indicates, was done with Dussaq practically anonymous. "René found and selected Fidel [as the leader to support]," he writes. "But Fidel was unaware of his [full involvement]…He was able to persuade, guide and influence from a distance, remaining only partly known as a contributor and enthusiast. He also protected Fidel by removing competitors—the dirty ambitious, etc.—plus actual Fidel enemies. René managed the most difficult role I ever imagined. He got Fidel credit [for presumably positive actions]…strengthened his reputation, blunted blame…But remained [largely] 'just a contributor' which was tantamount to anonymity…He was aware of Fidel's weaknesses [not given but which he deemed] unimportant [for the time being]…I think he would have eliminated Fidel had he felt him 'wrong.'"[8]

With Castro thus tapped, Dussaq pressed hard for Bazata to join him—and with good reason.

Since the war, Bazata, staying in Europe rather than returning home, had done quite well as a clandestine. Leaving OSS with an outstanding record[9]—but staying in the army—he was first assigned to interview high-level German prisoners about D-Day preparations and the 1944 plot to kill Hitler. Such access had taught him much "of the dirt about the war" and given him valuable connections with various clandestine intelligence agencies and spies. But his real job for the Army, as the OSS evolved into the CIA, was spying on the French, whom he admittedly admired. He did that but also given the opportunity, he began working for the French—and any other foreign intelligence agencies he fancied or which offered him clandestine jobs he liked, including the CIA.[10] He'd become almost a man without a country, although he still considered himself an American. In the meantime, he'd grown his Co-Op into a group of some twelve trusted operatives, some ex-OSS, some from other intelligence agencies—all tough, experienced men who could assassinate, kidnap, rescue, infiltrate and exfiltrate persons, especially agents, and successfully accomplish other high-risk missions. He was the group's mysterious contact and organizer, known by the hirers only by a code name.

"I was doing things in the manner I liked—merely saying yes or no when asked to perform some act. I never dealt directly with a contractor [usually through middlemen]. I watched the expensive CIA [effort against communism in the Third World] degenerate to a trickle and smiled sadly while we 12 sailed smartly onward. We contracted to the CIA and all leading agencies and none ever knew [who we were]. They would ask [for a job] from an 'Andres de Faubourg, seldom knowing Andres' full name, nationality or abode. I was Andres or Bertrand or Carlos or just Carl...I was not as idealistic as René. I have little faith in man. I could only weed...quickly...quietly...and usually for a fine fee...Kill the mad dog. That was usually my solution...."[11]

As cover he had gone to school at Paris's Institute Agronomique under the recently (then) passed GI Bill. He had received a degree in Oenology, the science of wine and wine making. That, and his suave, flamboyant personality—when he wanted it—had landed him a job as chief of staff at Mumm's main vineyards at Johannisburg on the French-German border not far from Frankfurt.[12] It was basically a castle with grounds, an ideal location for his and the Co-Ops's clandestine activities throughout Europe, the Mediterranean rim, and behind the Iron Curtain, including the Soviet Union, which he entered on jobs, he writes, many times. Eventually, he would add to that cover by becoming a celebrated artist whose modernist paintings would be touted by Europe's high society jet-setters. For instance, Princess Grace of Monaco and the Duke and Duchess of Windsor each gave him one-man shows. World renowned artist Salvador Dali, with whom he at times hobnobbed, would paint a portrait of him as Don Quixote—all of them apparently unaware of his true enterprise, clandestiny and special ops.[13] A colleague told me he used Mumm's "compost heap" to dispose of bodies.[14]

"What we want," said Dussaq, pressing Bazata to help "are young toughs with experience. We have a long, hard war ahead. A lot of blood will be lost. You and I are getting a bit overripe for sleeping in the rain and eating lizards. We need young men with years still left in their futures." Bazata didn't necessarily agree, not only because he himself was still operating, often like a fearless Jedburgh, but because "René was superbly fit and ideal for rain sleeping and lizard meals. And that's exactly what he [would do] for years to come..." So Dussaq kept after him. While in the army Bazata, because of his early background in the Caribbean, had devised plans for an invasion of Cuba. Dussaq knew that and wanted that expertise. He especially wanted Bazata's skills as a marksman. He knew how good a shot Bazata was. "Will you do it, Lebeau?" he kept asking. "Will you help us fight for our freedom? You know Cuba. You know what has to be done."

It was his friend asking him, a person Bazata admired greatly—and there weren't many of those.

He finally gave in.

"I told him I would teach and train. But I wanted to know only the plans, problems and students, not the country, politics or targets—not from hypocrisy but because such was the number one rule in clandestiny. [The less you know, the safer you are.]"[15]

Reluctantly, writes Bazata, he came on board.

30

Swiss Bank Account

In the next few years, writes Bazata, he would increase his aid to Dussaq. He would secure forged papers for him from "Germany and France— a simple matter." He and the Co-Op would "spring chaps" from prison, possibly, it appears, for the JFK assassination, which had initially set me on this search. Bazata gives no details of such "springings" except that the operations were "reasonable" and "easy."[1] He and Dussaq would meet in Europe, the U.S., and Mexico. They did so, he reveals, traveling under assumed names, faking their presence at expected, unsuspicious locations, while secretly meeting elsewhere.

Eventually, writes Bazata, he would funnel Dussaq weapons, train men in Europe for the assassination—that's what he was writing—and raise considerable cash—not for Dussaq personally, but for the cause. "René took nothing for himself, only expenses. He had a certain [unspecified] outside profession that pays a fairly decent living."[2] The money, it appears, was first for liberating Cuba and helping Castro, but, eventually, for the assassination which would stem from his Cuba passion and require ever larger sums. Dussaq, writes Bazata, had been fundraising since the late 1940s, possibly before. "Early donors" didn't know "his true aims [nor apparently did he—they hadn't yet been fully formed]. Later they would otherwise be persuaded...I know not how...We devised several schemes, Baden-Baden being headquarters for rich Cubans 'living apart.' They 'contributed.'"[3]

Bazata's parenthesis around "contributed" meant "donations" obtained by means other than voluntary—cheating, stealing, intimidation, kidnapping, and torture—methods justified, in Bazata's eyes, either by the "donor's" excessive wealth or how he accumulated it. Sleight of hand at Baden-Baden's casino, he wrote, was "Kid stuff. One of my guys, an amateur [magician]...would pass his hand over [other bets] while making his own...removing chips, or even entire stacks of chips [to be cashed in later]—absolute child's play, impossible in Monte Carlo." If they deemed the mark "evil"—such as an art thief, weapons trafficker, drug dealer, or war profiteer—Bazata had no compunction in using violence to force a "donation." Such was the case with an arms merchant in Monaco. Posing as local thugs and paying the jurisdictional police to ignore their crime, they abducted the man, sliced his scrotum, punched him as he screamed, and got a thirty thousand dollar "contribution"— and possibly more later because of the victim's fear of a repeat.[4]

At some point, he indicates, he and Dussaq went to Switzerland, Dussaq's former home, and opened a secret Swiss bank account. It would keep accounts hidden and enable anonymous payouts. Bazata gives no other details about the account—at least not at this point. And, in fact, as I was to discover, there existed, or still exists, a secret Swiss account in the name of "René Dussaq, AKA René Dussag," thus giving further credence to this part of Bazata's story.[5]

The account came to light as a result of recent international litigation for Nazi Holocaust victims of World War II. The Nazis had stolen much from primarily eventual Jewish concentration camp inmates whom they arrested, imprisoned, and murdered before and during the war. Swiss bank accounts, notoriously private and secure, were used to stash much of the stolen wealth. As a result of a growing international outcry reaching its crescendo in the 1990s—especially by American survivors of victims—investigations were launched. The Swiss resisted and still resist, but eventually an accord was reached after an "Independent Committee of Eminent Persons [ICEP]," headed by Paul A. Volcker, former chairman of the Federal Reserve, determined that some thirty-six thousand secret Swiss bank accounts "probably or possibly" belonged to Holocaust victims whose heirs should be compensated.[6] The Dussaq account, which could be found on an Internet-posted investigation list as late as 2016, is one of those.[7]

Bazata clearly indicates that Dussaq'a account was opened after World War II, probably in the early 1950s. So how could it have gotten on this list which presumably deals only with WWII accounts? The war ended in 1945. The "probably or possibly" designation of the ICEP could explain it. A mistake was made—at least as far as when the account was active. Dussaq's account, which should have remained secret, might have been accidentally put into the Holocaust mix. The committee had to have sifted through enormous numbers of accounts, possibly millions, to come up with its thirty-six thousand "possibles." No one is perfect, especially when dealing with such vast numbers and bureaucracies.

But could it be another René Dussaq?

It could. But René Dussaq is a very uncommon name—except amongst René's family. It's unfortunate the middle name or at least an initial is not provided—if there was one. René's older brother, Maurice, had a son he named René E. Dussaq. René E.—René A.'s nephew—is now an international sales manager for a large packing company. He wrote me in 2013: "I don't know anything about Uncle having a Swiss account. I did have one in the early 1990s but closed it 10 years ago." It's understandable that the ICEP might have mistakenly mixed an account opened shortly after World War II—for instance in the early 1950s. But I doubt it would have looked at accounts from the 1990s. That's some forty years later.

And why would Dussaq open an account in his name? Wasn't the point to be secretive?

The only other "René Dussaq" I could find was apparently René A.'s uncle or grandfather, listed only as "René Dussaq" in scattered documents, newspaper stories, and ancestral archives. He was French and apparently was one of the Dussaqs—if not *the* Dussaq—who settled in Cuba around the time of the Spanish-American War and founded—or at least was part of—the Dussaq family businesses there. By the early twentieth century, he was a recognized Cuban business leader, written about in maritime journals as an agent of seagoing ship insurance and travel, and a backer of notable ventures.[8] He was important enough to the U.S. State Department that the American embassy in Cuba, in a dispatch titled, "Political Characteristics of Mr. René Dussaq, Havana, Cuba," reported home that he died on May 27, 1942. Was this Dussaq the owner of the mysterious Swiss account? It's possible. But my attempts to learn more from the Swiss, the WWII Holocaust account officials, and others have yielded nothing. Books are closed. Privacy is cited.

Meanwhile, back in 1950s Cuba—specifically on July 26, 1953—Fidel Castro, in a brazenly fearless act, led a small army of revolutionaries, estimated variously as from 80 to 130 fighters, in an attack against the Moncada Barracks, a Batista government military fort near Santiago on the southern tip of Cuba. It contained more than one thousand soldiers. The attackers hoped to get the fort's approximate three thousand weapons. But the attack failed. Most of the rebels, novices at such action, were killed or wounded. Castro escaped into the countryside for a few days as Batista's troops tortured and executed many of those they caught. Castro and a small band with him were eventually tracked down, tried, and sent to prison on the Isle of Pines in the Caribbean Sea south of Havana. The trial, in which Castro, a lawyer by then, acted as his own defense attorney, rallied many Cubans to his cause and exposed the brutality of the Batista regime.

But prison was rough.

"Fidel had a hard time," writes Bazata. "Cuban jails are often totally inhuman. I speak from the closest observation—having once done a little time there myself. But Fidel was/is strong. He matured while in jail"—a judgment verified by Castro himself in *Fidel: My Early Years*.

Castro wrote that his cell was little more than a dank cave. He wrote and studied classics of revolution there, like Victor Hugo's *Les Miserables*, illuminated only by candlelight. When storms hit, he was drenched. "I did what I could to protect my books by putting them inside the suitcase and covering it with a blanket...the bed got soaked; the floor was flooded; and the cold, wet air penetrated everywhere. Wet and chilled to the bone," he persevered.[9]

The ordeal, he writes, strengthened his resolve and prepared him for the struggle ahead.

Then, on May 15, 1955, after Castro had spent nearly a year and a half in confinement, Batista, usually cunning and ruthless, did something uncharacteristic (historians might call it stupid in light of Castro's eventual 1959 triumph). In an attempt to gain favor with the Cuban public clamoring for Castro's release, the dictator granted Castro and the others imprisoned because of the Moncada attack a pardon.

By early July, they were all out of jail.

Castro, free but harassed by Batista, wasted little time exiting Cuba and going to Mexico, a traditional haven for runaway revolutionaries,[10] where he resumed plotting Batista's overthrow. Bazata writes that Dussaq, "who saw to all things," helped him in the move. He doesn't say how, only, "Instantly René and Fidel and a tight band of his followers in Mexico went straight to work. They continued as if they had never left their underground war."[11]

By this time—late summer 1955—Dussaq, home from Germany, was settled back in Los Angeles. It was only a few years after his known secret trip, or trips, into Mexico for the FBI. He was a short distance from the Mexican border. Even his wife Charlotte hadn't known his whereabouts until informed of them by the FBI. Mysterious travel was one of his fortes. He'd apparently broken with the Bureau under still mysterious circumstances. Did they know something not publicized? Was he making trips to Mexico again—perhaps as Bazata alleges—as a double, even triple, agent for a variety of intelligence agencies, like the CIA, but secretly working for or with Castro, or elements helping him?

Almost immediately after reaching Mexico, Castro began planning an invasion of Cuba. He was seeking help. He met Ernesto "Che" Guevara, a medical doctor and traveling revolutionary. The two meshed and Che joined Castro's expatriate forces. Guevara was from Argentina, Dussaq's birthplace. Was there any connection? Bazata doesn't give any. Shortly, Castro began training an invasion army at secret sites outside Mexico City. Was this what Bazata "sprang" men from prison for? Who they were and where they were sent is never clear. Given the need for military expertise, Dussaq would have been a perfect trainer. But the only military trainer mentioned by Castro or his biographers that I've been able to discover was a Cuban veteran of the Spanish Civil War—not Dussaq.[12]

By fall, only a few months after he had arrived, Castro began a tour of the U.S. to garner support and, of course, raise money. It is known he toured the East Coast—New York, Tampa, New Jersey and Connecticut. The American press praised him, publicizing his stops and pronouncements. He was a hero; Batista, the villain. But what did Castro do in secret during that tour? He would have been foolish not to tap Los Angeles, which had, after Miami, one of the world's largest Cuban émigré populations. But if he had, it's doubtful he would have exposed Dussaq who, Bazata says, was aiding him with arms and other illegal supplies.

Not until early 1956 does Bazata again put Dussaq and Castro together. Around that time, he writes, Dussaq and he met at an unidentified location. Dussaq wanted information from Bazata about invading Cuba. Bazata reiterates Dussaq knew Bazata had studied the problem during World War II. Then in February, in celebration of Bazata's forty-fifth birthday, the two traveled to Mexico and met Castro—Bazata for the first time. "No big deal," he says. He had "no real impression" of the Cuban revolutionary; apparently they met only briefly. Bazata remained anonymous, he stresses, "as was always my habit…mumbling or mispronouncing" whatever name he used.[13] He relates nothing of Dussaq's interaction with Castro. But that was soon to be revealed.

31

Sailing with Castro

Sometime during the summer of 1956, writes Bazata, he and Dussaq met in Washington, D.C. René informed him that Castro was going to invade Cuba. Having advised him on the matter, Bazata wasn't surprised. But then Dussaq told him he, Dussaq, was participating in the invasion.

"I strenuously objected. If Castro is slain or captured," he argued, Dussaq could "get another Fidel." He had a roster of them, Bazata reminded. "But if you [are killed], then what happens? You are the soul of this movement.[1] [If you're eliminated] it's back to the Sugar Barons."

No, said Dussaq, "We won't fail...Our plan is perfect, the men are perfect. I have to go to demonstrate my total devotion to the...active, physical element, to clear away those stares that say, who is this mysterious guy who flits around yakking but never does anything," never "risks even a finger."

Dussaq had to prove himself to overcome the suspicions of the doubters.

He added a complication. "I can't be certain but I think we've been infiltrated." He'd narrowed down the suspects to several who might have learned of the secret planning. "As an outside operator, I intend to catch these bastards."

To do so might reveal his "covers," warned Bazata—"CIA, MI6" (British intelligence) and other agencies Bazata believed Dussaq had infiltrated and was spying on as a double, even triple, agent for Cuban independence. If they learned the truth they'd target him.

"Possible," said Dussaq. But it would be a "fair price." He'd be careful. "Don't worry, Lebeau, I am wide-eyed" but "I have to go." One more thing, he added: "We require a great rifle shot—you."

It was another in the continuing invitations to get Bazata directly involved.

Again, he balked. "No thanks, René. But I don't want you [killed] so here's some advice." He speculated the informants might be "Germans" whom he presumably had funneled to Dussaq. Were these the men he'd sprung from prison?

Dussaq, notes Bazata, reacted with an uncharacteristic "Damn!" Apparently he hadn't considered that possibility.

Bazata offered a solution: Batista probably knew the plans. He had good spies and may have penetrated Castro's secrecy. At the last minute, he advised, change the invasion date and location. It would catch the enemy off guard. "Make some big speeches" about leaving in four weeks, but in reality make it two weeks. That's enough time for essentials. But don't tell the Germans.

The plan was risky, Bazata acknowledged. The chances for mistakes increased. But "you fuck everyone, including Batista."

Dussaq "seemed to buy it" and "was soon off."[2]

■ ■ ■

Leading what he now called "The 26 July Movement"—patriotically re-labeling the Moncada disaster—Castro launched for Cuba from Mexican shores near Vera Cruz. It was November 26, 1956. He did so in an aging, sixty-foot yacht christened *Granma* with some eighty or more fighters packed in and on it. The *Granma* was built in 1943 to carry only twelve.

The launch was at 2 a.m. Winter storms were brewing in the Gulf of Mexico. They had some 1,200 miles to go. Within hours, giant waves were pounding the vessel, drenching the revolutionaries not only in bone-chilling water, but fear and vomit. Many of the men on board had never been to sea. Almost all became seasick with no antidote on board.

Fear was personal, debilitating.

In the open sea, as water crashed in incessantly for days, they almost sank several times. A man accidentally was hurled overboard by the rough seas and believed lost. No one could find him in the swells. But Castro wouldn't abandon the search. Circling, he was eventually spotted—and alive! The slow speed of the vessel put the invaders days behind schedule. They had little food. Critical coordination with a planned uprising in Santiago was lost. There was no landing to inspire the nation. Those who continued with the uprising were caught and killed or imprisoned. When the invaders finally beached in Oriente Province, December 2, they had to slog through hours of mangrove before reaching dry land—a problem for which they hadn't planned. The slogging rubbed their booted feet raw and caused them to abandon needed ammunition and supplies.

Then the already dire situation really deteriorated.

Before leaving, Castro had publicly boasted that he was returning to Cuba. Did that alert Batista? Or had they not purged all the spies? In any case, Batista knew they were coming. His search planes and a coast guard ship found the beached *Granma* and attacked it. This sent the invaders, who were alerted, fleeing to sugarcane fields, which became killing fields. One of their own, acting as an advance guide, betrayed them to troops hunting the area. By then, having fought sporadically, they had little ammunition left. By December 5, most of the rebels had been killed by arriving planes or soldiers. Only a small group, evading the hunters, reached the mountains. But miraculously they would eventually grow into the force that would overthrow Batista in 1959.

The above is from a variety of sources—principally Castro's and Che Guevara's memoirs, as well as other accounts.[3] They differ in details, and, in fact, there is still mystery about precisely what happened. Even the exact number of invaders is uncertain. The numbers range from eighty men to over one hundred—which leads me to Bazata's next point. He writes Dussaq was among them. He was injured but escaped.

As the debacle ensued, Bazata writes he was "nervously back in safe Germany"—apparently not informed about what was actually happening—but "rooting" for René, who, he learned, "had it very bad" at the invasion. "He was wounded, etc., but recovered and slipped out to Guatemala," one of the countries closest across the gulf, "and then to Mexico and Paris."[4]

How exactly Bazata knows this, he doesn't disclose. But presumably he learned it later from Dussaq. It is very hard to track Dussaq's whereabouts at this time. There is scattered information that gives clues. Prudential, for whom he worked and which might have pertinent knowledge, will not help. Those few still alive who knew Dussaq at that time can't pinpoint dates. But if newspaper reports are accurate, Dussaq had a reasonable window in which to fit this adventure. A *Los Angeles Times* article, dated November 9, 1956, informs he was scheduled to address a local women's club on "espionage" on November 14, 1956.[5] But I could find no follow up story about him actually making the speech. Even if he did, he would have had almost two weeks afterwards to slip into Mexico and join the invaders. And following the Cuban landing, there is no available information on his whereabouts until seven months later—July 1957—when, interestingly, a letter from his files shows him dealing with the veteran's administration on payment for a knee injury.[6]

Checking a list of "Granma Expeditionaries" in Che Guevara's *Episodes of the Cuban Revolutionary War*, Dussaq's name does not appear. But is that unexpected? He probably wouldn't have used his real name and those in power in Castro's army, including Castro himself, would probably not have wanted him to be known. In any case, such rosters are scarce. Che's was the only list I found in public references. Similarly, escaping to Guatemala seems especially logical for Dussaq. He has been rumored to have participated in the Guatemalan revolution. He may have had contacts there. Guatemala was also where his older brother, Maurice, living in Cuba with his family, would relocate following Castro's 1959 takeover.

Similarly, escaping to Paris, rather than Mexico, is not as illogical as it sounds. If injured, he probably would not have wanted to return to Los Angeles and have to face questions. In Paris he could have recovered in relative secrecy.

■ ■ ■

Later, in 1957, writes Bazata—after the Granma failure and as Castro was safely in the mountains rebuilding his eventual conquering army—he heard from Dussaq, "who wasn't very [happy]." There's a possibility this may have been when Dussaq was recuperating. In any case, Dussaq, writes Bazata, told him that the rebels, as would be expected, now "needed [more] money, medicine, arms, clothing, especially boots." Bazata and the Co-Op obliged. They returned either to the same Monte Carlo arms dealer they had earlier robbed, or to a new war profiteer. Whichever, the arms dealer tapped this time had valuable paintings in his mansion. "We helped ourselves, sold them below decks and gave René the full take," then, he adds, "had the fun, joy and relaxation of replacing them"—a trick using Bazata's artistic talents.

Although he took himself seriously as an artist—and enjoyed the work immensely—Bazata's painting was also a cover for clandestine activities. For instance, a canvas, he explains, was an ideal hiding place for drugs. He would conceal the substance behind thick paint on a canvas. It would thus be transported to a buyer even by respected, but unknowing, art dealers. He was so good at abstract that he'd already earned a reputation among Europe's elite as an ascending modern artist. Self-taught, he was perfectly positioned for success by virtue of connection to Mumm, one of the continent's acknowledged "Great Houses." Already his oils adorned the walls of some of Europe's richest residents and eventually would hang in French and English museums and the Monaco casino.[7]

Unknown to all but a few, however, was his talent for faking.

"I had already painted over 20 Van Goghs, one Cezanne for a great Paris jet setter and several Matisses," he writes about the job for Dussaq. Apparently, following the theft, Bazata had painted excellent fakes of the stolen paintings. Then they'd arranged with the police, for part of the take, to return the fakes to the grateful profiteer as the "recovered" paintings while selling the originals on the black market. Such chicanery was rampant on the continent. "To this day," writes Bazata, "I believe the four [stolen] originals were phony. So it was phony being slipped in for phony"—his apparent justification for the crime. "Neat, yes? Anyway, all went well."[8]

But it wouldn't remain so.

32

The Scorpions Are Waiting

Around 1959—Bazata is not clear about the year—the Co-Op suffered a crippling loss. Five of the group's members were killed in a "car crash...obviously arranged."[1] They believed it was murder. "That left four plus myself." As a major mercenary group, "we were pretty-much done." The remaining mercenaries met somberly at a restaurant in Aix-en-Provence in the south of France and after paying respects to their lost colleagues, vowed "one last job—kill those responsible." It took "6 weeks," writes Bazata, but they found each one— "French" or possibly "Corsican" enemies—and took their revenge.[2]

The death of his colleagues was a blow to Bazata. But he was basically a loner anyway.

"For me, the strength of courage is to do it alone...go into an unknown totally unsung, unrewarded, unapplauded." He called it "beautiful courage." The "true clandestine" is "always alone with his target"— "no [Hollywood cameras], no audience, no thanks—nothing but total self-singularity." He liked it that way—spur-of-the-moment, live by your wits and skills. Get on with it. "I could spend long periods alone—at sea, in prison, gardening, soldiering." And he scrupulously obeyed the rules. "Remember to keep silence, Kid. Play it dumb and dizzy." Double-talk and triple-talk were his defenses, especially if he accidentally slipped up. "Did I say that? Goodness, I meant to say this. No—that...Be careful, Kid...The scorpions are waiting."[3]

■ ■ ■

Also in 1959—in the year's first dawning moments—Castro was victorious. His revolutionaries entered Havana while New Year's celebrations were happening. Batista fled. Bazata had reason to suppose Dussaq would be satisfied. But he was wrong. If anything, Dussaq became even more motivated.

Things weren't as Dussaq wanted them.

Meeting clandestinely, says Bazata, Dussaq informed him that Fidel had his problems. It was becoming clear he was a communist. Dussaq was not—at least that's the way it appears. Dussaq, his wife Charlotte told me, if anything, was mainly a "constitutionalist." He mostly championed individual rights. Bazata writes he did not believe in the communist "equality"[4]—everyone is the same, everyone gets the same—that Castro was espousing. What he passionately believed in was equal opportunity—and the right to use it free from outside interference. Now, he fumed, not only was Fidel courting communism—a minor problem—but, worse, the U.S. was stepping up its interference in Cuban affairs.

"René was aware of Fidel's weaknesses," writes Bazata. They were not so important to him "at this time." What *was* important to him was that U.S. President Dwight Eisenhower, whose CIA had already engineered in 1953 the overthrow of Guatemala's socialist government, had now in response to Castro's turn authorized the invasion of Cuba.[5] He knew CIA intentions long before the public because of his penetration of the agency.[6] "We can't conquer the U.S." Bazata says Dussaq lamented.

Cuba was too small. What chance would it have? "Why can't they leave us alone...Freedom is for all men," not just Americans.[7]

Bazata himself had lost a friend in the Guatemala coup.[8]

They discussed remedies, some of which made Bazata leery. He didn't want to get more involved: "1. Stop local incursions. 2. Seal off infiltration and penetration. 3. Protect the leader [Castro] and [other] leaders. 4. Elicit help" (as Dussaq did from him) from other nations, "like the Soviet Union just as the U.S. [had done] in World War II...You use weapons [at hand] in war. You are not required to love these weapons." And 5: "Call attention to the inconsistencies of America"—trumpeting that it's for democracy but manipulating democracies for its own benefit.[9]

Bazata says they met clandestinely four times in 1960. At one point during their discussions, the possibility of assassinating Eisenhower arose. "René took a violent turn, as he said, of necessity," writes Bazata. The idea was to use assassination as a warning to America that its leaders were on an "evil" path—meddling, bullying, and depriving Cubans of their right to self-determination. Dussaq believed such a drastic action would shock Americans, basically good and repentant, into realizing their country's "folly." But he quickly nixed the idea in regard to Eisenhower, who he said was too much a "kindly grandfather figure," too loved. Ike's public persona was a façade, they both believed. Guatemala proved that—as did much they knew about him from their experience in the war.[10] But, because the American people saw him sympathetically—even heroically—killing him would backfire. Assassination in Dussaq's mind, writes Bazata, would only be effective in changing America against a leader who was clearly wrong and evil—someone, he believed, like up-and-coming John F. Kennedy, who Dussaq, according to Bazata, was by then already predicting would be the next president (aided by his obsessed father, Joe Kennedy, who was determined to rule America and thus dominate the world through his sons).

John Kennedy, Joe's second son, was, by 1959, almost president already. A handsome returning war hero in 1945, he was quick on his feet, witty, and rich. The monetary demands of running for office were not a problem for him. His father was underwriting his campaigns. A Democrat,

"JFK" had been elected to the House of Representatives from Massachusetts in 1947. In 1953, he'd graduated to the Senate, a more prestigious and
visible office. In 1960, he represented a new, "fresher" type of politician,
young, vibrant, more relevant—a new breed—a welcome change from the
older, stodgier—however beloved—World War II figures like Eisenhower.
But the presidential election of 1960 was close. The Republican candidate,
Richard Nixon, may have won the popular vote (it's debatable) but he lost
the vital electoral vote that actually decides presidential elections. Illinois,
especially Chicago, was crucial. Run by Democrats, some historians
believe that Joe Kennedy bought the Chicago votes, possibly with the help
of the Mafia. Kennedy himself would joke about it in private.[11] At forty-
three and succeeding seventy-two-year-old Eisenhower, he would be at
inauguration the youngest U.S. president ever elected.

"The [Kennedy] campaign had...assembled the finest, slickest organization in the history of democracy," writes Bazata. The press and polls
"portrayed a fine family"—a wonderful candidate—"but not one mention of what K stood for or how he would achieve it. René kept showing
me these tear-jerkers"—the press fawning over Kennedy—how great he
was and would be for the country. "Did he feel I was wavering," tiring
of what he was telling me, "reticent?...We were both clandestines" both
of the same outlook. "Yet...of one thing I was certain. René would kill
any man who stood in his way to stop his life-long dream"—and not
only him [Bazata] but Kennedy. The fearful specter of assassinating the
next president scared Bazata. "René knew K would be president." He'd
known "this way back in 1948 or he'd started to know it...Just as Joe
planned the political overthrow of America, René was planning the
overthrow of [Joe's] evil way...Joe would enslave us all, turn all of us
into zombies by manipulation...deception...by his unique power and
brilliance," his "indomitable will...His boys were well suited to his
assigned slavery. But unbeknownst to Joe, he had a very special student
tracking his every move"—Dussaq—"So let Joe show it all...bring forth
his evil fruit...[Joe's] Frankenstein would be caught in the ultimate act."
Dussaq, he writes, "talked this way [about the Kennedys] for years before
I even could grasp it all."[12]

At one point, Bazata asked, "René, are you trying to convince me to devote my life to [changing] America [like] you are [trying to change] Cuba?" What Bazata meant was, he says, are you looking for a U.S. revolt, even to kill the new U.S. president? He was startled when Dussaq said "Yes," nothing more, calmly and expectantly. "I had expected...No"— and explanations that would allow him to exit Dussaq's obsession. But it didn't happen. Dussaq, in what Bazata relates was his calm but persuasive manner, talked of their similarities, their brotherhood, their shared outlook—all compelling arguments to Bazata. "I sat dumbfounded." Had René "catalyzed me to a form bordering on treason...I sipped [my drink] in very considerable gulps...Was I beginning to approve of disposing of my president other than by election?...elections that all of us know [are] subject to infinite questions, doubts and deceptions...Or was I so hardened...by prior activities," for instance, caring about little, having no real cause or ambition, so much so that it left him aimless and without purpose? "In fact, what the hell was I doing, slipping about, leading several lives randomly aimed at [exterminating] random shits—[terrorists and such] not even worth the risk."[13]

He agreed with Dussaq.

He would continue to help him—even in this drastic turn.

At some point during or closely after these discussions, Dussaq told him an alarming fact. There already was a plan to assassinate JFK if he continued Eisenhower's intentions of invading Cuba. It was called "Hydra-K." The organization and money to do the assassination was already in place and growing. Then he made a strange request of Bazata. In order to eliminate the need for such drastic action—and in order for Bazata to be "right with his country"—he wanted Bazata to warn U.S. officials of what would happen if they continued their meddling. It was a last-ditch attempt to avoid the worst—a kind of clandestine diplomacy.[14]

Bazata accepted. It was risky but better than what he'd expected. He had contacts in the spy world who he thought could get the message to those who needed to hear it.

33

"Sincerely, Luigi"

I f the word "legend" applies to any CIA agent, Lucien Conein is certainly in the running. "Black Luigi" or "Three fingers Lou"—he was missing several—is perhaps the most storied agent in true modern spy lore. He's as close as they come to a two-fisted movie action hero. Amazon alone lists his CIA exploits in 186 nonfiction books. Tough, shrewd, deadly, Conein, who died in 1998, lived a life as swashbuckling and full of danger as any fictional clandestine. His legend includes fighting in the French Foreign Legion, parachuting into World War II heroics behind German lines, Cold War missions against the Soviet Union, and the scary CIA "Phoenix" program during the Vietnam War. Phoenix was an effort to intimidate North Vietnamese spies. They were hurled alive and screaming from high-up helicopters and otherwise terrorized.

The Left scorns Conein as a cold-blooded assassin and unbridled mayhem-maker—an Ugly American who enjoyed the destruction he wrought. The Right praises him as a righteous, needed warrior the country was lucky to have.

The truth is probably somewhere in the middle.

Conein was a close advisor-enabler from the Kennedy Administration to the rebel South Vietnamese generals who murdered their president, Ngo Dinh Diem, on November 2, 1963 —three weeks before JFK himself was assassinated. He had jumped into Nazi-held France to steer resistance fighters killing Germans after D-Day. He was awarded the DFC and Silver Star for these exploits. After the war, he helped the French against the Viet Minh, the early Viet Cong, and joined the newly-formed CIA, where he ran spies and missions behind the Iron Curtain, a dangerous business which saw many on both sides die. He was a hard drinker and carouser who, like Bazata, was not intimidated by rank or position. He said what he felt regardless of the consequences, and part of the reason he's so legendary is that he was summoned before Congress regarding his Vietnam War activities and thus his exploits were introduced to the public.

He was a key military advisor to the Shah of Iran during the Shah's glory days, and eventually leaving the CIA—or being booted out—(the official record is unclear)—he would join in 1972 the Nixon Administration's newly-created Drug Enforcement Agency (the DEA), where he became its notorious "Dirty Tricks" boss. Conein headed a unit that under its cloak of official immunity committed acts in pursuit of drug dealers that could land ordinary citizens in jail or worse.

Conein was not ordinary. And he was a good friend of Bazata's.

They had met at Ft. Benning during WWII when both were Army instructors. They had much in common. Big and tough, Conein enjoyed a fight. It's an understatement to say he took chances. He'd been born in Paris, but at age five had been sent to an aunt in Kansas City, where he grew up. He spoke French fluently. He'd joined French forces fighting the Germans before France fell. That's possibly the origin of the French Foreign Legion stories. Somehow he'd gotten back to the U.S., where his language skills and fighting ability got him into the OSS, where he joined other recruits like Bazata. They trained together in England as Jedburghs—with

Dussaq in that mix—performed hazardous missions in Occupied France and elsewhere, and were reunited in Germany after the war when Conein had transitioned to the CIA and Bazata worked with the Co-Op. Conein had probably given Bazata and the Co-Op CIA jobs. They spent a lot of time together. Conein, according to CIA documents I have, stayed with Bazata on occasions at the Mumm estate.

They respected each other.

When Dussaq had asked Bazata to warn the U.S. about Hydra-K, Bazata, careful not to name Dussaq but use the alias "Paul," had decided Conein would be the person he would approach—the agent who would get the message to those who needed to hear it. Conein was at that time advising Iran's Shah (the country's monarch and leader) on military matters, and a document in Bazata's secret papers confirms the Hydra-K contact.

Dated "July 1971, Mclean," Conein writes in a memo I found amongst Bazata's secret papers: "Baz: This will confirm...our mutual records pertaining to the assassination of President John F. Kennedy in Dallas, Texas on November 22, 1963...You referred to this assassination as 'The Execution' noting always that your source of information was an anonymous 'Paul,' whom you obviously knew extremely well. You also referred to this tragedy as 'Operation Hydra-K.'"

Conein then mentioned five times that Bazata had warned him of Hydra-K and what he'd done with the warnings.

"You wrote to me in either very very [sic] late 1959 or the earliest days of 1960; to Teheran; my then current station...[Conein's periods, as are all in this declaration] I, as noted, passed the word; so notifying you by mail to Johannisberg, Germany; chez les Mumms...Next; we met at the downtown Prunier for Oysters on Christmas Eve [1960 or 1961 according to Bazata's diaries], where again you made this violence known to me. Again, I passed the word and wrote confirmation to you at Brat's/Madelaine [apparently the Mumm mansion again as "Madelaine" was Baron Mumm's wife's first name; a woman with whom Bazata was at one time allegedly having an affair].

"Our third such correspondence came from you to me while stationed in Saigon...You seemed 'alarmed' that official contact to you was very bizarre...I did as you asked; so writing to you chez Brat/Madelaine...The last exchange took place via a letter (coded as agreed) from you to me while still in Saigon...This was about mid-July of 1963...In this note you mentioned a 'fixed' date...Throughout these four notices; the plans were altered considerably; but number four gave out a final solution to the plan 'Hydra-K' of your Paul...Of course I specifically recall this fourth note; as it coincided with the peaking of the task assigned me here in Saigon [liaison with the generals who murdered Diem]...I therefore invited you to come out 'earliest'...for full discussions; possibly with superior participation? You agreed! That was it until we met again in Paris; January of 1964...when both slayings had been accomplished...The lengthy parallels of our careers struck me harder than ever before [probably meaning how they both are involved in major assassinations]...You will certainly recall our most vivid conversations at that time! You will well recall, also, our concern for each other!"

By this time (1964), John Kennedy had been murdered and the two of them, according to this memo, were on record with authorities as having known about plans prior to the act. That was damning, and they apparently decided they needed the memo for their protection, intending to confirm that all they were doing was trying to stop the assassination.

This Hydra-K document is hard evidence of what Bazata alleges. There is very little other "outside" documentation that supports his story—although one can argue lack of documentation would be expected in such a secret and monumental conspiracy.

Further, there is independent evidence that the memo itself is authentic, and that is another reason to present it here in its entirety.

Lou Conein is dead. He cannot be questioned. But there is much newly-released material about him that has now been declassified by the CIA. The thumbnail portrait I've written about him at the beginning of this chapter comes partially from some of that. And while at the archives, I saw numerous documents with his signature on them. In my opinion, based on more than ten such documents, the signature on the "July 1971 Mclean" is authentic.

Conein wrote it.

Also, while at the archives, I found independent documentary evidence that the memo is authentic. It's a letter from Conein to the Veterans Administration dated September 1977.

Bazata, as is common for most combat veterans, had to verify his injuries that resulted from service in order to get later treatment and compensation. In an effort to help Bazata with that chore, Conein, a retired lieutenant colonel himself, wrote to the administration: "I definitely recall several instances [in which Bazata mentioned war wounds] as Bazata and I had some important and memorable business to attend to. I refer here to correspondence in late 1959 while I was posted in Teheran...to a Christmas Eve dinner we both participated in in Paris in 1960. To some vital correspondence we shared in 1962 while I was stationed in Saigon...."

He wisely does not inform the administration what that "important and memorable business" was. Why bring on the wolves when it's not needed? He continues instead about Bazata's medical claims that he says were discussed or noted during these contacts. But given the dates, places, and urgency he expresses, it certainly sounds like he's referring to Bazata's Hydra-K warnings.

34

Settling Scores

Lucien Conein wasn't the only person Bazata writes he contacted about Hydra-K. He warned other officials about the possible assassination.

"I dribbled out info to several [persons] of different countries...I contacted six highly placed CIA chaps, including 2 directors...I got through to very important Germans, French, English and Russian [contacts]...A few doubted me ... a few failed to grasp the message" or understand his confusing "double" and "triple talk." All, he says, reacted with disturbing silence or inaction. He was running "astronomical" risks, he writes. Not only was he making himself a target for government reprisal, but "René's great loose consortium," members of which were purposely not informed about this René-originated part of the plot, would be incensed to learn what he was doing. "Here was a loud-mouth"—me—"calling their signals. Stop him! Shut the noisy bastard up. If they could target [Kennedy] they certainly could target...Bazata."

He contacted Frank G. Wisner, a Mississippi-born former OSS vet like himself, who, at the time—roughly 1959 to 1962—headed the CIA's anti-communist clandestine operations from a headquarters in England. An Olympic hurdler and New York lawyer, Wisner had been sent by the OSS to Turkey during World War II. After joining the newly-created CIA after the war, he had worked first in Romania and then in Germany, where Bazata was headquartered. One of the problems for Bazata and Conein was that both were considered mavericks by the CIA. Disdainful of authority, they were not part of the predominantly Ivy League-educated, Eastern establishment, anti-communist insiders who ran the agency. Wisner "considered Baz both odd and dangerous," writes Bazata about himself. He felt the same about Wisner, calling him "an American menace." Why is not stated. But Wisner, to the "[detriment] of America…did not pass along the several 'bombs' Baz presented."[1]

Wisner, who retired in 1962, died in 1965—his death officially ruled a suicide. He shot himself with one of his son's shotguns. The story goes that following mental problems that led to his retirement, he became progressively depressed over the morally questionable acts and ambiguities of the secret operations he ran.[2]

Bazata believed he was murdered.[3]

Did his death have anything to do with what he'd learned from Bazata?

Answer unknown.

Other CIA officials Bazata mentions contacting about the warning were Tracy Barnes, a close associate of Wisner, and Allen W. Dulles, former head of OSS operations in Switzerland during the war and the CIA's director from 1953 to 1961.

Barnes had practiced law with Wisner in New York. During the war he'd joined the OSS and, like Bazata and Dussaq, parachuted into occupied France in 1944. He had been awarded a silver star for the action. Following the war, at Wisner's request, he had joined the CIA, where he'd participated in the coup that overthrew Guatemala's president, Jacobo Arbenz, as well as other CIA operations in Latin America. Apparently Bazata and Barnes were friends. He writes that they had "dealings since 1943 continuing until Barnes' death" in 1972. He makes terse reference to Barnes being "vital" but with no explanation.

With Dulles the contact was clearer. Bazata writes he "personally telephoned" the director to tell him about the plot in both "New York City" and "Washington DC" in "1959 and 1960–1961" but was "rebuffed." "'What do you want?'" the director asked "in a decidedly angry tone." The conversation, indicates Bazata, went no further.

Another contact was columnist and author Stewart Alsop, a political analyst and writer for major American newspapers and magazines. Alsop was also an OSS veteran who had parachuted into France. He regarded Bazata among the unique and rare "crazy brave"—a reference to his authentic fearlessness.[4] Bazata writes they had a "relationship" for "30 years" but concerning Hydra-K he kept the columnist at a "necessary distance." Apparently when Bazata had inquired about good CIA contacts, Alsop had referred him to his friend and colleague, Tom Braden, another OSS veteran and CIA agent working at the time with Wisner and Dulles. Braden and Alsop co-authored the highly-regarded *Sub Rosa: The O.S.S. and American Espionage*, and Braden, after leaving the CIA, would eventually participate in CNN's "Crossfire" and author *Eight is Enough*, the book behind the hugely-popular 1970s television show of the same name.

But Bazata and Braden clashed. "Stew nagged me," writes Bazata, "'Give [Braden] a chance.' I did—many." Using his paintings as cover, he writes that he told Braden to pretend he wanted a canvas. They set up a code-phrase exchange on the pretext of buying one. Bazata then sent him, in the canvas, painted-over information about Hydra-K. But "he was just too damn dull," writes Bazata. Braden didn't pick up on the double or triple talk or, worse, purposely disregarded the messages. "I never heard from him again." It made Bazata mad. "That canvas contained one of the biggest pre-scoops in American history...poor, dumb CIA. No wonder Colby [former CIA director William E., a reformer of the agency] inherited such a tangle."[5]

Later, around 1969, when Bazata decided to exit his activities on the continent and return to America for good, he writes that Alsop told him,

"Stay alive, friend—go back to Europe." His life, Alsop indicated, was in danger. The implication was it involved, among other things, the Alsop-Braden connection. But this is never explained. Bazata says he brushed it off and had a chance confrontation with Braden as the ex-CIA agent prepared to deliver a speech at an institution. Bazata was at the event with Colby, his longtime friend. Braden came over to talk with Colby and greeted Bazata, "Hiya Bazzzz." Bazata, still smarting from their failed liaison, shot back, "You're a coward and a liar." Braden, apparently shaken by the confrontation, was subsequently a "fiasco on the lectern"—so much so, says Bazata, that Colby asked, "What's wrong with Tom?" Bazata replied, "I fixed him for you. I gave him an L-tablet [suicide pill]."[6]

Meanwhile—back in the pre-assassination period—falling flat with his attempts to warn U.S. officials, Bazata writes he continued aiding Dussaq, forwarding important intelligence to him and handling his bank transactions.

Basically, the financing for Hydra-K remains a giant, unsolved mystery. Bazata indicates the money came from a "complicated consortium" of mostly Americans and Cubans "meshed into innumerable cutouts"— whatever that means. Some in the consortium, he writes, did not know its ultimate purpose. Were they supporting him just to help bullied Cuba, or perhaps Castro, whom they admired? Whatever their understanding, Dussaq ultimately raised, according to Bazata, approximately twenty-five milliion dollars, almost all of which he applied to Hydra-K activities, keeping only for himself the bare minimums needed. "He told me he could have had $250 million—it was that easy," writes Bazata. But "he refused a penny more because of caution." He was afraid of "slip ups when stakes get too high."[7]

And there *were* slip ups.

In one, a trusted courier to Marseilles absconded with $500,000. The money apparently was consortium-raised to be turned over to Bazata for deposit in the Swiss account (or accounts). "It took René three months —with the help of you know who," writes Bazata, "to locate this 'nice' kid…The main fear was what this ape might say? He didn't know much [except that] a huge U.S. company was paying some low-level guy in Marseilles for some low-level dirt. Was it enough to trigger an investigation?...I spent approximately 21 days full time on that shit using [the Co-Op], the French police, the Swiss police—all with under the table money...Altogether it cost René nearly $200,000 to get back [the $500,000]—a net of $300,000."[8]

And the courier wasn't the only worry. Apparently he had two accomplices connected to the Swiss banks who were going to help him steal the money—"all three buried at sea," writes Bazata, indicating he had a part in their demise—"one in Lake Zurich," a second "off Hawaii," and a third "off Florida." They could run but not hide. He was not, however, he writes, involved in the Hawaii or Florida killings—"only as a listener...But I wander into irrelevant detail." The point was things "got thick and sticky."[9]

Twice that he knew of, writes Bazata, "guys tried to kill René. In one attempt, he "got shot in a kidney causing much discomfort." "And he was stabbed in the back three times...The first occurred in Paris so I had the opportunity of visiting him in the American Hospital" where, he writes, Dussaq stayed for three weeks. "I visited him twice daily...He recovered at a friend's house in Southwest France—a Basque friend who remained unknown to me although I drove him down to Saint-Jean-de-Luz," a French Basque seaside resort on the Atlantic. René "never confided the whos, whys or wheres of the stabbings. There were many other similar obstacles..."[10]

The Basque connection would coincide with Dussaq's training of Basques at the end of World War II. He'd made friends among them. The reported shootings and stabbings gave me a chance to check. I wrote the American Hospital in Paris asking for verification. A staffer there, Rebecca Allaigre, wrote back, "Unfortunately, we do not have medical records going back that far." I also contacted Dr. Melvin T. Monsher of Encino in Los Angeles. He signed René's death certificate and possibly had attended Dussaq before and during his final illness. My hope was that he could tell me if René had gunshot or stab wounds on his body. Despite numerous attempts to interview him via letter and the phone, he would not talk with me, although at one time he called back and left a taped message that he would. Then when I called back he seemed irritated.

Why the stonewall?

I was as courteous as I could be.

At one point, according to the diaries, Dussaq had a falling out with the consortium and money was cut off—to what degree is unclear. Bazata, if he knew them, gives few details. But the break caused stress. "René was in considerable trouble. He had cut off all contact with several of the leading personalities...of the consortium." These apparently were the donors who did not know "the true target. Thus they are mostly absolved...innocent...However [some or all] funds ran out. René was forced to alter his...methods and means." This caused "tenseness as the vital year approached. He came to me more often. He surely must have visited his other 'Peers' more often." He looked "tired." He'd "lost weight. Our visits were sometimes abruptly broken off."[11]

The effect, writes Bazata, was to cause "René's fever" to grow in him as well. The doubts started again. "Tho [sic] René held himself calm—low key...and considerate; I got the message. I did not like it. It was now all black —total war." The requests for aid (because of the consortium breakup) came more often. Bazata had to finance more of his help to Dussaq himself. "René tried not to press me but I certainly was pressed. America was unprepared for extreme roughness. She wanted the security of Hollywood's good guy ending to her devil's tales...the bright-tooth-paste-smile of knowledge that all would [eventually] be in Madison Avenue heaven...America had never been vaccinated against self-monstrosity." He worried the country—if Hydra-K was activated—"would have hissed, grown angry...and killed me." So he resisted silently—fighting a mind of doubts—and stayed alive unashamedly, eating garlic and goat cheeses, bumping kid-evils (terrorists) and fearfully wondering, "What will René bring next?"[12]

35

"Dear God, Guide Us"

This was it. The dreaded day had arrived. "We will kill your Kennedy," Bazata writes that Dussaq announced. He could see the conviction in René's face. It was in retaliation. The president had authorized the killing of Castro. They knew it for sure. All hope for accord was abandoned.

"I was startled," wrote Bazata. "I shouldn't have been. I knew it would come to pass. But clandestines are secret…not to protect their information," selves or sources—even the "Motherland. But to simply stay alive…It's the best way so far discovered. Shut up, lay low, lock all the doors and count the chickens. Don't even trust grandma—ever."[1]

Yet here it was. René was telling him without reservation. It was serious. Decision Day. He knew Dussaq wanted to know where he stood. He could get up and walk out, sever ties forever. He'd be free, never to think of this madness again—but maybe get a bullet in the head. There was that concern. But "give me a day of peace filled only by aromas of herbs and girls and laughter," he wrote. To walk was enticing. It was the decision of his life.

Dussaq saw his concern. "You don't have to do it, Douglas."

Bazata stared blankly, incredulously. Don't? Was he crazy? "I was deeply enmeshed in telling," warning—probably had already gone beyond the point of no return. Besides, he believed in Dussaq's cause and, most importantly, his ability to pull it off. René was unique. There were few more skilled, more dedicated, more determined. It was a chance to finally do something important and meaningful—something he'd wanted to do for a long time despite his often aimless wandering—his weeding.

Actually, he realized, the job could be done reasonably easily by a competent professional—someone like himself. "Hit [the victim] with a tiny, delayed activated pellet-bullet." That was the weapon of choice amongst pros. Literally undetectable—at least in theory—and with some luck. The tiny pellet is strategically shot into an unclothed body fold, crevice, or mark, so as hard to be seen—behind the ear, in the fingers, hand, or wrist; leg if it's exposed, like if the victim is jogging in shorts. The recipient thinks it's a bug bite or branch scrape. The entry wound quickly seals and heals, leaves little to no trace, nor does the poison. It vanishes quickly in the body's processes. The autopsy misses it. "History then calls [the death] a heart-attack…unknown causes." A professional could get away with it.

He was rolling. But René stopped him.

No. The assassination had to be public. Everyone had to witness it, know what had happened—and why. "David did indeed stop Goliath [an apparent reference to tiny Cuba's shocking victory at the Bay of Pigs invasion]. But Goliath kept returning. He must be destroyed…as Hitler might have been at his early takeovers." If not, "Kennedy might take over all of South America, then Canada—the entire Hemisphere." His father had made him that evil. Bolstered by success, he wouldn't stop. JFK was more determined than ever now to punish Castro. "Power is such…It will ever be so…The power mad…must always be killed—ere it's too late."[2] And the American people must know why. This would be Bazata's job, to tell them and the world what happened on that fateful day at the proper time. The story must be told. It was very important that Americans would know that espousing democracy at home but usurping it elsewhere was evil. Spotlighting it was the only way the evil would end.

If Bazata didn't want to participate in the actual assassination, telling the story was all René would ask.

That made it an easier decision.

Bazata doesn't give a date for this conversation (which will continue shortly). It appears to have occurred around the Bay of Pigs invasion, the failed attempt by U.S.-backed Cuban exiles to retake the island shortly after Castro's 1959 takeover. The Bay of Pigs was in mid-April 1961. More than one thousand exile fighters were killed or injured—slaughtered really—the survivors taken prisoner or shot. It was a debacle, humiliating to the U.S. and especially Kennedy, who, at the last moment, had refused to order crucial air cover.

Since Kennedy was assassinated on November 22, 1963, this "Kill Kennedy" conversation obviously occurred prior, probably a year or two prior. The CIA trained and supported the Bay of Pigs exiles. Dussaq, according to Bazata's diaries, was involved in the planning of the invasion. As a double agent, writes Bazata, Dussaq ostensibly was helping the exiles. But as a secret Cuban agent, he was actually helping to sabotage the invasion. Exactly how, Bazata doesn't explain. But in addition to aiding Castro, Dussaq "was most eager" to have the invasion flounder so there would be an excuse for Hydra-K. That excuse, Bazata explains, was JFK's expected frustration over the failure and, as a result, his targeting of Castro. Such targeting was—at least in Dussaq's mind—an unequivocal violation of international law and morality, and thus justification for like-minded retaliation.

"René was fully 'in' on both sides of the Bay of Pigs," writes Bazata. "He had penetrated CIA long before…Thus he was a contributor to [those who wanted the invasion] and an insurer [for Cuba] against its success…He diverted those that claimed to welcome this invasion, and he kept the 'rightful' defenders [Castro] well alerted. This maneuver is surely unique in history"—one of the great coups. All through this deception,

Dussaq remained relatively anonymous, writes Bazata, but "he was most eager to have [the invasion] launched—and fail" and yield its "great giant break"—its "miracle"—the justification to kill JFK.[3]

While I have not found Dussaq's name in any of the rare documents available concerning the invasion's planning, there are indications beyond Bazata's diaries that he was involved.

First, his wife, Charlotte, before her death, told me he was asked to participate but declined. "It was a government thing," she said. "I don't know whether it was OSS [sic] or what, but he was asked specifically if he would prepare men for this Bay of Pigs thing. He contacted his brother [Maurice, now deceased, and asked], what do you think? What should I do? [Maurice] said don't get involved." If you do, "you'll be a mercenary...He never went into war for anything but patriotism and for his love [of the cause]...If you do it," she said Maurice told him, "in a year's time [Cuba] will be right back to Batista days...back to the same decadence as before."[4]

The fact that he was asked—if true—indicates he had more involvement with Cuba than is publicly known. Was it the CIA that asked him? OSS was already gone, having been disbanded in 1946. Charlotte didn't seem to know that. But she hadn't known he had worked for the FBI either—or had made secret trips to Mexico—until FBI agents told her. Obviously—as all good clandestines often do to keep their wives or loved ones safe from reprisal—he kept things from her.

Additionally, on May 3, 1961—right after the Bay of Pigs—Dussaq wrote a letter to David J. Cathers, secretary-treasurer of the Executives Dinner Club of Pomona (California), at whose function he was scheduled to speak in a few weeks. I found the letter among his papers at his home. "I just returned from a trip back East," he wrote Cathers. "You might be interested to know that during that trip I became, for a period of four days very closely acquainted with our recent debacle in Cuba. I had occasion to personally contact leaders of the underground as well as representatives of the CIA."

The CIA, as I've earlier stated, will neither confirm nor deny Dussaq's association with it, or that it has any documents concerning him—the standard way the agency hides what it wants from the public. But the Cathers letter indicates he at least had access to them. He went on to tell Cathers, "I will probably draw on some of my past experiences as a revolutionist...deepsea diver...teacher...soldier and...businessman to illustrate the point that we are continually living within new frontiers"—an immortalized JFK phrase—"both as individuals and as business-men."[5]

Further, Castro, however he might have learned of it, historians agree, knew the Bay of Pigs invasion was coming. There were rumors of it in the press, of course, but he often boasted about his many spies. In 1965, for instance, the *Miami Herald*'s Jim McGee reported, "His spies, posing as 'anti-Castroites,' slip into 'the ranks of the enemy' and sabotage the exiles." McGee quoted State Department Cuban expert Wayne Smith thusly, "I can only say [Cuban agents] have infiltrated most, if not all, anti-Castro organizations."[6] Similarly, in his book *Castro's Secrets* (2012), former CIA agent and Latin American specialist Brian Latell writes that not only was Cuban intelligence "running what was probably the largest and long-lasting double-agent operation in the annals of modern spycraft," but the Bay of Pigs invasion was "an operation...thoroughly penetrated by Cuban intelligence."[7]

Was Dussaq, as Bazata writes, one of those penetrators?

Whatever the fact, it's certainly true, as Dussaq announced to Bazata, that the Kennedy administration, following the Bay of Pigs disaster, targeted Castro for "elimination"—obsessively so, according to many investigators.[8] For instance, according to Gus Russo and Stephen Molton, authors of *Brothers in Arms*, a 2008 book about the Kennedy-Castro conflict, Joseph Califano, a then young State Department official, exited a Robert Kennedy-chaired meeting about handling Cuba with the impressions that (1) "murder was the agenda," (2) Bobby was "reckless with regard to Fidel," and (3) "Castro was a walking dead man."[9] Califano was shocked. And that meeting was held in February 1961—several months *before* the Bay of Pigs.

In the short time span between 1960 and 1965—encompassing the relatively brief Kennedy Administration—no fewer than eight plans to kill Castro were hatched by the CIA alone, according to numerous sources.[10] The most infamous involved the Mafia and Cuban exiles, two groups badly hurt by Castro's revolution and thus likely to want to see him removed.

Johnny Rosselli was a dapper, silver-haired West Coast gangster. He had apprenticed under Chicago's Prohibition Era crime kingpin Al Capone. Robert A. Maheu was a tight-lipped lawyer and former FBI agent who handled business affairs for movie and aviation tycoon Howard Hughes. All three frequented Las Vegas. In September 1960 the CIA sought a secret way to kill Castro. Maheu knew Rosselli. The CIA asked him if he could solicit Mafia help. Rosselli arranged a meeting with Cosa Nostra bosses Sam Giancana and Santo Trafficante. The mob liked the idea. They had Cubans on the island who could do the hit. Giancana thought a poison pill in Castro's food or drink would be best. The assassin had more time to escape that way. Giancana had a Cuban on his payroll with access to Castro. But after several failed attempts, the Cuban got scared and backed out. Another assassin was readied but the hit was canceled in eager anticipation of the Bay of Pigs invasion killing Castro.[11]

So Dussaq's claim that the Kennedys were targeting Castro was true. He and Bazata appear to have met at a restaurant. Bazata writes Dussaq continued: "We will kill Kennedy not in Paris, not in easy Berlin by delayed pellet...not by tampering with medicines used for his [indecipherable but probably Kennedy's Addison's] disease...But openly in the sunshine—in full view of the entire world—within the strong bounds of the strongest USA."

Bazata balked, nervous about such a discussion. "This was not like a request like the others...I certainly didn't want to talk about [murdering the U.S. president]"—not there, not in a public space. But they looked around, saw they were sufficiently alone, and "shared...that awful nod." Okay, Bazata acknowledged, "[You were describing this] fairly simple guy [JFK], vain, victim of Devil Joe [his father], victim of himself, strutting about, posing, carefully toweling his hair, grinning, acting, acting, acting..."

Dussaq interjected: "You mean lying, deceiving, distorting, ruining other men, competitors, rather decent men...aiming only to win...unlimited power. Not just political…oval office power, but…madman power… Hitler power…I will continue to observe and study and learn and prepare my organization. The direction of Joe and John and RFK is fixed—the dice have been thrown…The scorpion has surfaced…He must be killed…It is now merely a question of time."[12]

But why kill in broad daylight?

"René smiled. 'Lebeau, it ain't easy. The system has solidified. You can't crack it without joining it… You, Lebeau, won't [join the system. You are an outsider—in effect, not corrupted.] Your fire remains constant. [But most are not like you. They are not listening.] We are all surely tempted to relax—to sample a few luxurious hours. But we cannot and must not [relax. The evil] will not end by vote or oratory or example. No one will look or listen or hear—never. Thus our plan—our shock deed.'" Only that will lead to "movement, new life, new creation. Only [Hydra-K] will reach the few who will induce the many."[13]

How could he be so certain?

Dussaq replied: "I am not certain—so many unforeseen happenings can divert and sidetrack us. But I am quite confident of what I can control. If Joe [JFK's father] can control John, then so can I…I will maneuver him precisely at the last hour…He has clearly shown he can't take it—all those protected years [money and power of the Kennedys] plus his weak and compulsive nature…He has few convictions and no profound ethics…Remember my marvelous contacts within your government's heart? These patriots—strong thinkers, believers, men of action—detest [America's] meddling and are not hypnotized by Kennedy or bought by Joe or bullied by 'The Kid' [RFK]…These fine men are our frontline scouts—the bravest of all—fearless—devoted not to a poppycock Kennedy—but to America and to…free men" everywhere.[14]

Was he blaming the sons for the father's sins?

Dussaq "shook his head. Don't read good into evil. You don't have to study crabs and clams to understand doves. Some extremes are just that—extremes. Your president wasn't compelled into office. He was not ordered to listen to [his brother Robert], the CIA—to evil. He is the president. He gives the orders. He alone is responsible. He should have said 'No', 'Never', 'Get out!' He should have quietly cleaned out the evil, including his own brother—all the 'Chosen'...He should have come at once to Cuba...directly to Castro, saying 'Forgive me'...Castro wanted that. He wants to forgive and forget. [But Kennedy didn't.] He must be killed. I will do this...We must be free...And you, LeBeau" must communicate why.[15]

Bazata wrote, "I must confess I get moved when this calm master unfolds his intricate puzzles." After listening awhile, "I suddenly saw that I had alone drunk two full bottles of a fine red Burgundy, was on my third...René had sipped possibly two glasses."[16]

As Bazata continued to listen, Dussaq, he writes, struck certain chords with him. "Instead of admiring Castro for his courage—for fighting on fearlessly against the giant's pressures...America grew livid, hissed, screamed and used more bully pressure, including the ultimate"— invasion, assassination. "Is this not the worst of hypocrisy? Is this not the most dastardly dangerous? What remains but to truly fight to the death—and death it became."[17]

Dussaq recited the CIA kill-Castro plots to him—"laid bare...almost instantly, one after another—most small and vicious and silly"—all of them unknown to the public.[18] "I was startled, ashamed, disgruntled and angry." He recalled his friend's death in Guatemala and a meeting with a CIA official in which he accused the CIA of killing the friend. "We fenced around for about 15 minutes. Finally he [the official] said, 'Come to think of it, so-and-so did die down there...Then he pointed to me, saying, 'You take good care, won't you?' It was a tone of warning...Fratricide lives on 'oh so elegantly.'[19]

"Slowly, bit by bit, my logic and credo...pointed me with René— away from the Kennedys, the meddlers, the brutes...imposing their wills and whims. They weren't Americans of quality anymore...They were the manipulators of the Senate, the Wall Street crooks...I felt great warmth for this strangely dedicated man—all alone, the steadiest of fighters. Fortunate is he that has René for a friend or colleague—fortunate Bazata. Fortunate Fidel. Unfortunate Kennedy.

"That was a long, long evening. I was truly exhausted. But I found no sleep. Over and over I marveled at man and men—contriving through their days and nights and hours...like chess pieces—for astronomic stakes—lives—countries—peoples. I felt like a little kid caught playing in the sandbox. I was embarrassed and deadly chilled. I wanted to play [too]. I thought of Ft. Benning—Oh I thought of many things that interminable night—[How he'd delivered a lecture on Gen. Lee who] studied his military enemies, knew everything about them." Still, he lost. But "deep down I felt—no, I knew—René was right. Let's carve out this evil, cut it away, let man be free. Ah if only you didn't have to carve...To kill!—to stop a life from living—no matter how evil. Dear God, guide us."[20]

36

Five Triggers

With the future decided, Dussaq seemed bolstered. He was "at the height of activity…He had a religious air…not fanatic or martyr or zealot" but "happy." He now had a "solution" for "freeing Cuba"—justified (in his opinion) assassination. The shocking act would "wake" America, "cause her to [take] a profound pause" and "ordain a new democracy…for all people," not just Americans.[1]

Bazata wasn't so sure. On the one hand, "I was thinking less and less of myself—the Co-Op [his livelihood], and the [implications of Hydra-K]." But "sometimes, after communication with René, I'd wake up perspiring, [feeling] a damp chill"—something "no doctor can proscribe for."[2]

He records that they plotted at meetings in both Europe and America. One was at Paris's luxurious Tremoille Hotel on the famed Champs-Elysees. They had dinner there. Bazata lamented his failed efforts to get American officials to respond to his warnings. Dussaq consoled him.

"They didn't listen because they *wouldn't* listen—because of their mind-set, they *can't* listen." René "then proved he was still in CIA," or at least had penetrated the agency. He amazed Bazata by recounting almost word for word what Bazata had said privately to CIA agents.

They discussed hitmen to be used—an area of Bazata's expertise. "Dussaq, ever polite," called the killers "craftsmen"—no "stupid profanity or wild adjectives" like he writes he might use. While continually stressing that Castro should not be connected to the plan in any way, Dussaq called the Cuban dictator "Boss." This impressed Bazata: "This was the first time he had referred to Castro like that." Bazata, still leery— perhaps frowning at Castro's communist ideology—told Dussaq, "Well I'm about 80 percent for your 'Boss' but 20 percent against [him]."

A group from San Remo, a resort city on the Italian Riviera near France, stopped by their table because, Bazata notes, "They wanted to chat for a few minutes...I was amazed at René—so polite, smiling, interested in San Remo." Yet he had "the most momentous weight on his back since the planning for the Lincoln assassination."

When the group left, Dussaq and Bazata returned to the hitman discussion and a particular professional Bazata didn't like—not because he wasn't good. According to Bazata, the hitman was one of the best. But he gave even Bazata the creeps. Bazata called him "Piatogorsky," a pseudonym that Bazata apparently created and used derisively, possibly because he thought the scowling killer had Russian-Polish origins or ties.

He was to be the "Third Trigger" in the plot.

Bazata: "I did something most unusual for me: I blurted out, 'René, take extreme care. I neither trust nor like that dirty, cold son-of-a-bitch. [He's] a hateful bastard...nothing but a trigger finger...I suspect a Russian...a KGB boy'...I had already mentioned he was MI6's number one killer. René laughed aloud. 'Yes he is'"—as if that sealed the deal. "You can't disturb René. He knows no fear—a lonely gentleman alone in an alien world."[3]

Mostly, writes Bazata, he and Dussaq conferred in America. He gives scant details. For instance, on December 14, 1962, he writes: "Bazata to New York...with René" on the French luxury liner SS *France*. But both used phony names and passports, he adds, so it's almost impossible to check.[4] By March 13, 1963, he records that he returned to Europe on the Queen Elizabeth specifically to be seen and recognized while secretly both of them flew back and forth using phony names and identification to discuss more details.

Bazata writes that "they"—he and apparently what was left of the Co-Op—trained some in Europe for the assassination. "We went over and over [details that could be practiced] "until it seemed letter perfect." They could do no more, he writes, as the exact time and location for the assassination was not yet set. "We set up a dummy area in a town in France and walked through it dozens of times."[5]

At one point, a security risk was discovered—"some chap in René's group talked too much." At their next meeting, Bazata confronted Dussaq with the need to take action. "He put his hand on mine signaling quiet. 'All is well,' he said slowly, 'Yes. He is already silenced.'" Again, Bazata was impressed. "Oh yeah, René was way ahead." But he was still uneasy. "What about the others"—anyone who might have caught on because of the talker? No matter, answered Dussaq. "The plan has been changed." But the target, it might leak out? Dussaq calmly replied: *you* tried to tell them and what did they do?

Dussaq was always ahead, marveled Bazata.

■ ■ ■

As they conferred, details of Hydra-K emerged. From what Bazata deduced, Dussaq seemed in charge. But he was never sure. Sometimes it appeared there were others giving orders. For instance, Dussaq didn't want Lee Harvey Oswald involved.[6] He thought Oswald, "who selected himself by constant self-pushing," was dangerous and "uncontrollable." His "unpredictability" was a threat to the plan. Dussaq, writes Bazata, wanted to "liquidate" Oswald. But "CIA meddlers" saw the brazen ex-marine as a needed "patsy"—the one on whom the assassination would be blamed, thereby keeping themselves safe and hidden. René "didn't like patsies" but "he had no choice."[7]

As "far back as 1961," writes Bazata, René said Texas was the preferred choice for the execution and Dallas the preferred city. This was
mainly because of the state's proximity to "the Mexican haven" which
allowed relatively easy entry and especially, in the heat of pursuit, escape.
René knew Mexico well. In addition, Texas was rightfully the place. It
was the most "bombastic" state, "crying out for just such a macabre
canonization."

Dallas was preferred because it was a "flag-waving," anti-Kennedy
"hothouse for murder" with "one of the most corrupt and ridiculous
police forces in America, fully purchasable at bargain prices...Every-
thing goes." The city boasted "a bizarre assortment of 'bought' [sic] FBI
chaps and their stooges—informants, plants, patsies: ditto the CIA [and
other federal officers] all independently corrupted yet...needing each
other...for a price...a deal, a favor...or just silence."[8]

The plotters were sure Dallas would be the site "possibly about mid-
June [1963] or maybe a bit later," writes Bazata. He says they had insider
information. "Dallas Mayor [Earle] Cabell was the brother of [Air Force]
Gen. [Charles] Cabell [former deputy director] of CIA." The general "had
been one of the most vital CIA backers of the Bay of Pigs" and was "fired
from his high post by [JFK]"—and thus had it in for the president. "René
knew both well. The mayor was specifically instrumental in mapping
[Kennedy's November 22, 1963] motorcade route."[9]

Bazata's mention of the Cabell brothers is not in a vacuum. They are
listed in *Who's Who in the JFK Assassination*, a standard reference to
the killing. It relates, "After his dismissal, [Gen.] Cabell worked for
Howard Hughes" and "was involved with Robert Maheu in [the CIA-
Mafia] plots to kill Castro."[10] Wim Dankbaar, a Dutch researcher and
film-producer about the assassination, implicates General Cabell in his
book, *Files on JFK*, a relatively new (2008) investigation. Believing the
assassination a combined CIA-Mafia hit, Dankbaar writes, "Where the
plan originated...is unclear." But during the president's funeral, a group
"was in General Cabell's house, watching JFK's funeral on television...with beer and all that." The implication was that they were cel-
ebrating JFK's death.[11] The *New York Times* reports that after the

assassination, Earle, as mayor, sided with others in the city opposing a Dallas memorial honoring Kennedy—implying he too disliked the president.[12]

As to why General Cabell, who worked with the CIA on various plots aimed at killing Castro, would have collaborated with pro-Cuba Dussaq—if in fact the Cabells *were* involved—remains unclear. Were they unaware of Dussaq's true motivations and affiliations? According to Bazata, René was a masterful double-agent, a chameleon believed to be on one side while actually working for another. Assuming that's true, the Cabells could have been hoodwinked. Additionally, there's the ancient adage to consider: "The enemy of my enemy is my friend." Having been cashiered by President Kennedy, General Cabell may have regarded Hydra-K as a prime opportunity for revenge.

■ ■ ■

"René ordered five triggers," writes Bazata, "each with a second standing behind" him. "However, these so-called 'seconds' were, in fact, COs"—commander-managers—in place to make sure the "trigger-sharpshooters" did their jobs.

Each CO was "armed with [a German] Carl Walther P38 9mm Waffenfabrik Ulm/Do" pistol with silencer affixed. Each had "splendid Binoculars…Their word was COMMAND FINAL [Bazata's caps]." In the event a trigger did anything off plan, like refuse to shoot, the CO would kill him. Each CO had at his disposal a "Cyanide 'inflictor,'" which Bazata writes he personally "procured from East Germany," and which he believed "even the CIA didn't have." It "killed instantly." It's unclear whether this was a bullet in their pistols or a separate weapon. But "no trigger was aware of this precaution."[13]

It's important to note that Bazata writes he was not part of the assassination team. He says he was in Europe when Kennedy was executed. His description therefore—if what he says is true—is, at best, second hand, probably gotten from Dussaq, whom he says he met with after the assassination. He doesn't have all the details of that fateful day, and there are minor inconsistencies in his account (which appear to stem from lack of eyewitness knowledge more than anything else).[14]

The following is the gist of his account—at least what I can discern with some certainty.[15]

He identifies five primary "triggers" or sharpshooters in Dallas on the day of the assassination. They are: René, Oswald, the code-named "Piatogorsky," and two unnamed CIA hitmen, variously described. He discusses other Hydra-K functionaries used in the assassination—backup shooters, "five" doubles for Oswald, random "pointers" and "shouters"—but does not identify any of them beyond their purpose in the plot.

The final plan, he writes, was the result of multiple changes as Hydra-K evolved right up to the assassination. It had numerous deceptions, as well as alternatives in case the motorcade route was changed at the last moment. "It was a complicated system," writes Bazata. It employed "bought" philosophically-driven public officials, phony policemen and secret service agents, accomplices posing as uniformed security, strategically placed spotters to alert and aid the shooters, and "obstructors" to slow the authentic police and any others possibly detrimental to the plan. These "extras," he writes, did not know more about the plot than their assigned jobs and many of them died mysteriously following the assassination.[16]

Multiple disguises were used, as were ruses employed to confuse the immediate situation and later investigations. For instance, phony "bullet nicks" were "installed" (not otherwise explained) as misleads in Dealey Plaza. This was done, in some cases, "almost 2 weeks" before the motorcade passed by. Deceiving pre-recorded audio was used—apparently played at specific times when needed. There were "plants" and "patsies" in the crowd to shout misleads, such as "Look over there!" These were to make "innocents" think they'd heard or "seen things they really hadn't seen"—the "magic," as Bazata terms it, "that would soon become myth, then legend...The deception that continues until this very day [1977]."

Each shooting duo (trigger and CO) "had a good field of fire. Each had absolute orders and sequences to adhere to"—unless something "unforeseeable" happened. Then the commander could improvise along lines "talked about beforehand." The shooters too had plans in case the

COs were incapacitated. The CO's main job, besides monitoring the shooters, was situational awaRenéss—know what was happening around them so they could react in a planned way, especially if discovered. Dussaq had complete confidence that no principals would talk if arrested. They were "professionals." The CO would talk to the shooters "for calming effect" and to keep them abreast of what was happening as they tracked their target. The command for cleared to fire was a finger to the trigger's neck.

Dussaq's role in the killing was almost "religious," writes Bazata. It was in "evil Lyndon Johnson's Texas,"[17] a place viewed as needing spiritual redemption. Dussaq was compelled to participate, like an apostle at the Last Supper. He himself had to fire the telling shot or the act wouldn't be sanctified. "Cuba must be freed by her own hand—not a substitute," Bazata quotes him as saying. Once, as justification, he "recited the Lord's Prayer to me," i.e., "Thou shalt not trespass," meaning America on Cuba, or any lesser nation—and "an eye for an eye...I felt he was quite serious... 'I must be there,' he said. 'I must take this risk.'"[18]

Dussaq arrived in disguise. Bazata doesn't say how, from where, or what kind of disguise—only that it was "simple." He entered a building, similarly not defined. Several plotters were waiting. One was "an American of Cuban origin living in Miami and New York...who contracted to the CIA." Another was an unnamed "assistant" of Dussaq's "from California" about whom, Bazata writes, he "knew nothing." A third was "a Texas policeman being paid who did some work with the CIA and FBI." Bazata speculates that the California assistant was there to "watch" the policeman. All were armed and had binoculars. Dussaq "appraised the situation for any unexpected obstacle or danger" and determined "all well."[19]

■ ■ ■

On November 22, 1963, half past high noon, Hydra-K commenced.

As the motorcade approached, René, preparing to shoot, readied his weapon. Bazata doesn't say where he is, only that he was a "great distance" from his target. He is "in front" of the motorcade. His soon-to-be-fired shot, however, would not be the first. It would be the second. The first shot, according to Bazata, would be by Oswald—who, most accounts agree, was at this same moment also aiming a rifle from a sixth floor window in the Texas School Book Depository. He is above and—unlike Dussaq—*behind* the slow-moving motorcade.

Here, however, Bazata's account deviates from the standard.

Since Dussaq didn't want Oswald in Hydra-K but was forced to use him, he devised a "brilliant" (according to Bazata) alternative plan to use Oswald to his own advantage, i.e., in the fulfillment of his quest for Cuba. Oswald, in effect, would become Dussaq's patsy. Oswald believed himself to be an important part of the assassination plan. Dussaq didn't have faith in or trust the unstable Oswald. He was, after all, tabbed to be the patsy. Dussaq surreptitiously had Oswald's rifle armed with duds, blanks, which Oswald would fire harmlessly at Kennedy. This ploy, this "red herring," Dussaq believed, would later be discovered and serve to exonerate the patsy and undermine and thus misdirect all "official" investigations, clearing a path for Bazata's subsequent planned revelations. Far-fetched, perhaps, with too many variables, but that's how I understood the plan from Bazata's recounting of it decades later.

The blanks were actually "combustible cartridges." These were seemingly genuine cartridges in appearance. The bullet would disintegrate shortly (approximately fifteen yards) after exiting the rifle. They were essentially harmless. Oswald's CO secretly inserted the dummy cartridges (or cartridge—it's not clear) in Oswald's rifle. But after firing the first shot—the signal to the others that the assassination plan was now in motion—Oswald realized something was amiss. It appears, from Bazata's recounting, the shot's report didn't ring true. "He heard his shot was far sharper—abrupt—than a normal explosion," writes Bazata. "Also there was an instant snapping 'echo' in front of him. Instinctively Oswald knew something was wrong."[20]

Apparently already suspicious of his handlers, Oswald was prepared. He purposely let a "clip" (or possibly something else—it is not clear) fall from his rifle, pretending to be flustered and drawing the CO's attention to it with some excited words. Thus, with the CO fleetingly distracted, he pulled a slight of hand, retrieving what had fallen and surreptitiously inserting a real cartridge into the rifle and fired a second shot—an authentic bullet—before the CO, realizing something was amiss, could wrestle the rifle from him. "Os, the odd ball sly, had fooled them all, including René to this extent." Bazata writes that Dussaq learned this later from his "eyes-ears" in the "Dallas jailhouse...I do not know exactly what transpired here...René only stated what I here repeat."[21]

Meanwhile, the actual execution began. Oswald's first shot—the dummy shot by him from behind—drew the attention of onlookers in Dealey Plaza at the rear of the motorcade as per plan. Dussaq, a "superb shot"—presumably unseen because of the onlooker diversion—now squeezed off the first lethal shot of the assassination from his lair in *front* of the motorcade. The grassy knoll? The overpass they were gliding toward? A manhole in the street ahead? Bazata doesn't say.[22] "René...had no CO behind him but did have two seconds. They are described as having their binoculars on the target to make sure JFK was mortally hit. The plan was to "execute Kennedy only"—and they took pains not to injure "innocents."

Almost simultaneously, "as René fires from the front," writes Bazata, another trigger [described only as "CIA"] fires from the rear"—as Oswald had done only seconds earlier. Bazata does not pinpoint exactly from which location in the rear this trigger fires, but does write that both he and Dussaq are aiming for the "the exact same hole"—and the shot from behind (the fourth shot, the third with real bullets) "is slightly higher in the head."

Was this to confuse later forensics by producing entry wounds from both directions? Bazata hints at that but doesn't really say it. His diary entries are not clear on this point. However, he indicates that in addition to the earlier planted "bullet nicks," phony bullets or fragments of bullets were possibly planted in the area and perhaps elsewhere (i.e., the hospital floor or the gurney carrying the dead president's body) by other Hydra-K players in the shooting's wake to create more confusion and misdirection.[23]

All shooters wore gloves and special face coverings to prevent incriminating "powder debris" from landing on their skin. All told, writes

Bazata, four shots were fired; three real, only two consequential, and one dummy—the combustible shot by Oswald.[24] Removal of weapons and incriminating material was accomplished by "experts," and there was a "squad" to remove "all persons." Was this an extrication squad or was it an execution squad organized to eliminate post-assassination problems? It remains unclear.

Dussaq and his assistant left Dallas shortly after the assassination and "reached Mexico by private boat," writes Bazata. Others in the plot remained, "having solid cover-reasons to be there."

In snippets scattered piecemeal, Bazata gives the following additional details about the triggers:

The so-called "Piatogorsky" was "a British professional killer, well known to René and Baz. His origin is supposedly Polish but Baz [suspects he might be] Russian [or at least working largely for the KGB]." He was "a better shot than me...one of the coolest, greatest hit men known to the trade." He "did not fire at Dallas...It was not necessary." Only if René had missed or not killed the president would Piatogrosky have fired. "Still he was paid $100,000...$50,000 in advance and [the other half] awaiting him in Switzerland after the execution." Several times Bazata cautions *himself* in discussing Piatogorsky. "Baz does not intend to cross the Brits or syndicates!"

The gunman firing the other actual shot from behind the motorcade was "a self-employed clandestine who quite often contracted to the CIA." In one description Bazata indicates he might be a former U.S. Marine, but other entries indicate he may be writing about the other unnamed trigger (listed below as the "fifth" trigger). "None of us 'seem' to know or care if he was in CIA...as we all know it is very difficult to be sure of [who is who] even on the part of fellow CIAians [sic]...Baz feels he was of British or French origin."

The "fifth trigger" was either a CIA "contract" or probably "a fellow CIA colleague of René's...Superb shot...He did not know Piatogorsky was there...He too did not fire. Not needed."

Oswald did not shoot Officer Tippit as is widely believed, writes Bazata. "Tippit was slain by a fairly reasonable [Oswald] look-alike." Oswald, as explained earlier, was supposed to survive his arrest and later trial in order to be found innocent and thus aid in the even later Bazata-revealed "revelations" about the assassination. But an "insider" tipped Hydra-K operatives still in Dallas that, while in custody, he was "talking out of turn." Jack Ruby, who Bazata writes was connected to some of the plotters and was promised "protection" and "rewards" by them for killing Oswald, was then dispatched. "It was lucky they got him."

37

"Lunched with Two Mafias"

azata writes that he learned of the Kennedy assassination on Europe's American Forces Radio Network.[1] "I heard that music. The announcement had already been made. They were giving details." Among his first thoughts were, "Am I a patsy too?" What would those he warned think—that he was there? But Dussaq, he reports, was quickly ("at once") in Paris to offer reassurance. "He was concerned that I should not be held a party to [the assassination] in any way." To this end, he told Bazata, "Everything went as planned...only a few minor hitches. There can be no identification [of those who were there]. We were all disguised...no fingerprints."[2]

Oddly, Bazata says he was in the U.S. by December 1963—only several weeks after the assassination. According to personal letters he sent years later, December 1963 was when his friend and colleague Salvador Dali, the famous Surrealist artist, painted a canvas of him in New York

City. "Exactly 15 years ago this month," he writes in a "5 December 1978" post to an overseas friend, "Dali made a painting of me as Don Quixote, the sole [such painting] he ever did for any fellow artist...It was done in the St. Regis Hotel in Dali's 6th floor apartment." The *New York Times* mentions the painting in Bazata's obituary, accompanied by a photo of the two artists together "in 1963."[3]

I mention this oddity because if Dussaq met with Bazata in Paris right after the assassination, and Bazata was in New York by December, it seems there was unnecessary travel by Dussaq. If Bazata was going to be there, why not meet in the U.S., perhaps in New York City? That's much closer than Paris. Might Bazata's claim of a quick Paris meeting be subterfuge? Was he in the U.S. when Kennedy was killed? Had he actually participated in the assassination and written the diary entries for protection?

It's possible.

Regardless of his whereabouts on November 22, 1963, Bazata writes that afterwards he spent "considerable time" in New York between December 1963 and an undisclosed date in 1968. This was "to reach accord with René on the revelation" he'd agreed to make about the assassination: "what he would tell," which names he'd reveal, "how he would tell it," and especially "when?"

In one vein, he writes, Dussaq continued to be "delighted with the outcome" of the investigations, i.e., "J. Edgar Hoover's stubborn, bull-headed insistence on a single assassin" theory and the Warren Commission's echo of that finding. He was "happy" no others died at Dealey Plaza, and that "there was no fall out on Castro and Cuba." He was "content with the elimination of Oswald and Ruby. Both had enormous quantities of [information] to reveal;" ditto "with CIA middle-men" who decided to "flee" and "stay quiet."

On the other hand, "he made it known [the task] was not finished... He was far, far [sic] less cheerful than at any time in the past 37 or 38 years I'd known him. I felt he considered much had not succeeded." Castro was still "persecuted" by the U.S., and Cuba was not free of American meddling. "But I didn't ask" about these issues. "We agreed

I should wait until 'other vital events' had occurred, then wait until America was prepared [for the revelations] by time and information via leaks, confessions, investigations and informants."[4]

There is little more about this four-year period in Bazata's diaries and letters. Around 1968, he abruptly left mainland Europe for England and then Vietnam where, ostensibly in the middle of the Vietnam War, he would study a specific ancient Asian painting technique called "lacquers"—the use of tree sap for paint. Baron Mumm, head of the Mumm Estate, the site of his clandestine cover for over two decades, had committed suicide under mysterious circumstances. Bazata had married his third wife and was beginning to feel his age. In a field where a clandestine mercenary needed peak vigor and fighting skills, he had lost a step or two. His succinct yet mysterious explanation: "I was forced to shift base for security reasons."[5]

In Vietnam, he and his French wife, Marie-Pierre, a tall, soft-spoken beauty, lived with American Ambassador William Colby, who after the Vietnam War would become director of the CIA, and who himself would die mysteriously.[6] Bazata and Colby had been OSS Jedburghs together. They were longtime friends. In Vietnam, Colby was running an anti-Viet Cong program called "Phoenix." As previously noted, Phoenix was designed to terrorize Viet Cong spies and infiltrators. Congressional estimates say between ten thousand and forty thousand suspected insurgents were slain under the program. Bazata, he writes, participated "lightly" in the program but became "disgusted" and quit. He couldn't tell "who was guilty and who was innocent."

He and Marie-Pierre left Vietnam and settled first in Pennsylvania, where Bazata had been born, then in the Maryland woods, near D.C., where he took up bird-raising at what was probably a CIA safe house. He'd expected to get a well-paying job from the agency, something he felt he'd been promised for past work. But he was shunned. The CIA he came home to was a different CIA than the one he'd worked with prior to the Kennedy assassination. Officials he'd known had been purged. There was no paperwork for most of the work he'd done. He was asked to "prove" his work record, which infuriated him. "We don't keep records." In addition, attempts were made on his life. Marie-Pierre told me: one night the birds started squawking. She turned on a light in their bedroom. Baz shouted, "Shut it off!" As she did, shots crashed through the window. He ran outside and found himself engaged in a firefight. Returning unscathed, he cautioned, "Don't ask." She didn't.[7]

It was around this time that Bazata apparently sought the July 1971 letter from Lucien Conein confirming that at four different times before the assassination he had warned Conein it was going to happen.[8]

Was he nervous that certain plotters had turned against him and were trying to kill him? It doesn't seem he believed Dussaq was the culprit. Without giving details, he writes that he and René met several times at his remote bird farm "discussing what to do next." But the contacts were few and far between. At one point it appears they had an argument over his lack of money to, in effect, do Dussaq's bidding. Dussaq basically told him to tough it out, which Bazata reluctantly did. After a while, the "threats and attempts" on his life "suddenly stopped." He writes he never took them seriously anyway, labeling the attackers "bumbling fumblers trying to be spies." His only worry was that one of them "might get lucky." At one point, it appears, he lost track of Dussaq, who, he writes, "had his own concerns." He wondered what had happened to his friend. But ultimately, his journals indicate, they apparently got back in touch because "we decided to float a few trial balloons."[9]

It seems the strategy was to ease into the Hydra-K revelations by first using his life saga to garner interest and establish credibility—the Renégade son of a minister, shipped out to the Caribbean as a teenager, followed by being a Depression-era train-hopping hobo and bare-knuckle fighter, a world-class marine sharpshooter, rough and tumble WWII saboteur and hero, OSS assassin, and Cold War spy. He began setting pen to paper. I have one hundred or so rambling, sometimes confusing manuscript pages. He made ultimately futile contacts with publishers. His writing was often egotistical, boastful, and probably hard to believe. And Bazata resented demands to provide hard evidence for his claims, not only because he regarded such requests as challenges to his honesty, but also because the documentation was mostly secret and inaccessible.

However, word spread. Features about him appeared in the Washington papers. "Douglas Bazata—A Many-Faced Man" was the headline on a 1972 story in *The Sunday Star and Daily News*; "From the OSS to an Easel" headlined another story a few weeks later in the *Washington Post*. By 1975, he was profiled with several other clandestines in an *Esquire* magazine piece entitled "Six Good Spies." They pictured him looking dark and sinister on his bird farm. The short article, set like a CIA dossier, noted that he "scored highest officer rating in history of Fort Benning, higher than MacArthur and Eisenhower."[10]

There was some interest in his story from *Time* magazine, but ultimately his double and triple talk and penchant for coyness and caution made potential buyers leery. John Greenya, who would eventually write five books of his own and collaborate on many others, was approached by Bazata to help him better the half-done manuscript he'd so far produced. "I recall him as a real character whom I really liked," Greenya responded to my query. "I vaguely recall him mentioning the JFK assassination, but, alas, no details...I remember him showing me journal pages, apparently in his own handwriting, but I don't remember their content. My biggest question at the time went to his veracity, was he simply a charming raconteur? I never got the answer to that question...he could not afford to hire me and my rates were very reasonable back then."[11]

Not until he was connected with author and *Newsweek* columnist Ralph de Toledano did anything along the lines of what Dussaq wanted begin to happen. Toledano, a former OSS agent, had written, among many other books, a 1967 book about Robert F. Kennedy entitled *The Man Who Would be President*. JFK's brother, Robert, was eyeing a run for the White House. Toledano was convinced the Warren Commission was covering up facts about JFK's slaying. A founding reporter for William F. Buckley's *National Review*, Toledano believed Castro and the Mafia were behind the assassination. How he connected with Bazata is not clear, other than possibly their OSS connection. But a 1999 Toledano column offers a stronger possibility. Toledano wrote that in the 1970s a professor friend called him and said, "I've got someone here who was a hit man [for the] OSS...He's got a tremendous story to tell—and everything that is susceptible of proof about what he alleges checks out. He wants to do some articles and a book. I'm sending him to you." Toledano, protecting his source, continues, "I sat with this man—call him 'Ishmael'—and he described a plot to kill President Kennedy in complete detail, and how it was done. He was thoroughly convincing, but no magazine or book editor was ready to give him a contract. 'Where's the proof?' they would say. And I would answer that conspirators don't send memos to each other."[12]

By 1977, according to Bazata's papers, he, Toledano, and the *National Enquirer* were in talks for the two to write an article about Hydra-K. I have a three-page outline Bazata wrote for Toledano in that year and a contract Bazata apparently had a lawyer draw up covering the terms of their collaboration. It indicates they were hoping to get fifty thousand dollars or more for the collaboration. In 2005, two years before Toledano died at age ninety, I contacted him about the matter. He remembered it. He said at that time he and a partner were writing a book about the assassination, and Bazata knew who had staged it. Bazata showed him a document that cinched it for him, he said, but he, alas, no longer had it to show me. I asked him if it could have been the Conein letter? His memory was dim. He couldn't be sure—maybe yes, maybe no. But he was convinced Bazata knew the truth—until Bazata himself nixed the collaboration and the deal fell through.

I'd already guessed the breakup from some terse entries in Bazata's journals: "Ralph de T. just rang," he wrote, listing the time and date: "0950, 19 May 1977. I explained drop it [the story and their collaboration] for 6 weeks, maybe 2 months"—maybe more depending. He'd "lunched with 2 Mafias" who "noted 4 boys had been killed last week, including Nardia, etc." It was an obvious threat. If he made a mistake in the retelling, he'd end up like the recent four "boys." Days before he'd written another entry: "Friday the 13th of May '77. I can note this day that all the JFK triggers[13] are still alive and are about 99.99 % free from revelation or persecution. I cannot say the same about informants-fingers-betrayers-patsies, stand-ins, decoys and witnesses, both planned and inadvertent. Their mortality rate is unique in the crime world and will so continue."[14]

It appears Bazata had decided disclosure—at least at this time—was not worth the risk.

■ ■ ■

In 1979, Toledano wrote a syndicated column arguing that while the recently concluded House Assassinations Committee had—in a dispute with the Warren Commission—concluded that there indeed had been a conspiracy in the death of John F. Kennedy, it (the committee) still had not gotten things right.

"First," he wrote, "there was a film showing that someone was with Oswald when he allegedly fired the shots at the president's motorcade." The committee had "suppressed a report that at least one shot had been fired from a grassy knoll" and that another shot had come "from a boxcar on the railroad tracks over the underpass that President Kennedy was approaching." That boxcar was only yards from the grassy knoll, he noted. "The Dallas Police Department is also attempting to muddy the waters," he added, and "no attempt seems to have been made to question the former CIA officials who, if my information is correct, can give a detailed account of events." All of this showed, he concluded, that "Oswald did not act alone... The basic fact that the assassination was organized and inspired by Castro's Cuba is now beyond doubt... But for some reason there are political forces in this country which are determined to place all the blame on a single individual."[15]

Toledano was an anti-communist. It's likely he was bolstered in his arguments by at least some of what he'd learned from Bazata—specifically, the CO monitoring Oswald,[16] the grassy knoll or railroad boxcar as the site of Dussaq's "great distance" shot,[17] and the Castro-Cuban indictment.[18]

PART 4

AFTERMATH

38

Enigmas

I f what Bazata secretly wrote is true—even if only partially—then Dussaq did a masterful job of deception which, of course, is what masterful clandestines do. By all public accounts, and in the minds of most who knew him, René was a respected and talented leader, a war hero and patriot, a responsible member of the Los Angeles business community, an admirable husband and father. I think most who knew him—even some of those who worked with him undercover—would be shocked to learn what Bazata alleges.

I was.

Yet those close to him, a very small group consisting of certain relatives, friends, and business colleagues, admit Dussaq was a mysterious man. Even his own wife, Charlotte was in the dark about his clandestine activities until the FBI informed her. "He was very reticent," she said. There were times when he would just "black out," go "totally blank" when she asked—for instance, why was he screaming in his sleep? She assumed it was because of the war.

But was it?

His former daughter-in-law—son Maurice's ("Toro's") first wife, Kathleen, when I spoke with her, recalled René as very tight-lipped. "He told you what he wanted and nothing more." He was "tough" and "fascinating," a man she surely admired, but mysterious nonetheless. "He would have been very happy if the world would [have left] him alone and he could [have stayed] back in his room"—an office in his Encino home—"reading and exercising. He was a wonderful man but a self-contained man."

Toro's second wife, Gina, echoed Kathleen. "René didn't talk a lot," she told me. "Neither did his son"—her deceased husband, Maurice. René's only child, Toro grew up to be physically larger than his father, served in the Air Force during the Vietnam War, and with Gina became a business owner in Nevada. Tragically, he died of cancer in 2009. I never got to interview him. Walter Puth, René's closest Prudential associate—and he wasn't close to many—agreed that there was mystery to his colleague—as did René's nephew, René E. Dussaq, now a veteran salesman for an international firm. As a teenager, he lived with his uncle (whom he was named after) and Charlotte for several years until early 1963, shortly before the assassination. "I'm grateful for him. He taught me many things. His life was like you see in the movies… He did everything…He was fearless…A life like his creates an aura, a mystique…I was always in awe."

Throughout the Kennedy presidential years—as well as before and after—Dussaq conducted business for Prudential, building the company's worth, especially in Los Angeles. He was good at it but "he hated working there," said Kathleen, his former daughter-in-law. "He said, 'I have a family. I have to support them. What can I do?'" His agency colleagues never saw or heard the negative remarks. Just as he'd inspired ROTC students, and hard-to-impress warriors like Bazata, he did the same at Prudential. "He was tremendously smart," recalled Jack Hines, a young, former naval officer when hired there, whom Dussaq recruited into the company. "He'd use his military experiences to teach...I was just enthralled...His physical presence was something else. He had a magnificent physique, mustache, crewcut, French accent. He would sunbathe every weekend. He had a gorgeous tan..."

Dussaq continued public speaking, a talent he obviously enjoyed and used, enhanced by his sense of humor, to advance himself. Sometimes he spoke to civic groups, other times to insurance professionals, often on patriotic subjects, always urging those in his audience to better themselves; to be cognizant of their freedoms and constitutional rights. When one looks at his speaking engagements, however, there is a drop off during the months preceding JFK's assassination—hardly incriminating but nonetheless worthy of note. He was promoted to manager of the San Fernando Valley office just months before the assassination, in September 1963. It was an important personal upgrade for him. Along with more money—which he always said he didn't care about—came more responsibility. But it worked both ways. He became more his own boss, with more freedom to come and go as he pleased and set his own schedule should he ever need such cover.

His love of physical fitness and athletics never waned. He was often at Southern California tennis courts, surprising unsuspecting young hopeful braggarts by casually challenging them to a match and then beating them soundly. He had a gym set up in his backyard with a climber's rope dangling thirty feet from a large oak. He regularly ascended the rope with Olympic precision. Rick Weber, a young Prudential agent then, remembers: "He invited me over for a drink after work. He was fascinating and I felt privileged to accept. He took me outside and showed me the rope. 'Climb it,' he said. 'Then I'll pour you a scotch and water.'"[1] Weber did and they became friends, with Dussaq becoming like a mentor.

In the late 1960s, when he was almost sixty, Dussaq would go downtown to a well-known gym and box toughs still in their prime. "One time he went there before doing his Christmas shopping," remembers colleague Puth. "He was driving a '67 Chevy convertible," a flashy car, one of many through the years for which he was known. "He parked and locked it and went into the gym. He told me that when he came back, unfortunately, one of his countrymen"—presumably he meant a Hispanic—"had opened the door and was rifling through his glove box. He said something to him. The guy jumped up and took a swing at him. He shouldn't have done that. He put the guy out with one punch and they took him away in an ambulance."[2]

Researching Dussaq's life, I found only a few instances of genuine distress and turmoil of which his friends and relatives were actually aware.

One was an argument he had with Sidney "Monty" Montague, the former Canadian mounted policeman, author and outdoorsman, with whom he and Charlotte lived when they were first married, and whose name they honored by including it in their only son's name—Maurice *Montague* Dussaq. "Monty was a dear friend," said René's nephew, René E. "He knew a lot about Uncle René. When I lived with [them] Monty used to come over and take Toro and me places like Disneyland. They [the Montagues] thought of Toro like a son...Not only were [René and Monty] good friends but I think it went beyond...There was something about both of them...I never heard anyone yell at Uncle René before but I saw Monty at one time get very mad at him. Very mad."

For what?

"I don't remember the circumstances but it was in the house in [Encino] where we lived. I didn't know what it was all about but I thought they were going to come to blows. Monty [a large man] was right up to him and Uncle René backed down. I don't think he would have backed down from anything except that what Monty was telling him was true."

What was the problem? This was close to the time of the JFK assassination. René and his son, Toro, are said to have had issues. But they mainly centered on the Vietnam War.[3] This confrontation was before Vietnam became controversial. Had the former Mountie discovered something he objected to in René's activities? Or, more likely, was it simply a disagreement over one of a myriad of relatively benign issues about which two headstrong men of action could have disagreed?

Montague died in 1971—I had no chance to interview him—and René's nephew could shed no more light on the matter. Further, as a young high school student at the time, he said he didn't know his uncle's politics. René never spoke to him about them. But "he was an avid digester of the news...He would come home and watch and read...He was keeping up."

What did his uncle think of Fidel Castro? The question is pertinent because the reason young René E. was living with the Dussaqs was that Castro shortly after the 1959 revolution had confiscated most of René's older brother's holdings—René E.'s father, Maurice—forcing the family, including young René, to leave Cuba. "Whenever he talked about Castro," said his nephew, "he'd say the reason he came to power was because of the great distance between the upper and lower class. There was no middle class. That fed the revolution. Uncle René was never critical of Castro.... It was like he admired him."

Again, that is not, by itself, incriminating. Most people have opinions about the Cuban dictator—especially those with ties to Cuba. They are as varied as all political discourse. But considering the Dussaq family's catastrophic loss of property and holdings, René E.'s remembrance is hard to simply dismiss.

■ ■ ■

Dussaq retired from Prudential in 1970[4] but periodically kept in touch with at least one colleague, Walter Puth. One day Puth was surprised to see Dussaq enter the office looking shaken. It was during the 1979 Iranian Hostage Crisis—a time of great turmoil in America. Islamic militants had taken control of the American Embassy in Teheran and were holding fifty-two Americans hostage—ultimately for a year. A Carter Administration rescue raid had failed. Dussaq signaled Puth into Puth's private office and then quietly broke down. "I said, 'What's the matter?' In soft tones, he said two guys had been at his house for three days trying to get him to go to Iran." Puth thought they might have been

FBI but wasn't sure. "They wanted him to parachute at night into Iran to see if he could help free the hostages. I mean he was what—nearly 70? It was after he'd retired. He was in good shape but parachute into Iran? He said, 'I can't believe it. Didn't I do enough? They made me feel so small.'"

It's doubtful that the agents pressing Dussaq were from the FBI. The Bureau normally handles crimes only perpetrated in the United States and Latin America—not overseas. However, it can jump to international areas with Justice Department approval—as several administrations have done following terrorist acts against U.S. sovereign interests abroad. Also, the U.S. Embassy in Teheran was, under international law, U.S. territory. More than likely, however, the agents Puth reports on were from the CIA. Regardless, it's startling that either agency would solicit help from a seventy-year-old for what had to be a young man's mission. But Dussaq was unlike most seventy-year-old men. He was physically fit and his record spoke to his expertise and courage. Unfortunately, neither the FBI nor the CIA would provide further information. The FBI says it's released all documents concerning Dussaq, and there is nothing about such a mission among them. Similarly, the CIA will not confirm or deny his affiliation. So it's back to square one on such a matter—which is the way the agencies prefer it.

In 1986, Dussaq again nixed publicity about his life as he had in the early 1950s when he withdrew his approval from a radio broadcast based on his experiences. John Champion, the late Hollywood writer, had turned producer and wanted to make a movie about René's exploits. Champion had credits like *Airplane*, a major box office smash. Champion had become familiar with René's life after penning the earlier proposal, *The Katherine Keeler Story*, based on the life of René's first wife. The new film was tentatively titled *Captain Bazooka*. As he had before, René initially agreed to the deal but soon backed out.

Why? Was he laying low? Did he not want publicity that might reveal, however inadvertently, events René was committed to keeping secret?

Whatever his reasons, he remained fearless, undeterred by the prospect of danger. At age eighty-three, he announced he would jump into the skies over France during the fiftieth anniversary commemoration of the D-Day invasion. He was immensely proud of having been a paratrooper. He would jump with a group of other veterans who had parachuted into Normandy on that fateful day. When his turn came, he was blown off course just as he had been in 1944. Fortunately, when he landed, unlike in 1944, he was located quickly and taken to a pub to celebrate. His well-honed humor was still intact. "You know," he told the *Washington Post*, "you say I look good for my age but I've been coming to pieces in the last few years. I had a cancer operation, a collapsed lung, a hernia and a bad leg. The other day the doctor said to me, 'René, you must reconcile yourself...you'll never feel like you did when you were 80.'"[5]

Whether he wanted publicity or not, he received a great deal of it during the D-Day anniversary year (1994). Most of the major U.S. newspapers included him in their stories, some featuring him alone. He was the "elder statesman" of the jumpers, doing something most of them, years younger, wouldn't attempt. "Dussaq might be 83, but he looks 20 years younger," said the *Cleveland Plain Dealer*. He's "a trim 160-pounder with thick white hair complemented by a California tan."[6] He was typically vague about his past. "I've repressed the memories totally," he told the *Post*. "Many things happened in those days that were not pleasant."[7] Similarly, he told the *New York Post*: "What I'm telling you [about his past] is what [I've read] from reports ... I have read [them] again and again, and for the life of me I don't remember. It's like I'm talking about somebody I don't know."[8]

Two years later, on June 5, 1996, René Dussaq died of cancer. The certificate of death reads "respiratory failure, hemolytic anemia" and "metastatic prostate cancer." His doctor would not call me back so I could not learn more. A relative told me he questioned his Catholic faith at the end—"but only questioned." I know from documents I found at his house that he was a "member in good standing" of the "Sufi Order" in later years. So his father's influence was still with him. The *Los Angeles Times* ran a short obituary noting some of his exploits, but with little hint of the extraordinary life his had been.

If you go on the Internet today and click on "Who's Who at Croft"—the South Carolina infantry center where Dussaq served in 1942—he's one of those "bragged" about among the camp's notable graduates. The piece is a quick composite of his known life—a good one at that. It ends with the following: "In retirement, Dussaq, who 'was once a man of violence' found adventure enough tending his garden. 'You know what they say,' he's quoted as telling them, 'When the Devil gets old, he retires to a monastery.'"

■ ■ ■

Because most people alive at the time remember exactly where they were when Kennedy was shot, and because the assassination occurred during a work day, I asked several of those still alive who were at Dussaq's Los Angeles office that fateful day to describe the scene when they heard the terrible news. I didn't mention Dussaq. I wanted them unprompted to recall him being there—that would be evidence that he was not in Dallas.

Puth said: "I was in the agency office in West Los Angeles [where Dussaq was a supervisor]. We heard it. My boss [a man named Joe Kenney] was there with his wife. She broke down and was crying. We had to console her. It was a real shocker. We went to lunch with some of the other guys."

Was René there?

"I don't remember. I'm sure he was but I don't remember."

Jerry Wasserman was another surviving Prudential agent who knew René well. I asked him if he recalled the day. "Of course. I know exactly where I was." He said he was with a client who repaired auto bumpers downtown. "I'd just left his factory, gotten in the car and turned on the radio. That's when I heard it. It was a terrible day."

Wasserman went home to be with his wife. "Later, or the next day," he said, "I went to the office and it was the topic of discussion. Everybody was so shocked. I'll never forget it. I remember Joe Kenney, my division manager. He and I discussed it." "Was René there?" He didn't remember "but I'm sure he was," he said. "He was the assistant manager. I just don't remember him specifically."

Jack Lines, who had joined Prudential in 1957: "Yes...I walked out of my office and someone...said Kennedy was killed. I was just, 'What!' It was total shock. Everybody was that way."

"Did you talk to René about it?"

"No. I don't remember talking to René about it."

"So on the day Kennedy died, you don't remember seeing René?"

"No."

I wish I could ask others who were there too. But none of those still alive could give me additional names of surviving agents and managers. I've not been able to find other colleagues. These responses don't prove Dussaq wasn't there or elsewhere at the critical times. And equally they don't prove he was involved in the JFK assassination. Neither do they by any measure contradict Douglas Bazata's assertions that René Dussaq was involved and instrumental in JFK's assassination.

■ ■ ■

Toward the end of his diaries, Bazata concludes: "You either believe me or not. I care not one fig...I merely set down all that happened...It is totally true...Readers seeking facts and proofs...had better stop now...No clandestine keeps proofs." If he does, he dies. "Am I afraid? Absolutely...I've survived these 50 years through skill, foxy nastiness and strong action...But I never once talked...not ever...I agreed to be René's historian—a tough role for me. I've always been a creature of action"—bring it on, let's get on with it. "It's difficult for me to merely 'tell.' I do it for René...to bring his plan to near completion. It remains for [America] to finish."

But he neither published nor broadcast the story publicly as he had promised. Only now with my recounting here have his diaries told the tale.

Douglas Bazata died at his home in Chevy Chase, Maryland, in 1999. He had been ill for a while. It was three years after his close friend and fellow warrior René Dussaq had died.

39

The Cuban Question

Was René A. Dussaq hero or villain, champion or dark knight?

It's a question I've asked myself repeatedly. When I began researching this work, I could barely believe Douglas Bazata's claims. Now I'm not so sure. I want to believe Dussaq was admirable. So much of what he did in his long and illustrious career was for the good. But life is complex, as are people.

Douglas Bazata was deeply embedded in the world of secrets, especially those surrounding JFK's death. As a Jedburgh, he was there at the birth of the CIA as an early and major player in that murkiest of worlds. He often hired himself out to the agency as a contractor. He was close friends with former CIA Director William Colby, a former Jedburgh, which afforded him rare and special access. He was an insider.

Dussaq, too, was part of that shadowy, opaque world. He had been a revolutionary, a spy, an assassin, a saboteur, and an FBI undercover agent. Considering what I've learned through my research, I need no further convincing that he was also deeply involved with the CIA. He even alludes to his connection in a letter,[1] and the CIA's refusal to confirm or deny his association indicates, to me, that the tie existed.

Bazata and Dussaq maintained a close, decades-long friendship, one that's independently verified through official records and personal correspondence.[2] Bazata's diaries are rich sources that underscore the two clandestines' connections. They are detailed, factual, and verifiable. The story they tell is credible and I believe they are what they purport to be—Douglas Bazata's honest but secret recollections.

Could they be fantasy, concocted by Bazata for purposes unknown? Sure, and if so, an attempt to conjure a saleable story from which to profit? But how? Having known him, such a longterm master plan would have been thoroughly out of character and probably beyond his abilities or inclinations. He wasn't a glory seeker hungering after fame, nor did he aspire to become a writer. Secrecy was ingrained in his personality. And with the exception of attempting to interest someone in publishing the story he believed René Dussaq wanted him to publish, he loathed writing, finding it tough, tedious, and boring work. Money? He had several chances to profit from the JFK story but ultimately opted not to. In 1978, he writes, he was offered one million dollars by the *National Enquirer* to unmask the JFK plotter he'd disguised as "Peter" or "Paul." He refused to do so.[3]

Further, I doubt the diaries would ever have come to light if I hadn't interviewed Bazata at the right time. He was aging rapidly and had suffered a stroke. His defenses, which served him well as a keeper of secrets, were weakened and down. In 1996, when I spent a week with him at his home, he simply said, "Take what you want." He was feeling remorseful, not only for the life he'd led—his father was a Presbyterian minister whom he revered—but also, perhaps, that he'd failed his cherished friend, Dussaq, by not fulfilling his pledge to inform America of the truth behind the November 22, 1963, assassination of JFK.

Then there's the Lucien Conein letter, independent evidence supporting Bazata's allegations. The legendary CIA and DEA operative testified in writing that on four separate occasions Bazata warned him of the impending JFK murder, and that they discussed it in a fifth meeting following the assassination. For reassurance, I searched in the National Archives and found numerous documents with Conein's signature that matched up with the signature on Conein's letter to Bazata. Moreover, the times and places mentioned in the letter checked out. Conein clearly refers to his meetings with Bazata in his 1977 letter to the Veterans Administration—further confirmation of the letter's authenticity.

Dussaq unquestionably maintained strong ties to Cuba—essential to the plot described in the diaries. His beloved father was Cuban, as were others in his family. He spent considerable time on the island. As mentioned earlier, he'd become a celebrated Cuban tennis star and a participant in the Machado Revolution. His bond with Cuba was so strong that although Argentinian by birth, he sometimes claimed Cuban citizenship in official documents. All of this is well-documented and verified. Also, according to his wife and other accounts, he was asked to participate in the Bay of Pigs invasion and discussed its feasibility with the CIA. Those events alone tie him to Castro's Cuba—although, given Bazata's information,[4] in which way and on whose side remains unclear.

Was Dussaq pro- or anti-Castro?

He gave little indication where he stood—at least in the public or private record. Was that by design, a spy's evasion? His nephew recalled Dussaq's admiration of Castro even after Castro's 1959 Revolution, the dictator's declared allegiance to communism, and his confiscation of Dussaq's family's land and holdings that drove his brother from Cuba. One would logically expect anger and resentment but the opposite was the case. His was, to say the least, a puzzling reaction.

Could Dussaq philosophically have been a communist?

I don't think so. Although the Army suspected him of being such—as did several in his audiences at his pre-war speeches—he was too much an outspoken champion of liberty and individual rights, although those same beliefs could have made him protest, as it has been alleged, the anti-communist witch-hunts during the 1950s. It should be noted that I never uncovered documentary proof that he openly opposed these anti-communist efforts.

Yet even as he was working as an undercover FBI counterspy supposedly rooting out communist subversives, according to his wife Charlotte, he remained friendly with the blacklisted Mexican actress, Dolores del Rio. Earlier, in 1940, he had courted and praised the Peruvian communist leader, Victor Raul Haya.[5] And during a lecture tour, he'd appeared on the same program with the U.S. State Department's chief of Latin American affairs, Laurence Duggan, the same official later exposed as a spy for the Soviet Union.[6]

How could someone assigned to hunting and prosecuting communists be so comfortable in their company on so many occasions? Was he that adept an undercover agent that his infiltration of the communist party movement attracted no notice? Or was he a fellow traveler, a double—or even a triple agent?

If only the now-infirm Fidel Castro himself would or could shed light on the mystery (or mysteries surrounding René Dussaq). Obviously, this will never happen for if he, or his successor(s), disclosed what they know of Dussaq's role on behalf of the Castro government—if in fact he acted on its behalf—the arguably excellent clandestine apparatus Cuba has in operation would be undermined, possibly hurt badly. And if it provided confirmation that Dussaq was involved in the Kennedy assassination on its orders—even without—it might be tantamount to a declaration of war, the endgame of which is rather obvious. Of course, only an unveiling comparable to the revelations that emerged from the Venona Project would bring it all to light.

Reading and deciphering Douglas Bazata's 1970s coded diaries—and in view of what the CIA has since revealed—it's no wonder that Fidel Castro could justify the killing of President Kennedy. According to official records, now public but still secret in the 1970s, Kennedy approved several plots intended to kill Castro. The Bay of Pigs, a follow up to those CIA assassination efforts, was an undisguised attempt to topple Castro's regime and seize the island. Castro was ferocious, fearless like Dussaq, not prone to forgiveness, and vengeful.[7] There were no cooler heads in his inner circle to prevail. Fidel Castro wanted his revenge.

Dussaq returned from Germany, disgusted and at odds with the Army and his own country's foreign policy, at approximately the same time the Cuban government exiled Fidel Castro to Mexico, the very country in which Dussaq had worked undercover for the FBI. In fact, he may well have still been secretly working in Mexico simultaneous with Castro's exile there.

Castro was in dire need of money, supplies, and expertise in guerrilla warfare. Dussaq was virtually at his doorstep, a decorated soldier trained in all the required combat skills, including assassination and sabotage. René was an avowed Cuban patriot who also had fled the island after an earlier uprising. Dussaq had exactly the sort of experience and background that Castro required.

Had the two met, come to an understanding?

Beyond the entries in Bazata's diaries, there is no independent, corroborating evidence. Still, the question lingers. Castro toured the U.S. seeking support for his movement. Even in its nascent stages, Castro and his circle ran an effective and diligent intelligence operation. Dussaq was not an unknown quantity. It's impossible to accept that he, or certainly one of his trusted aides, had no contact with a potential ally as prized as René Dussaq.

Here's another puzzle:

In 1977, Bazata wrote in his diary that Dussaq "told me [he] had a man, very gifted, break in selected houses [and] make 'arranged' long distance calls to 'Mark' [to] aid misdirection [of the JFK assassination investigation]. The call," writes Bazata, "was to Jose Antonio Cabarca of Mexico City," not otherwise described. According to secret CIA cables, a Mexico City lawyer named "Jose Antonio Cabarca," was arrested in Mexico City on November 24, 1963, two days after the assassination, following his placing a phone call to a Miami-based Cuban stating, "With [the] assassination [of] Pres. [sic] Kennedy, Castro's plan has been realized. The next one to go would be 'Bob.'"

This secret cable was not declassified and available to the public until 1992, when the House Select Committee on Assassinations (HSCA) released it. During the next few years, the CIA declassified and released other related cables.[8]

How did Bazata know that an obscure figure like Jose Antonio Cabarca was connected to the slaying as early as 1977?[9]

One answer is that his diaries are factual. Dussaq said as much.

There are caveats, of course. Who is "Mark?" He remains unidentified. And if Dussaq didn't want suspicion to fall on Castro, why would Cabarca declare that the assassination was Castro's plan? I have no answers, but we're all aware that the secret world is filled with misdirection, dead ends, and lies—a veritable wall of mirrors, as it's often been described. Perhaps Cabarca got carried away after Dussaq's "man" phoned him? Maybe Bazata erred in recounting what Dussaq told him? The diaries easily could have errors. I'm cognizant of that possibility. But if not hearing it directly from Dussaq, how would Bazata know Cabarca's name when the secret cable wasn't declassified until 1992?

Dussaq himself wrote that he was an actor. He lied to his teacher and loved the successful subterfuge. What other secrets had he hidden from view? Had he participated in other uprisings and revolutions? What actually happened in the crash off Mulholland in 1932 in Los Angeles? Was he acting as a spy during his diving ventures in the run-up to World War II? And, if so, for whom? What had compelled his first wife to hide her assets just prior to her death? How had the OSS lost track of Dussaq as he fought with the Maquis? What was the mysterious medical operation René's father wrote Charlotte about in the early 1950s? What precisely had happened while he'd been undercover in Mexico? Had he really run guns over the border for a communist group in Cuernavaca, as he'd told his nephew, Francois? Or had the smuggling been designated for Castro himself? And had he really "put down" a union member, a clear case of murder even if he'd done it during an FBI-sanctioned operation?

What really occurred in Germany on that cold Cold War border? Both the military and the FBI seemed to suddenly, inexplicably turn against him. Why? The question has never really been satisfactorily answered and without access to military and CIA records, we can only speculate. Why does there exist a Swiss bank account in his name? Bazata specifically mentions it. A great deal of Dussaq's pre-war speaking engagements focused on and emphasized America's domination of Latin America's nations. This theme dovetails precisely with what Bazata insisted was Dussaq's primary, even obsessive concern. And, most importantly, of course is where René Dussaq was when John F. Kennedy was murdered.

So many questions still lack definitive answers.

I've often wondered, in light of several of his diary entries, if Bazata himself was in Dallas on that fateful day. Occasionally it appears as if Bazata himself was researching the how-to of the assassination. But wouldn't he have done that if he was personally tasked with a role in it—whether there or not. I can't drum up another reason for him to do so.

A recent television documentary noted that there are approximately two thousand books that have been published about the Kennedy assassination. Seventy percent of Americans believe the murder was a conspiracy. Over a million tourists each year visit Dallas' infamous Dealey Plaza. The assassination of JFK has become an industry unto itself. I'm less an expert on the assassination, but I've studied enough about it to know that what Douglas Bazata said and wrote in no way contradicts the more sober current prevailing theories. The Cuban government could certainly have been involved, along with rogue CIA agents, and New Orleans Mafia figures. Bazata, in the diaries, unites all the elements, tying up many of the loose ends. And he had the basic story outlined by 1968, and confirmed by 1976. The diaries, with the dates in them pinpointed, underscore this, which is certainly reason enough to now consider them seriously. With the release of official material related to the assassination over the past several years, it's become easier to connect the dots and pursue the appropriate lines of inquiry. The Bazata diary's contents, bits and pieces that originally defied connections and failed to provide a coherent picture now, in light of newly released information, may do so today.

A little known—and today—lost fact:

In the horrible days immediately following JFK's murder, the administration was convinced Fidel Castro was behind the assassination. Bobby

Kennedy, who had so relentlessly tried to kill Castro, was consumed with guilt, convinced he'd caused his brother's death. Jacqueline Kennedy, JFK's widow, wrote Russian Premier Nikita Kruschev that she was convinced Castro was the culprit.[10] Castro, alerted by his network of double agents about the continuing plots against him, had only days before JFK's death warned that if the plots continued, "your leaders are not safe."[11] Gen. Alexander Haig, who would become secretary of state under Ronald Reagan, wrote in his memoir, *Inner Circles*, that the day after the assassination, President Lyndon Johnson said, "Kennedy tried to get Castro, but Castro got Kennedy first." Johnson himself is now suspect in recent speculation. But Haig adds that he also saw in those terrible days a secret report that said Oswald had been in Cuba with Cuban intelligence officers several days before Dallas, arranged through the Soviet embassy in Mexico. The detailed report, writes Haig, "would not have reached so high a level if others had not judged it plausible enough to merit the consideration of high officials." But instead of bringing it into the investigation, he was told to destroy it "and never mention it again." The fear, he writes, was that if pursued the U.S. would have to invade Cuba and thus begin World War III.[12]

So the first suspect, Fidel—the primary suspect—was eliminated before even the first commission began investigating.

René Dussaq led a long, eventful life, much of it shrouded in shadow and secrecy. Although there's no conclusive evidence, no "smoking gun" so to say, confirming his presence in Dallas on November 22, 1963, there are surely many indications that he may well have been there. And if Dussaq was there, as Bazata testifies, he might well have fired the fatal shot or shots that brought down John F. Kennedy, the thirty-fifth president of the United States.

I hope not, for there is much that is admirable in his saga. But I can no longer dismiss the accusation. The persistent stonewalling by the U.S. government (and the Prudential Insurance Company, too, among others), in refusing to accede to my repeated requests for further documentation and answers only serves to arouse more suspicion rather than quell it. In weighing the circumstantial evidence I've collected and provided here, ultimately it's up to the reader to judge whether René A. Dussaq was implicated and, if he was, the extent of his complicity in the commission of the greatest unsolved crime of the twentieth century.

ACKNOWLEDGMENTS

This book did not start out as a book. It was just an inquiry. After writing and publishing *Target: Patton*, my first "Target" book, I had lingering questions about passages in Douglas Bazata's personal diaries. There was a mystery in them concerning René A. Dussaq, his friend from World War II. To my surprise, Dussaq lived near me. Unfortunately, he'd died just months before I learned this. But his wife was gracious and gave me access to his documents, especially an unfinished manuscript about his life. Without that, this book probably would not have been written.

My cousin, Tim Wilcox, head of International Investigators, introduced me to Douglas Bazata. Needless to say, if I had not met Bazata, this book also probably would not have been written. My longtime agent and friend, Jim Trupin, encouraged me throughout the research and writing. He saw the potential. A former editor, his advice and suggestions were always good.

My wife Bego never refused to read a chapter even if she didn't feel like it. She was my gauge of whether I was on the right or wrong track. My son Robert was the same. My daughter Amaya, too far to read daily pages, was always supportive. It helps to have family in the lonely battle with words.

In addition, I'd like to thank Alex Novak at Regnery for acquiring the book. This will be my third book in a row with this fine publisher. Dan Allott did a superb job editing the book. At the National Archives (NARA), Mary Kay Schmidt was a big help with research. Also aiding were NARA's Eric Voelz, Eric VanSlander, Bill Cunliffe, and Leroy W. Gardner. At the British National Archives, David Harrison was very helpful. In France, Catherine McLean at the Musee de la Resistance d'Anterrieux, and Gerard Crevon helped with Maquis history. Guillermo Tabernilla aided with facts about the Basque training outside Paris.

Thanks also must go to Dussaq family members who answered questions, especially his nephews who lived with him, and Gina Dussaq, wife of René's only son, Maurice, who unfortunately died before I could interview him. I also want to thank Northwestern professor Ken Alder, the Katherine Applegate family, René's Prudential colleagues who spoke with me, Nick Pinhey, historian Thomas L. Ensminger, Kathi Neal at UC Berkeley, the Los Angeles County coroner's office, Peter Vollheim, and Bill Davies. All helped in different but important ways.

Sources

BOOKS

Alder, Ken. *The Lie Detectors*. New York: Free Press, 2007.

Alsop, Stewart and Thomas Braden. *Sub Rosa: The OSS and American Espionage*. San Diego: Harcourt, Brace, 1946.

Anonymous. *The Man on the Grassy Knoll*. Palm Beach: Grey Knight Press, 2011.

Argote-Freyre, Frank. *Fulgencio Batista: From Revolutionary to Strongman*. New Brunswick: Rutgers University Press, 2006.

Beavan, Colin. *Operation Jedburgh: D-Day and America's First Shadow War*. New York: Penguin Books, 2006 .

Benson, Michael. *Who's Who in the JFK Assassination: an A to Z Encyclopedia*. New York: Citadel Press, 1993.

Binney, Marcus. *Secret War Heroes: The Men of Special Operations*. London: Hodder Paperbacks, 2006.

Bown, Wayne H. *Spain During World War II*. Columbia: University of Missouri Press, 2006.

Braden, Thomas. *Sub Rosa: The OSS and American Espionage*. San Diego: Harcourt, Brace, 1946.

Bradley, David. *No Place to Hide 1946/1984*. Lebanon: Dartmouth/ New England, 1983.

Breuer, William B. *Vendetta: Castro and the Kennedy Brothers*. New York: Wiley, 1997.

Carroll, Peter N., Michael Nash, and Melvin Small, eds. *The Good Fight Continues: World War II Letters From the Abraham Lincoln Brigade*. New York: NYU Press, 2006.

Castro, Fidel. *My Early Years*. Melbourne: Ocean Press, 2005.

Castro, Fidel and Ignacio Ramonet. *Fidel Castro: My Life: A Spoken Biography*. New York: Scribner, 2006 .

Chambard, Claude. *The Maquis: A History of the French Resistance Movement*. Indianapolis: Bobbs-Merrill Company, 1976.

CIA. *CIA Targets Fidel: The 1967 secret assassination report by the CIA Inspector General*. Melbourne: Ocean Press, 1996.

Colby, William. *Honorable Men: My Life in the CIA*. New York: Simon & Schuster, 1978.

Craig, John D. *Danger Is My Business*. New York: Simon & Schuster, 1938. (For January 1946 epilogue see articles by John Craig.)

Creed, Virginia. *France*. The Fideler Company, 1971.

Dankbaar, Wim. *Files on JFK*. Independent Publishers Group (IPG), 2007–2008.

Dunlop, Richard. *Donovan: America's Master Spy*. Skokie: Rand McNally & Co., 1982.

Dussaq, René A. *Adventure To Order*. Unfinished, unpublished manuscript. I have two of these, a long one and a short one. I got the short one from his home when his wife Charlotte gave me access. I got the longer one from Gina Dussaq, widow of Toro, René's only son, when I visited her in 2010. For outline purposes, the short is "A," the long is "B." It appears to have been written either in the late 1930s or early 50s. One page on the shorter one seems to have his agent's imprint on it. Page 139 of B makes me think it's late 30s. He also mentions Squalis (submarine) as "recent." The sub sunk in May 1939 on its first test. Twenty-six died and thirty-three were rescued.

Elliot, Geoffrey. *The Shooting Star: Denis Rake, MC, A Clandestine Hero of the Second World War.* London: Methuen, 2009.

Ensminger, Tomas. *Spies, Supplies and Moonlit Skies: The French Connection, April–June 1944.* Xlibris Corp, 2004.

Escalante, Fabian. *JFK: The Cuba Files: The Untold Story of the Plot to Kill Kennedy,* Ocean Press, 2006.

———. See *CIA's Inspector General's Report* for Escalante testimony given to them.

Fiester, Sherry P. *Enemy of the Truth: Myths, Forensics, and the Kennedy Assassination.* JFK Lancer Productions & Publications, Inc., 2012.

Fleming, E. J. *Hollywood Death and Scandal Sites: Sixteen Driving Tours with Directions and the Full Story from Tallulah Bankhead to River Phoenix.* Jefferson: McFarland & Co., 2000.

———. *The Fixers: Eddie Mannix, Howard Strickling and the MGM Publicity Machine.* Jefferson: McFarland, 2004.

Fontova, Humberto E. *Fidel: Hollywood's Favorite Tyrant.* Washington, D.C. Regnery, 2005.

Ford, Corey. *Donovan of OSS.* New York: Little Brown, 1970.

Ford, Roger. *Steel From The Sky: The Jedburgh Raiders, France 1944.* London: Weidenfeld & Nicholson, 2004.

Geyer, Georgie Anne. *Guerrilla Prince: The Untold Story of Fidel Castro.* New York: Little, Brown and Company, 1991.

Guevara, Ernesto Che. *Episodes of the Cuban Revolutionary War 1956—1958.* Atlanta: Pathfinder Press, 1996.

Hadley-Garcia, George. *Hispanic Hollywood: The Latins in Motion Pictures.* Secaucus: Carol Publishing Group, 1990.

Haig, Alexander M., Jr. *Inner Circles: How America Changed The World: A Memoir.* New York: Warner Books Inc., 1992.

Johnson, Haynes. *The Bay of Pigs: The Leaders' Story of Brigade 2506.* New York: W. W. Norton & Company, 1964.

Jones, Howard. *The Bay of Pigs.* Oxford: Oxford University Press, 2008.

Kahn, Gordon. *Hollywood on Trial*. New York: Boni & Gaer, Inc., 1948.

Keeler, Eloise. *Lie Detector Man*. Telshare Publishing, 1983.

Kirkpatrick, Sidney D. *A Cast of Killers*. Boston: E.P. Dutton, 1986.

Kornbluh, Peter, ed. *Bay of Pigs Declassified: The Secret CIA Report on the Invasion of Cuba*. New York: New Press, 1998.

Kurlansky, Mark. *The Basque History of the World*. New York: Walker & Co., 1999.

Latell, Brian. *Castro's Secrets: The CIA and Cuba's Intelligence Machine*. New York: Palgrave Macmillan, 2012.

Marquez-Sterling, Manuel. *CUBA, 1952-1959: The True Story of Castro's Rise to Power*. Wintergreen: Kleiopatria Digital Press, 2009 (advance edition).

Matthews, Herbert L. *Fidel Castro*. New York: Simon & Schuster, 1969.

Millar, George. *Maquis: The French Resistance at War*. Cassell Military Paperbacks, 2003 (first published by Wellington House, London, 1945).

Nesmith, Robert L. *Dig For Pirate Treasure*. New York: Bonanza Books, 1958.

Porter, Darwin. *Hollywood's Silent Closet*. Georgia Literary Association, 2001.

Rake, Denis. *Rake's Progress*. London: Leslie Frewin, 1968.

Rasenberger, Jim. *The Brilliant Disaster: JFK, Castro, and America's Doomed Invasion of Cuba's Bay of Pigs*. New York: Scribner, 2011.

Rathbone, John Paul. *The Sugar King of Havana: The Rise and Fall of Julio Lobo, Cuba's Last Tycoon*. New York: Penguin Books, 2011.

Rawlinson, Andrew. *The Book of Enlightened Masters: Western Teachers in Eastern Traditions*. Chicago: Open Court Publishing Company, 1997.

Roush, Col. John H. Jr. *World War II Reminiscences*. Reserve Officers Association of the U.S., Calif. Dept., 1995.

Royal Historical Society. *Transactions of the Royal Historical Society: Sixth Series, XIII*. Cambridge: Cambridge University Press, 2003.

Russell, Dick. *On the Trail of the JFK Assassins: A Groundbreaking Look at America's Infamous Conspiracy.* Skyhorse Publishing, 2008.

Russo, Gus and Stephen Molton. *Brothers In Arms: The Kennedys, the Castros, and the Politics of Murder.* New York: Bloomsbury USA, 2008.

Russo, Gus. *Live by the Sword: The Secret War Against Castro and the Death of JFK.* Baltimore: Bancroft Press, 1998.

Sauer, Francois W. *Relearn, Evolve, and Adapt.* Bloomington: iUniverse, Inc., 2008.

Schecter, Jerrold and Leona. *Sacred Secrets: How Soviet Intelligence Operations Changed American History.* Sterling: Brassy's, Inc., 2002.

Swarengin, Phil. *The Carpetbagger Project: Secret Heroes.* CreateSpace, 2007.

Thomas, Evan. *The Very Best Men: Four Who Dared: The Early Years of the CIA.* New York: Touchstone, 1995.

Thomas, Victoria. *Hollywood's Latin Lovers: Latino, Italian and French Men Who Make the Screen Smolder.* Santa Monica: Angel City Press, 1998.

Troy, Thomas F. *Wild Bill and Intrepid.* New Haven: Yale University Press, 1996.

Wake, Nancy. *The White Mouse.* New York: Macmillan, 1986.

Waller, Douglas. *Wild Bill Donovan: The Spymaster Who Created the OSS and Modern American Espionage.* New York: Free Press, 2011.

Warren Commission. *A Concise Compendium of The Warren Commission Report on the Assassination of John F. Kennedy.* New York: Popular Library, 1964.

Weiner, Tim. *Legacy of Ashes: The History of the CIA.* New York: Doubleday, 2007.

Werth, Alexander. *France 1940–1955.* Boston: Beacon Press, 1966.

Wilcox, Robert K. *Target: Patton: The Plot to Assassinate Gen. George S. Patton.* Washington, D.C.: Regnery, 2008.

ARTICLES

"Adventurer Sees Greater Thrill in Pan-Americanism." *Kirksville Daily Express*, March 7, 1940.

"At End of 200-foot Plunge." *Los Angeles Examiner*, Febuary 24, 1933.

Beck, Jan. "Katherine Applegate Keeler Dussaq: The First Woman Document Examiner." *The American Society of Questioned Document Examiners, Inc.*, 2, no. 1 (June 1999).

Brooks, Jeanne Freeman. "Big step taken back toward Normandy." *San Diego Union*, February 19, 1994.

Bryan, F. MacDonald. "Test Descent is Rehearsal For Attempt." *Washington Post*, December 5, 1937.

Chaplin, Gordon. "I Learned To Keep A Secret—And it was torture." *Potomac*, June 6, 1976.

Clay, Hiland and Jack DeSimone. "René Dussaq, Son of Cuban Diplomat, Has Packed Varied, Colorful Experiences in 30-Year Span." *Spartanburg Journal*, May 23, 1942.

Craig, John D. Epilogue to *Danger Is My Business*, excerpt. *Coronet*, January 1946, 160–61.

———. "I Was Scared Stiff." *Wings* (March 1938).

Davis, Fred. "Veteran re-lives D-Day action." *Bear Valley Springs, Ca.* 16, no. 7 (July 1994). From Dussaq papers via his second wife, Charlotte.

DeCarvalho, George. "Capt. Bazooka, a Character, But Not One in a Comic Strip." *San Francisco Chronicle*, February 14, 1951.

Dussaq, René. "Sunken Treasure Curse Scorned by Searchers." *Daily Boston Globe*, July 15, 1939 (one of a series by Dussaq syndicated by *North American Newspaper Alliance*).

"Friends Go To Moreno Last Rites." *Los Angeles Times*, February 26, 1933.

Hughes, Les. "The Special Force Wing." *Trading Post* (July–September 1988).

Jameson, Betty. "WASP Head Wants to Start New Air Race." *San Antonio Light*, September 19, 1944.

Katz, Jesse. "Welcome to Hotel California." *Los Angeles Magazine* (March 2004).

"Makes His Mark." *Washington Post*, May 9, 1942.

McCarthy, Dennis. "Old Soldier Hung on for Ride of a Lifetime." *LA Daily News*, June 11, 1996.

McGee, Jim. "Informants scuttle plots against Cuba." *The Miami Herald*, June 19, 1983.

McKinney, Delores. "Looking Back: A Woman of Independent Means." November 26, 2004.

Mio, Lou. "At 83, He's still ready to jump; Elder statesman parachuted into France to help Resistance." *Cleveland Plain Dealer*, February 20, 1994.

"Moreno Driver Absolved." *Los Angeles Times*, February 25, 1933.

"Mrs. Moreno Auto Death Inquest Set." *Los Angeles Examiner*, February 24, 1933.

"Mrs. Moreno's Death Accident, Jury Rules." *Los Angeles Examiner*, February 25, 1933.

"Mrs. Moreno's Death Quiz Set." *Los Angeles Times*, February 24, 1933.

Pope, Polly. "René Dussaq, Who Sells Insurance in The Mile, Could Write Quite a Book." *LA Independent*, July 11, 1949.

Rasmussen, Cecilia. "Police Scandal Is Worst Since 1930s," *Los Angeles Times*, September 17, 1999.

———. "Tale of Wealth, Murder and a Family's Decline." *Los Angeles Times*, August 20, 2000.

Reynolds, Reg. "Rock Schoolboy Became Silent Screen Star." *Gibraltar Magazine* (November 2007): online edition.

Ringle, Ken. "The Golden Parachutists; 50 years later, Troopers prepare to relive the glory that was D-Day." *Washington Post*, February 21, 1994.

Rodriguez, Mikel. "The case of Basque Commandos." Euskonews & Media 99.zbk (2000/11/10-17), Euskonews.com.

Russo, Gus. "The Dallas-Cuba Connection – 2009 Update." *Secrets of a Homicide*, August 6, 2009, http://jfkfiles.blogspot.com.

Smith, Kyle. "D-Day paratrooper ready to jump again—at 83." *New York Post*, April 27, 1994.

"The Stunt man became a military professor." *Mail*, February 10, 1951.

"Treasure Vessels Found on Sea Bed." *New York Times*, September 13, 1939.

"Victim Happy Before Death, Antonio Moreno Tells of Phone Conversation With Him at 7 o'clock Night of Tragedy." *Los Angeles Examiner,* February 5, 1922 (on Bruce Long's Taylorology site; http://www.taylorology.com).

"Waldo H. Logan Kills Himself in Miami Hotel," *Chicago Tribune*, January 12, 1957.

Watson, Elmo Scott. "Again is Revived the Romantic Story of the 'Hispaniola Treasure.'" *The Ironwood Times*, December 2, 1938.

Wise, David. "[CIA] Covert Operations Abroad: An Overview." CIA document "Approved for Release," 2004, acquired at National Archives.

DOCUMENTS

"A Short Autobiography of René A. Dussaq, CLU, Manager, Prudential Insurance Co." From Dussaq documents.

"Verification of Lt. Dussaq's Report." HQ OSS Detachment, European Theater, US Army, SO/WE section, dated 4 December 1944 and signed by George A. Schriever, First Lt. (two-page document copied from Dussaq docs).

Adjustment of Dussaq's birth date in military records. Department of the Army, office of the adjutant general, Washington, D.C., signed by "W. James," Adjutant General. (Copied from Dussaq docs).

War Department. "Permission" for "Captain Dussaq, Inf." to "visit Cuba." It's from adjutant general's office, Washington, D.C., dated August 27, 1945.

OSS France office, July 18, 1945. Permission to visit parents in Geneva, Switzerland at end of July.

Application for enrollment in Army courses. Dated May 28, 1947. (From Dussaq material at his home).

1953 Separation papers from the army. DD form 214. (From Dussaq material).

Organized Reserve Corps Questionnaire filled out June 13, 1949. (From Dussaq material).

Typed seven-page statement by René Dussaq to FBI agent Vincent W. Hughes about allegations that he said things about the FBI and his undercover work for them. It discusses his undercover work in LA, Mexico, and Germany with and against communists; names various intelligence Cos; and charges he did "strong arm" missions for the FBI and was present when Red was "manhandled." It is signed by Dussaq and dated October 14, 1954, LA, California. (From Dussaq material).

HQ 532D Military Intel Battalion order, October 22, relieving René of assignment with battalion, by order of Maj. Krieg. (one page)

Dussaq Army Separation Qualification Record. (form 1001945)

Dussaq's application to Veterans of O.S.S. (From Dussaq material)

Army Separation Qualification Record (form DA 493) signed by Grace Womble and dated December 17, 1953.

Packet of documents (twenty-five pages) about Dussaq entering OSS, including an OSS job application with lots of personal information. Starts with OSS memorandum on Dussaq to Lt. John M. Shaheen from Percy Wood. Dated March 25, 1943. Sent to me by U.S. National Archives. Record Group 226, Entry 92a, Box 34, Folder 512.

Two-page confidential OSS memo from George K. Bowden to Lt. Col. E.C. Huntington, Jr. It's dated November 30, 1942 and explains why they want to recruit him. Sent with D13 by U.S. National Archives, Record Group 226, Entry 92a, Box 34, Folder 512.

Packet of documents (thirty pages) about trying to get Dussaq in OSS. There is resistance from his superiors who are about to go overseas and want his services and possibly Dussaq himself because he wants to get into action ASAP. His wife is consulted. U.S. National

Archives, RG 226, Entry 93A, Box 34, Folder 512 (attached post-it
note says "Part 2 of 3 ... ").

Apparent file on Dussaq beginning with British evaluation of him dated
July 17, 1943. It describes him as "flamboyant, verbose, self-centered
and not recommended." But also includes note that he "left for field
22.5.44" and is part of the "Freelance" circuit. Three pages from
UK National Archives, HS 9/462/3.

Packet of twenty-five pages, formerly top secret docs (some dupes) from
U.S. National Archives postmarked on the envelope, May 16, 2008.
These have to do with his service in WWII, including drop into
France and selection to special forces. I presume they came over from
CIA. They are from: RG 226, Entry 168(N or A), Box 15 (folder
number illegible but possibly 11) They appear to be reports and other
relatively immediate processing when René came back from Free-
lance in the fall of 1944. Some done in Paris.

Packet of thirty-seven pages, formerly top-secret docs, from U.S. National
Archives, postmarked on envelope May 21, 2008. These have to do
with Dussaq's service in WWII, including wife's death, his DFC,
promotion to captain, parachute training in '45, and Far East training. I presume they came over from CIA. They are from RG 226,
Entry 92, Box 34, Folder 512.

Certification by Cuban Sec of State Orestes Ferraca y Marino that
twenty-one-year-old René Dussaq is Cuban national. Given January
13, 1933 in Cuba. Has picture of petulant René.

Certificate of naturalization as American, dated July 24, 1942.

Petition for naturalization, dated July 21, 1942 (two pages from Ances-
tryLibrary.com).

Certificate of Service, November 5, 1945.

Seventy-nine-page Army Air Force booklet about the special air transport
unit used at Bikini atom bomb tests. Main title is "Air Transport
Unit" with (Green Hornet), Roswell-Kwajalein and Fifty-Eighth Wing
variously elsewhere on cover. No date but has to be post mid-1946.

Thirteen-page Post Project Crossroads report entitled, "The Role of
Army Air Forces Radio—Controlled Aircraft in Project X-Roads."

Thirty-nine-page packet of pages apparently from British archives about "Freelance" activities in France. It is labeled "Freelance Gaspard Circuit" in big letters, and "Vol.3....Western Europe" in smaller letters across the top. There is a map of the pertinent area boxed on the front. At the bottom is a citation "(1338) War Diary Vol. 11 p. 90," which could be the larger volume from which this packet was taken. The first few pages are selected cover pages. The next excerpt is pp. 221–26 of "Vol. 3 April, May, June 1944 Western Europe." Then pp. 798–824, 837, 847 of the same which deal specifically with "Freelance" for a few pages and then Dussaq's activity report which which I received from Ensminger. For citation purposes it is called: Activity Report of First Lieutenant René A. Dussaq (Anselme), Freelance Gaspard Circuit, Vol. 3, Western Europe, F-Section; Book 5 (July, Aug, Sept, 1944) from British National Archives.

Dussaq's actual report of his mission in France from May–Sept 1944. It is entitled "Report of Activities—1ˢᵗ Lt. René A. Dussaq (Anselme)." Twelve pages with maps. From Tom Ensminger's website.

René's instructions from Brits before he jumps in. Several pages, perhaps not complete. Titled "Operation Instruction No. F. 133 – Part 1.

Fake ID of "Alexandre René Lacoste", used by René in France. Date of stamp is June 3, 1944." It says that he's a professor, born May 6, 1908.

Report on "Freelance-Gaspard Circuit," "History of Organization." Three pages, small type, and starts with a graph on Gaspard and then continues with a date-by-date entry log of events. It apparently (according to an Internet search) comes from Lt. Col. EG Boxshall, *Chronology of SOE operations in France with the resistance DURING World War II*, 1960, typescript (copy from the library of Pearl Witherington Cornioley, available at the Library Valençay). Voir sheet 30B, FREELANCE-GASPARD CIRCUIT . See sheet 30B, FREELANCE GASPARD-CIRCUIT. Mine has the 30B in right-hand corner. This document can be obtained from Tomas L. Ensminger's excellent research at http://www.801492.org/Agents/TeamInsertions/FREELANCE-GASPARD.pdf.

Letter from Bernard M. W. Knox, former Jedburgh, with Dussaq gondola jump, written for Bazata to veterans board on Harvard letterhead and dated April 25, 1978.

Swiss Overseas Immigration permit for November 1930 departure to Havana, Cuba from Boulogne s/M. Residence is Geneva, Switzerland.

One page OSS Memo date September 21, 1945 to "The Director" (General Donovan) from E. W. Andrews, Lt. (j.g.), USNR. It accompanies Beldarain report on Basque training. From National Archives packet, sent 2013.

Four-page OSS report from General Beldarrain to "Don Jose Antonio de Aguirre," exiled Basque president in New York City. Dated "Paris, 17 August 1945." From National Archives packet, sent 2013.

Formerly "Top Secret" five-page OSS memo on Basque training dated April 7, 1945. "Subject: Operation Airedale. To: Commanding officer, OSS, ETO." From National Archives (2013).

Formerly "Top Secret" six-page OSS memo, "The Basque Situation." Dated April 14, 1945. It's to "Mr. Whitney Shepardson" from Lt. (jg) Edward W. Andrews, USNR. RG 226, WN# 25922, Box 2, National Archives (2013).

Formerly "Eyes Only Secret" CIA memorandum entitled "Family Jewels" about CIA-Mafia plot to kill Fidel Castro. It's by Howard J. Osborn, CIA Director of Security, dated May 16, 1973. National Archives.

PERSONAL PAPERS

Letter to René from his father, undated, beginning with "My beloved Son" (four handwritten legal pad pages).

Bazata letter to Ralph de Toledano, dated September 7, 1980, proposing Toledano write his book (in Toledano file).

Outline of a book Bazata was going to write with de Toledano. I have several pieces of it which I call P3-1, P3-2, etc. P3-1 is labeled "The Doorway." P3-2: "Operation 'Hydra K.'" P3-3 "K: Op 'Hydra….'" This is in "Assassination plan" folder under JFK "subject."

Outline of a book Bazata wrote labeled "Outline One" and dated "10 Oct 1976." It comes from Bazledg28 pp. 51–64.

Continuing outline for book. This one has "ONE Chapter Outline: for 'Florida': 20 Feb 77" at top (has previous "BL-2" in top right corner). Two pages.

May 6, 1977 Bazata paper entitled "An extreme brief for Roy..." It concerns Hydra-K and seems to be an overview. I have a five-page document and it incorporates parts P-3.

Eight lined pages torn from small Bazata spiral notebook labeled "Specifics Chapter–K."

Single-family book page filled out about René by wife Charlotte for their grandchildren. It tells things the kids might want to know about their grandfather, such as his background and when and where he and Charlotte met.

Over 156 personal letters overwhelmingly between René and Charlotte while he was in the Army, mainly while he was in Germany during the Korean War. They span three years, from November 1950 to November 1953. They also include a few letters from the decades beyond. These were saved by Charlotte. A few of the envelopes contain more than one letter, which is why their actual number is over 156. I've numbered each letter and refer to them as P8 (plus the number, e.g., P8-28).

First two chapters of a proposed ghostwritten biography of Douglas Bazata. Writer is not clear. From markings on the envelope in which I found it, it appears to have been written in 1976. The envelope has a return address of Charles Neighbors, Inc., a New York literary agent. (It's in "Baz Bio Documents" file, which is in Box 3 of Patton files.)

Personal letter to René from Daphne M. Freile, of West Redding, Ct. She was secretary to Jed CO Col. G. Richard Musgrave and tells how she listed him as "Known to be deceased." She died in 2008, according to an obituary in the *North Haven Citizen*.

INTERVIEWS

Francoise Brun-Cottan, Jean-David Coen's sister and family friend of René and Charlotte, in an interview with the author, 2009 and September 2013.

Jean-David Coen, family friend of René and Charlotte, in an interview with the author, September 2009.

Harry Drucker and his mother, Miriam, neighbors of René and Charlotte, in an interview with the author, April 2013.

Charlotte Dussaq, René A. Dussaq's second wife, May 1997, June 1 and 27, 1997, plus follow-ups.

Elena Dussaq, René A.'s niece, in an interview with the author, March 15, 2014.

Gina Dussaq, René A.'s son, Maurice "Toro" Dussaq's second wife, in an interview with the author, April 13, 2010, May 19–21, 2010, plus follow-ups.

Kathleen Dussaq, René A.'s son, Maurice "Toro" Dussaq's first wife, in an interview with the author, May 4, 2008.

Maurice Dussaq, René A.'s nephew, in an interview with the author, April 13, 2008.

René E. Dussaq, nephew of René A., in an interview with the author, March 11, 2014, plus follow-up.

Sean Dussaq, son of René A.'s nephew Maurice, in an interview with the author, April 12, 2008.

Jack H. Lines, Prudential colleague, in an interview with the author, February 2, 2011, and September 9, 2014.

John J. Maloney, former journalist and PR man who earlier interviewed Dussaq, in an interview with the author, June 1997 and 2013.

Walter Puth, Prudential colleague, in an interview with the author, May 5, 2008, June 10, 2008, and September 11, 2014.

Gorden Ramsden, Western Prudential administrator in 1960s–1970s, in an interview with the author, December 28, 2011.

Francois W. Sauer, René A.'s nephew, in an interview with the author, 2009, plus follow-ups.

Gen. John K. Singlaub, fellow Jedburgh (OSS) with René A., in an interview with the author, March 3, 2012.

Jerry Wasserman, Prudential colleague, in an interview with the author, June 29, 2008, and September 2014.

Rick Weber, Prudential colleague, in an interview with the author, February 8, 2012 and July 7, 2012.

INTERNET SOURCES

"Fidel Castro." DiscoverTheNetworks.org, http://www.discoverthenetworks.org/.

Items about Antonio Moreno mentioning René Dussaq in "Some Rumors," ed. Bruce Long. *Taylorology* 57 (September 1997): 22–23, http://www.silentera.com/taylorology/issues/Taylor12.txt.

"Harrington Joes." *The Carpetbagger Archives*, http://www.801492.org/index.html. This is part of Thomas L. Ensminger's extensive research site on drops of agents in WWII.

"The Maquis of Mount Mouchet." Translated from French.

Sierra, J. A. "History of Cuba," www.historyofcuba.com.

"Who's Who at Camp Croft," U.S. Army Infantry Replacement Center at Camp Croft, South Carolina, http://www.schistory.net/campcroft/people/whoswho.html.

Notes

Introduction

1. I wrote extensively about him in *Target: Patton* (Washington, DC: Regnery, 2014), my recent book about the possible assassination of Gen. George S. Patton.

1: The Commando

1. Pilot's report #456 (Merrill), Stationer 113 Operation, 22/23 May 1944, Harrington Agent Non-Team Insertions, British National Archives via Tom Ensminger's "Carpetbagger" website records.

2. Activity Report of 1st Lieutenant René A. Dussaq (Anselme), Freelance Gaspard Circuit, Vol. 3, Western Europe, F-Section, book 5 (July, August, September, 1944), p. 802, from British National Archives.

3.   Kyle Smith, "D-Day Paratrooper Ready to Jump Again—at 83,"
      New York Post, April 27, 1994.

4.   Hiland Clay and Jack DeSimone, "René Dussaq, Son of Cuban
      Diplomat, Has Packed Varied, Colorful Experiences in 30-Year
      Span," *Spartanburg Journal*, May 23, 1942.

5.   OSS Interoffice Memo to Major David K. E. Bruce, November
      30, 1942, 13032.

6.   Page fourteen of an unfinished biography of Bazata, ghostwritten
      for him in 1976. The writer is identified only as "Bud" or
      "Buck." The same feat—although, so far, I've been unable to
      find a 1943 press or newsreel about it—is mentioned in Roger
      Ford, *Steel from the Sky* (London: Weidenfeld & Nicolson,
      2004), 28.

7.   November 22, 1943, memo from Lt. (j.g.) H. G. Nickles, USNR,
      to Lt. Col. Joseph F. Haskell, U.S. National Archives, Rec. Grp.
      226, Entry 168A, Box 15.

8.   Bazata's unfinished biography, 14.

9.   Bazata diary (#41), 51. The numbers are mine, not Bazata's, who
      only gave the ledger-like diaries titles like "Don't think. React"
      or "No name. No title. No nothing." They are mostly spiral
      bound notebooks that remind me of ledgers. I assigned each
      ledger-like diary a number according to the sequence in which I
      read it. Thus, Diary 1 was the first I studied; Diary 41, near the
      last. As far as I know, Bazata kept these diaries secret until he
      gave them to me. As far as I know, no one else has ever read
      them.

10.   Roger Ford, *Steel from the Sky*, (London: Weidenfeld &
      Nicolson, 2004), 23.

11.   Written statement to a veterans' injury board by Bernard M. W.
      Knox, Harvard University professor of Hellenic Studies and
      former Jedburgh. The statement is dated April 25, 1978. It was
      taken from Bazata's papers, and confirmed by Bazata in person
      and Knox by phone.

12.   Bazata's unfinished biography, 14.

13. Ibid.
14. British National Archives SAB report regarding Dussaq dated July 17, 1943, Ref. HS 9/462/3, which I was able to get declassified.
15. Nancy Wake, author of the successful autobiography *The White Mouse* (New York: Macmillan, 1986), died in 2011.
16. Geoffrey Elliot, *The Shooting Star* (London: Methuen, 2009), 176; also see "Emile Coulaudon" at *Wikipedia*, https://en.wikipedia.org/wiki/Émile_Coulaudon.
17. Report on "Freelance-Gaspard Circuit," "History of Organization," sheet 30b, British National Archives.
18. Activity Report of 1st Lieutenant René A. Dussaq (Anselme), Freelance Gaspard Circuit, Vol. 3, 803.

2: "I've Come for a Room"

1. Ibid. One article, "Veteran re-lives D-Day Action" by Fred Davis, quotes Dussaq as having been dropped 150 miles from the drop zone. But that distance seems too far given the fact that his report says he reached a nearby destination that night.
2. *Adventure to Order*, Dussaq's unpublished autobiography, 18. As well as newspaper and other stories about him. These include The Racine (Wisconsin) *Journal Times*, Oct. 28, 1941, and "Who Was Who at Camp Croft" on the Internet. However, he was not, to his youthful chagrin, called on to participate, and thus is not listed on the rosters.
3. Most Jeds and SOE agents parachuted in as teams—usually three together—and landed behind enemy lines in military uniforms.
4. May 4, 1944 authorization by Col. David K. E. Bruce, head of the OSS office in London, obtained from NARA (RC226, Entry 168A, Box 15, Folder 11. The document sent to me has the citation penciled in. It appears to be Folder 11 but because of hasty handwriting, I can't be sure.
5. "Operation Instruction No. F. 133—Part 1," instructions for "Operation DRUGGIST," given to Dussaq by SOE. A printed

instruction for "Druggist." There is no notation on the back of where it is from but several copies I have, including what appears to be a frayed original, lead me to believe it came from Dussaq's house and is probably available from the British National Archives.

6. Activity Report of 1st Lieutenant René A. Dussaq (Anselme), Freelance Gaspard Circuit, Vol. 3, 803

7. Political Report of: Lieutenant René A. Dussaq, National Archives, Record Group 226, Entry 168 A (or N), Box 15, Folder (11).

8. Marcus Binney, *Secret War Heroes: The Men of Special Operations Executive* (London: Hodder, 2006), 256. Binney's account appears to have been taken directly from Dussaq's "Activity Report." The estimate is found in "Appendix to Dussaq ITG," attached to his activity report cited previously.

9. Activity Report of 1st Lt. René A. Dussaq, Freelance Gaspard Circuit, Vol. 3, 804

10. Les Hughes, "The Special Force Wing," *Trading Post*, July–September 1988

11. "René Dussaq, Who Sells Insurance in The Mile, Could Write Quite a Book," Los Angeles Independent, July 11, 1949.

12. Thirty numerous articles repeat this, with slight variation of the ages and titles. For instance see, "Capt. Bazooka, a Character, But Not One in a Comic Strip," San Francisco Chronicle, Feb. 14, 1951

13. Fred Davis, "Veteran re-lives D-Day Action." See Sources.

14. Dussaq's papers, including his June 13, 1949 "Organized Reserve Corps Current Status Questionaire" (Form 401)

15. The colleague is Walter Puth, a fellow Prudential worker, who told me in an interview what Dussaq had told him about the incident. Among the reporters was Davis in "Veteran Re-lives D-Day Action". The scriptwriters are Jack and Gretchen Sharp who wrote "The René Dussaq Story" for the Adventurer's Club program which is dated, Jan 3, 1947.

16. Wake, *The White Mouse*, 122.

3: The Redoubt

1. Wake, *The White Mouse*, 122–23.
2. Alexander Werth, *France: 1940–1955* (New York: Henry Holt, 1956), 164.
3. War Diaries, History of Organization, Freelance-Gaspard Circuit, Sheet 30B (from British National Archives).EG Boxshall, *Chronology of SOE operations with the resistance in France during world war II* , 1960, document dactylographié (exemplaire en provenance de la bibliothèque de , consultable à la bibliothèque).
4. Personal communication from Gerard Crevon, son of Henri Crevon, one of the Maquis leaders, who interviewed surviving Maquis.
5. There is controversy about this. Gaspard had earlier met with a British forerunner of Freelance. He had interpreted the meeting's outcome as a promise that, in conjunction with the redoubt plan, the Allies would send paratroops and heavy weapons. But the British agent with whom he had conferenced—according to some accounts—did not have the power to authorize such reinforcements.
6. Activity Report of 1st Lieutenant René A. Dussaq (Anselme), Freelance Gaspard Circuit, Vol. 3, 805.
7. Ibid.
8. Some sources say less but the majority, especially French historians, give this figure up to eleven thousand.
9. Wake, *The White Mouse*, 123.
10. To be explained later.
11. Ibid.
12. Ibid.
13. Activity Report of 1st Lieutenant René A. Dussaq (Anselme), Freelance Gaspard Circuit, Vol. 3, 806.

14. Ibid., 805–6. There are various explanations for how Dussaq got the nickname in articles written about him after the war. This one seems the best because 1) it comes from his own writing, and 2) it was written closest to the time in which he got the nickname.

15. Ibid., 806–7.

16. Geoffrey Elliot, *The Shooting Star* (London: Methuen, 2009), 198–99.

17. Report on "Freelance-Gaspard Circuit", "History of Organization," British National Archives, sheet 30b, page 2.

18. Activity Report of 1st Lieutenant René A. Dussaq (Anselme), Freelance Gaspard Circuit, Vol. 3, 807.

19. Ibid.

20. Ibid., 809.

21. Wake, *The White Mouse*, 128.

22. Activity Report of 1st Lieutenant René A. Dussaq (Anselme), Freelance Gaspard Circuit, Vol. 3, 808.

23. Wake, *The White Mouse*, 128.

24. Ibid.

25. Ibid., 129.

26. Ibid.

27. Ibid., 130.

28. Werth, *France: 1940–1955*, 164.

29. Wake, *The White Mouse*, 130.

30. Activity Report of 1st Lieutenant René A. Dussaq (Anselme), Freelance Gaspard Circuit, Vol. 3, 810. Ibid., 810–11.

31. Ibid., 810–11.

32. Ibid., 809.

33. Wake, *The White Mouse*, 117, 125.

34. *Adventure to Order*, unfinished, unpublished autobiography by Dussaq given to me by his second wife, Charlotte, 30.

35. Interview with Charlotte Dussaq, June 1, 1997.

36. Activity Report of 1st Lieutenant René A. Dussaq (Anselme), Freelance Gaspard Circuit, Vol. 3, 822.

37. Elliot, *The Shooting Star*, 193.
38. *Denis Rake, Rake's Progress* (Frewin, 1968), 246–47.
39. Ibid., 247–48.
40. Ibid., 249.
41. Ibid., 250.
42. More on that in the manuscript later.
43. Activity Report of 1st Lieutenant René A. Dussaq (Anselme), Freelance Gaspard Circuit, Vol. 3, 809.
44. Elliot, *The Shooting Star*, 202.
45. Ibid.

4: The Lion

1. I have two copies. One came from his office drawer in his Encino, CA, home. His second wife, Charlotte gave it to me along with other papers shortly after he died. A second one, with a few more chapters than the first, was given to me by his daughter-in-law, Gina Dussaq. The particular quotes cited are on page twenty.
2. That's my opinion based on his mentioning Daisy in the manuscript but nothing about the tragedy.
3. *Dussaq, Adventure to Order*, 13.
4. Ibid., 6a–6b.
5. Ibid., 6b.
6. Ibid. 15–16.
7. Ibid.
8. Ibid.
9. Ibid., 17.
10. Ibid.
11. Andrew Rawlinson, *The Book of Enlightened Masters*, (Chicago: Open Court, 1997), 371.
12. Dussaq, *Adventure to Order*, 1, 3.
13. Ibid., 25–26.
14. Ibid., 26.
15. Ibid., 26–27.

16. Ibid., 68–69.
17. Ibid., 41.

5: Maquis

1. Activity Report of 1st Lieutenant René A. Dussaq (Anselme), Freelance Gaspard Circuit, Vol. 3, 823.
2. Wake, *The White Mouse*, 130–135.
3. See "Resistance, Reprisals and Community in Occupied France" by Robert Gildea in *Transactions of the Royal Historical Society*, 2003, for a full discussion of the retaliation.
4. Activity Report of 1st Lieutenant René A. Dussaq (Anselme), Freelance Gaspard Circuit, Vol. 3, 811.
5. U.S. National Archives, RG 226, Entry 168 (N or A), Box 15.
6. Political Report of Lieutenant René A Dussaq, October 16, 1944, U.S. National Archives, 1.
7. Ibid.
8. Activity Report of 1st Lieutenant René A. Dussaq (Anselme), Freelance Gaspard Circuit, Vol. 3, 812.
9. Ibid.
10. Ibid.
11. Gerard Crevon, whose father served with the Maquis.
12. Activity Report of 1st Lieutenant René A. Dussaq (Anselme), Freelance Gaspard Circuit, Vol. 3, 812.
13. Ibid, 813.
14. Ibid.

6: "Crashing the Door"

1. Dussaq, *Adventure to Order*, 33.
2. Ibid., 33–34.
3. Ibid., 36.
4. Ibid. (This is also mentioned in an article about him in the *Detroit News*, January 16, 1942.)
5. Ibid., 36.

6. "The Golden Parachutists: 50 Years Later, Troopers Prepare to Relive the Glory," *Washington Post*, February 21, 1994.
7. Dussaq, *Adventure to Order*, 36–37.
8. The record, Swiss Overseas Emigration, 1910–1953, is written in German. I got it from AncestryLibrary.com. It says he left Boulogne-sur-Mur, France on that date and his "Port of arrival" was Havana, Cuba.
9. "Pearl of the Antilles," *Time*, January 26, 1959. Also, Ernst Halperin, "Fidel Castro's Road to Power," (Cambridge: Center for International Studies, MIT, 1970), 10.
10. Confidential memo from G.K. Bowden to Lt. Col. E.C. Huntington, dated November 30, 1942, U.S. National Archives, RG 226, Entry 92a, Box 34, Folder 512.
11. Dussaq, *Adventure to Order*, 37.
12. For instance, as a student, in June 1896, he wrote for the *Harvard Monthly* an impassioned call for war entitled "The Case of Cuba Against Spain."
13. Antonio Moreno, "The True Story of My Life," *Movie Weekly*, November 8–December 13, 1924.
14. According to Dussaq's second wife, Charlotte.
15. *Dussaq, Adventure to Order*, 37.
16. Ibid., 38.
17. Ibid.
18. Ibid., 39.
19. He apparently tells a reporter this in "René Dussaq, Son of Cuban Diplomat, Has Packed Varied, Colorful Experiences in 30-Year Span," *Spartanburg Journal*, May 23, 1942.
20. For a good description of the still standing building see, Jesse Katz, "Welcome to the Hotel California," *Los Angeles Magazine*, March, 2004.
21. Dussaq, *Adventure to Order*, 40.
22. Ibid., 96–99.

23. Through the years, these included Errol Flynn, Douglas Fairbanks Sr., Mary Pickford, Humphrey Bogart, Mae West and Clark Gable. See Wiki entry for more.

24. Victoria Thomas, *Hollywood's Latin Lovers*, (Santa Monica: Angel City Press, 1998), 42.

25. Coroner's report on accident, dated 23 February 1933 (File no. 45205, Register 251, 32). Other sources, including newspapers, report her age variously as forty-five to forty-nine.

26. "Moreno Driver Absolved" *Los Angeles Times*, February 25, 1933.

27. "Mrs. Moreno Auto Death Inquest Set," Coroner's Register, File no. 45205, Department of Coroner, County of Los Angeles; *LA Examiner*, February 24, 1933.

28. Ibid.

29. I traveled the road trying to determine which one. But today, over seventy-five years from the event, it's almost impossible. It's been repaired, paved, and homes and residential developments have been built along it.

30. "Mrs. Moreno Auto Death Inquest Set," *LA Examiner*, February 24, 1933.

31. Estimates vary from two hundred to three hundred, depending on newspaper and date of story.

32. William B. Molony, M.D. who later treated him and wrote a description of his injuries to Dussaq's father.

33. Coroners's report.

34. "Moreno Driver Absolved," *Los Angeles Times*.

35. "Mrs. Moreno Auto Death Inquest Set."

36. "Mrs. Moreno's Death Quiz Set," *Los Angeles Times,* February 24, 1933.

37. "Mrs. Moreno Auto Death Inquest Set."

38. Coroner's Report.

39. "Friends Go To Moreno Last Rites," *Los Angeles Times*, February 26, 1933.

40. E. J. Fleming, *Hollywood Death and Scandal Sites* (Jefferson: McFarland & Co, 2000); "Rock Schoolboy Became Silent Screen Star," *Gibraltar Magazine*, November 2007; Fleming, *The Fixers* (Jefferson: McFarland & Co, 2004), 56–57.

41. "Mrs. Moreno's Death Accident, Jury Rules," Los Angeles Times, February 25, 1933 (from LA Times film reel 651).

42. Nicholas Pinhey, who believes Moreno is his grandfather from an affair Moreno had with his grandmother, has understandably been researching the actor's life. He's a former California water official with a distinguished record. He told me a Crestmount handyman who worked for the Morenos told him Antonio had, during an argument, pushed Daisy down some stairs. Pinhey wonders if that was the source of the "arm" injury which precluded Dussaq driving Daisy's car.

43. Vidor had hidden it because he didn't want to hurt persons still alive.

44. "Victim Happy Before Death…" *Los Angeles Examiner*, February 5, 1922.

45. "Rock Schoolboy Became Silent Screen Star."

46. Numerous sources confirm this; movies, like *Chinatown*, are based on it. This *Los Angeles Times* quote is from an article headlined, "Police Scandal is Worst since 1930s," run September 17, 1999.

47. "Tale of Wealth, Murder and a Family's Decline," *Los Angeles Times*, August 20, 2000.

48. The Paramour Sessions: Music: Papa Roach.

49. "Canfield-Moreno Estate," Wikipedia, https://en.wikipedia.org/wiki/Canfield-Moreno_Estate.

50. Proof of his leaving Daisy out of stories about his life can be seen in the following: a story in advance of his speaking in Tennessee in the Memphis Press-Scimitar, February 13, 1941; a feature about him in the San Francisco Chronicle, February 4, 1951; and the current Camp Croft profile of him on the Internet. There are

more. In all such stories, the crash is a movie stunt with no death involved.

7: "I Will Kill You Myself"

1. Activity Report of 1st Lieutenant René A. Dussaq (Anselme), Freelance Gaspard Circuit, Vol. 3, 814.
2. "Political report of Lt. René A Dussaq," October 16, 1944, U.S. National Archives, RG 226, Entry 168 (A or possibly N) Box 15, Folder 11.
3. Ibid.
4. Activity Report of 1st Lieutenant René A. Dussaq (Anselme), Freelance Gaspard Circuit, Vol. 3, 814.
5. Ibid., 816.
6. Operation Anvil-Dragoon had begun on August 15.
7. Activity Report of 1st Lieutenant René A. Dussaq (Anselme), Freelance Gaspard Circuit, Vol. 3, 816.
8. Ibid., 817.
9. Ibid.
10. Ibid., 817–818.
11. The details about the flag and car are not in Dussaq's after-action report, although the use of both are. The car's origin, the flag's creation, and the display are variously in: an "Appendix to Dussaq, ITG" entitled "Recent activities," which is in his OSS records (RG 226), and two newspaper stories: Polly Pope, "René Dussaq…Could Write Quite a Book" and George deCarvalho, "Capt. Bazooka, a Character, But not one in a Comic Strip," *San Francisco Chronicle*, February 4, 1951.
12. Activity Report of 1st Lieutenant René A. Dussaq (Anselme), Freelance Gaspard Circuit, Vol. 3, 818-819.
13. Ibid., 819.
14. Ibid., 819–820.
15. The number of 120 prisoners is what he reports in the after-action. The numbers get larger in official retellings—not by Dussaq.

16. Activity Report of 1st Lieutenant René A. Dussaq (Anselme), Freelance Gaspard Circuit, Vol. 3, 819–820.
17. Ibid., 820.

8: A Dangerous Business

1. Personal letter from Emilien Dussaq to the doctor, dated March 9, 1933, Dussaq documents.
2. Letter to "E.T. Dussaq" by "W.R. Molony", dated March 22, 1933, Dussaq documents.
3. Interview with her at her house, June 1, 1997.
4. Dussaq, *Adventure to Order*, 127.
5. Ibid., 158.
6. The first sentence is from "René Dussaq, Who Sells Insurance…" *Los Angeles Independent*, July 11, 1949. The rest is from deCarvalho, "Capt. Bazooka, a Character, But not one in a Comic Strip."
7. This is in numerous articles about him and his OSS recommendation cited in chapter two.
8. This appears to be the 1934 Spanish film version of Guy de Maupassant's *The Woman of the Port*, titled in Spanish, *La Mujer del Puerto*. Dussaq's second wife, Charlotte, said he once doubled for Mexican-born actor Gilbert Roland. In February 1942, syndicated columnist Walter Winchell, in an item about Dussaq, also wrote he'd doubled for Roland. But Roland is not listed in *Mujer*'s credits. My guess is that Craig got the film's name wrong and Dussaq did the dives in "Our Betters," a 1933 picture adapted from a play of the same name by W. Somerset Maughhm. The film, about high society and lavish parties, lends itself better to such a scene and Roland played one of the main characters.
9. John Craig, *Danger Is My Business* (New York: Simon & Schuster, 1938), 232.
10. Dussaq, *Adventure to Order*, 147.

11. Dussaq's undated, multi-page "Application for Employment and Personal History Statement" which he filled out for OSS. I received it from the National Archives, College Park, along with other papers apparently from Record Group 226, Entry 92a, Box 34, Folder 512.

12. Although Nohl and Crockett can be found on the Internet, these thumbnail portraits are largely from Craig's *Danger is My Business*.

9: "Adventure to Order"

1. A word he used to describe it.

2. Craig, *Danger Is My Business*, 161.

3. Created from a terse description of the incident in *Adventure to Order*, 159.

4. Craig, *Danger Is My Business*, 173.

5. Ibid., 279–280.

6. Robert I. Nesmith, *Dig For Pirate Treasure* (Prineville: Bonanza, 1958), 91–92.

7. Dussaq, *Adventure to Order*, 84–85.

8. Ibid., 76.

9. Ibid., 77.

10. Ibid.

11. Ibid., 78.

12. Ibid.

13. Ibid., 79.

14. Ibid., 80.

15. Ibid., 159.

16. Ibid., 82.

17. Ibid., 159.

18. Ibid., 160.

19. "Treasure Vessels Found on Sea Bed," *New York Times*, September 13, 1938.

20. deCarvalho,"Capt. Bazooka, a Character, But Not One in a Comic Strip."

21. *Dussaq, Adventure to Order,* 124.
22. Ibid., 125.

10: Sunken Treasure

1. Craig, *Danger Is My Business,* 236–241.
2. In researching the John S. Dwight, I encountered varying stories concerning the details about what happened to the ship at various Internet sites, but none in such detail as Craig's account. I chose to go with his because he was closer in time to the sinking and, unlike those writing the other accounts, actually dove on the wreck.
3. "Test Descent Is Rehearsal For Attempt," *Washington Post,* December 5, 1937.
4. Craig's involvement with the Lusitania comes mainly, except for verifications, from *Danger Is My Business,* 247–261.
5. Dussaq, *Adventure to Order,* 44–46.
6. Craig, *Danger Is My Business,* 262.
7. "Test Descent is Rehearsal For Attempt," December 5, 1937.
8. Ibid. Estimates vary greatly. One insurance claim was for fifty million dollars, but most sources say between one and two million, a king's ransom regardless of the correct figure.
9. René Dussaq, "Sunken Treasure Curse Scorned by Searchers," *Daily Boston Globe,* July 15, 1939.
10. Epilogue to "Danger is my Business," an excerpt from the book in the magazine's January, 1946 edition. Coronet ceased publication in 1971.
11. Front page, *Norfolk Ledger-Dispatch,* August 9, 1939.
12. He was an Argentine or Cuban, it's not entirely clear. And during this time he was making periodic trips back to Cuba. Was he still connected to the revolutionary forces that caused him to flee? Or was he simply keeping in touch with family?
13. "Titanic Facts, History and Biography," Encyclopedia Titanica, www.enclopedia-titanic.org/titanic-biography/thomas-whiteley.html.

14. One of the few men to survive the Titanic, Whiteley, according to the encyclopedia, was left to die on the sinking ship but swam out to an overturned life raft. Men already on the raft fought to keep him off but he eventually got on and survived. He is believed to have been a mercenary in the Boer Wars in South Africa. A Brit, he served with British fighter squadrons in World Wars I and II. He probably met Craig in Hollywood where he had small parts in MGM films. The site has pictures of Craig and Whiteley together.

15. Dussaq, *Adventure to Order*, 118.

16. Craig, *Danger Is My Business*, 245–246.

17. Ibid., 22.

18. Ibid., 148.

19. Ibid., 278.

20. Ibid., 50–52.

21. "I Was Scared Stiff," *Wings* (March, 1938).

22. The gear eliminated telltale bubbles from underwater saboteurs allowing them to swim undetected.

23. Author Robert L. Nesmith interviewed Logan for his 1958 book, *Dig for Pirate Treasure*. In it, on pages 102–3, he quotes Logan saying, "Did I get the treasure? No. I was reluctantly forced to discontinue operations and withdraw…because of the imminence of war. A little later, a German sub surfaced off shore and fired more than twenty shells into the [the island] apparently thinking [it was] part of some army installation."

11: Legend

1. Activity Report of 1st Lieutenant René A. Dussaq (Anselme), Freelance Gaspard Circuit, Vol. 3, 820-821.

2. The critically-acclaimed film was produced by American director and comedian Woody Allen.

3. "Political Report of Lieutenant René A. Dussaq," National Archives, Record Group 226, Entry 168n, Box 15, Folder 11., page 3

4. Ibid.

5. The letter, accompanying a Jedburgh map on the stationary, was written to Dussaq "4 September 1987" by Friele of West Redding, CT., who has since died. She says that as "Col. Musgrave's F.A.N.Y. secretary...I know you jumped alone and having listed you as 'known to be deceased' I am overjoyed to find you are alive." She explains that after his return from France, she and all the other Jedburghs had lost him again—until just recently being informed of his address. Apparently he had been so silent in the intervening years that she and others had, for a second time, assumed he had died.

6. *New York Times,* December 1, 1944. Also Special Forces Roll of Honour on the Internet.

7. Fred Davis, "Veteran re-lives D-Day action"; deCavalho, "Capt. Bazooka, a Character, But Not One in a Comic Strip."

8. Schriever's report entitled "Verification of Lt. Dussaq's Report," December 4, 1944, with letter head, "Hq & Hq Detachment, OSS, European Theater of Operations, U.S. Army, SO/WE section." I got it from Dussaq's personal papers.

9. Dussaq's name is sometimes misspelled in references to him as "Dussac" or "Dussacq" —even in official papers.

10. Ibid.

11. Unfortunately, working on a prior book, I wasn't that interested in Dussaq, and only copied the page. I hope to go back and find the document so I can cite it correctly.

12. Dunlop's Donovan, pg. 472. Unfortunately, Truman did not like OSS or Donovan and dissolved the service on the same day he cordially received Dussaq.

13. Personal correspondence from Gerard Crevon to me.

14. I have corresponded only with Gerard Crevon who has cited Martres's writings.

12: A Man of Many Talents

1. Dussaq, *Adventure to Order,* 86–87.

2.   *Kirksville Daily Express*, March 7, 1940. The story says his
     partner was "Beatrice Dix, a niece of Richard Dix, of movie
     fame." But I could not verify that.
3.   Most of this dancing episode comes from *Adventure to Order*,
     179–89, a hard-to-decipher hand-written tag-on at the end of the
     manuscript.
4.   *Kirksville Daily Express*, March 7, 1940.
5.   Dussaq, *Adventure to Order*, 67.
6.   Spartanburg (S.C) Herald, Mar 19, 1942.
7.   "Walter Winchell. The Private Papers of a Cub Reporter,"
     Wisconsin State Journal, April 8, 1940.
8.   "South America Dreams of Union, Native says," *Wisconsin State
     Journal*, February 23, 1941.
9.   "Solidarity of America's Seen As Example for Torn World by
     Town Hall Lecturer Friday," *Beaumont Journal*, January 9,
     1942.
10. "South American Dreams..."*Wisconsin State Journal*, February
     23, 1941.
11. Blanchard, Frances, "Federation of Women's Clubs In
     Convention at Swampscott," May 12, 1942. (This was from a
     clipping I found at Dussaq's house. The periodical is not given).
12. "Warns That South American Unity Only Forced by Threat of
     Hitler," January 30, 1942, article about Dussaq's speech with
     newspaper uncited.
13. Charlotte Dussaq, Interview, June 1997
14. "Beach Speaker Branded As Phony By Consulate," *Miami
     Herald*, February 7, 1941.

13: Katherine

1.   Eloise Keeler, The *Lie Detector Man* (Telshare, 1983), 88.
2.   Ken Alder, *The Lie Detectors: The History of an American
     Obsession* (New York: Free Press, 2007), 141.

3. Shannon Applegate, Skookum: An Oregon Pioneer Family's History and Lore (Corvallis: Oregon State University Press, 2005).

4. Kristin Applegate-King, whose mother is Katherine's niece.

5. Ibid., 24.

6. Alder, *The Lie Detectors*, 84.

7. The word "mules" is used on a resume I have that's supposedly written by Katherine.

8. Keeler, *The Lie Detector Man*, 87–90, from which most of the following account is taken.

9. The account is taken mostly from Keeler, *Lie Detector Man*, 87–90. The 137 convicted figure comes from Katherine's resume.

10. Alder, *The Lie Detectors*, 142.

11. Ibid., 115.

12. Ted Leitzell, "The Camera Goes to Court," sent to me by the Texas Women's University but without a date or in what magazine it was published.

13. "Katherine Applegate Dussaq: The First Woman Document Examiner", Journal of the American Society of Questioend Document Examiners, Vol. 2, no. 1 (June 1999).

14. "10/3/39 – 10/13/39," according to Alder, a professor of the history of science at Northwestern, *The Lie Detectors*, 171, 297.

15. Alder, *The Lie Detectors*, 136.

16. Ibid., 171.

17. Ibid., 172.

18. Ibid.

19. Keeler, *Lie Detector Man*, 143.

20. Ibid., 144–145.

14: My Beloved

1. *Field Museum News*, October 26, 1940.

2. Keeler, *Lie Detector Man*, 119.

3. It's two pages long, typewritten, and appears to have been created by Katherine.

4. U.S. National Archives. Record Group 226, Entry 92a, Box 34, Folder 512.
5. "Veteran re-lives D-Day action," by Fred Davis, *Bear Valley Springs, Ca.*, July 1994. See Sources.
6. New York dancer and choreographer Agnes deMille, *The Lie Detectors*, 173.
7. US National Archives, Record group 226, Entry 93A, Box 34.
8. See Katherine Dussaq's bio at Texas Woman's University library under "Woman Airforce Service Pilots," or the website with her profile at http://wasp-wwii.org/wasp/38/38.htm.
9. "Katherine Applegate Keeler Dussaq: The First Woman Document Examiner," 54.
10. Keeler, *Lie Detector Man*, 173.
11. Ibid., 146.
12. Alder, *The Lie Detectors*, 178.
13. "WASP Head Wants to Start New Air Race," *San Antonio Light*, September 19, 1944.

15: Into the Night

1. My account of the flight and crash comes mostly from the twenty-three-page official Army Air Forces accident report of Katherine's death. I received it from Mike Stowe, Accident Reports (accident-report.com), 1322 W. Main St., Millville, NJ 08332. Earlier I had received an abbreviated report from Texas Women's University.

16: Shadows

1. de Carvalho, "Capt. Bazooka, a Character, But Not One in a Comic Strip."
2. Unheaded memo to "Major McLallen" from National Archives, Record Group 226, Entry 92N, Box 34, Folder 512.
3. The request is in the same thirty-seven page group of OSS papers from the National Archives listed in footnote three hundred. The

separation certificate is headed "Military Record and Report of Separation Certificate of Service." It was amongst the papers I found at Dussaq's house. It is dated "5 Nov 45."

4. Personal email to me from Penny Eckert dated August 13, 2012.

5. Ibid.

6. Personal email to me from Penny Eckert dated August 14, 2012.

7. "Dussaq Rites Are Conducted," Walla Walla Union-Bulletin, December 6, 1944.

8. So much so that she didn't want to discuss it with me and referred me to her daughter Kristy instead.

9. Letter to Mr. C. K. Merrill, 630 Fifth Ave., NY, NY. National Archives Record Group 226, Entry 92A, Box 34, Folder 512

10. Petition for Letters of Administration, Estate of Katherine Applegate Dusaq (sic), Probate Court, Cook County, Illinois, December 1944.

17: The Basques

1. Volunteer fighters, who, along with communists, fought against the Spanish dictator.

2. This comes from one of Bazata's diaries, number 28 in my system of numbering them. (See endnote 9 of Chapter 1 for more on my numbering and the diaries.)

3. The unit is named for the ancient Basque town, Guernica, which is a symbol for Basque freedom. It was bombed by Nazi warplanes on April 26, 1936, and as such became a rallying cry for the Basques during the Spanish Civil War and beyond.

4. April 7, 1945 memo from Gerald E. Miller, chief, Special Operations Branch, OSS, "Subject: Operation Airedale," received from the National Archives under FOIA request.

5. Formerly "Top Secrret" OSS memo from Lt. (jg) Edward W. Andrews, USNR, to Mr. Whitney Shepardson, dated April 14, 1945, and entitled "The Basque Situation." National Archives.

6. Dussaq's "Application for enrollment" to Army extenstion courses. Dated May 28, 1947, it's among the documents I found at his house.

7. For a good article about him, see Allen Pittman, "W.E.Fairbairn: British Pioneer in Asian Martial Arts," Journal of Asian Martial Arts, Vol. 6 no. 2 (1997), http://www.journalofasianmartialarts. com/product/asia/pioneers/william-e.-fairbairn-british-pioneer-in-asian-martial-arts-detail-135.

8. Basques I have contacted say Beldarrain was a lieutenant colonel, commander of a Basque division, which in the U.S. military is usually a general. Dussaq may have simply assumed he was a general. The Basque sources also say his last name is spelled with two 'Rs', rather than one as in U.S. reports.

9. This comes from two declassified documents I received from the National Archives. One is a September 21, 1945 memo to Gen. Bill Donovan, addressed to "The Director" from "E.W. Andrews, Lt. (j.g.), USNR"; and from a second document attached to which is the Beldarain report, dated "Paris, 17 August 1945."

10. Lararreta's "Memoirs of a 'Mugalari' (Basque for a political border crosser), can be found, it appears, in Rodriguez's *The Guerilla in the Basque Country.*

11. His ancestors appear to have come from southern France.

12. The exact citation for this is unclear. Apparently Professor Rodriguez interviewed Paco Perez Lazarreta and wrote up what he said under the title of "Memoirs of a 'Mugalari.'" This was published in the professor's book, *Memory of the Basques in World War II* (Pamiela, Pamplona, 2002) and/or in an article whose only citation I can discern from the Google-produced translation is "History 16 #357, Jan 2006." This is probably a Basque journal of some kind. I think the problem here is in the computer-generated translation. While helpful and appreciated, such translation is often wanting.

18: Radioactive

1.   "Bikini," *Newsweek*, July 1, 1946. There is no author attached. It appears to be by the editors. Bikini is the magazine's cover subject that issue. The copy of the article I obtained is at http://www.bikiniatoll.com/ Newsweek 1946.html.

2.   July 18, 1945 letter from Lt. Col. Lewis M. Gable, OSS Euro Theater.

3.   He had died in 1927.

4.   There is debate about whether and how badly Noor was physically tortured. This account comes from the Wikipedia article entitled "Noor Inayat Khan." It is well detailed. She was eventually awarded England's George Cross, one of Britian's highest medals for gallantry, and a bronze bust of her was erected in London.

5.   The "Autobiography"—that is its title—can be found at http:wahidduddin.net in a section of the work headed "Biographical Sketches of Principal Workers."

6.   Interview with Charlotte, June 1, 1997 and "Top Secret" OSS interrogation of René by Maj. Wm. T. Hornaday, Paris, September 1944 (National Archives, Entry 168n, Box 15, Folder 11).

7.   July 19, 1945 letter from Maj. Stuart O. Pusey to Adjutant OSS, "Jump Status of Captain René Dussaq."

8.   Front page of *Semaine* Lausanne, Switzerland, July 31, 1945.

9.   Permission letter from War Department August 27, 1945 signed by adjutant General W.E. Fitzgerald.

10.   Richard Dunlop, *Donovan: America's Master Spy* (Skyhouse, 2014), 472.

11.   Not only did he give Logan's address as his when discharged but a November 7, 1945 article in the *Chicago Daily Tribune* noted he'd attended an Opera Guild benefit with the Logans.

12.   Thomas E. Mahi, *Espionage's Most Wanted* (Sterling: Potomac Books, 2003), 248.

13. Ibid. One of their executives, Stanton Griffis, had been an agent in Finland.

14. Short at end of syndicated Bob Thomas column titled, "Curtain Calls: Mere Man says Woman Can't Shop,"*Oakland Tribune*, March 5, 1946.

15. Article about Dussaq's upcoming speech to a Los Angeles civic group by Jack Alger, editor of *The Crenshaw Rotator*, undated but probably early 1950s; also implied in a July 11, 1949 article about Dussaq in Los Angeles's *Independent*.

16. Wikipedia article on John D. Craig, https://en.wikipedia.org/wiki/John_D._Craig.

17. David Bradley, *No Place to Hide* (Lebanon: Dartmouth, 1983), 19.

18. I found a copy of the original script in Dussaq's papers.

19. At first I thought the signature was "William Robinson." Subsequent research, however—to be dealt with in the next few paragraphs—turned up Runinson. The entire letter is handwritten and hard to decipher. The signature is the worst. The letter is dated June 13, 1946, approximately a half month before the test. The envelope has a P.O. Box number and "New Mexico" printed on its corner. But handwritten on the letter is "Kwajelien, Radition Lab." It's possible it was penned on the island and then mailed from New Mexico. My efforts to locate either William Robertson or William W. Runinson were fruitless.

20. Tony Smith, "A-Fleet Will Get Final Search for Stowaways," *The Binghamton Press*, May 14, 1946.

21. I found copies of this story in numerous papers across the country. Only one of them gave a by-line: Charles McMurtry. But it got a lot of play.

19: "Juanita"

1. John Maloney, a Connecticut writer who interviewed Dussaq years later for a proposed book about the OSS, told me he had

the parachute in case there was an emergency and he had to jump to protect the films.

2. New York Office of The Mail, "The Stunt man became a military professor," Adalaide, Australia, February 10, 1951.

3. At the time she told me this she didn't go further. And when I later realized I should find out what she meant, she had died.

4. Pope, "René Dussaq, Who Sells Insurance in The Mile, Could Write Quite a Book."

5. Some say his older brother, Maurice, contributed money to help the buy.

20: Counterspy

1. In contrast, he told a reporter (Polly Pope) in 1949, "I enjoy my work. No work is dull unless you make it so." But what was he supposed to say? His boss, no doubt, would see the story.

2. Public proof was hard to come by and was often disputed. But mounting confessions by Soviet spies like Elizabeth Bentley, who revealed her clandestine activities to the FBI in the late 1940s, and whose life as a "mole" was published in the bestselling book, *Out of Bondage* (Literary Licensing, 2013) showed the depth of infiltration. Revelations in the recently released Venona papers, detailing America's breaking of the Soviet codes during and after World War II, unequivocally have shown that many accused spies and communists were, in fact, justly accused and prosecuted. The Rosenbergs and Alger Hiss, two of the most defended by the Left, are prime examples. Venona proves they were Russian agents. For instance, see *American Betrayal (New York: St. Martin's Press, 2013)* by Diana West, or my own work, *Target: Patton*: The Plot to Assassinate General George S. Patton (Washington, DC: Regnery, 2008).

3. There are bits and pieces in his personal papers. For instance, in the "how did you earn a living" space in a form for his grandchildren, he penned, "FBI 2 yr undercover."

4. Application for Enrollment, Army Extension, "3rd Bn. 361st 91st. Inf.," dated May 28, 1947.

5. Dussaq's reserve questionnaire, form 401, dated June 13, 1949.

6. Memo to "Director, FBI" dated April 11, 1950, and November 3, 1949, "Memorandum Re: René Alexander Dussaq Summary," no other identifying information given.

7. This and what follows about Dussaq's counterspy activities at the end of the 1940s and into the early 1950s is based on some seventy pages of formerly classified documents released to me by the FBI in mid-2009.

8. Havana News Agency, PO Box 1617, Havana, Cuba. Examination of the news agency's files, says the investigation, "reveals correspondence from 1939 to 1941 from René Dussaq."

9. The Brigade was made up of mostly leftist volunteers from America.

10. I have a file full of nebulous indications, nothing proving it, but things like Sen. Prescott Bush, father of the two later presidents, having served on Prudential's board; a supposedly former CIA agent, Gunther Russbacher, given a job as a Prudential agent as a cover (www.rumormillnews.com/cgi-bin/archive. cgi?read=127611); former clandestines I know having worked for Prudential, and one spy source I'm using who confirmed the suspicion. "It's a longtime cover," he said without hesitation.

11. My letter to Prudential Chairman and CEO John Strangfeld yielded this polite refusal: "Although we are not able to release any personnel records pertaining to Mr. Dussaq's time with Prudential, we wish you every success…" Contacting Strangfeld was just one in a long line of frustrating attempts I've made to see Dussaq's records.

12. This will be detailed in an upcoming chapter.

13. One of the first of over one hundred I've collected from René's files, Charlotte, and other sources. They deal mainly with the early 1950s when he was away during the call-up.

14. This FBI report is from the Internet page "Bob Feldman 68," which cites a declassified FBI memo dated "4-30-50 at Los Angeles entitled 'Factionalist Sabotage Group,' Internal Security-C." The memo and source can be found at http://feldman68.blogspot.com/2007_06_21.

21: Red Scare

1. Letter four in my numbering system of them, dated December 1, 1950.
2. Handwritten letter given to me by Dussaq's good Prudential friend Walter Puth. It's dated 12/5/96. Unfortunately, in copying it, I mistakenly cut off the writer's name. But he was a Prudential employee who had read an article about René in a company publication.
3. de Carvalho, "Capt. Bazooka, a Character, But Not One in a Comic Strip." Carvalho also writes that Dussaq said he was "twice" recommended for the Medal of Honor, the nation's highest military decoration. I'd not heard that or encountered it in my research. But such honors, unless awarded, are probably not part of the official record.
4. Ibid.
5. Letter 42 in my numbering, René to Charlotte, Mar 19, 1952. I numbered the letters by date; that is, from November 4, 1950 through 1969. Most of the letters are from the early 1950s, mostly written by René. But Charlotte does write back and when she does, I count her letter as a number in sequence, i.e., if René writes number 50 and Charlotte returns in the next letter which I've arranged by date, her return is number 51. If she returns his a week or two later, there might be several letters from him— numbers 51, 52, 53 etc., before her return. In that case, her return would be 54. These numbers are only for my own organization and retrieval of the letters which otherwise would have been harder to work with.
6. Letter 5, René to Charlotte, December 10, 1950.

7. Letter 42, René to Charlotte, 19 March 1952.
8. Letter 152, René to his brother, December 27, 1962.
9. Dated February 6, 1952, it's not signed, although the name again, in copying, may have been cut off at the end. The letter head is "Glee Club and Treble Clef Society," indicating a cadet of varied interests. But it's accompanied by letter from his commanding officer, Col. T. L. Waters, "Artillery," to whom it was addressed and who forwarded it to René with his compliments.
10. June 4, 1952, to Col. Walters, signed by fourteen cadets. Dussaq'.
11. Letter from Lt. Col. Silvio E. Gasperini, Jr., Chief, Infantry Section, dated June 16, 1952.
12. I tried to find more on this but that is all officials of the UC system could find.
13. Letter 39, postmarked March 5, 1952.
14. Husband and wife who maintained their innocence to their executions.
15. He was a top diplomat. Richard Nixon, then a congressman, played a key part in his demise.
16. Certain of René's relatives have confirmed his appearance before the committee but without evidence or details.

22: Letters

1. Letter 30, from René to Charlotte, dated September 12, 1951. This date, as is the case unless stated otherwise, is the postmark on the envelope, not the date of the letter itself. The date of the letter itself, when given, is usually a day or two earlier. The letter number is my own, according to the way I organized them usually by date sequence, earliest letter "1," next "2," etc.
2. Letter 57, René to Charlotte, September 20, 1952.
3. Letter 58, René to Charlotte, September 29, 1952.
4. Letter 61, René to Charlotte, October 4, 1952.
5. Ibid.

6. Letter 62, Charlotte to René. The date appears to be October 22, 1952 but I can't be sure. If so, it's out of sequence datewise with the next letter cited in these endnotes (my number 63)—an inevitable consequence of time gone by and faded numbers.
7. Ibid.
8. Letter 63, René to Charlotte, the envelope date is unreadable but the letter itself is dated "6 Oct 1952."
9. Ibid.
10. Ibid.
11. Letter 64, Charlotte to René, October 6, 1952.
12. Letter 65, René to Charlotte, October 16, 1952.
13. Ibid.
14. From two letters, number 66, from René to Charlotte, postmarked October 18, 1952, and number 67, René to Charlotte, postmarked October 26, 1952.
15. Letter 67 (see above).
16. Letter 65 (see above).
17. Letter 67 (see above).
18. Letter 68, Charlotte to René, October 30, 1852.
19. Ibid.
20. The story is an interesting one. *Wikipedia* says she had an argument with studio authorities because she wanted a boyfriend to star in the Tracy picture, titled *The Mountain*, which was to be shot in France. But the *San Diego Union*, in response to her obituary in 2012, has a comments letter from her son, Stephen Southerland, a minister, saying it was her conversion to Christianity, brought about by evangelist Billy Graham, which caused her break with the movies.
21. Letter 68 (see above).
22. Letter 71, René to Charlotte, letter dated "10 Nov 52."
23. Ibid.
24. Ibid.
25. Letter 74, René to Charlotte, letter dated "21 Nov 52."
26. Ibid.

27.   Letter 75, Charlotte to René, November 24, 1952.

28.   Letter 76, René to Charlotte, letter dated "2 Dec 52".

29.   Letter 81, René to Charlotte, letter dated "22 Dec 52".

30.   Letter 90, René to Charlotte, letter dated "1 Jan 1953".

31.   Letter 91 from Charlotte to René, postmarked Jan 6, 1953.

32.   Letter 92, from René to Charlotte, postmarked Jan 8, 1953.

33.   Ibid.

34.   Letter 94, René to Charlotte. This letter has "15 Jan 52" penned in at top but considering the content and arrangement in the batch of letters I received, I think that is a mistake—one commonly made when the year ends. The postmark is obliterated by a German stamp.

35.   Letter 96, René to Charlotte, letter dated "17 January 1953."

36.   Letter 98, Charlotte to René, post marked January 25, 1953.

37.   Letter 108, René to Charlotte, letter dated "9 February 53."

38.   Letter 110, Charlotte to René, letter dated February 15, 1953.

39.   Letter 113, Charlotte to René, letter dated February 21, 1953.

40.   See Ian Sayer, and Douglas Botting, *America's Secret Army* (Franklin Watts, 1989), for more on this FBI-like agency.

41.   Letter 116, René to Charlotte, letter dated "3 March 1953."

42.   Letter 119, René to Charlotte, "17 March 1953."

43.   Letters 123, René to Charlotte, postmarked April 3, 1953, and 128, René to Charlotte, letter dated "24 April 53."

44.   Letter 140, René to Charlotte, letter dated "12 June 53."

45.   Letter 142, René to Charlotte, letter dated "15 June 1953."

23: Accusations

1.   I made three separate FOIA requests to different army branches.

2.   Dussaq's Report of Separation (form DD 214) dated December 20, 1953.

3.   December 18, 1953 from Clary to René; number 150 in the Korean War Letters.

4.   Letter 148.

5.   Ibid.

6. The following is from some fifty pages of formerly classified documents I received in June 2009 under a FOIA request to the FBI. They detail their investigation of Dussaq after his return from Germany.
7. Ibid.
8. Ibid., Memo from the Baltimore FBI office to "Director, FBI," dated 9/23/54.
9. Memo to "SAC, Los Angeles" from "Director, FBI" dated October 4, 1954.
10. The seven-page statement, signed by Dussaq, is part of the June 2009 FOIA release to me. I also found an identical copy in René's papers given to me by his wife.
11. Ibid.
12. This is from the FBI files on folksinger Woody Guthrie, specifically NY 100-87247, pg. 17. It was sent to me by Mary Kay Schmidt, National Archives archivist, with the larger designation: RG 65, 100-HQ-29988, Box 1739.
13. "George Haggerty," Abraham Lincoln Brigade Archives, www. alba-valb.org/volunteers/george-haggerty.
14. Michael Nash and Melvin Small, *The Good Fight Continues* (New York: NYU Press, 2006), 88.
15. His name is listed in the "In Memoriam" column of the University of Nebraska Alumni Association newsletter of October 2003. His career can be followed through documents at the National Archives and Records Administration.
16. Page four of a five-page memo to "Director, FBI" from "SAC, Baltimore," dated 9/23/54—one of the documents sent to me by the National Archives in June 2009.
17. One-page document (my page sixty) in the many sent by the National Archives in June 2009.

24: Secret Diaries

1. The exact date is unconfirmed. Bazata writes variously 1925 to 1928. It was a long time ago. Exact dates are hard to recall,

which presumably is the problem. Penning it down is even harder.

2.   For more about the diaries, see endnote 9, Chapter 1.

3.   Readers can learn more about him in my 2008 book, *Target: Patton.*

4.   In the diaries and newspaper and magazine stories about him, many of which are in *Target: Patton.*

5.   Bazata's military background is part of his official record, which I verified in the National Archives and other sources and is in greater detail in *Target: Patton* and his diaries.

6.   They also, he claims, discussed killing Franklin D. Roosevelt.

7.   This refers to the entire plan involving actions after the assassination. Diary 18, 9.

8.   I've identified over fifty such similarities and ties to Dussaq in diary entries pertaining to the plotter/shooter.

9.   Diary 28, 26–28 and Diary 34, 3–4.

10. Diary 34, 63.

11. The death of Gen. George Patton, the subject of *Target: Patton.*

12. From this point on in the narrative, unless otherwise stipulated, I will use "René" or "Dussaq" where Bazata has used "Peter" or "Paul."

25: "Little Time for Whiners"

1.   IMPORTANT: Keep in mind that if the names "Peter" or "Paul" occur in Bazata quotes, they are code names Bazata uses for Dussaq. I've changed all such references to René.

2.   Such conversation brings up the question of Dussaq's English. In his biography he said he didn't speak English well until after he arrived in America. But once there he was quickly hobnobbing with Hollywood's elite, some of whom, like Daisy Moreno, presumably did not speak Spanish. Yet he conversed with her well enough to be her driver and friend, and with police, doctors, and reporters only a month after he arrived. Reporters quote him in the paper. Without knowing exact dates for this first meeting

between Bazata and Dussaq, no precise judgment about the question can be made. Is Bazata remembering later conversations? Was Dussaq's memory wrong about his mastery of English? Are there lies or exaggerations being told by either one? It's part of the mystery.

3.   A more detailed description of this grisly fight is in *Target: Patton.*

26: Hitman

1.   Cuban politics at this time were extremely complicated with various groups backing various leaders and much violence. For an indepth look at Batista's role see Frank Argote-Freyre, *Fulgencio Batista: From Revolutionary to Strongman* (Rutgers University Press, 2006), a former journalist in Cuba at the time and now an American history professor.

2.   Again, one of his two pseudonyms for Dussaq.

3.   "LeBeau" is a codename Bazata used throughout his career. The origin is obscure. But before reading this I assumed it came from his time in France as a Jedburgh with the Maquis. Apparently he used it earlier.

4.   It's never explained whether he had a uniform on or not—but presumably not.

5.   Bazata's term, not mine. The "Keystone Cops" were the Bungle Brigade in silent movie comedies.

6.   He actually writes ten minutes. But 17:45 to 17:50 is five minutes. He was wrong on one of the two. It was a long time ago. Either works. The point is, as often happens in such tense situations, time seems much longer than it actually is.

7.   Understandably there are no public records of this event. Probably, by now, any records about it have been destroyed. But sometime around 1980 he received, as a result of his probing his own secret records, a "Letter of Commendation," signed by Rear Admiral C.S. Freeman, commander of U.S. forces in Cuban Waters, 1933-34. I have a copy of it. It says, in part, "For services

performed in connection with intelligence operations during the Cuban situation." And as Bazata then added to his official biography—which presumably was part of his hiring by Defense as an aid to John Lehman—the citation was for his work regarding "Fulgencio Batista." The citation is dated January 30, 1934.

27: A Seed is Planted

1. Gordon Chaplin, "I Learned To Keep A Secret," *Potomac*, June 6, 1976.
2. Ibid.
3. This had to be—if Bazata is recalling the right restaurant— sometime after December 1941 which, according to records, was when the restaurant first opened.
4. Here's the mystery of Dussaq's spoken English again. In his unfinished biography, *Adventure to Order*, Dussaq indicates he didn't speak English, or at least not well, until after he arrived in the U.S. in the early 1930s. Bazata's writings indicate he spoke very well in the late 1920s.
5. His wife crashing into trees was part of how Katherine Applegate Dussaq died. As the reader will see, Bazata knew of her death.
6. Diary 34, 66, and Diary 41, 70.
7. Diary 20, 87–92.
8. True. Before Pearl Harbor, the U.S. was secretly giving aid to Britain and the Soviet Union in lend-lease and in flat out shipments of war materials to Russia.
9. Ibid.
10. One need only read some of the new books about Venona, the super-secret breaking of Russian codes by U.S. spymasters to learn the scope and depth of this infiltration. In addition to books I've already mentioned in footnotes, see Leona and Jerrold Schecter, *Sacred Secrets: How Soviet Intelligence Operations Changed American History* (Sterling: Potomac Books, 2002), Sudoplatov, Pavel, et al., *Special Tasks*, (New York: Back Bay

Books, 1995), John Earl Haynes and Harvey Klehr, *Venona: Decoding Soviet Espionage in America*, (New Haven: Yale University Press, 2000), Allen Weinstein and Alexander Vassiliev, *Haunted Wood: Soviet Espionage in America—The Stalin Era*, (Modern Library, 2000), and Diana West, *American Betrayal*.

11. Diary 20, 92, also Diary 15, 4–5.
12. For more on this see *Target: Patton* or Thomas Troy, *Wild Bill and Intrepid: Donovan, Stephenson, and the Origin of CIA* (New Haven: Yale University Press, 1996).
13. His papers and witness as detailed in *Target: Patton*.
14. As described in this book at the end of chapter eleven.
15. For more details see David Nasaw, *The Patriarch: The Remarkable Life and Turbulent Times of Joseph P. Kennedy* (New York: Penguin Books, 2013), his biography of Joseph Kennedy.
16. The quotes concerning Joe Kennedy come mainly from Diary 29, 28–30.
17. Copeland's letter and Kennedy's reply are part of Bazata's CIA file which Bazata received after a Privacy Act request following his return to the U.S. in 1970.
18. Diary 29, 30–31.
19. Diary 34, 50.

28: Incubation

1. Bazata is not precise about the date. The town today, in the Rhone-Alpes Region of France, is called Amberieu-en-Bugey.
2. The details are in *Target: Patton*.
3. More detail about this miraculous ride can be found in George Millar, *Maquis: The French Resistance at War* (London: Cassell, 2003), or my book, *Target: Patton*.
4. "Makes His Mark," *Washington Post*, May 9, 1942. Bazata showed me a copy of the target, clearly labeled "record" by "Pvt. Bazata."

5. The "Sugar" story comes from, among other sources, former CIA Director William Colby, a fellow Jedburgh with Bazata. He mentions it in his book *Honorable Men: My Life in the CIA* (New York: Simon & Schuster, 1978). Bazata's widow, Marie-Pierre, told me about the duffle bag ruse, confirmed by others as well.

6. Diary 18, 15, and Diary 28, 54.

7. Although this is the codename Bazata writes, it's unclear whether it was the actual codename or one made up for the diary.

8. Diary 41, 50–51. Bazata identifies the officer as "Gen. Wharton-Cates...commandant." Clifton B. Cates was commandant of the corps in 1951 and Franklin Wharton was commandant in 1818. Perhaps Bazata confused the two.

9. Diary 13, 19–20.

10. Diary 29, 39–46.

11. Wilcox, *Target: Patton*, 93–94.

12. Ibid., 93; Diary 34, 113a–114a.

13. Diary 29, 32–33.

14. Bazata letter to "Greenya/van Roijon," dated July 27, 1972—apparently John Greenya, a prospective writer of a book about his life that Bazata was trying to generate but never finished. This is on page four of some sixty pages, plus notes, he typed, single-spaced, which I've filed under "Baz Book 1," one of four manila envelopes full of such remembrances. These are in addition to his diaries.

15. The information is on page four of a five-page memo to "Director, FBI" from "SAC, Baltimore," dated 9/23/54. It is one of many sent to me by the Bureau in response to an FOIA request about René.

16. Diary 11, 57-62.

17. More of that is in *Target: Patton*.

18. Ibid.

29: "Will You Join Us, LeBeau?"

1. Diary 28, 11–12.
2. Ibid.
3. Diary 28, 3–4.
4. Diary 28, 9–10.
5. Chibas's story can be found in various sources including Fidel Castro, *Fidel: My Early Years* (Melbourne: Ocean Press, 2004), and Castro, *Fidel Castro: My Life: A Spoken Autobiography* (New York: Scribner, 2009). A detailed account of Chiba's self-shooting can be found in Georgie Anne Geyer, *Guerrilla Prince: The Untold Story of Fidel Castro* (New York: Little, Brown and Company, 1991). Bazata writes about it in Diary 41, 126.
6. Castro, *Fidel: My Early Years*, 104; and Castro, *Fidel Castro: My Life: A Spoken Autobiography*, 27–28.
7. Castro, *Fidel Castro: My Life: A Spoken Autobiography*, 104.
8. Diary 34, 171a–172a.
9. It can be viewed today at the National Archives in their OSS collection.
10. When I first met Bazata, he showed me his CIA file, which he got through his own personal request. Although the CIA will neither confirm nor deny his work for them, it is quite extensive.
11. Diary 9, 40–42; Diary 28, 6–7.
12. It was also rumored he was having an affair with Baron Mumm's wife.
13. See *Target: Patton*, 53.
14. Interview with Joe Lagattuta, former DEA agent, now deceased, who served in intelligence in Europe after WWII and knew Bazata.
15. Diary 28, 12; Diary 34, 59a and 52a.

30: Swiss Bank Account

1. Diary 18, 16; Diary 34, 78; Diary 42, 16.

2. Prudential insurance salesman? The source is Bazata in the diaries. In an earlier chapter I talk about Dussaq being a Prudential agent. This is a reference to that.
3. Diary 18, 17.
4. For more detail see *Target: Patton*, 83–84.
5. See CRT-II Claims Resolution Tribunal Deposited Assets Claims, http://www.crt-ii.org/2001_list/publication_list1_D.phtm.
6. For details see http://en.wikipedia.org/wiki/World_Jewish_Congress_lawsuit_against_Swiss_banks
7. http://www.crt-ii.org/2001_list/sba_publication.pdf—look under "D."
8. For instance, a plan to generate energy from the Gulfstream flowing by Cuba with a giant one million dollar tube generator, reported in the *New York Times*, June 28, 1930.
9. Victor Hugo, *Les Miserables* (New York: Signet, 2013), 170–71.
10. For instance, Russian communist revolutionary Leon Trotsky exiled there until Stalin's henchman found him in 1940 and one murdered him with an axe.
11. Diary 28, 13–14.
12. Albert Bayo, living in Mexico at the time. Bayo died in Havana in 1967.
13. Diary 18, 16; Diary 27, 13; Diary 28, 55.

31: Sailing with Castro

1. I don't think he meant of Castro's revolution. He meant of Dussaq's wish to free Cuba.
2. Diary 28, 14–17.
3. *Fidel: My Early Years, Episodes of the Cuban Revolutionary War*, articles on Castro in *Wikipedia*.
4. Diary 28, 18.
5. "Van Nuys Women's Club to Hear Medal Winner Speak on 'Espionage,'" *Los Angeles Times*, November 9, 1956.

6. Letter to Dussaq from the VA's LA office dated July 12, 1957. In order to have the money he would have had to say the injury was service connected.
7. For further information on his painting career see his *New York Times* obituary, "Douglas DeWitt Bazata," August 22, 1999, and especially the article, Joy Billington, "Douglas Bazata—A Many Faceted Man," *The* (Washington) *Sunday Star and Daily News*, September 17, 1972.
8. Diary 28, 18–24.

32: The Scorpions Are Waiting

1. In one reference he says the five died in two separate incidents but doesn't elaborate.
2. Diary 5, 66–68.
3. Diary 11, 17–19, 125.
4. Diary 34, 176.
5. For details on the CIA operation see CIA study, "*Operation PBSUCCESS: The United States and Guatemala 1952-1954*, available on line at the National Security Archive, George Washington University.
6. Diary 18, 18.
7. Diary 34, 53a–54a.
8. Diary 28, 260.
9. Ibid., 176a–177a.
10. For instance, Eisenhower's participation in the assassination of Vichy leader Jean Darlan. For particulars see *Target: Patton*, chapter fourteen.
11. From a Wiki article on JFK's father, Joseph P. Kennedy—"When Jack was asked about the level of involvement and influence that his father had held in his razor-thin presidential victory, John would joke that on the eve before the election, his father had asked him the exact number of votes he would need to win: there was no way he was paying "for a landslide. John Kennedy's presidency was a victory for his father."

12. Diary 29, 65–68.
13. Diary 34, 178a–180a.
14. Among others, personal letter by Bazata to "Dear John"— otherwise unidentifiable—dated June 24, 1978.

34: Settling Scores

1. Diary 39, 49–51.
2. See *The Very Best Men* for an examination of Wisner's CIA life.
3. No details given. Diary 39, 44–50.
4. This was in an article about Watergate. Alsop contrasted what he called the "phoney-tough" who talk a lot with the "crazy-brave" who do things that should get them killed but don't.
5. Diary 5, 91–92.
6. Diary 39, 95–97.
7. Diary 15, 14, Diary 34, 171.
8. Diary 34, 171–172.
9. Ibid, 174.
10. Ibid, 175.
11. Diary 34, 169–170, 197a.
12. Diary 34, 183a–186a.

35: "Dear God, Guide Us"

1. Diary 34, 186a–187a.
2. Diary 34, 54a–55a, 58a.
3. Diary 27, 19; Diary 42, 32–33; Diary 29, 65.
4. Taped interview 2b with Charlotte.
5. Cathers is dead. I located his son in Washington State who couldn't provide more information. "New Frontiers" was a concept used by Kennedy to launch his administration.
6. "Informants scuttle plots against Cuba," *Miami Herald*, Sunday, June 19, 1983

7. Brian Latell, *Castro's Secrets: Cuban Intelligence, The CIA, and the Assassination of John F. Kennedy* (New York: St. Martin's Press, 2012), 10.

8. Numerous authors and historians attest to this fact, including University of Alabama Prof. Howard Jones in *The Bay of Pigs* (Oxford: Oxford University Press, 2010); Tim Weiner, Pulitzer Prize winning New York Times reporter in *Legacy of Ashes* (New York: Anchor, 2008); and, most recently, Jim Rasenberger in *The Brilliant Disaster* (New York: Scribner, 2012) about JFK and the Bay of Pigs.

9. Gus Russo and Stephen Molton, *Brothers in Arms: The Kennedys, the Castros, and the Politics of Murder* (Bloomsbury USA, 2008), 246. Califano later became Secretary of Health and Human Services under President Jimmy Carter.

10. See JFK researcher Mary Ferrell's extensive Internet archive on the matter; https://www.maryferrell.org/pages/JFK_Assassination.html.

11. Formerly "Eyes Only" CIA memorandum entitled "Family Jewels" May 16, 1973.

12. Diary 29, 69–70.

13. Diary 41, 113–115.

14. Diary 29, 73–74.

15. Diary 34, 188a–192a.

16. Diary 29, 74–75.

17. Diary 18, 25.

18. This conversation allegedly took place prior to November 1963, when Kennedy was killed. None of the plots were publicly known then.

19. Diary 28, 259–261.

20. Diary 28, 261; Diary 34, 190a; Diary 29, 75–77.

36: Five Triggers

1. Diary 18, 24–25.

2. Diary 15, 11; Diary 28, 197.

3. Diary 34, 92–96.
4. Diary 42, 64–65. This is one of the few times in the diaries he slips and actually writes "René," instead of Paul.
5. Diary 34, 126.
6. Arrested for the murder and identified by the Warren Commission as the sole assassin.
7. Diary 42, 39–40, plus indications in a three-page typed book outline Bazata prepared about the assassination P3 under "Personal Papers" in my Sources.
8. Diaries 34, 150–151 plus "Chapter: Operation 'Hydra K," page 1, written by Bazata and dated January 20, 1977. My designation for it is P3-2.
9. Same chapter outline referenced above (my P3-2).
10. Michael Benson, *Who's Who in the JFK Assassination: An A to Z Encyclopedia* (New York: Citadel, 2003), 68.
11. Wim Dankbaar, *Files on JFK* (Trine Day, 2008), 19.
12. "Dallas Comes to Terms with the Day that Defined it," *New York Times*, November 20, 2003.
13. "Chapter: Operation 'Hydra K," Page 2, written by Bazata and dated January 20, 1977. My designation for it is P3-2.
14. For instance, in one recounting—as opposed to multiple others—he has the managing COs equipped with .45 pistols rather than the German P38s. His diaries were written between seven and twenty-five years after the fact and in this case 1979, sixteen years after the fact. So faulty memory or understandable mistakes could be at fault.
15. The accounts are scattered and piecemeal in various diaries and sometimes leave a lot unsaid.
16. This coincides with many JFK researchers' assertions that witnesses and others concerning the assassination may have been murdered to silence them. See http://spartacus-educational.com/ JFKdeaths.htm for a pro and con discussion. For instance, John Simkin, Spartacus creator, cites Jim Marrs' 1976 book *Crossfire*

that 103 people connected in some way to the killing had died "under mysterious circumstances."

17. Johnson is mentioned several times as if he might somehow be involved in the plan, possibly as a source of motorcade intelligence. But the accusation is unsupported.

18. Diary 34, 96a–97.

19. Diary 42, 21–22.

20. Diary 41a, 6–8.

21. Diary 42, 40—Given this account, it should be noted that Oswald, once arrested, repeatedly said, "I'm a patsy."

22. Although in discussing the assassination he writes he would like to visit the "grassy knoll."

23. Most of the assassination scenario, from Dussaq's arrival in Dallas through the shooting, comes from Bazata's Diary 41, 163–168; other sources were: Diary 34, 97a–98a, Diary 15, 27–28, and several personal letters. It's in bits and pieces throughout many of Bazata's Diaries.

24. Most JFK researchers believe at least three shots were fired. Entry and exit wounds are a source of debate. All agree the wounds were to the head and the neck areas, but exactly where varies. There are charges of autopsy cover-ups, even surreptitious surgery following the killing to alter the wounds.

37: "Lunched with Two Mafias"

1. Aka "Armed Forces Radio Network."

2. Diary 18, 29–30; Diary 34, 95a, 98a–99.

3. I have at least three Bazata letters in which he mentions being with Dali in December 1963. The painting Dali did about him apparently was titled "Homage to Bazata." Dali must have respected Bazata as an artist—and certainly as an iconoclast like himself. Being a rebel, he probably looked romantically on Bazata's anti-establishment personality and lifestyle, whatever he knew of it.

4. Dairy 42, 117; Diary 28, 62.

5.   D 28, 63. For more detail on Bazata's exit from Europe and his life afterward see *Target: Patton*, especially pages 380–383.

6.   In 1996, Colby was found near his home dead on a marshy riverbank. The canoe he'd been rowing was nearby. The autopsy presumed he had a heart attack or stroke and drowned. Bazata believed he was murdered.

7.   *Target: Patton*, 382–383.

8.   A fifth meeting mentioned in the document occurred after the assassination.

9.   My own speculation based on interviews with Bazata and research about him. Plus, Diary 18, 22, 32, 50, 53.

10. "Douglas Bazata—A Many-Faced Man," Joy Billington, *The Sunday Star and Daily News*, September 17, 1972; "From the OSS to the Easel," Henry Mitchell, *Washington Post*, November 3, 1972; "Six Good Spies," Esquire, 85 (June 1975).

11. Email from Greenya August 2014.

12. Toledano, "Were U.S. Allies in CIA Sights?" *Insight on the News*, February 15, 1999.

13. This quote uses the number "five"—five triggers are still alive. But Oswald was dead. Elsewhere he refers to "principal" triggers, allowing for others to be principals. In still other passages he relegates Oswald to a status other than "principal." So perhaps he's elevating a managing CO to the fifth trigger? This quoted passage was written nearly fifteen years after the assassination so faulty memory also could be at play.

14. Diary 11, 117–118.

15. "JFK Assassination Probe Bungled," *Ludington Daily News*, January 26, 1979.

16. Who might have been the person in the film he mentions which, however, I have not been able to locate.

17. Many assassination investigators now locate fatal shots from the grassy knoll and/or railroad boxcar area.

18. Castro has always been one of the primary suspects in supposition about who was responsible for JFK's death.

38: Enigmas

1. Interview with Rick Weber, 2012.
2. Interview with Puth, 2008.
3. Some in the family feel Toro wanted to prove he was as war-capable as his father. That was one of the reasons he enlisted in the Air Force. Toro's first wife, Kathleen, felt father and son were estranged. Gina, his second wife, disagreed. Time had passed and she felt they'd become closer as both got older.
4. The exact date, even year, is not certain, although 1970 seems right. Several articles, including one in the *Los Angeles Daily News*, give that year, but there is indication he continued working, probably as a private financial advisor to select clients.
5. Ken Ringle, "The Golden Parachutists: 50 years later, Troopers Prepare to Relive the Glory That Was D-Day," *Washington Post*, February 21, 1994.
6. Lou Mio, "At 83, He's still ready to jump," *(Cleveland) Plain Dealer*, February 20, 1994.
7. Ringle, "The Golden Parachutists."
8. Kyle Smith, "D-Day paratrooper ready to jump again—at 83," *New York Post*, April 27, 1994.

39: The Cuban Question

1. The May 3, 1961 communication to David J. Cathers about an upcoming speech (chapter thirty-six).
2. I have the records and the letter. It's from Bazata's niece. He sent it to her while on leave. Dussaq was with him and wrote and signed a greeting.
3. The letter, addressed to "Chere Wendy/Jon," is dated "17 Feb., 1978." It was typed from his farm in Dickerson, Maryland. I wrote the *Enquirer* asking if they could confirm or deny the offer. Since it's so far back, and since Generoso Pope Jr., owner of the weekly, is now dead, that was a long shot. I have not heard back.

4. Bazata avers that he was a double agent, working for Cuba.

5. This is in a personal letter from Dussaq dated "September 16th 1940." It's addressed to Luis-Alberto Sanchez, a Leftist editor who arranged an interview with Haya for Dussaq.

6. This was at a November 2, 1940 "Hemisphere Defense" luncheon-discussion in New York City. Duggan, who died mysteriously in 1948, was later shown to have been a Russian spy in decrypted Soviet telegrams.

7. This is not just my opinion but that of many who knew and wrote about him, for instance in Geyer, *Guerrilla Prince: The Untold Story of Fidel Castro*, one of the most acclaimed biographies about Fidel Castro.

8. The cables can be seen at Mary Ferrell's extensive Internet archive on the Kennedy Assassination. (They are also at the National Archives.) She obtained them from the House Committee in 1993, and then later duplicates of the cables in other releases, such as the CIA's in the late 1990s.

9. He is only found on the Internet in connection with the arrest— and that only in Kennedy archives compiled after the 1990 releases. Gus Russo, in his excellent *Live by the Sword* (Baltimore: Bancroft Press, 1998), believes that Robert Kennedy felt the plots he directed against Castro caused his brother's death. That is why, Russo believes, the information about Cabarca was not released.

10. Humberto Fontova, *Fidel: Hollywood's Favorite Tyrant* (Washington, DC: Regnery Publishing, 2005); in an article about Castro on Discoverthenetworks.org, 12.

11. Alexander M. Haig, *Inner Circles: How America Changed the World* (New York: Grand Central Publishing, 1994), 113.

12. Ibid., 115–116.

Index

189–90, 192–93, 195, 320,
322, 340
Dussaq, Rene A., xi–xv, 3–8,
11–14, 16, 46, 48–49, 157,
175, 182–99, 241–47, 320–29
and Basque fighters, 139–44
and Bikini Atoll, 145–56
and Cuba, 210–11, 217–19,
223–30, 249–55, 263–64,
270–71
and Daisy Moreno's death,
51–59
and JFK's assassination, 213,
236–38, 272–73, 277, 281,
284–95, 297–307, 310, 312,
319, 330–37
at Prudential, 160–61
at UC Berkeley, 176–79, 181
childhood, 32–35
dancing, 101–2
deep-sea diving, 68–70,
73–92, 99–101
in World War II, 18–29,
39–42, 61–66, 93–97, 239–
41
lecturing, 103–6, 158–59
marriage to Katherine Applegate, 106, 108, 112, 115–19,
129–35
spy activity, 164–73, 201–6,
231–36, 257–62, 266–68
Dussaq, Rene E., 259, 320, 322–
23

Dussaq, Sara ("Shanti"), 148,
183, 189, 198
Dussaq & Company, 35
Dussaq & Toral, S.A., 35, 195

E

Eckert, Dorothy, 118, 124
Eckert, Penny, 131
Eisenhower, Dwight, 18, 187–88,
234, 270–73, 313
Embassy Row, 232, 235
Empire State building, xiv, 5, 145,
179, 244
Encino, California, 161, 195,
285, 320, 322
Encyclopedia Titanica, 90
Ensminger, Thomas, 7
Ernest, Jim, 71
Esquire, 313

F

Factionalist Sabotage Group, 166,
170–71, 201, 206,
Faggian, Luigi, 88–90
Fairbairn, W. E., 142
Falco, 88–90
Farmer, John 8–9, 18, 23–24, 28,
39, 41, 42
Federal Bureau of Investigation
(FBI), xiii, 163–72, 179, 201–
6, 245, 261, 290, 292, 300,
303, 319, 324, 329, 332–34

Z